W9-BFP-538

RAND McNALLY

ATLAS OF WORLD HISTORY

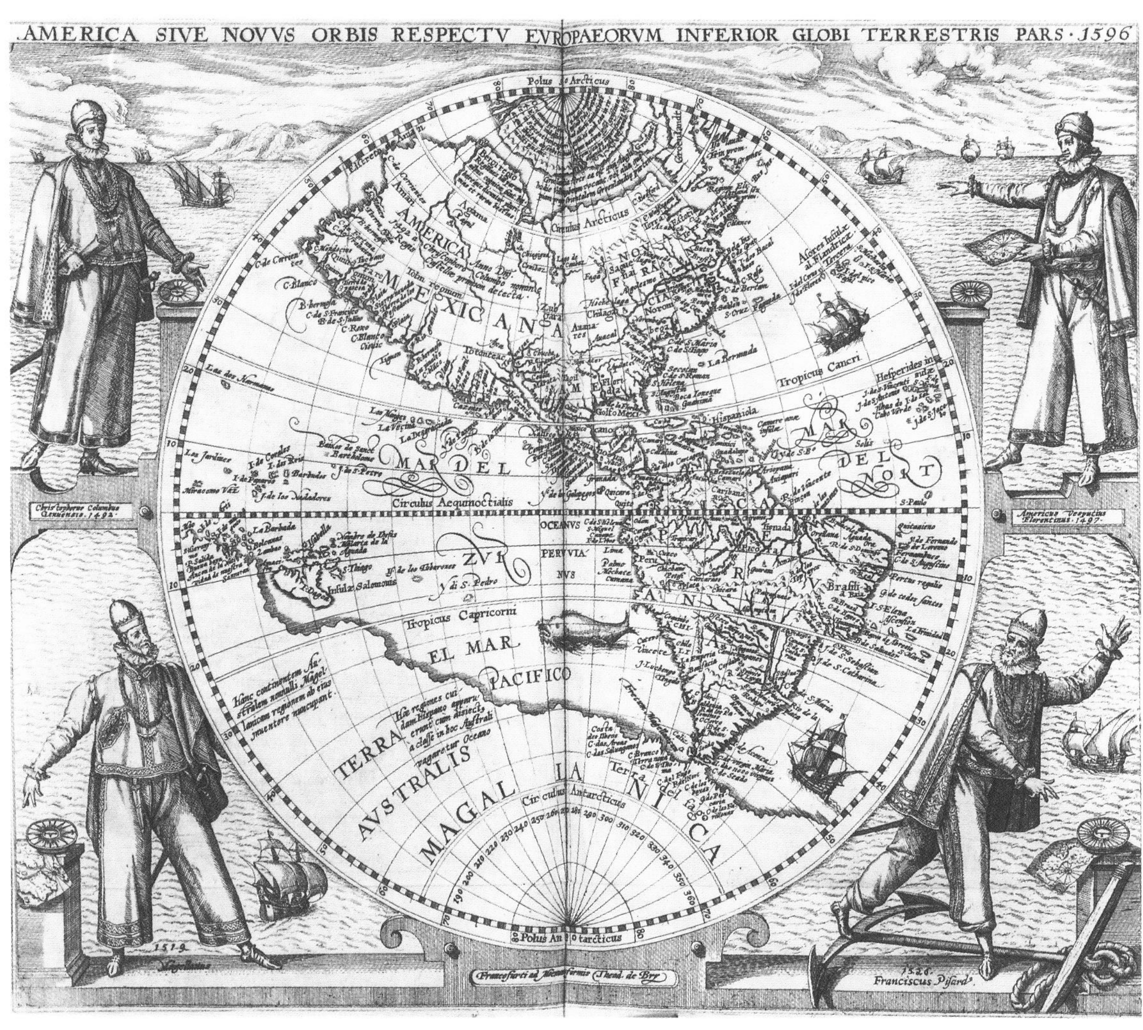
AMERICA SIVE NOVVS ORBIS RESPECTV EVROPAEORVM INFERIOR GLOBI TERRESTRIS PARS. 1596
Polus Arcticus
Circulus Arcticus
Tropicus Cancri
MAR DEL
MAR DEL NORT
Circulus Aequinoctialis
Tropicus Capricorni
EL MAR PACIFICO
TERRA AVSTRALIS
MAGAL IA NICA
Circulus Antarcticus
Polus Antarcticus
Franciscus Drake
1596

ATLAS OF WORLD HISTORY

RAND McNALLY

Frontispiece: The western hemisphere as it was known or imagined at the end of the sixteenth century. It is flanked by figures of Columbus, Vespucci, Magellan and Pizarro

Rand McNally
Atlas of World History

This edition published 1995 in England under the title of the Philip's Atlas of World History by Philip's, an imprint of Reed Books

Revised edition 1995

Original cartography by Creative Cartography Limited: Nicholas Skelton and Terry Allen.

Produced by Mandarin Offset
Printed and bound in Hong Kong

Library of Congress Cataloging-in-Publication Data

Atlas of world history
p. cm.
At head of title: Rand McNally.
Includes index.
ISBN 0-528-83779-6 (pbk) – ISBN 0-528-83780-X
1. Historical geography – Maps. I. Rand McNally and Company.
G1030.R36 1995 <G&M>
911 – dc20
95-6576
CIP
MAP

The emergence of the modern world

United States Historical Maps

SURVEY OF MAPS BY DATE AND REGION

This chart shows the rough chronological span of each map, and serves as a guide to the coverage of each region's history in this atlas. As well as the maps indicated for each specific region, information about that region may also be found on the maps of the relevant continent, and on the world maps.

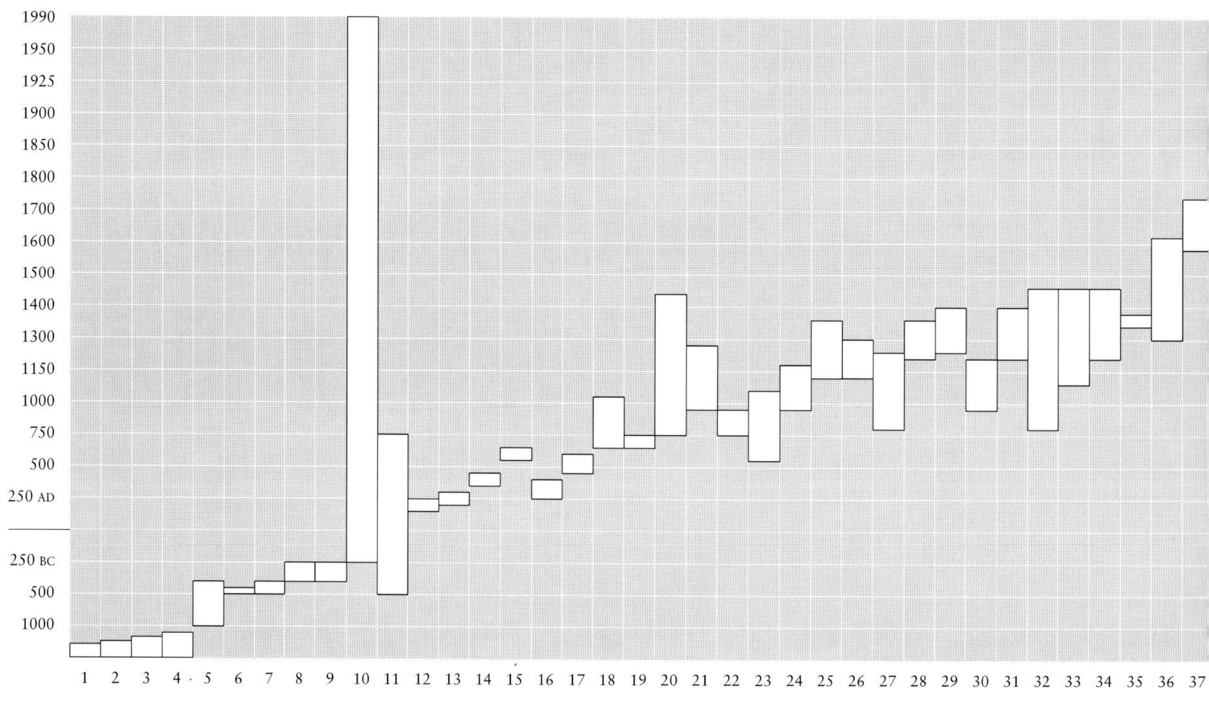

	upto1000BC	1000-460BC	460-246BC	246-1BC	AD 1-246	246-460	460-746	746-1000	1000-1146	1146-13
THE WORLD	1,2,3									
THE AMERICAS										
North America										
South America										
EUROPE				8,11	12	14	17		20	28
Scandinavia									23	
Germany and Central Europe									24	
Western Europe										25
France and the Low Countries								22		
British Isles									23	25
Spain and Portugal										
Italy										
The Mediterranean		5		8	12	14	17,19		27	
Eastern Mediterranean	4						18			26
Greece and the Balkans	4	5	7				18	21		
AFRICA				11					20	
North Africa	3						19		27	
EURASIA				11					20	
Russia								21		
Persia and Asia Minor	3	6		9		15	19		27	
INDIA	3				16					
THE FAR EAST				11					20	
China					10	13			30	
Japan										
AUSTRALASIA	1									

upto1000BC 1000-460BC 460-246BC 246-1BC AD 1-246 246-460 460-746 746-1000 1000-1146 1146-13

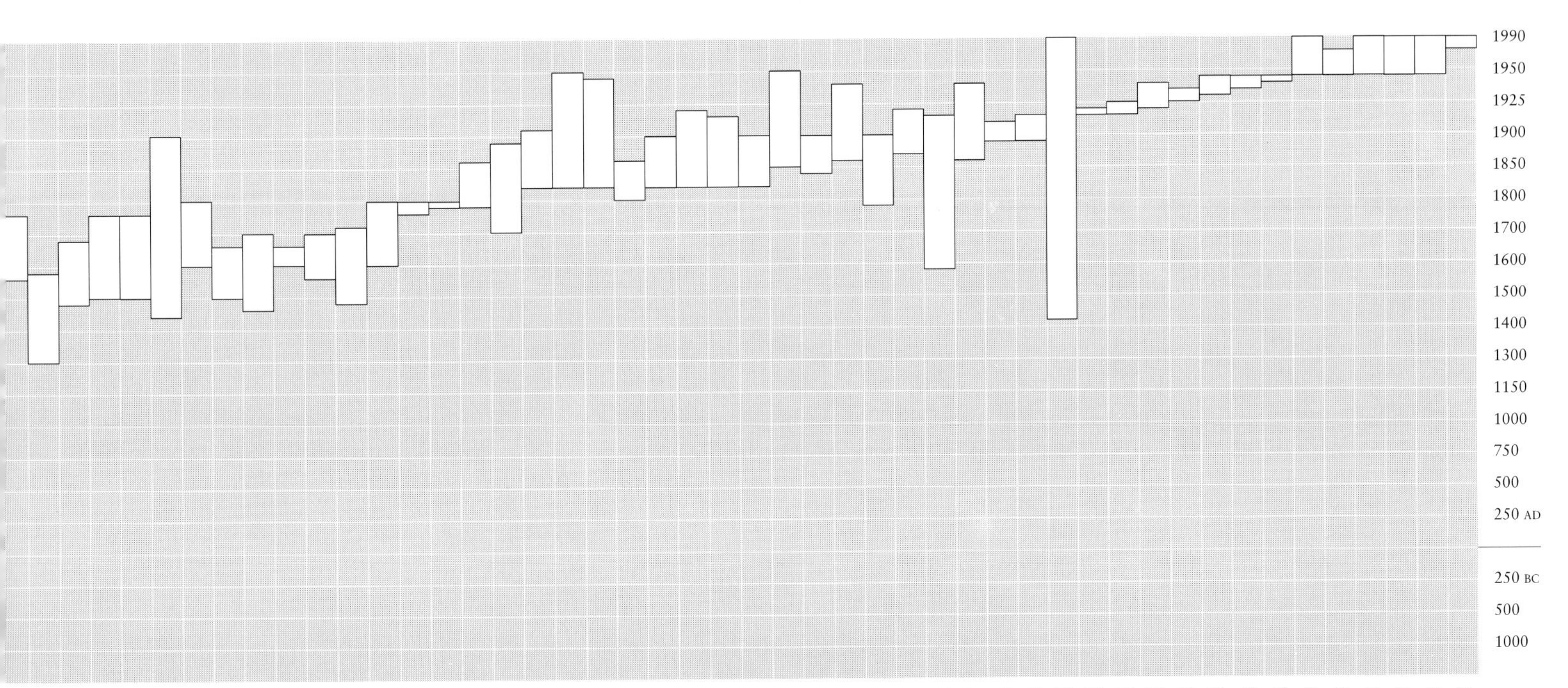

300-1400	1400-1500	1500-1600	1600-1700	1700-1800	1800-1850	1850-1900	1900-1925	1925-1950	1950-1990	
	36		46			58	67		83,84,87	**THE WORLD**
				45						THE AMERICAS
			44	53	68	69		78		*North America*
			43		59					*South America*
	35	48		52	55,60	57	75	78,80,81	82	EUROPE
			50							Scandinavia
34		42	49		61		76	77		Germany and Central Europe
		42,47								*Western Europe*
			51	54						France and the Low Countries
					56					British Isles
32										Spain and Portugal
33						62				Italy
								81		*The Mediterranean*
	39								86	Eastern Mediterranean
						63				Greece and the Balkans
			46		66		74			AFRICA
								81	86	*North Africa*
31										EURASIA
	41				70		71,76			Russia
									86	Persia and Asia Minor
29			40			65			85	INDIA
			37			64	73	79	85	The Far East
			38							China
						72				Japan
			46			67			87	AUSTRALASIA

300-1400 1400-1500 1500-1600 1600-1700 1700-1800 1800-1850 1850-1900 1900-1925 1925-1950 1950-1990

'Show me the map of a region,' a great French geographer used to say, 'and I will tell you its history'. The greatest historians, from Herodotus in the fifth century BC to Idn Khaldun in the fourteenth century AD and Fernand Braudel in the twentieth, have emphasized the interaction of environment and human development. Enduring characteristics of states and societies have been shaped by their climate and natural resources, their topography and communications. We could no more attempt to understand the past without maps than without records.

The first business of any historical atlas is to show the development of human society in its physical setting. Ideally it should contain, in addition to historical information, much of the material of a geographical atlas, which is also indispensable for every student of history. It might show, for example, the relief, climate, soils and vegetation of the world in detail not only as they are today, but at appropriate moments in the past. But although historians, geographers and (especially) archaeologists have made great strides in these directions even since the first edition of this Atlas appeared in 1981, it is not possible to do that job systematically. The history of climate is only now taking shape. Some of the changes in the world's coastlines over the centuries, or in the courses and deltas of its rivers, have been studied in very great detail; others hardly at all. Still more distant, though by no means unattainable, are comprehensive accounts of the changes in vegetation, natural and cultivated; in the animal populations from which humans have taken food, clothing, labor and transport; in the insect ones which have ravaged them with disease, and prevented or limited their access to many areas of the globe right up to the present. All of these things are represented in this Atlas, but we are still far from the day looked forward to by the great English historian F W Maitland, when we will know enough about our ancestors to make their 'common thoughts of common things become thinkable once more'.

Nevertheless, while the maps in this volume are intended to be informative to the experienced as well as accessible to the beginner, they unhesitatingly give priority to clarity. They are meant to be attractive, to encourage the reader to linger, pondering the connections between, say, access to precious metals and the rise of the Abbasid empire, or between the aggrandisement of the French monarchy in the eighteenth century and the dissemination of French ideas. They are meant to stir the imagination as well as inform, and to provide a constant reminder of the real world in which the conflicts and controversies of the history books have taken place. Full-page or double-page maps of as many areas as possible show one or two points in the history of those areas in depth rather than many superficially; multiple insets crowded with valuable but invisible detail have been avoided wherever possible.

The selection of maps is designed to illustrate subjects which are of particular interest and importance in themselves, but also to assist the reader to form a general view of human history as a whole. Accordingly, the text offers neither detailed commentary on particular maps and the subjects which they illustrate nor a compendium of facts and dates, but a series of essays on some of the larger themes and questions, which individually may provide a historical context for a particular group of maps. Together, the text and maps present a scaffolding upon which the reader may begin to construct her or his own understanding of world history. Both maps and text are therefore selective. In principle the problems of selecting and defining subjects for treatment, of soundness of evidence, permissibility of inference and objectivity of judgement, are exactly the same in presenting world history through maps as through a written narrative. In practice they are often starker. It may be impossible to explain that two sets of apparently comparable data are of quite different orders of reliability. The fortifications of Justinian's Africa or Norman Wales, the shrines of classical Greece or Gupta India, the linguistic minorities or mining areas of nineteenth-century Europe - the members of almost any set of information - are far too numerous to be shown in full. Selection cannot be evaded: a decision to show some of the places which were bombed during the Second World War, or whose bombing had a particular tactical or strategic significance, is equally a decision not to show the bombing of many other places which might quite reasonably be held to have been equally significant or horrific. One must, therefore, approach these (or any other) maps at least as critically as one would a textbook, remembering that more exact truth about any subject than can be contained in the limits of plain statement is to be found only by consulting the specialist works devoted to them.

The theme which has guided our selection of subjects is a very simple one. At most periods of history scores, even hundreds of human societies have lived on this planet quite oblivious of one another's existence and quite unaffected by one another's doings. Today we live in a world which is inescapably, however unhappily, a single community. Its peoples increasingly tend towards uniformity in their culture and ways of life, and are inextricably bound together in their political destinies. The maps have been chosen with this inter-relationship in view, and concentrate on the forces which have contributed most directly to it. The distances between peoples have been bridged by the expansion of communities, by exploration and trade, by the search for land or precious metals. The differences between them have been broken down, often with the utmost brutality, by the imposition of domination, by conquest and the construction of systems of government, as well as by the simple necessity of cooperation; by the promulgation of religious and political ideologies which have absorbed or eliminated innumerable cults and regimes; and by the creation of literate cultures which have expressed and perpetuated the values, ideas and common bonds of ruling groups.

Concentration upon such themes inevitably seems to produce another version of the old story that history is about winners. Among the omissions, those of the many societies, especially of the ancient world, of Afria, the Americas, central and southeast Asia and Oceania, which have been the victims rather than the beneficiaries of these unifying processes, are most conspicuous, and very much to be regretted. Yet however regrettably, any view of the development of human society is inescapably dominated by the evolution, the achievements, and simply the presence of the great civilizations. It is not so easy to strike a balance between them. Europeans no longer claim the lion's share of world history as confidently as they did even a generation ago. Yet it remains true, for better or worse, that the impact of Europe on the rest of the world has been great. The formation of the world community is very largely the consequence of European expansion, imperialism, technical inventiveness and industrialization, products of the conditions and internal development of European societies. Consequently most readers will have a greater need for maps illustrating the domestic history of Europe than of other regions. Nevertheless, we no longer inhabit a world which wishes, or dares, to understand its history in terms of only one of its parts. That too is reflected in the contents and design of the volume.

The 23 contributors to this Atlas have benefited from the help and advice of several times that number of friends and colleagues in many academic fields, including the staffs of many libraries, and they have relied on the tolerance and encouragement of many wives and families, whom it is impossible to list by name.

The editor's debts are enormous; foremost to the contributors, whose willingness to undertake a novel and difficult task in a short time, many of them at the request of a stranger, has been equalled by the patience with which they have dealt with his questions and quibbles since. To say that responsibility for all errors rests with the editor alone is no mere formality, for among his many debts to the contributors not the least is for the forebearance with which they have accepted his suggestions and submitted to his judgements.

The associate editors have performed a thankless task with inexhaustible grace and good humor. Without their knowledge and judgement and their readiness to undertake the execution of a very large proportion of the maps and text, the editor's task would have been quite impossible; they are responsible for many of the Atlas's virtues and none of its defects.

I cannot sufficiently express my personal gratitude to all those who have made it possible for me to complete it, and especially, for everything they have put up with, to my wife and daughter.

Preface to the revised edition

As far as possible this edition of the Atlas is up to date to the end of 1994, but recent events, especially in the USSR, Eastern Europe and the Middle East, remind us sharply that History always moves too fast for historians to keep up with it.

GENERAL EDITOR

RI Moore *University of Newcastle upon Tyne*

ASSOCIATE EDITORS

Mark Greengrass *University of Sheffield*
Bernard Wasserstein *Brandeis University*

CONTRIBUTORS

Graeme Barker *University of Leicester*
Julian Birch *University of Sheffield*
Keith Branigan *University of Sheffield*
JG de Casparis *University of Leiden*
Gordon Daniels *University of Sheffield*
JF Drinkwater *University of Nottingham*
Mark Elvin *St Antony's College, Oxford*
Richard Fletcher *University of York*
Bernard Hamilton *University of Nottingham*
Peter Hardy *SOAS, University of London*
Robert Irwin
Colin Jones *University of Exeter*
Edmund King *University of Sheffield*
DO Morgan *SOAS, University of London*
TA Reuter *University of Southampton*
Francis Robinson *Royal Holloway and Bedford New College, University of London*
J Roy *University of Nottingham*
John Stevenson *Worcester College, Oxford*
David Turley *University of Kent*
A Wasserstein *The Hebrew University of Jerusalem*
Henry S Wilson *University of York*
John Woodward *University of Sheffield*

The ancient world 1

THE BEGINNINGS OF CIVILIZATION

Fossil remains of primitive forms of man have been discovered from sites in Africa dating to the beginnings of the Pleistocene Era (the first Ice Age), at least two or three million years ago, such as Lake Turkhana and Olduvai Gorge (see Map 1), but the process of anatomical development leading up to these 'hominids' can be traced back much further, to at least fifteen million years ago.

The earliest true member of our genus, called *homo erectus*, belongs to the Middle Pleistocene period, roughly half a million years ago. Like the ancestral hominids, *homo erectus* was confined to Africa and the frost-free zones of Europe and Asia.

From about 100,000 years ago Neanderthal Man (now commonly regarded as a member of the species *homo sapiens* rather than as a divergent species) occupied much the same area of world. He was replaced in Europe about 40,000 years ago by fully modern man, *homo sapiens sapiens*. Like the earlier forms of man *homo sapiens sapiens* was a hunter-gatherer, but culturally he was more advanced – at what is termed the Upper Palaeolithic stage. He was equipped with a stone and bone technology much more sophisticated than those of earlier hunters, as well as a conceptual repertoire that included systematic burial of the dead and adornment of the living, and a fertility ideology best known from the so-called 'Venus figurines' and painted caves such as Lascaux in France and Altamira in Spain.

Modern man spread rapidly over the globe. He probably reached North America about 20,000 years ago, by means of a land bridge that existed then between Siberia and Alaska (the plain of Beringia, where the Bering Straits are now) and a corridor between the northern ice sheets of Canada and Alaska. To reach Australia by about 35,000 years ago he must have used sea-going craft of some sophistication, for no land bridge existed across the Wallace Line. All the more remarkable, the rapid expansion of modern man over the world took place at the climax of the Ice Age, when many parts of the world were ice-covered and when the temperate regions of today were extremely inhospitable. Yet, well-adapted to these severe conditions, man the hunter had colonized nearly all the ice-free parts of the globe by the end of the Ice Age, 12,000 years ago.

Gordon Childe's use of the term revolution to describe the beginnings of agriculture has been criticized because we now know that agriculture took many thousands of years to evolve in different parts of the world. Nevertheless the development of food production remains the most revolutionary advance in prehistoric subsistence technique. The origins of agriculture probably lie in the highly specialized forms of hunting and plant collecting that had developed amongst many Palaeolithic societies by the end of the Ice Age 12,000 years ago. Three or four thousand years later there is clear evidence for farming communities in the hills of Palestine, Turkey, Iraq and Iran and in surrounding areas such as Greece and Crete, perhaps in Egypt, and in Turkmenia (*Map 2*). These regions are thought to have been the natural habitats of the wild ancestors of domesticated wheat, barley, sheep and goats – the staple crops and stock of the first farmers here. Although research has tended to concentrate in the Near East (because very early farming was expected here, given the development of the Sumerian and Egyptian civilizations by 3000 BC), current work in the Americas, the Far East and South-East Asia indicates that agricultural systems using different crops and animals may well have developed at similarly early dates, within three or four millennia of the end of the Pleistocene Era.

In the Americas, domesticated animals were by and large unimportant. Instead a wide range of plants was taken into cultivation in different areas, including avocado pears, beans, peppers, pumpkins, squashes, and maize which eventually became the major staple. In China pigs and millet were the staple resources of the first farmers, and people in New Guinea kept domesticated pigs, grew yams and taro. Later on rice became the staple crop in the Far East, and the first agriculture in sub-Saharan Africa was based mainly on cattle and millet.

Between 3000 BC, when urban life was beginning in Mesopotamia and Egypt, and the time of Christ, farming spread over the most accessible parts of the world. Many regions beyond these areas of early farming were still occupied by hunting and gathering societies, some of which have survived to modern times, such as the Aborigines of Australia and Bushmen of southern Africa. Within the farming world, also, some societies continued with the hunting and gathering way of life and

1 The human revolution
The earliest members of our *genus* were confined to Africa and the frost-free zones of Europe and Asia. About 40,000 years ago they were succeeded in Europe by *homo sapiens sapiens*, who spread across the world.

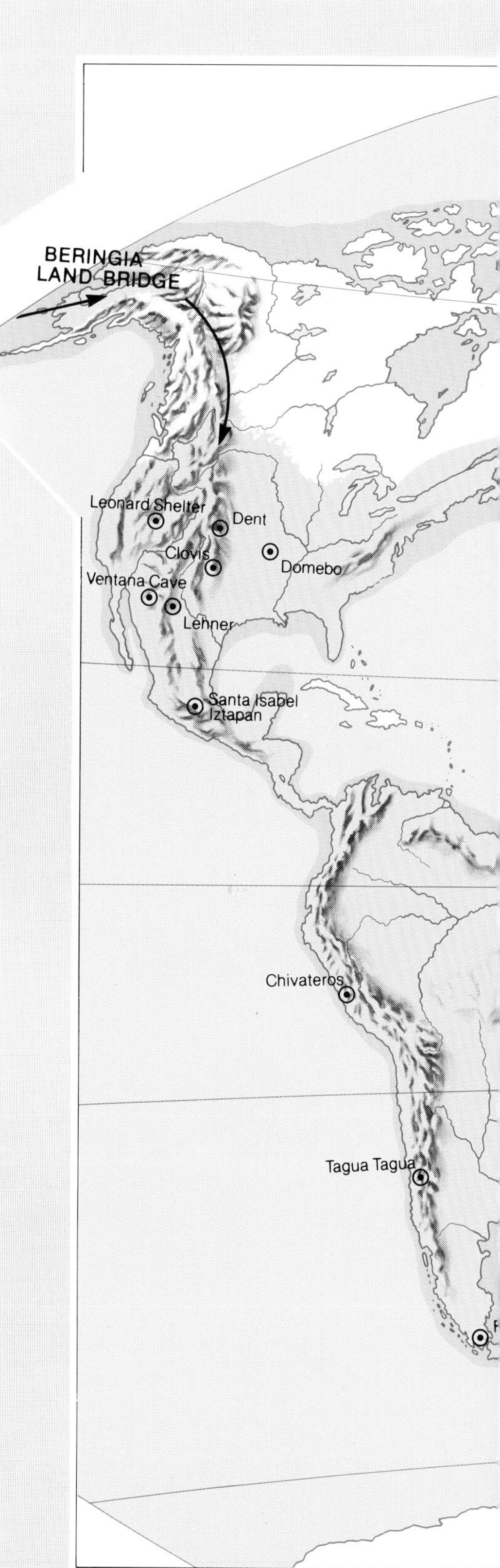

others practised both types of subsistence. On the fringes of the farming world there have always been other societies practising 'intermediate' economies like the reindeer herders of Lapland and Siberia, or the Bedouin camel herders of the Arabian and Saharan deserts.

In Europe the spread of agriculture from the south-east to the north-west between 6000 and 3000 BC has long been regarded as accompanying the movement of new people – the first farmers – into a sparsely inhabited environment. In recent years, however, it has become increasingly clear that a vigorous hunter-gatherer population was living in most parts of Europe, and that the development of prehistoric agriculture in Europe has to be understood as much in terms of the adaptation of existing people to new resources (for cereals and sheep and goats must have been introduced to temperate Europe from the eastern Mediterranean) as in terms of the arrival of colonist farmers. Similarly, the beginnings of farming in other parts of the Eurasian and African continents used to be regarded as the result of the diffusion of ideas or people or both from the 'hearth area' of early agriculture in the Near East, but the variation we now see between early farming peoples across the world – different crops and animals, different farming techniques, different timescales of development – makes it clear that many prehistoric societies in different parts of the world developed agricultural systems in the millennia following the end of the Ice Age without any major stimulus from each other.

Dry farming (that is, farming without irrigation) had developed in the hills of Mesopotamia by 6000 BC. In the next two thousand years, population pressure in these hills seems to have forced the colonization of the Tigris and Euphrates plains below, where rainfall was insufficient for dry farm-

MAP 1 THE HUMAN REVOLUTION

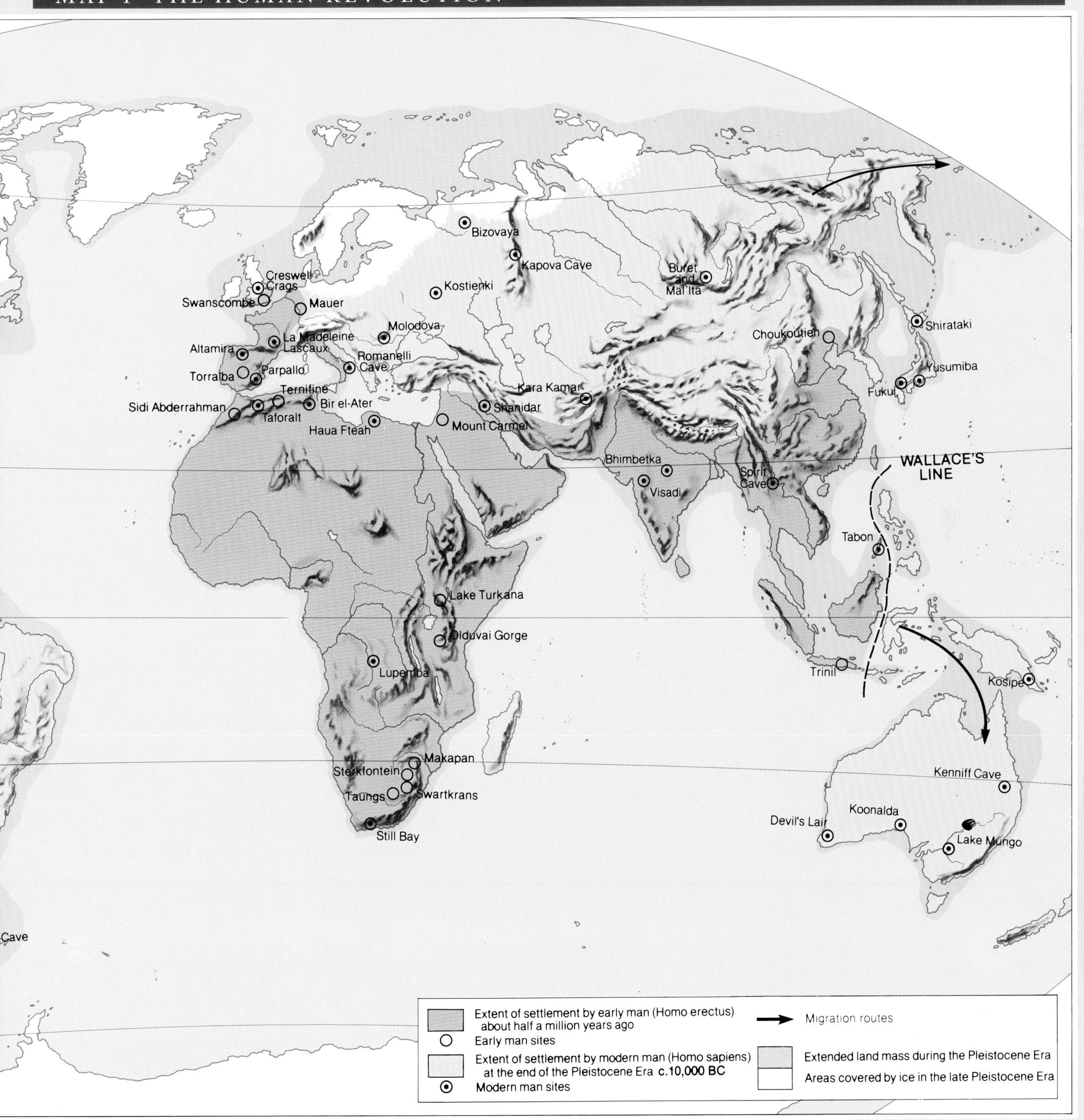

ing (*Map 3*). To survive, the new villages had to develop simple irrigation systems to farm the land of the Twin Rivers. The new technology both demanded higher levels of social and economic complexity and in turn allowed much higher levels of population than were possible in the hills. By 3500 BC the Sumerian civilization had evolved in lower Mesopotamia: it consisted of a collection of a dozen or so cities and their territories. The cities were dominated by temple complexes housing priestly élites who controlled a large part of the social, economic and ritual life of the city state. Writing systems were developed for accounting purposes, and craft technology attained a very high level of sophistication.

By 3000 BC a very different civilization was established in Egypt. There was a single state rather than a series of small city states, geared to the exploitation of the Nile valley by highly organized irrigation systems, controlled by a single ruler (the pharaoh) and his regional governors. By 2500 BC a third – as different – civilization emerged in the Indus valley, the Harappan. The nature of the leadership is not clear, but the cities were carefully planned on a grid system (quite unlike the Sumerian and Egyptian cities) with artisans' quarters and residential areas, well provided with drains and fresh water supplies, and with massively defended citadels containing public buildings.

These civilizations are so different from each other that the Egyptian and Indus cities must almost certainly be thought of as independent in origin rather than as the result of diffusion from Sumeria, although there is considerable evidence for systematic trade between Sumeria and both Egypt and the Indus valley. Civilization continued virtually uninterrupted in Mesopotamia and Egypt for thousands of years, up to the classical period, but the Indus state collapsed after only a few centuries, in about 1700 BC. The state system here depended on intensive irrigation agriculture, and over-exploitation of the valley may have led to soil deterioration, erosion and flooding, until the weakened state fell prey to outside attack.

The second millennium BC saw the emergence and florescence of complex state societies in Crete, mainland Greece and central Turkey (*Map 4*). In China, proto-urban societies may have developed by *c*.2500 BC, but the first dynasty recorded in the Chinese annals to be identified by archaeology is that of the Shang (traditionally dated 1523-1027 BC). Shang society, according to both documentary records and excavation, was extremely hierarchical and warlike. Subsistence was still based on millet and pigs rather than rice (irrigation was very limited), but craft techniques were highly sophisticated, particularly bronze casting, jade carving, pottery and silk weaving.

Left: The Black Obelisk. Obelisk of Shalmaneser III. King of Assyria 859-824 BC. The inscriptions record annals of the reign and show tribute being brought to the king by those he conquered.

In the New World, complex societies emerged in Mesoamerica and Peru at the end of the first millennium BC. The Maya civilization in Mesoamerica (Guatemala, Yucatan and Belize) achieved its climax between AD 300 and 900. Massive ceremonial centres were constructed in the rain forests by a stoneage society for a priestly élite which seems to have owed much of its power to its control of the ceremonial calendar and its ability to predict astronomical events. The centres were not cities, for the ordinary people were dispersed throughout the countryside. In Peru the ceremonial centres began in the first millennium BC, but the

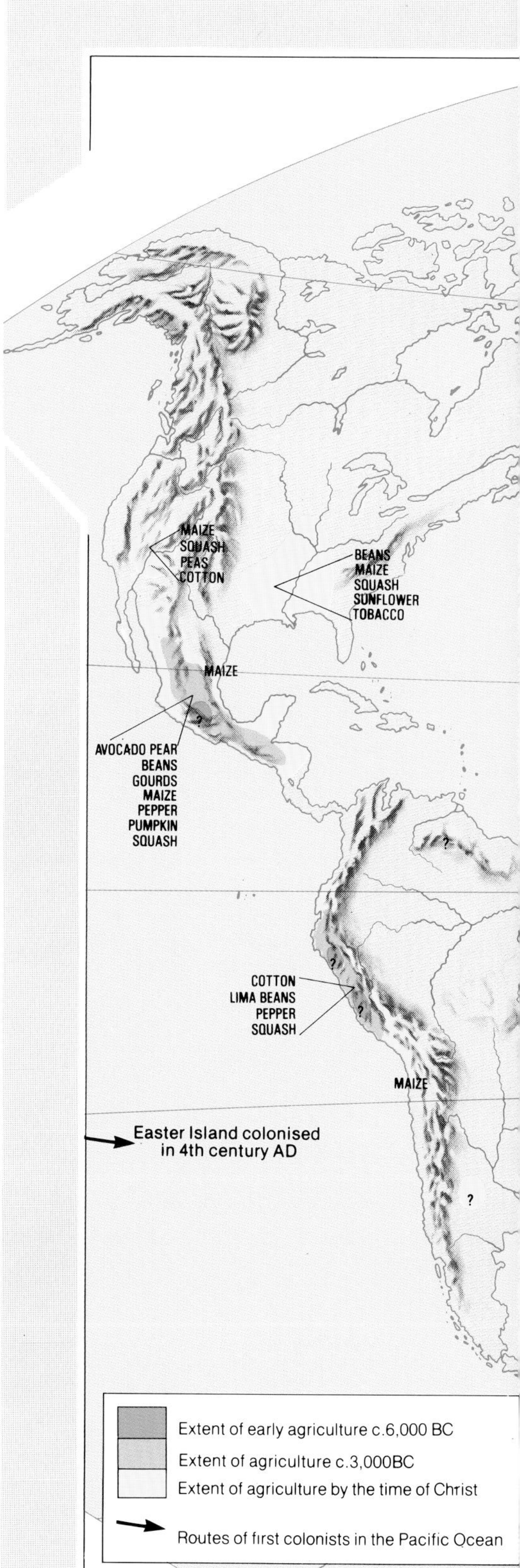

2 The Neolithic revolution
The great prehistorian Gordon Childe coined the term 'Neolithic revolution' to describe the transformation in prehistoric society represented by the beginning of agriculture: it was to be the springboard for early civilizations in several parts of the world.

Moche and Nazca states flourished at the same time as the Maya. Like the Maya they were founded on maize cultivation and were dominated by huge ceremonial centres, but on the other hand the Andean cultures were technologically more advanced, practising irrigation and bronze smithing.

By the beginning of the second millennium AD these early states had been replaced by the major imperial civilizations, the Aztecs in Mesoamerica and the Incas in Peru (*see also Map 36*). The fundamentals of these civilizations were much as before – monumental centres, obsessive and savage religions, all-powerful élite groups and relatively primitive technologies. Unlike the Maya, the Aztecs built true residential cities and intensive irrigation systems in the arid highlands of Mexico. Both Aztecs and Incas controlled large imperial domains, exacting tribute from subject states, but neither was able to organize effective resistance when the Spaniards invaded and their empires were swiftly dismembered, the Aztec in 1519-1521 and the Inca in 1527-1532.

In sub-Saharan Africa, two notable prehistoric states flourished between about AD 1000 and 1500, roughly contemporary with the Aztec and Inca civilizations. In Nigeria, stimulated by Arab caravan trade across the Sahara for gold, ivory and slaves (*Map 27*), complex hierarchial societies (like the Yoruba) developed in the savannah zone between the desert and coastal west Africa, best known today from the fine bronze heads of Ife made by the *cire perdue* technique of casting, a skill acquired from the Arab traders. In central southern Africa, the *zimbabwe* states developed *c.* AD 1200-1600 out of the preceding simple agricultural societies of the African Early Iron Age, in Rhodesia and in Mozambique. Cattle were a major source of wealth for the *zimbabwe* rulers, who traded with

MAP 2 THE NEOLITHIC REVOLUTION

MAP 3 THE URBAN REVOLUTION

The Major Early States

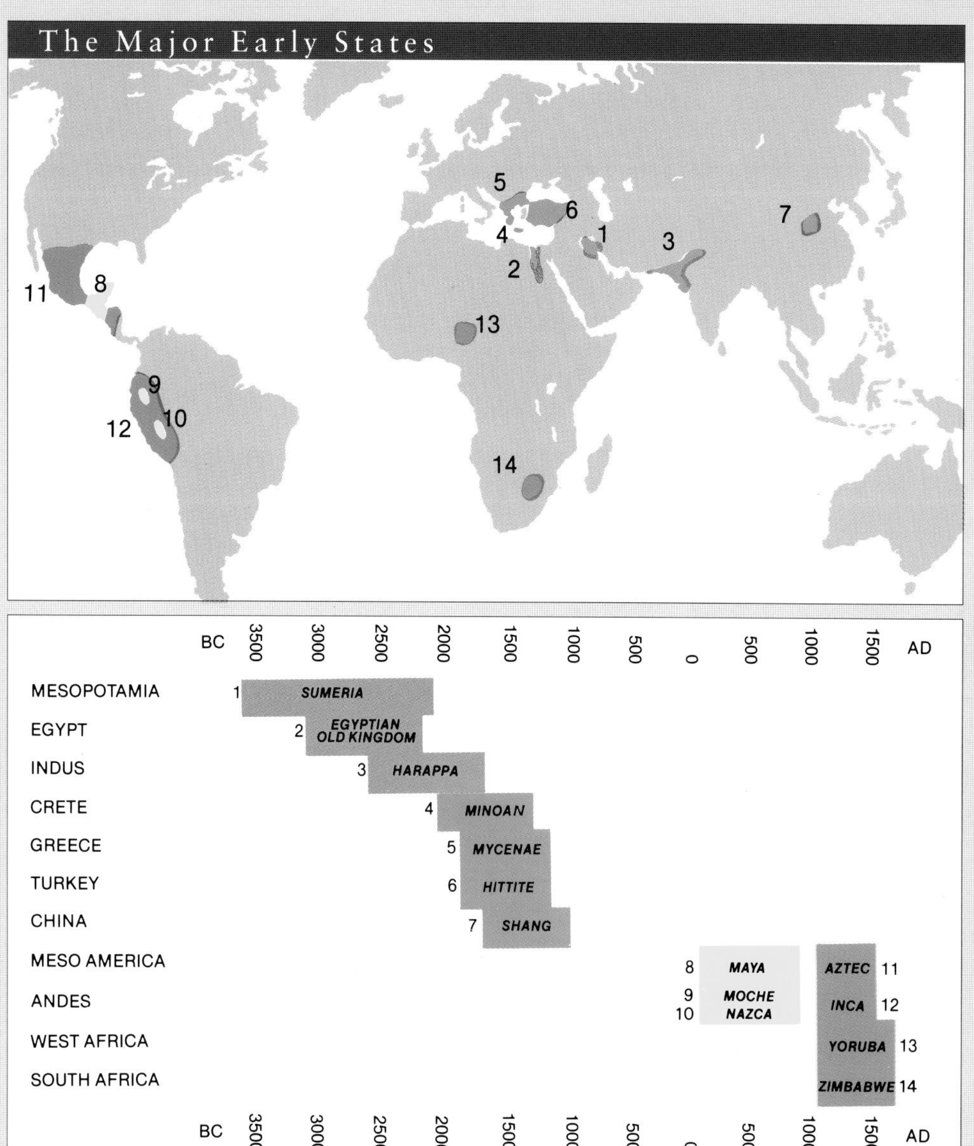

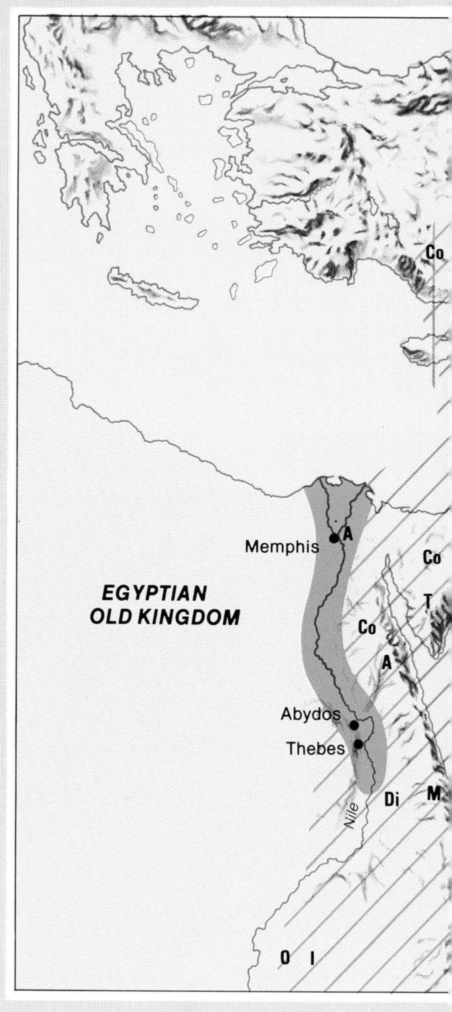

Below: More captives and spoil being brought to Ninevah (Kuyunjik), probably after the Assyrian conquest of tribes inhabiting Chaldaea or southern Babylonia.

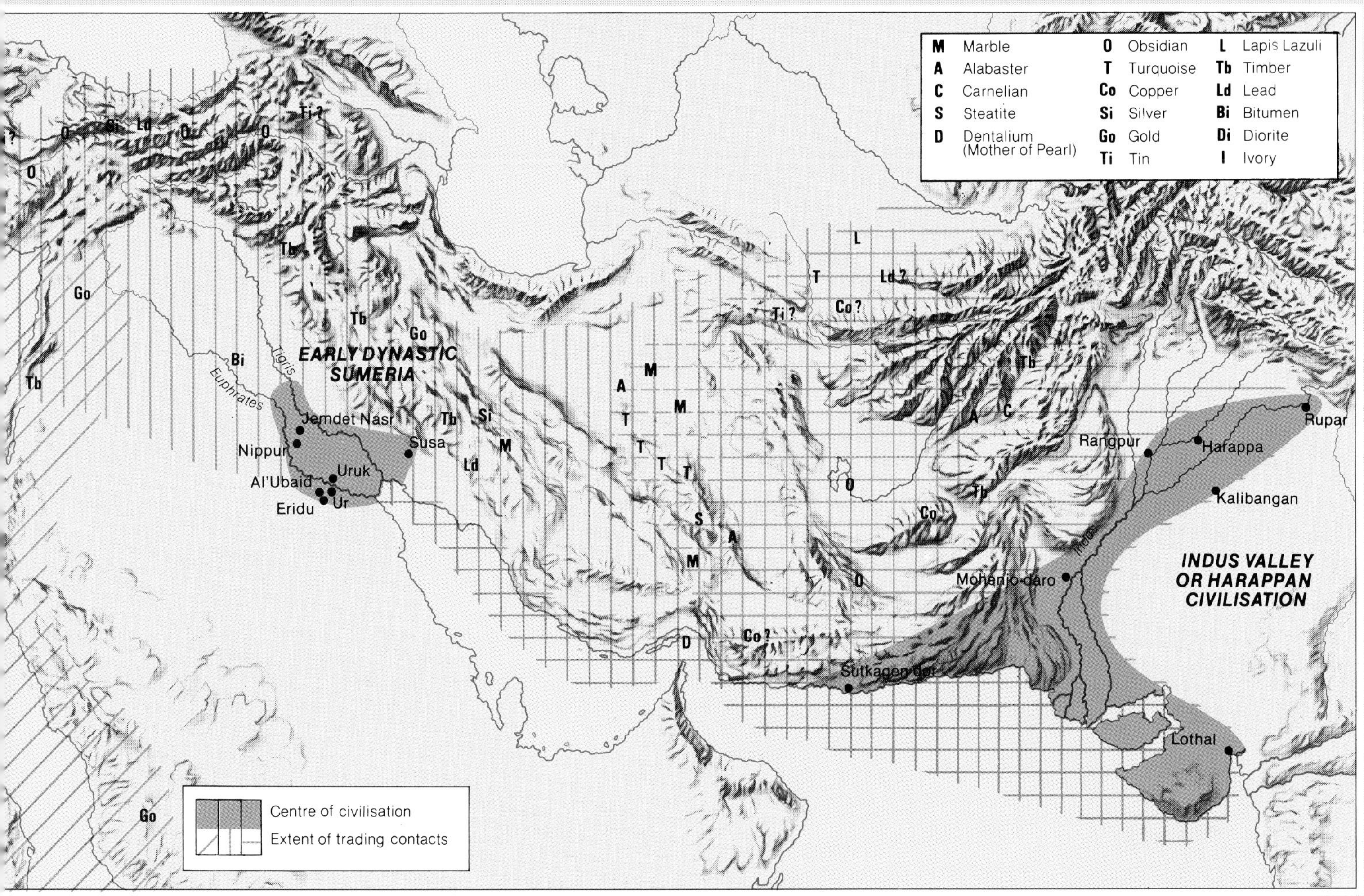

Arab and then Portuguese communities on the east coast for Arabian, Persian and Indian glass beads (and occasionally even Chinese porcelain) in exchange for gold, iron and ivory. Like the American civilizations the African states were unable to withstand European technology and military organization, although their destruction was less cataclysmic.

3 The urban revolution
Childe described the next major stage in the evolution of prehistoric societies as the 'urban revolution'. He referred mainly to the earliest civilizations of Mesopotamia, Egypt and the Indus valley, but the same revolutionary process also took place in other parts of the world.

Below: The ziggurat of the moon-god Nonna, built by Ur-Nommu (2250-2233 BC) at Ur.

Further reading: P. Mellars and C. Stringer, *The Human Revolution* (Edinburgh U. P. 1989); G. Barker, *Prehistoric Farming in Europe* (Cambridge U. P. 1985); J. Gowlett, *Ascent to Civilization* (Collins 1984); Charles L. Redman, *The Rise of Civilization* (Freeman 1978); J. G. D. Clarke, *World Prehistory in New Perspective* (Cambridge U. P., 1977); G. Daniel, *The First Civilizations* (Thames & Hudson, 1968).

The ancient world 2

THE ANCIENT MEDITERRANEAN

After some three thousand years of prehistoric settlement the Minoan civilization emerged in Crete around 2000 BC.

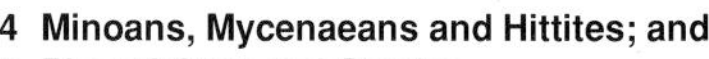

4 Minoans, Mycenaeans and Hittites; and
5 Phoenicians and Greeks
After about 2000 BC the shores and islands of the Mediterranean were gradually colonized by a succession of enterprising peoples who laid the foundations of the cultural and commercial unity upon which classical civilization was based.

The island was controlled by a series of palaces, of which the best known are Knossos, Phaistos and Mallia (*see Map 4*). Each palace, which was undefended, had a large courtyard at its focus, surrounded by elegant monumental buildings, often decorated with highly coloured frescoes. The palaces also housed workshops for craftsmen, who were especially skilled in the working of precious metals and stones, and substantial storerooms. The palaces were primarily administrative centres. Their officials organized agricultural production in the surrounding countryside, (particularly of sheep for wool, and cereals, olives and vines), the collection and storage of foodstuffs, the distribution of rations to craftsmen and agricultural workers, and trade with the outside world. The Minoan script, 'Linear A', still undeciphered, was presumably developed for the complex accounting which this 'palace economy' required.

In about 1450 BC, perhaps in the wake of a volcanic eruption on Santorini (Thera), Crete seems to have fallen under the control of the Mycenaeans, who had established themselves in mainland Greece at about 1700. Their palace architecture, craft skills and decorative arts were very similar to those of Minoan Crete. The Mycenaean script, 'Linear B', is an early form of Greek. It was also primarily an accounting device, for the administrative centres of Greece operated much the same sort of economy as those of Crete. However the Mycenaean centres were usually much smaller and closer together than the Minoan and had massive defences.

In their heyday the Mycenaeans not only controlled Crete and the Cyclades, but traded throughout the eastern Mediterranean, mainly in wine and olive oil. They set up colonies in Italy, Cyprus and the Levant. Some of the most remarkable evidence for their trade comes from a Mycenaean shipwreck with 'ox-hide ingots' (copper weights of a standard measure) discovered off Cape Gelidonya in southern Turkey. The wealth and power of the Mycenaean lords in life are spectacularly illustrated by the fabulous metalwork placed with them in death in the Shaft Graves of Mycenae.

Urban life in Anatolia began on a significant scale with the emergence of the Hittite state after 2000 BC. There had probably been petty chiefdoms in the area before that, for the treasures of the 'royal tombs' of Alaca Hüyük and Troy, dating from about 2500 BC, provide clear evidence of concentrated wealth, advanced craft skills and social hierarchy. However the process of social stratification in Anatolia was apparently accelerated by contact with the established civilization of Mesopotamia. The region was drawn into the trading networks of the higher cultures to the south-east. Shortly after 2000 BC an Assyrian colony was established outside the town of Kültepe (Hittite Kadesh) to organize the export of metal, particularly copper, back to Mesopotamia. The Hittites built a great capital city at Bogazköy (Hattusha), with massive defensive walls four miles in circumference. Perhaps their most significant achievement was their mastery of iron production, which gave them military supremacy in their time. They were far more warlike and expansionist than the Minoans and Mycenaeans, and at the height of their power sacked Babylon (destroying the Babylonian first dynasty) and defeated an Egyptian army near Kadesh.

The Minoan, Mycenaean and Hittite civilizations all collapsed in about 1200 BC, and in Egypt the system of government of the Pharaohs crumbled temporarily. The immediate cause in every region seems to have been military attack, but such raids should be regarded more as symptoms of internal disintegration than as a fundamental cause of collapse. Social and economic failure, compounded by natural disasters such as drought and disease, opened the way for the invaders. In addition, the fact that iron making had become very widely diffused in Anatolia and Asia Minor by 1000 BC not only contributed to the confusion of the following centuries, as one people after another bid for supremacy, but suggests that the loss of the Hittite monopoly of ironworking was one reason for their decline. Advanced civilization had lost its technological lead over its barbarian neighbours.

Whatever its cause, the collapse of 1200 BC inaugurated a long period of obscurity and confusion from whose debris the continuous history of Western civilization begins to emerge. By around 500 BC, the Eurasian landbridge of the Middle East and Anatolia had been subjected to a unified political domination which stretched to the edges of desert, sea and steppe, while the shores of the Mediterranean had been settled by colonists from the Levant and the Aegean (*Maps 5 and 6*). This contrast between the two great homes of classical civilization was not only geographical: the words 'Persian' and 'Greek' already stood, as they would continue to do, for 'despotism' and 'democracy'.

The Assyrian empire, which controlled the trade

Left: Phoenician ivory furniture panel depicting a lion attacking a slave, gilded and decorated with carnelians and blue enamel. The Assyrians collected Phoenician ivories. This one was thrown into a well during the sack of the Assyrian city of Nimrud in 700 BC and found 1951.

MAP 4 MINOANS, MYCENAEANS AND HITTITES

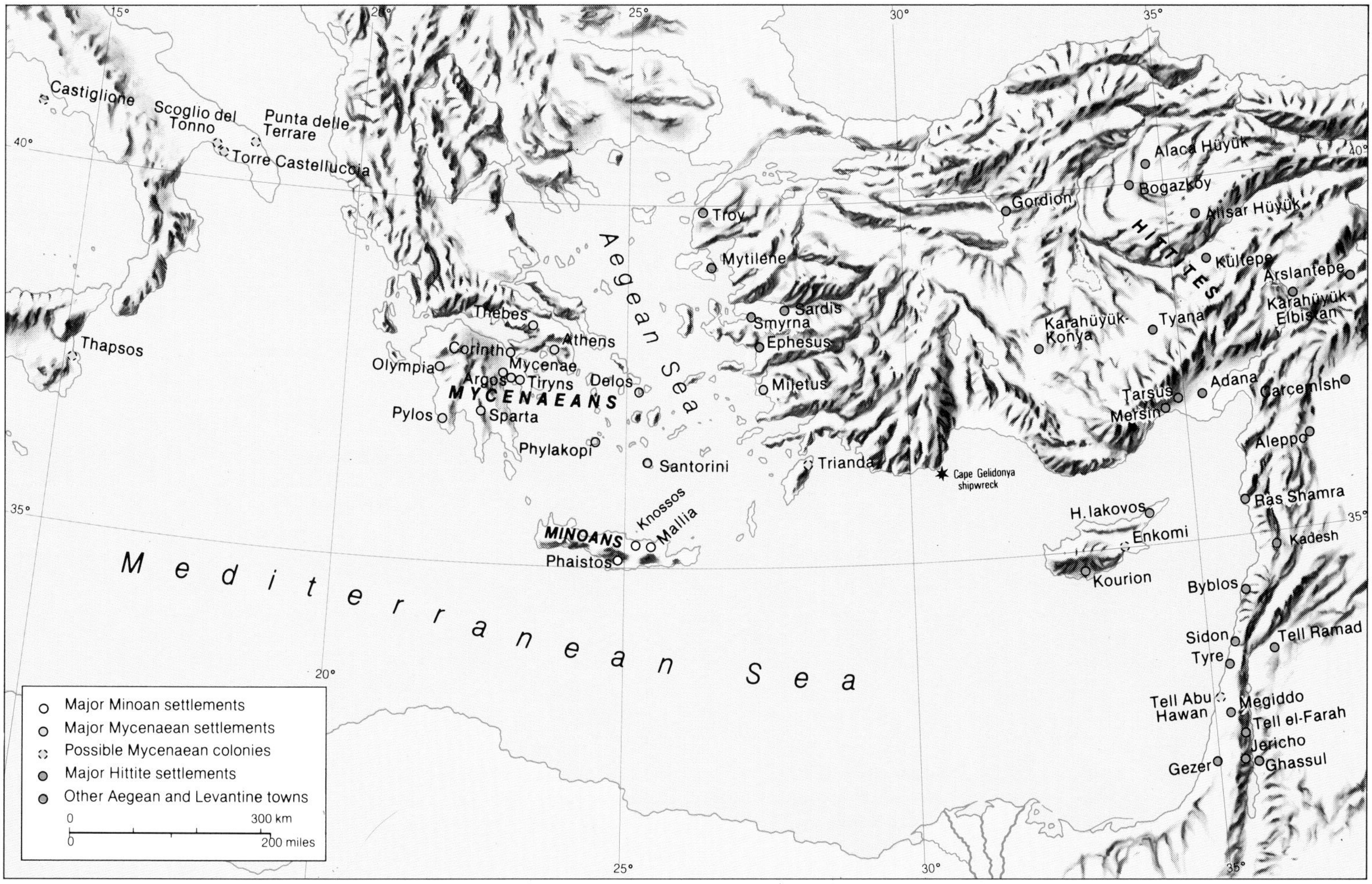

- Major Minoan settlements
- Major Mycenaean settlements
- Possible Mycenaean colonies
- Major Hittite settlements
- Other Aegean and Levantine towns

0 300 km
0 200 miles

MAP 5 PHOENICIANS AND GREEKS

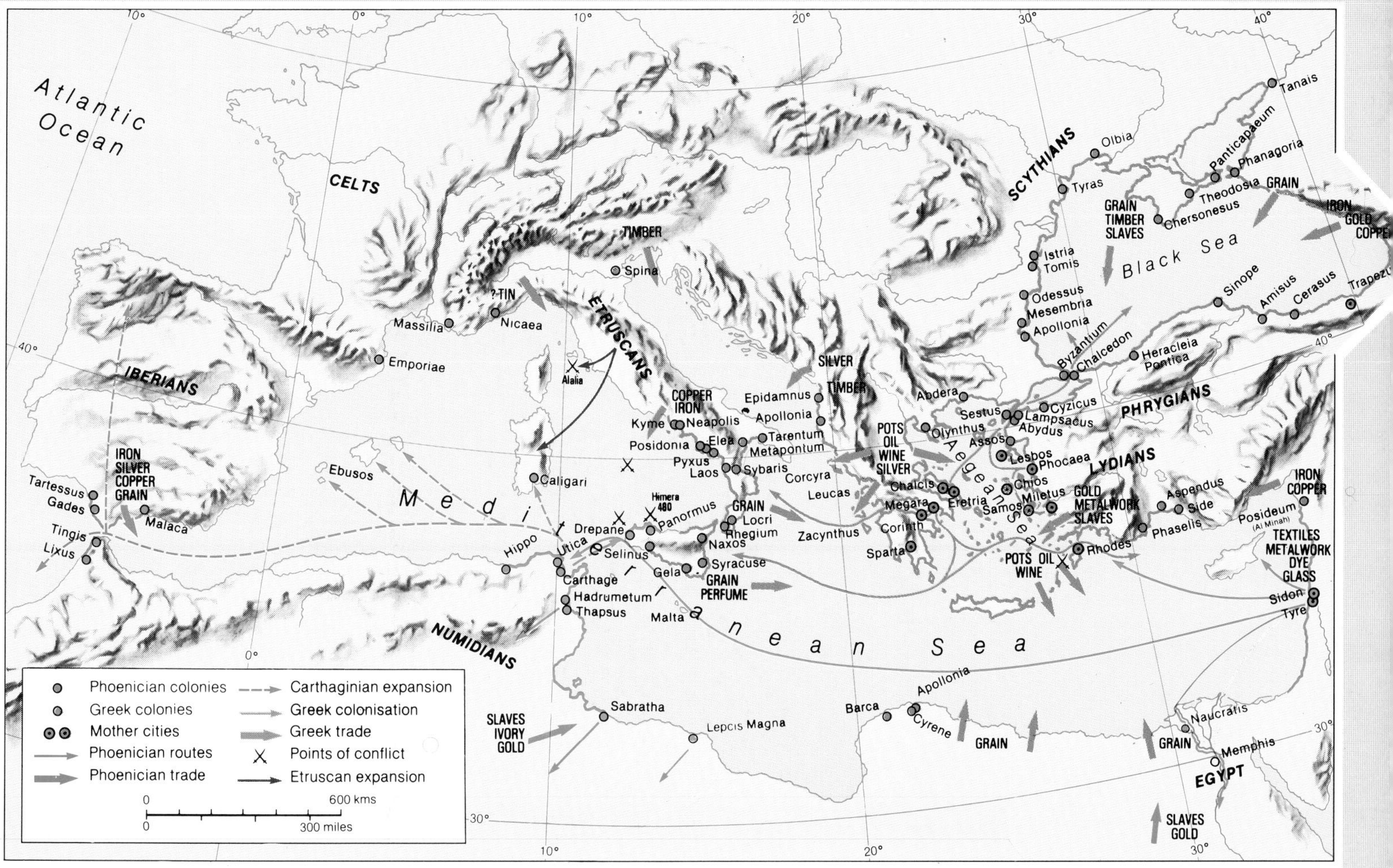

- Phoenician colonies
- Greek colonies
- Mother cities
- Phoenician routes
- Phoenician trade
- Carthaginian expansion
- Greek colonisation
- Greek trade
- Points of conflict
- Etruscan expansion

0 600 kms
0 300 miles

routes between Mesopotamia and the Mediterranean from the time of Ashur-narsi-Pal (*r*.883-859 BC) and conquered Egypt in that of Essarhaddon (*r*.680-669), provided the most centralized and the most brutal government that man had yet seen. Its populations were subjugated by mass murder, deportation and enslavement on a huge scale. Assyrian governors, supported by a professional and internationally recruited army, imposed a single code of law and administration. Even more than the Medes who overthrew them, destroying their capital of Ninevah in 612, the Assyrians were the precursors of the more enduring despotism of the Persian empire.

The Achaemenids had ruled Persia as tributaries since about 700 BC. Cyrus I (*r*.559-29) rebelled against the Medes, capturing their capital at Ecbatana in 550. He extended his rule to the banks of the Jaxartes and, with the seizure of the Lydian kingdom and the exaction of tribute from the Greek cities of the Ionian coast, to the shores of the Aegean. The conquests of Darius I (*r*.521-486) completed the empire (*Map 6*). He established a system of imperial government which gave a common institutional and cultural heritage to the whole region. Both from the administrative districts (satrapies) of the directly ruled empire and from his subject kings he demanded a fixed annual tax. A complex bureaucracy maintained a standing army and labour forces to construct vast temples and cities, extensive irrigation works, a common coinage and the system of royal roads – the most famous running from Sardis to Susa – which both symbolized and permitted a new degree of unity and coherence. The wealth and power of the king of kings were reflected in the magnificence of his palace, the elaboration of his court ceremonials, his proclamation as immortal by his subjects, (who prostrated themselves before him in the gesture which the Greeks would long regard with contempt as the supreme expression of oriental servility), and the proliferation of harems and later of the palace eunuchs whose sinister influence would play behind the thrones of this region for the next two thousand years and more.

Oriental despotism was founded upon the physical domination of those who cultivated the land through the ruthless and large-scale centralization which was necessary to create and maintain the vital irrigation systems. The bare, steep and deeply indented shores of the Mediterranean did not require irrigation on so large a scale nor did they permit the easy expansion of communities across large areas of land. The peoples who lodged around it were compelled to independence by their isolation from each other, and to inter-dependence by the constant need to exchange men and goods across the sea.

By comparison with these fundamental bonds, the larger political structures which the wealth of the Mediterranean basin periodically called into being were ephemeral. When the Roman Empire collapsed it became apparent that, among the components into which it crumbled, those which had been created by Greek colonization between 750 and 550 BC (*Map 5*) still remained distinct. They persisted, politically and culturally vital, for another thousand years (*see Maps 17 and 21*).

The Greeks believed that the maritime expansion of the Phoenician cities – Aradus, Byblus, Berytus, Sidon and, greatest of all, Tyre (*Maps 5 and 9*) – preceded their own. In fact there is no evidence that anyone traded between Greece and the Phoenician coast until the Greeks themselves founded a colony at Al Minah in the eighth century BC, or that the Greek colonies in Sicily displaced Phoenician ones. The early Phoenicians seem to have been content to trade where 'civilized' peoples had already settled, for example at Cyprus, Rhodes and Crete. The first proven colonies appeared after about 750 BC (probably following Assyrian attacks on the mother cities) in Sardinia, Sicily, Africa and Spain; those at Leptis Magna, Utica, Hadrumetum and Gades were among the first. And Gades, with its proximity to the Guadalquivir river and the metal deposits of Spain, suggests the motive. In a pattern that would appear again (*compare Map 27*) the Phoenicians exchanged for raw materials – slaves, ivory and above all metals – the fripperies of civilization such as metal ornaments, glassware, and the legendary purple cloth of Tyre. Phoenician colonization, in short, began at much the same time as Greek, and in much the same way, developing in response to pressures on the mother cities some time after a pattern of irregular trading had been established. Phoenician colonies, unlike those of the Greeks, were tied to their founders by an obligation to pay tribute. Carthage (traditionally founded in 814) became the effective leader of the western colonies when Tyre fell to the Assyrians in the eighth century; it then founded an empire of its own with the planting of a colony at Ibiza in 654-53 (*see Map 8*).

The extension of the Hellenic world to Sicily and the shores of the Black Sea was intimately bound up with the evolution of cultural unity and a measure of political co-operation among the Greeks. During the dark age around 1200, when the Dorian Greeks apparently moved southwards into Thessaly, Boeotia, Achaea, the Peloponnese and some of the islands, settlement apparently continued at some Mycenaean centres, including Crete and Athens (*Map 7*). According to tradition the re-occupation of the Ionian coast and islands was organized from Athens around 1000. The story may reflect a preponderance which Athens had already attained, for it was the first centre of iron-age culture in Greece.

Expansion beyond the Aegean basin followed in Mycenaean footsteps. From about 700 BC eastern goods, designs and ideas were brought from the Levant by the Euboeans. A little later they planted the first western colony at Cumae (Kyme). Others followed rapidly; the fact that Reggio and Messina were among the earliest, though not the most fertile or convenient spots available, suggests that securing supplies of metal from Etruria was an immediate objective. The unending search for metal took the Greeks to the Rhône delta, the Spanish coast and the shores of the Black Sea in the next century. Nevertheless trade was not the most important reason for their expansion. If there was a prime cause, over-population is the most likely. The severe limit which the poor soils, narrow plains and inhospitable hills of the Aegean basin set upon natural increase was perfectly clear to its inhabitants, and simple overcrowding as well as political dispute compelled many of the early colonists to leave their native cities.

Emigration produced a measure of co-operation among the Aegean communities. The colonies were founded by a relatively small number of cities. Samos, Phocaea and Miletus founded many settlements along the Black Sea and in the west, as did Chalcis and Eretria of Euboea, and Megara on the mainland. Corinth and Achaea contributed most of the colonies in Sicily and the toe and instep of Italy. Since it would be absurd to suppose that all the colonists came from these few places, they must be regarded as organizers and initiators of colonising activity on the part of others.

Westward expansion was checked by an alliance of the Etruscans and Carthaginians at Alalia, *c*. 540, a battle which marks the appearance of new powers in the western Mediterranean. Both would be succeeded in their turn by the Romans (*Map 8*). Commerce continued, however, and in return for their metals the Etruscans had already acquired, though they had not absorbed, a substantial inheritance of Greek culture in the form of metalwork, pottery and fresco painting far more advanced than they could have attempted themselves. This was what the Greeks had to exchange (in addition to their wine and olive oil, which were highly valued) for the extensive variety of goods which they imported.

The colonies not only provided the cities of Aegean Greece with an outlet for their surplus population but enabled them to support a greater one themselves, particularly as the great granaries of Sicily and Southern Italy, Egypt (through Naucratis) and the northern shores of the Black Sea were opened up. Rapidly increasing population provided the foundation for the achievements which ensured that the cultural influence of the Greeks would always surpass the limits of their political power.

6 The Achaemenid empire in Persia
The Achaemenids set up the Persian empire, established common legal and administrative arrangements and a common currency and built a system of royal roads linking the earliest centres of civilization.

7 The Greeks in the Aegean
'We sit around our sea like frogs around their pond', Socrates said of the Greeks. The people of the cities of island and mainland Greece began to come together for games and religious worship, united by a common culture and institutions rather than by political union.

Further reading P. Levi, *Atlas of the Greek World* (Phaidon 1970); J. Boardman etc., *The Oxford History of the Classical World* (Oxford U. P. 1986); M. I. Finley, *The World of Odysseus* (second ed. Viking Penguin 1978); J. Boardman, *The Greeks Overseas* (second. ed. Thames & Hudson, 1980.); N. Spivey and S. Stoddart, *Etruscan Italy* (Batsford 1990).

MAP 6 THE ACHAEMENID EMPIRE IN PERSIA

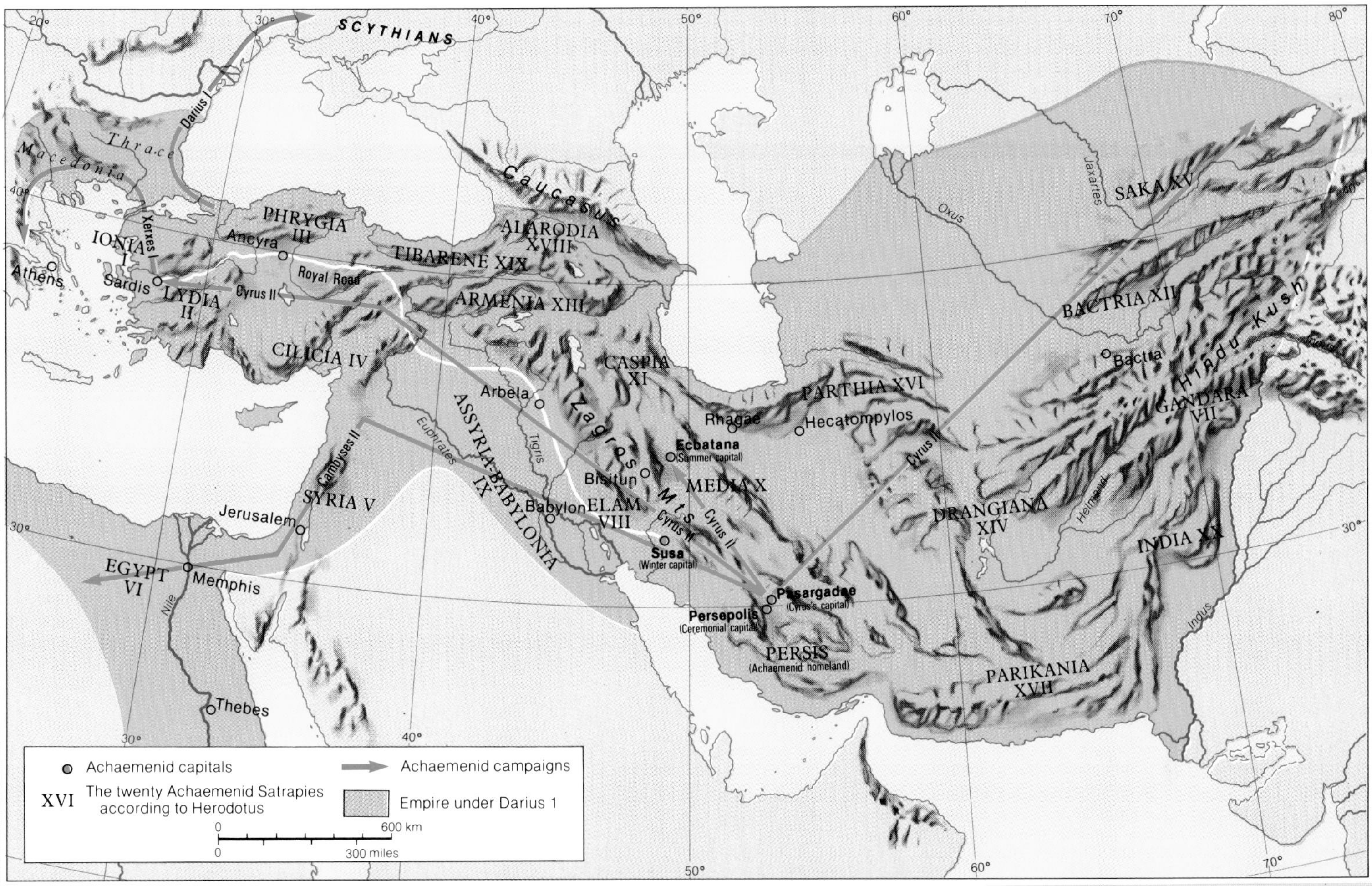

SCYTHIANS
Darius I
Thrace
Macedonia
Xerxes I
IONIA I
Athens
Sardis
LYDIA II
PHRYGIA III
Ancyra
Royal Road
Cyrus II
CILICIA IV
Caucasus
ALARODIA XVIII
TIBARENE XIX
ARMENIA XIII
CASPIA XI
Arbela
Zagros Mts
Tigris
Euphrates
ASSYRIA-BABYLONIA IX
Cambyses II
SYRIA V
Jerusalem
EGYPT VI
Memphis
Nile
Thebes
Babylon
Bisitun
ELAM VIII
Susa (Winter capital)
Ecbatana (Summer capital)
MEDIA X
Rhagae
PARTHIA XVI
Hecatompylos
Pasargadae (Cyrus's capital)
Persepolis (Ceremonial capital)
PERSIS (Achaemenid homeland)
DRANGIANA XIV
PARIKANIA XVII
Oxus
Jaxartes
SAKA XV
BACTRIA XII
Bactra
Hindu Kush
GANDARA VII
Helmand
INDIA XX
Indus

Achaemenid capitals
XVI The twenty Achaemenid Satrapies according to Herodotus
Achaemenid campaigns
Empire under Darius 1
0 600 km
0 300 miles

MAP 7 THE GREEKS IN THE AEGEAN

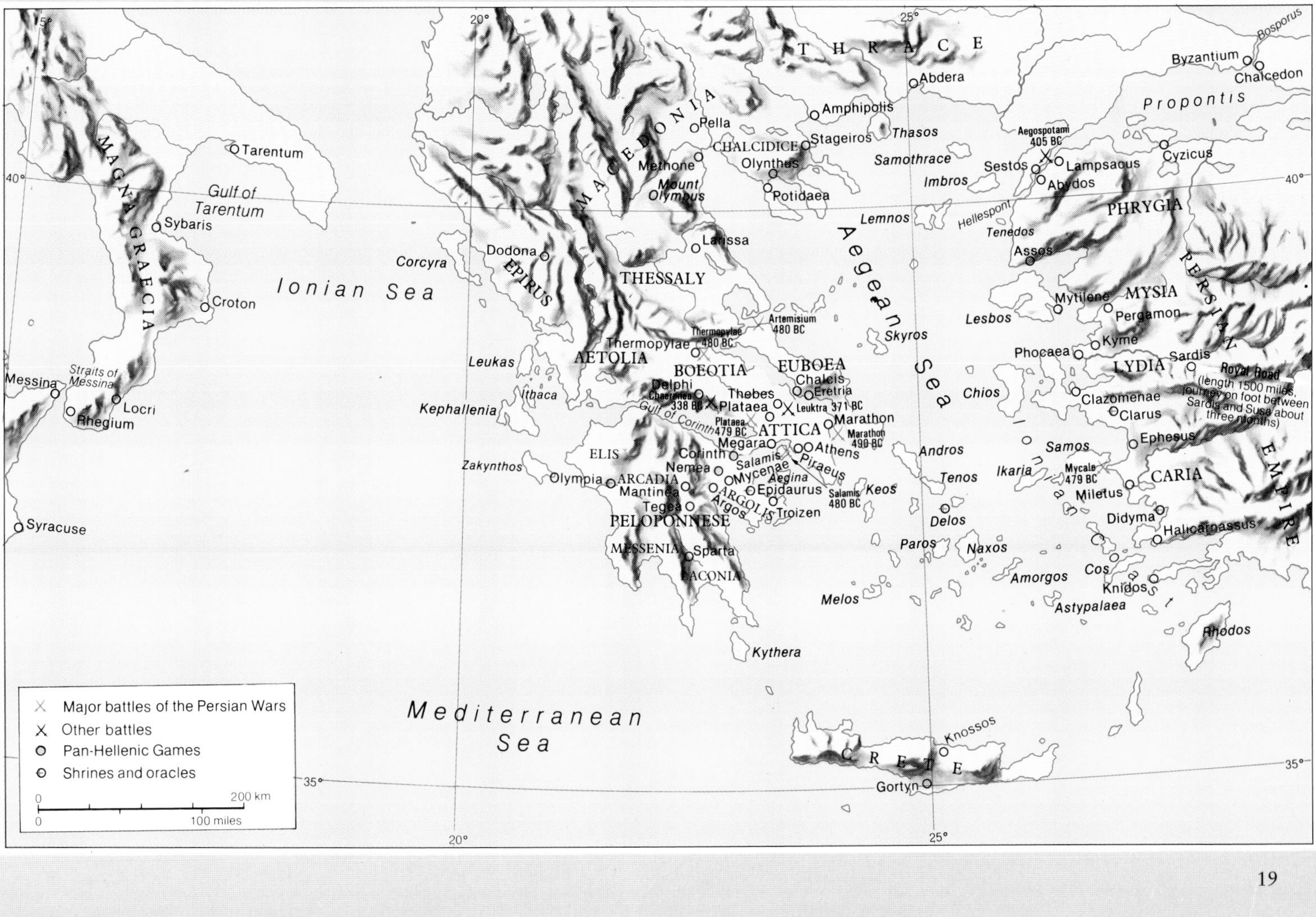

THRACE
Abdera
Byzantium
Chalcedon
Bosporus
Propontis
Cyzicus
Amphipolis
Thasos
Rella
Stageiros
CHALCIDICE
Olynthus
Potidaea
Methone
Mount Olympus
MACEDONIA
Samothrace
Imbros
Aegospotami 405 BC
Sestos
Lampsacus
Abydos
Hellespont
Lemnos
Tenedos
PHRYGIA
Assos
MAGNA GRAECIA
Tarentum
Gulf of Tarentum
Sybaris
Croton
Ionian Sea
Corcyra
Dodona
EPIRUS
Larissa
THESSALY
Aegean Sea
Lesbos
Mytilene
MYSIA
Pergamon
Kyme
Phocaea
LYDIA
Sardis
Royal Road (length 1500 miles, journey on foot between Sardis and Susa about three months)
PERSIAN EMPIRE
Messina
Straits of Messina
Locri
Rhegium
Leukas
Ithaca
Kephallenia
Thermopylae 480 BC
Artemisium 480 BC
Skyros
AETOLIA
BOEOTIA
EUBOEA
Chalcis
Eretria
Delphi
Chaeronea 338 BC
Thebes
Plataea
Leuktra 371 BC
Plataea 479 BC
Gulf of Corinth
ATTICA
Marathon
Marathon 490 BC
Chios
Clazomenae
Clarus
Ephesus
Megara
Corinth
Athens
Salamis
Piraeus
Andros
Samos
ELIS
Nemea
Mycenae
Aegina
Zakynthos
Olympia
ARCADIA
Mantinea
Argos
ARGOLIS
Epidaurus
Salamis 480 BC
Keos
Tenos
Ikaria
Mycale 479 BC
Miletus
CARIA
Tegea
Troizen
PELOPONNESE
Delos
Didyma
Halicarnassus
MESSENIA
Sparta
LACONIA
Paros
Naxos
Amorgos
Cos
Knidos
Melos
Astypalaea
Rhodos
Kythera
Syracuse
Mediterranean Sea
Knossos
CRETE
Gortyn

Major battles of the Persian Wars
Other battles
Pan-Hellenic Games
Shrines and oracles
0 200 km
0 100 miles

The ancient world 3

THE CLASSICAL CIVILIZATIONS

The belief of the Greeks that they inhabited an island of freedom in a sea of despotism was well founded. By 500 BC the monarchies and aristocracies of heroic Greece had mostly gone, to leave a world comparatively little marked by variations of wealth and privilege.

Its free citizens were accustomed to ruling their own lives, and, except in Sparta, many slaves differed little from them in the pattern of their everyday lives, the structure of their families and the range of their occupations. The Greeks began to express a sense of community when they came together for festivals of games and music – the Olympiads were reckoned from 776 BC – and at the shrines of the most famous oracles (*Map 7*); and many of them joined together, under the leadership of Sparta and Athens, to reject Persia's demand for a general submission after the brutal suppression of the revolt of the Ionian cities (499-94), and to win the ensuing war.

The plays, the histories, the philosophy of the golden age which followed are marked by an intense curiosity about the nature of man as a social animal, possessed of the power to shape his destiny and thereby obliged to define and seek 'the good'. 'We Athenians, in our own persons, take our decisions on policy and submit them to proper discussion', Pericles, the greatest of their leaders, told his fellow citizens. 'We give our obedience to those whom we ourselves put in positions of authority.' The quest for the highest good, to which the actions of free men should be directed, is ideally depicted in the dialogues of Plato (428-347), while the results of calm enquiry into the nature of the visible world are triumphantly set out in the writings of his pupil Aristotle of Stagira (384-22). Aristotle's works, surviving in effect as lecture notes collected by his pupils, lack the charm and grace of Plato's, but they cover every branch of the knowledge of his time, from aesthetics and politics to botany and physics. Their conclusions dominated western thought for more than 2000 years and their method still does. If we fail to be startled by Aristotle's close and dispassionate observations of diligently collected facts, from which conclusions are drawn with scrupulous attention to the soundness of argument and the legitimacy of

8 The rise of Rome
Three centuries of almost continuous warfare made Rome the first and last power to unite the shores of the Mediterranean under a single regime, overthrowing the empires of Carthage (destroyed 146 BC), the Seleucids (64 BC) and the Ptolemies (30 BC) and, especially in the west, garrisoning the conquered territories with colonies of Roman citizens.

MAP 8 THE RISE OF ROME

deduction, or to be astounded by the absence of any appeal to the supernatural to resolve the mysteries of nature, it is because the 'father of reason' has taught us to take reason for granted. Nor did this reason defeat itself by resting on instinct. Its basis in the nature of language and knowledge themselves was examined and set forth in the logical works which remain the foundation of all rational thought.

The conquests of Aristotle's pupil Alexander of Macedon (*Map 9*) constitute another remarkable monument to the curiosity of the Greeks. Beyond destroying a Persian empire already in decay they had little political purpose or importance. After Alexander's death in 322 his empire fragmented into a shifting assortment of successor (*diadochi*) states ruled by his generals and their descendants, of which the most important were those of Egypt under the Ptolemies and Syria-Iran under the Seleucids. But Alexander's journey represented an extension of Greek civilization from the Nile to the Indus. The Achaemenids had already done much to unite this area (*Map 6*). Although the Ptolemies adopted a lighter coinage which ran through the Nile valley and the southern and western Mediterranean – the Phoenician world – there was a great expansion in the volume and regularity of the exchange of goods across this great common market, now settled by Greek communities linked to one another by the ties of language and culture (*see Map 9*).

Some of the new cities were only glorified fortresses. In many others the Greeks (who, despite some intermarriage with the existing populations, remained socially and culturally dominant) built temples, gymnasia and theatres, educated their children in Greek schools and settled disputes before Greek judges according to Greek law. The universality of their influence is attested by the foundation of the two greatest libraries of antiquity, at (Egyptian) Alexandria and Pergamum, or by the inscription which records the arrival at the frontier city of Ai Khanum, in modern Afghanistan, of a visiting lecturer from mainland Greece.

The wealth and sophistication of the Hellenistic world are most familiar today through its dynamic and often tortuous sculpture, the Venus of Milo or the Laocoön, and its mechanical ingenuities such as the lighthouse at Alexandria, the screw of Archimedes, the steam engine invented by Hero of Syracuse or the water organs and animated dolls which amused the court of the Ptolemies. But failure to develop equal skill in metallurgy prevented most of these devices from becoming more than playthings, and the lasting achievements were still in the area of theory, especially in mathematics and physics. The work of Euclid (*c*.300 BC) and Archimedes (*c*.287-212 BC) in these fields was not surpassed until the age of Descartes and Newton.

The diffusion of Greek culture in the Hellenistic age multiplied the manuscripts in which it was preserved. Many of them were copied by the technique invented at Pergamum of writing on animal skins – parchment, much more durable than papyrus – which made it possible for their contents to survive the vicissitudes of a thousand years and be taken up again by the Arabs.

The Jews, whose kingdom had been founded about 1000 BC under David, split by rival claimants, crushed by the Babylonian captivity (586-538 BC) and revived under the protection of the Achaemenids, flourished in this age of cultural exchange. The destruction of Jerusalem by Nebuchadnezzar in 587 began the dispersal (*diaspora*) which became the continuous experience of the Jews (*see Map 11*). It also gave rise to the practice of regular collective reading of the scriptures and insistence upon close observance of the Law – for the Destruction was interpreted as divine punishment for its neglect – which have con-

9 The Hellenistic world
In the footsteps of Alexander the Great, the Greeks founded scores of cities in the old Persian empire, and absorbed others at economically and strategically vital points. They created a network which connected all the known civilizations of the world, and which was completed when the Chinese opened the silk route *c.* 112 BC.

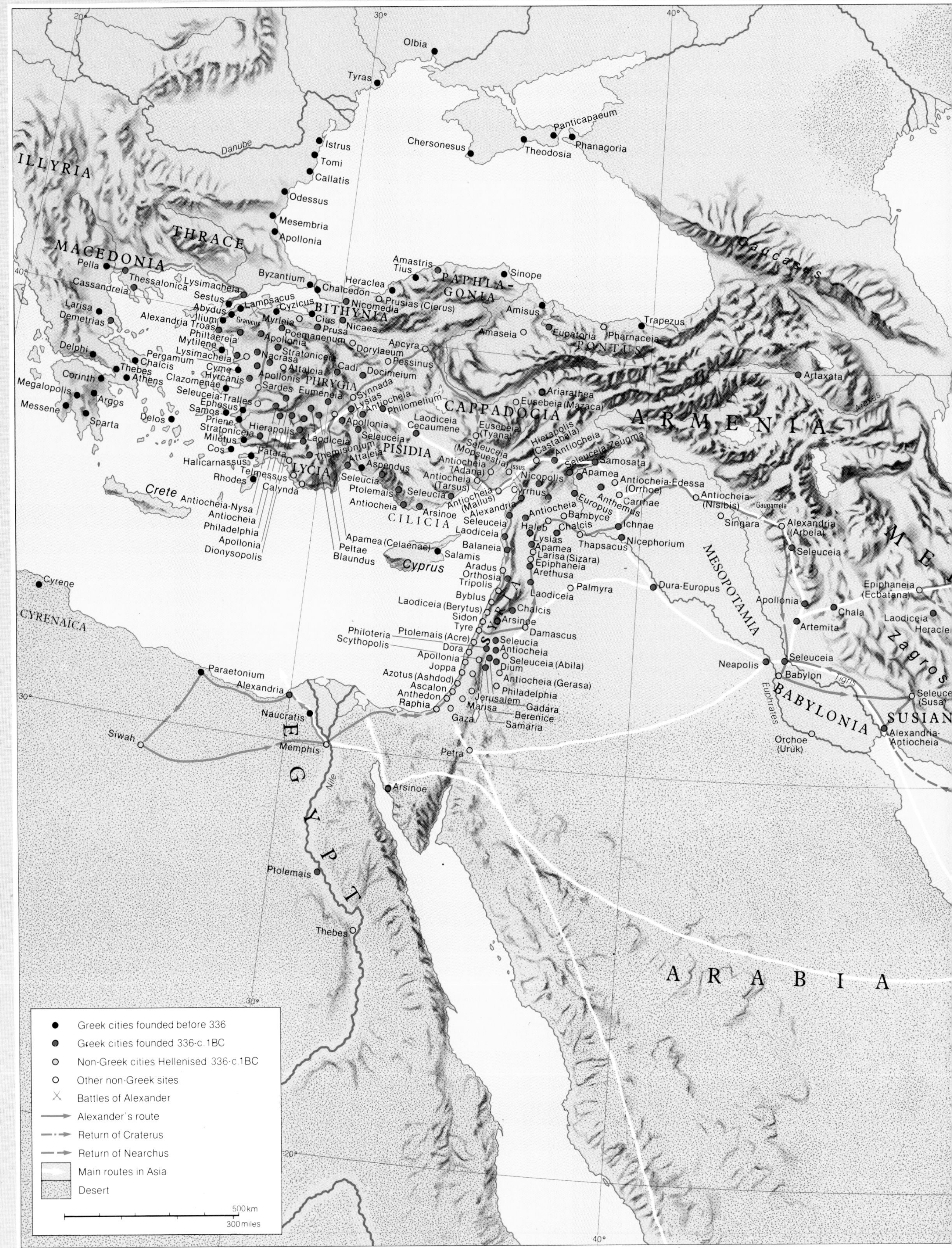

Greek cities founded before 336
Greek cities founded 336-c.1BC
Non-Greek cities Hellenised 336-c.1BC
Other non-Greek sites
Battles of Alexander
Alexander's route
Return of Craterus
Return of Nearchus
Main routes in Asia
Desert
500 km
300 miles
ILLYRIA
THRACE
MACEDONIA
BITHYNIA
PAPHLAGONIA
PONTUS
PHRYGIA
CAPPADOCIA
ARMENIA
PISIDIA
LYCIA
CILICIA
SYRIA
MESOPOTAMIA
BABYLONIA
SUSIANA
CYRENAICA
EGYPT
ARABIA
Danube
Caucasus
Zagros
Tigris
Euphrates
Araxes
Nile
Crete
Cyprus
Olbia
Tyras
Istrus
Tomi
Callatis
Odessus
Mesembria
Apollonia
Chersonesus
Theodosia
Panticapaeum
Phanagoria
Byzantium
Chalcedon
Heraclea
Amastris
Tius
Sinope
Amisus
Trapezus
Amaseia
Eupatoria
Pharnaceia
Artaxata
Pella
Thessalonica
Cassandreia
Lysimacheia
Sestus
Lampsacus
Abydus
Cyzicus
Granicus
Ilium
Alexandria Troas
Myrleia
Cius
Prusa
Nicomedia
Nicaea
Prusias (Cierus)
Poemanenum
Philtaereia
Mytilene
Apollonia
Stratoniceia
Dorylaeum
Ancyra
Pessinus
Larisa
Demetrias
Delphi
Chalcis
Thebes
Athens
Corinth
Megalopolis
Argos
Messene
Sparta
Pergamum
Lysimacheia
Nacrasa
Cyme
Hyrcanis
Attaleia
Cadi
Docimeium
Clazomenae
Apollonis
Sardes
Synnada
Eumeneia
Seleuceia-Tralles
Ephesus
Lysias
Antiocheia
Philomelium
Samos
Delos
Priene
Stratoniceia
Miletus
Hierapolis
Apollonia
Laodiceia
Seleuceia
Laodiceia Cecaumene
Cos
Halicarnassus
Patara
Themisonium
Attaleia
Aspendus
Telmessus
Rhodes
Calynda
Seleuceia
Ptolemais
Antiocheia
Antiocheia-Nysa
Antiocheia
Philadelphia
Apollonia
Dionysopolis
Apamea (Celaenae)
Peltae
Blaundus
Eusebeia (Mazaca)
Ariaratheia
Eusebeia (Tyana)
Seleuceia (Mopsuestia)
Antiocheia (Adana)
Antiocheia (Tarsus)
Seleuceia
Arsinoe
Antiocheia (Mallus)
Issus
Alexandria
Seleuceia
Laodiceia
Hierapolis Castabala
Antiocheia
Seleuceia-Zeugma
Samosata
Nicopolis
Apamea
Antiocheia-Edessa (Orrhoe)
Carrhae
Anthemus
Antiocheia (Nisibis)
Gaugamela
Singara
Cyrrhus
Antiocheia
Europus
Bambyce
Haleb
Chalcis
Ichnae
Thapsacus
Nicephorium
Alexandria (Arbela)
Seleuceia
Lysias
Apamea
Larisa (Sizara)
Epiphaneia
Arethusa
Salamis
Balaneia
Aradus
Orthosia
Tripolis
Byblus
Laodiceia (Berytus)
Sidon
Tyre
Laodiceia
Palmyra
Dura-Europus
Chalcis
Arsinoe
Damascus
Philoteria
Scythopolis
Ptolemais (Acre)
Dora
Apollonia
Joppa
Azotus (Ashdod)
Ascalon
Anthedon
Raphia
Gaza
Seleuceia
Antiocheia
Seleuceia (Abila)
Dium
Antiocheia (Gerasa)
Philadelphia
Jerusalem
Marisa
Gadara
Berenice
Samaria
Petra
Cyrene
Paraetonium
Alexandria
Naucratis
Siwah
Memphis
Arsinoe
Ptolemais
Thebes
Epiphaneia (Ecbatana)
Chala
Apollonia
Artemita
Laodiceia
Heraclea
Neapolis
Seleuceia
Babylon
Seleuceia (Susa)
Alexandria-Antiocheia
Orchoe (Uruk)

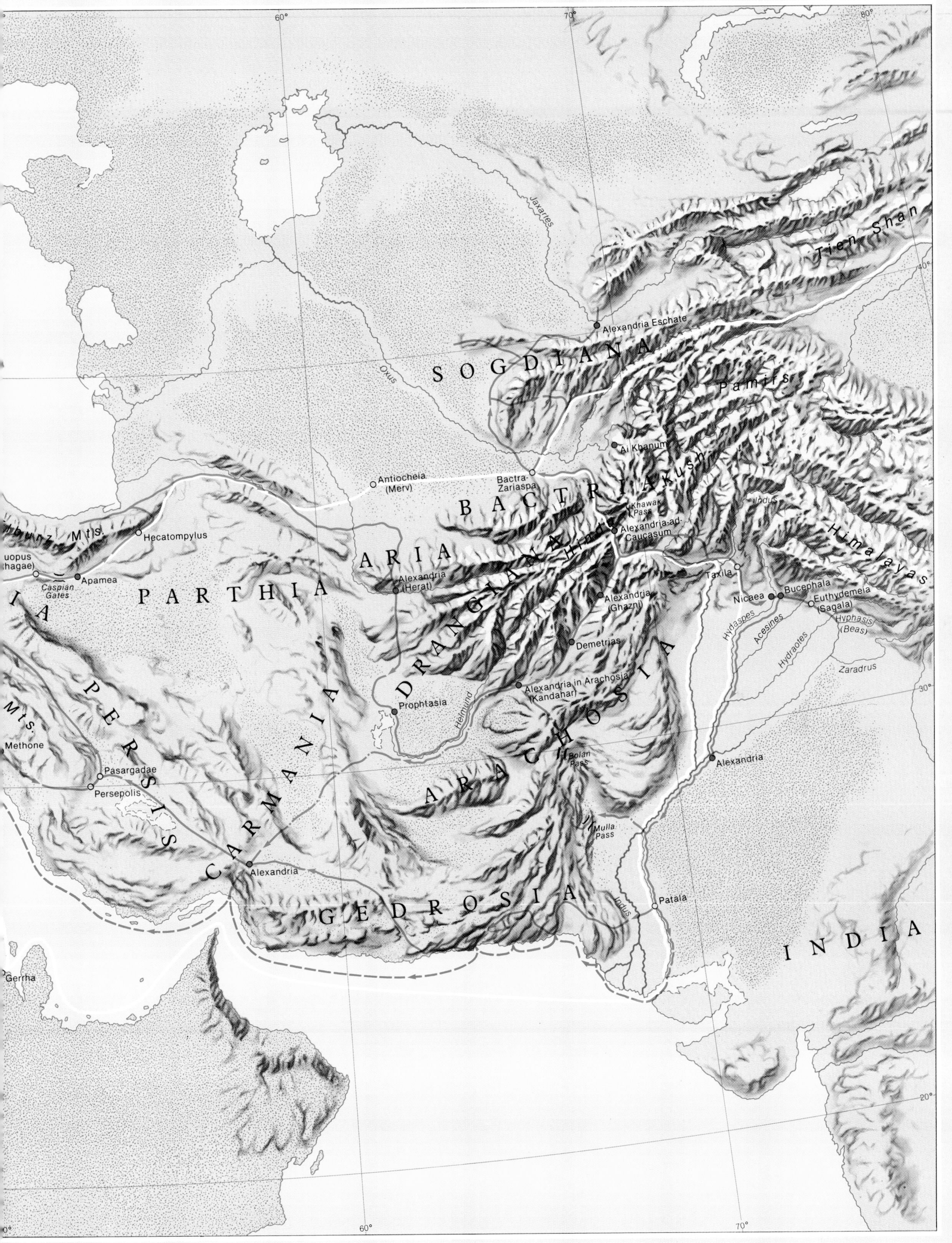

SOGDIANA
BACTRIA
ARIA
PARTHIA
DRANGIANA
ARACHOSIA
CARMANIA
PERSIS
GEDROSIA
INDIA
Alexandria Eschate
Jaxartes
Oxus
Tien Shan
Pamirs
Ai Khanum
Hindu Kush
Himalayas
Antiocheia (Merv)
Bactra-Zariaspa
Khawak Pass
Alexandria-ad-Caucasum
Hecatompylus
Apamea
Caspian Gates
Alexandria (Herat)
Alexandria (Ghazni)
Taxila
Nicaea
Bucephala
Euthydemeia (Sagala)
Hydaspes
Acesines
Hydraotes
Hyphasis (Beas)
Zaradrus
Demetrias
Alexandria in Arachosia (Kandahar)
Prophtasia
Helmund
Bolan Pass
Alexandria
Methone
Pasargadae
Persepolis
Mulla Pass
Alexandria
Patala
Indus
Gerrha
60°
70°
80°
40°
30°
20°

MAP 10 THE EXPANSION OF THE HAN CHINESE SETTLEMENT

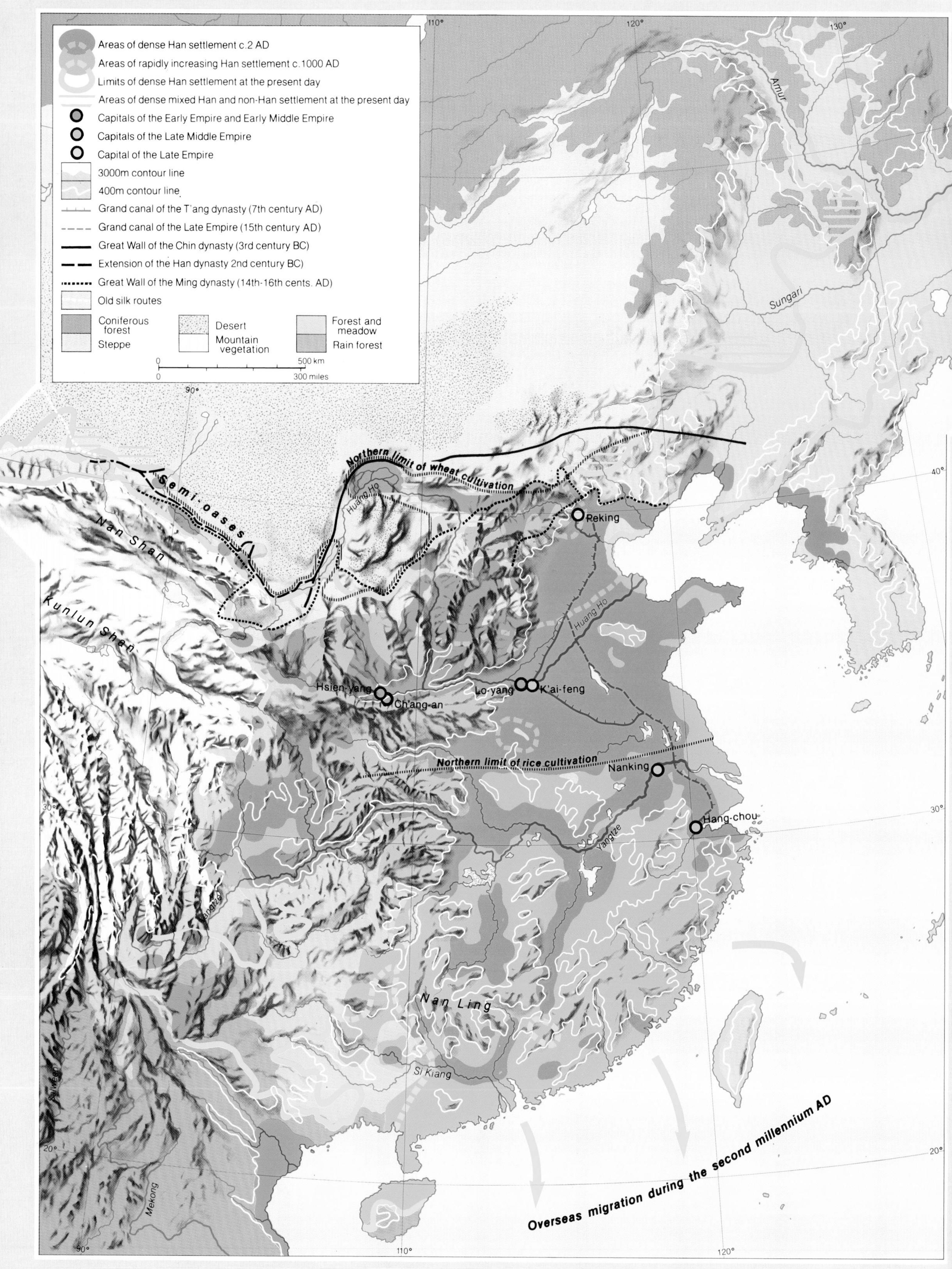
Areas of dense Han settlement c.2 AD
Areas of rapidly increasing Han settlement c.1000 AD
Limits of dense Han settlement at the present day
Areas of dense mixed Han and non-Han settlement at the present day
Capitals of the Early Empire and Early Middle Empire
Capitals of the Late Middle Empire
Capital of the Late Empire
3000m contour line
400m contour line
Grand canal of the T'ang dynasty (7th century AD)
Grand canal of the Late Empire (15th century AD)
Great Wall of the Chin dynasty (3rd century BC)
Extension of the Han dynasty 2nd century BC)
Great Wall of the Ming dynasty (14th-16th cents. AD)
Old silk routes
Coniferous forest
Steppe
Desert
Mountain vegetation
Forest and meadow
Rain forest
0
500 km
0
300 miles
Amur
Sungari
Northern limit of wheat cultivation
Semi-oases
Nan Shan
Kunlun Shan
Huang Ho
Peking
Hsien-yang
Ch'ang-an
Lo-yang
K'ai-feng
Northern limit of rice cultivation
Nanking
Hang-chou
Yangtze
Nan Ling
Si Kiang
Salween
Mekong
Overseas migration during the second millennium AD
90°
110°
120°
130°
40°
30°
20°

tributed so much to Jewish survival. In the Hellenistic age, according to the Jewish historian Josephus, 'countless myriads whose numbers cannot be ascertained' spread through Syria and Asia Minor to Armenia and the Crimea, and around the Mediterranean. The great Jewish community at Alexandria produced many distinguished philosophers and the first Greek translation of the Old Testament. This meeting of Jewish and Greek culture created the essential context, socially and intellectually, for the appearance and early development of Christianity.

Some time before the rise of the Achaemenids a new religion appeared among the peoples of the Iranian plateau. Its prophet, Zoroaster, is one of the most shadowy of religious leaders, every detail of his life and teaching being open to radically differing interpretations. Probably he preached in eastern Iran in the first half of the sixth century BC. His principal innovations were the monotheism which denounced the many gods of Iranian paganism in favour of Ahuru-Mazda, the creator, and the stark and uncompromising confrontation which he proclaimed between those who followed his teaching – the Truth – and adherents of the old cults – the Lie, perhaps reflecting the bitter hostility in eastern Iran in his time between the settled farmers of the plateau and the nomads of the steppes to whose depredations they were constantly exposed.

Zoroaster preached a universal faith commending 'good thoughts, good words, good deeds' (including either opposition to or great moderation of animal sacrifice) and offering eternal peace to the blessed and the torments of the damned to the wicked. There is little doubt that the Achaemenid kings from Darius I onwards accepted it as a religion of state, though its hostility to the older cults was considerably softened by the readmission of the worship of gods other than Ahuru-Mazda, in a subordinate position. Other religions were still tolerated, and this, together with the great extent of the Achaemenid empire, gave Zoroastrianism an influence on many other faiths, including both Judaism and Hinduism, and later Christianity and Buddhism (*see Map 11*). Its close association with the Persian empire persisted, and during the Sassanid revival (*Map 15*) it flourished again, championed from the time of Bahram I (*c.* AD 273-6) by savage persecution of the religious minorities which abounded in the Persian world. It was apparently during this second period of prosperity that Zoroastrianism, in common with Manicheism (which under Shapur I [*d.* 273] had almost supplanted it as the official religion and spread widely through the late antique world in spite of universal persecution) developed its prophet's delineation of the war between good and evil into a theological dualism which divided creation between the realms of Light and Dark, Spirit and Flesh, inspiring a radical asceticism which left its mark on most of the world religions.

The origins of Hinduism are lost in obscurity. It grew slowly from the Vedic religions of the Aryan peoples who conquered the Indus valley about 1000 BC, and did not attain a generally accepted theology until, perhaps, about AD 500, but hints of its unique institution, the system of caste, have been found in the Harappan as well as the Aryan civilization. As Hinduism expanded it absorbed the cults of many gods and many styles of religious life. But its essential character derived from caste, the belief that people are divided into self-contained and sealed groups, or castes. Into one of them each person is born, and will marry and die within it, living scrupulously in accordance with its particular rules, prohibitions and customs, to be rewarded if merit and fortune permit by reincarnation in a higher caste. The original groups were occupational – warriors (*kshatriyas*), priests (*brahmans*), cultivators (*vaishyas*) – and among them the brahmans quickly took over the first place by proclaiming the divine origin of kingly authority. A fourth caste, those of non-Aryan origin – *shudras* – appeared very early, and beneath these four a network of subcastes was elaborated, defined by occupation and, increasingly with time and Aryan expansion, by race. Essentially a device to preserve the racial purity of the Aryan conquerors by allowing them to absorb but not to mix with the conquered peoples, caste has remained until the present day the framework of Indian social and political life.

Above right: A stone-rubbing of a portrait of Confucius.

Resentment of brahman dominance first appeared among the *shudras* and the *vaishyas*, whose importance as landowners and as the leaders of an increasingly farflung trade conflicted with their low caste. The principles of Jainism appeared perhaps a century before the birth (*c.*540 BC) of its effective prophet, Mahavira, who won a substantial following in the Ganges valley. The core of his teaching was the renunciation of killing, upon which he insisted so absolutely that his followers not only refused to eat meat but wore muslin masks over their mouths to avoid inhaling insects. It was not a creed to appeal to farmers, but it attracted, and still retains, considerable support in the merchant community.

The teaching of Gautama Buddha (born *c.*566 BC, the son of a *kshatriya* prince) was also based on the renunciation of desire. The Buddha's path, however, was not that of bodily asceticism – which he tried and found wanting – but of meditation, directed to a balanced and moderate life, cleansed of the passions which were the cause of suffering. Salvation lay in *nirvana* (extinction), freedom from the cycle of suffering, death and rebirth. Buddhism rejected caste and the idea of a personal God. It was disseminated by monks who wandered from place to place begging for alms. The universality of its appeal was expressed in its repudiation of social and even sexual distinctions (which the brahmans were emphasising increasingly) in the egalitarian organization of Buddhist monasteries and nunneries.

The decision to undertake systematic proselytisation, which eventually made Buddhism the religion of east and south-east Asia, was taken at a great council at Pataliputra in 250 BC, shortly after the conversion of Ashoka, ruler of the Maurya

10 The expansion of the Han Chinese settlement
Beginning in the first millennium BC, the expansion of the Han Chinese people and of Chinese culture from the central river valleys has been continuous for more than two thousand years. It has been closely related to the ability of the Chinese to control and exploit an extremely varied natural environment.

11 The appearance of the world religions
Between about 1000 BC and AD 500 all the formative religions and philosophies of the world except Islam established themselves as the bases of the great civilizations. Here short-term fluctuations in their influence are ignored to show the relationship between the areas in which they began and those over which they exercised permanent influence.

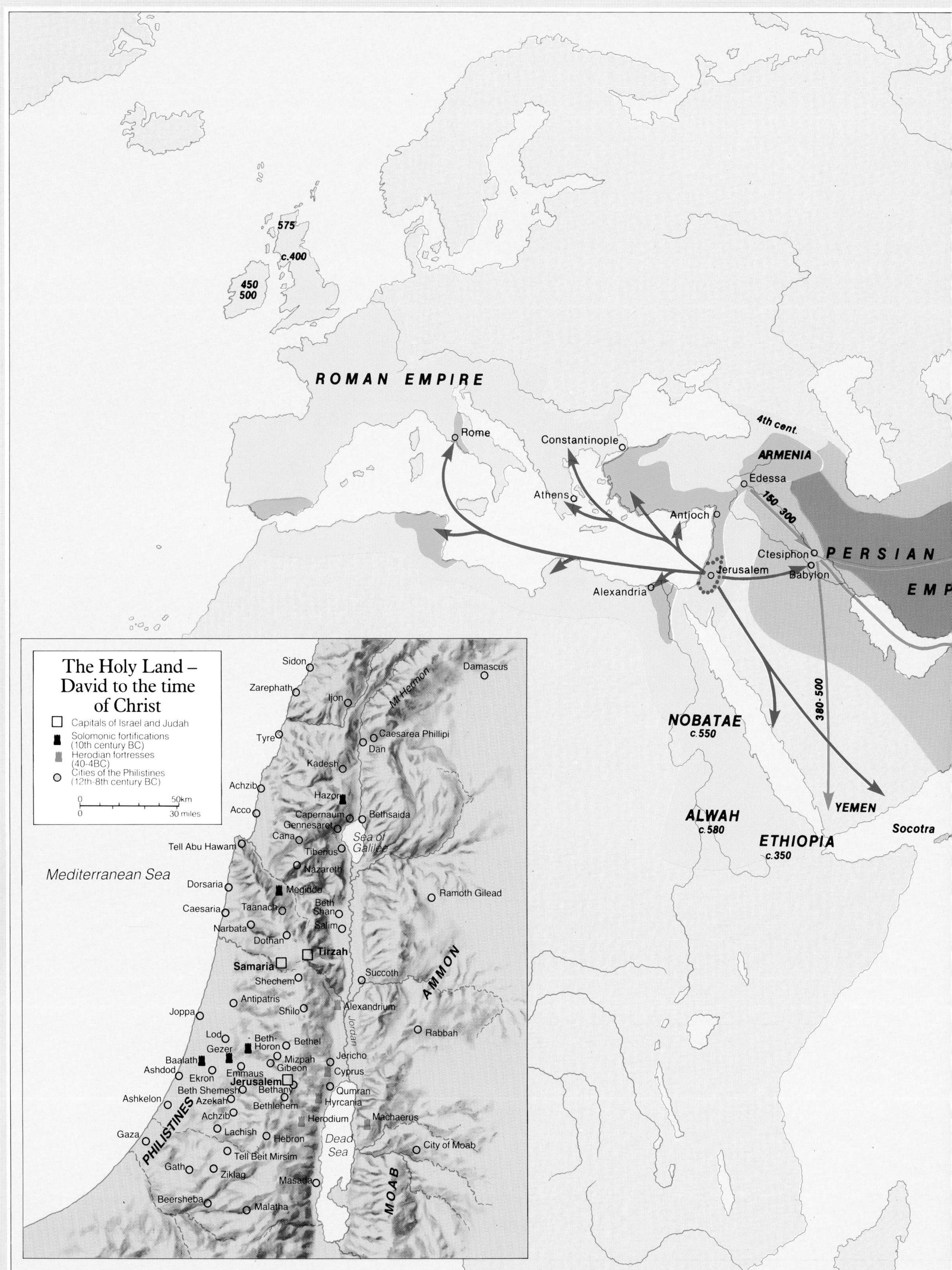
575
c.400
450
500
ROMAN EMPIRE
Rome
Constantinople
Athens
Antioch
Alexandria
Jerusalem
4th cent.
ARMENIA
Edessa
150–300
Ctesiphon
Babylon
PERSIAN
EMP
NOBATAE
c.550
380–500
ALWAH
c.580
ETHIOPIA
c.350
YEMEN
Socotra
The Holy Land – David to the time of Christ
Capitals of Israel and Judah
Solomonic fortifications (10th century BC)
Herodian fortresses (40-4BC)
Cities of the Philistines (12th-8th century BC)
0 50km
0 30 miles
Mediterranean Sea
Sidon
Zarephath
Ijon
Mt Hermon
Damascus
Tyre
Caesarea Phillipi
Dan
Kadesh
Achzib
Hazor
Acco
Capernaum
Gennesaret
Bethsaida
Cana
Sea of Galilee
Tell Abu Hawam
Tiberius
Nazareth
Dorsaria
Megiddo
Ramoth Gilead
Caesaria
Taanach
Beth Shan
Salim
Narbata
Dothan
Tirzah
Samaria
Shechem
Succoth
AMMON
Antipatris
Joppa
Shilo
Alexandrium
Jordan
Rabbah
Lod
Beth-Horon
Bethel
Gezer
Baalath
Mizpah
Gibeon
Jericho
Ashdod
Ekron
Emmaus
Cyprus
Jerusalem
Beth Shemesh
Bethany
Qumran
Ashkelon
Azekah
Bethlehem
Hyrcania
Achzib
Herodium
Machaerus
PHILISTINES
Gaza
Lachish
Hebron
Dead Sea
City of Moab
Tell Beit Mirsim
Gath
Ziklag
Masada
Beersheba
Malatha
MOAB

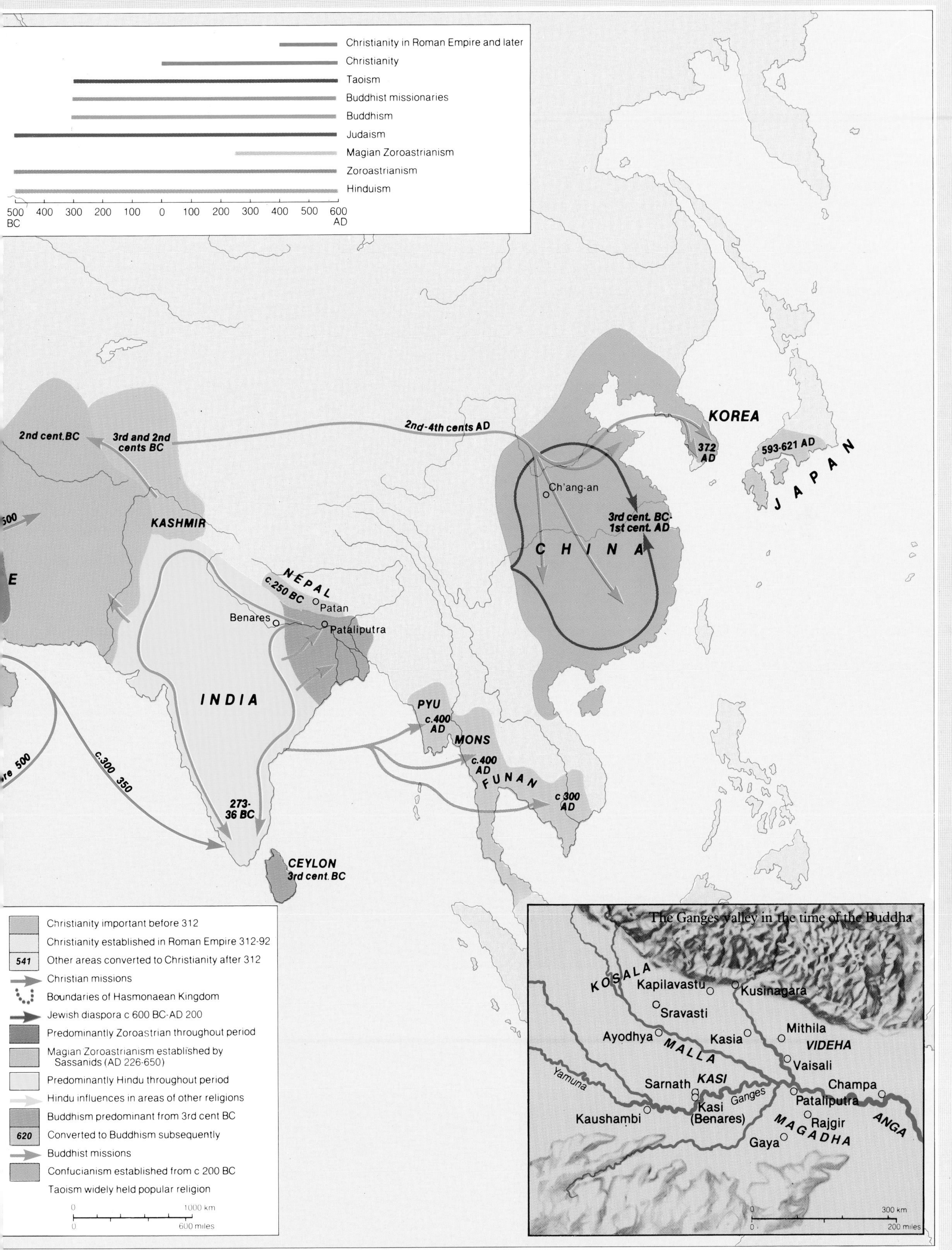

Christianity in Roman Empire and later
Christianity
Taoism
Buddhist missionaries
Buddhism
Judaism
Magian Zoroastrianism
Zoroastrianism
Hinduism
500 BC 400 300 200 100 0 100 200 300 400 500 600 AD
2nd cent.BC
3rd and 2nd cents BC
2nd-4th cents AD
KOREA
372 AD
593-621 AD
JAPAN
Ch'ang-an
3rd cent. BC-1st cent. AD
CHINA
KASHMIR
NEPAL
c.250 BC
Patan
Benares
Pataliputra
INDIA
PYU
c.400 AD
MONS
c.400 AD
FUNAN
c 300 AD
c.300 350
273-36 BC
CEYLON
3rd cent. BC
Christianity important before 312
Christianity established in Roman Empire 312-92
541 Other areas converted to Christianity after 312
Christian missions
Boundaries of Hasmonaean Kingdom
Jewish diaspora c 600 BC-AD 200
Predominantly Zoroastrian throughout period
Magian Zoroastrianism established by Sassanids (AD 226-650)
Predominantly Hindu throughout period
Hindu influences in areas of other religions
Buddhism predominant from 3rd cent BC
620 Converted to Buddhism subsequently
Buddhist missions
Confucianism established from c 200 BC
Taoism widely held popular religion
0 1000 km
0 600 miles
The Ganges valley in the time of the Buddha
KOSALA
Kapilavastu
Kusinagara
Sravasti
Ayodhya
MALLA
Kasia
Mithila
VIDEHA
Vaisali
Yamuna
Sarnath
KASI
Champa
Ganges
Kasi (Benares)
Pataliputra
Kaushambi
MAGADHA
Rajgir
ANGA
Gaya
0 300 km
0 200 miles

empire from about 272 to 231. Ashoka was converted through revulsion from the bloodshed of the wars he himself had waged to gain control of the trade routes to the south. He distinguished clearly between his personal conviction and his imperial duty, as he saw it, to treat all religions with impartial respect. Nevertheless the association between the evolution of the world religions and the appearance of great political structures is more than coincidence. Between the accession of Chandragupta Maurya in 321 BC and the death of Ashoka, the Mauryan emperors used their control of the Ganges and Indus valleys to bring under their sway an area which stretched from territory beyond the Indus, recovered from the Seleucids, to the far south of the sub-continent. The rock and pillar inscriptions of Ashoka not only show the extent of his influence (*Map 16*) but illustrate the spirit in which it was exercised. In several languages, including Greek, they command religious tolerance, respect for human dignity and gratitude for the benevolence of a paternal ruler. His messages were designed to promote unity in a heterogeneous kingdom hastily assembled, but ruled with a sophistication which stretched from collecting taxes and maintaining communications to creating an imperial espionage service and planting banyan trees along the road to give shade to travellers. This degree of political evolution, common to the cradles of all the great religions, not only created conditions in which they could spread and flourish, but rested on a degree of homogeneity among those who made the systems of government work, and their ability to express and share values which were necessarily more abstract and reflective than the blood-stained cults of warrior kings.

Chinese civilization too began to assume its familiar aspect during the first millennium BC. The Chou dynasty, which replaced the Shang probably in 1027, presided over a world effectively ruled by a nobility which gave it formal allegiance. Traditionally the nobles owed their lands to the king and gave him military service in return. The very emptiness of his power in practice suggests that it was some sense of community among the Chinese that led them to acknowledge his rule. This allegiance remained a fiction until the Age of the Warring States (481-221 BC) ended when the warrior state of Ch'in swallowed all the rest, to be replaced after only fourteen years by the real founders of imperial China, the Han (*Map 13*).

Behind these events the permanent features of Chinese society were already evident. The expansion of civilization which has been the central thread of 2000 years' development (*see Map 10*) was already in progress. Increasing activity in the Huang-ho valley by the seventh century BC was quickly followed by the first stages of the conquest of the south. The wealth of this warlike and sophisticated world was produced by a vast peasant labour force – this was already the world's most populous region – tied to the land in subjection to the nobles. To judge from the beauty of their pottery, painting and bronzes (the art of bronze-casting had been inherited from the Shang) and from the importance which they attached to literacy, this nobility was already more than a simple warrior caste. By 800 BC it had assumed the twin responsibilities of organising government and conducting the worship of its ancestors according to the traditional rites. In consequence China had no need of, and never developed, a specialized priestly class.

The preoccupations of the nobility shaped its philosophies. By around 500 BC three attitudes to the relations between the individuals and the state had become apparent: henceforth they would compete for influence over the government of China. Rejection was represented by the Taoists who, inspired by the fifth-century teacher Lao-tze, advocated complete withdrawal from worldly affairs to submit, in contemplative calm, to the Way (*Tao*), the cosmic principle that sustained the harmony of the universe. Lao-tze said that his disciple should know of the existence of villages beyond his own he would hear their cocks crow in the morning.

The Taoists in a sense sidestepped the great debate of the Age of Warring States. The Legalists sought order through a universal system of law to which all men should be held subject by the authority of a powerful, centralized state. On these principles the Ch'in dynasty (221-206 BC) made a determined assault upon the fragmentation which was blamed for the years of war. The old kingdoms were broken up and replaced by administrative districts with different boundaries; the nobles were transported and the peasants upon whom their power had rested were freed. To destroy local customs and loyalties all libraries in private hands were ordered to be destroyed. Uniform weights and measures were introduced, the script (which, by denoting ideas rather than sounds has enabled Chinese of different regions to communicate freely without being able to understand one another's dialect) was simplified and standardized, and the first Great Wall was completed to keep out the barbarian horsemen (*Map 10*).

The death of Shih Huang Ti, the First Emperor – as he justly called himself – in 209 BC was followed by rebellion and the fall of his dynasty, but he had already laid the foundations of the unity which the Han achieved. They adopted the principles of Kung Fu-tzu – Confucius (551-479 BC) – who had looked not to the force of law, but to the power and example of tradition, enshrined in scrupulous adherence to precedent and diligent observance of ritual. Confucius and his followers put their trust in the disinterested skills of bureaucrats, honest and modest in their conduct, and carefully inculcated with the values of loyalty and justice through the study of the literary classics. 'Documents, conduct, loyalty, faithfulness' were their watchwords. Under the Han, classical works were recovered and recopied, and a new literature created whose leading achievement was the inauguration of the series of official dynastic histories. By recording in detail the wise acts of successful emperors and officials, and the errors of foolish ones – as the Confucian historians saw them – these embodied the code of the official class and became the repositaries of a tradition of government which lasted until this century. Local officials were carefully trained, and though most were still appointed on the recommendation of nobles and other officials, recruitment by public examinations, perhaps China's most remarkable gift to the modern world, was begun.

The Confucian tradition, elaborated by generations of disciples (among whom Mencius, in the fourth century BC, emphasized that the welfare of all mankind must be the goal of good government) has been almost as much the formative thread of

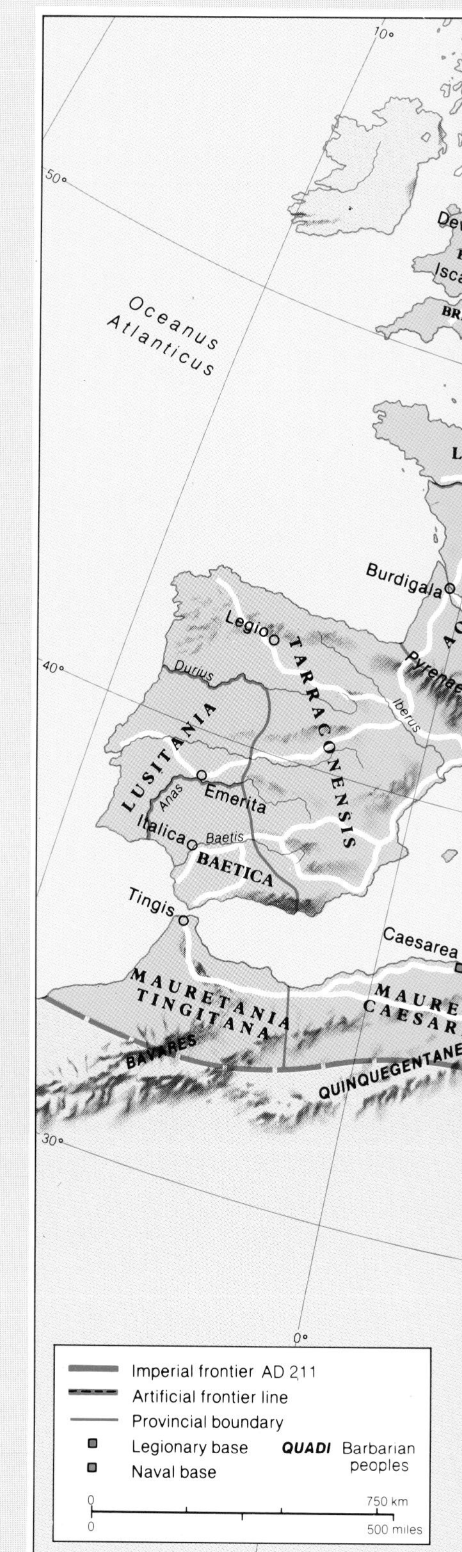

12 The Roman Empire at its height
By AD 211 the Roman Empire had expanded to fill its natural frontiers, completed where necessary by man-made barriers. Within them the whole empire was now subjected to a uniform system of administration whose important centres were connectcd by a network of roads radiating from Rome.

Chinese as Hinduism has of Indian history. In sharp contrast Confucianism has no interest in the supernatural. Even the worship of the ancestors is explicitly recommended as reinforcing the values of the ruling class, and of the here and now.

Confucianism and Legalism both took for granted what was already the most remarkable thing about China, the idea that the cultural unity of this vast area, with its great variety of soils and terrains, its extremes of climate and profusion of peoples, was more important than the political powers which rose and fell upon it. The Chinese, like the Greeks, defined barbarians as those who did not speak their language. Unlike the Greeks they were isolated from other advanced peoples by distance and the immense physical barriers which surrounded them. By the time their isolation was breached they were secure in the conviction of their superiority to the rest of mankind. This belief remained unshaken by the occasional necessity to submit to barbarian power until Chinese culture could absorb it. When the Chinese entered into contact with the European powers in the nineteenth century it was to accept not diplomatic relations, but tribute.

Further reading: C. Blunden and M. Elvin, *Cultural Atlas of China* (Phaidon 1983; Facts on File); R. Dawson (ed.) *The Legacy of China* (Oxford U. P. 1964); A. L. Basham, *The Wonder that was India*, (third ed. Sidgwick and Jackson 1978); A. Andrewes, *Greek Society* (Penguin 1971; Norton); R. Lane Fox, Alexander the Great (Allen Lane, 1973); R. Ghirshman, Iran (Penguin, 1978).

MAP 12 THE ROMAN EMPIRE AT ITS HEIGHT

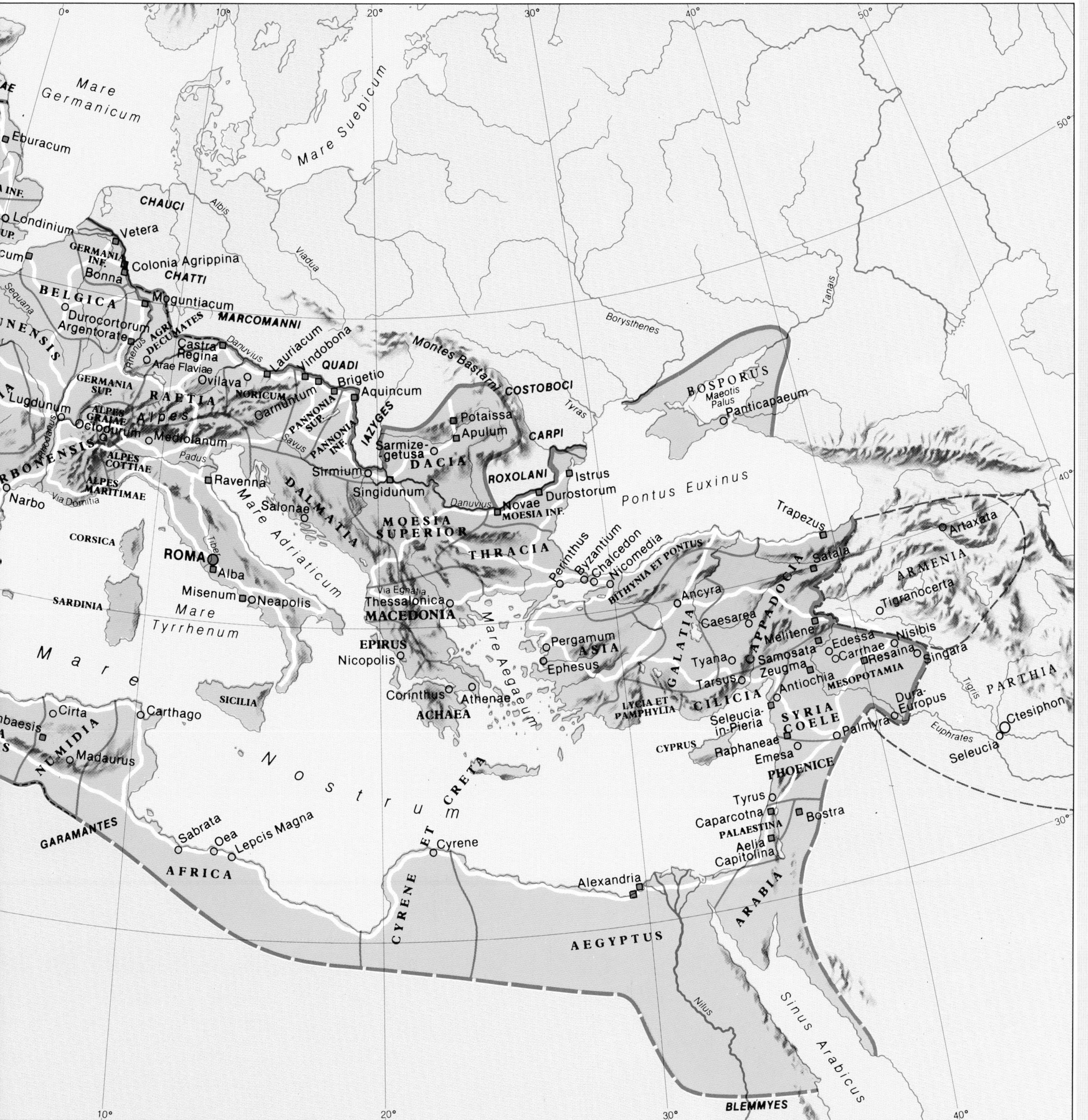

The ancient world 4

THE GREAT EMPIRES OF ANTIQUITY

By the last centuries BC the political systems of the regions of the most ancient civilizations (see Map 3) had proved able to survive their creators by absorbing conquerors. Iran was ruled by Greeks (under the Seleucids) and Parthians (from 247 BC to AD 227) much as it had been by the Achaemenids, whose tax-gathering system and claim to divinity were taken over with equal nonchalance.

The shores of the Mediterranean and the banks of the Ganges and the Yellow River now became in their turn the seats of empires which future rulers in those regions would strive to imitate and aspire to restore.

From 206 BC to AD 9 and from AD 25 to 220 the Han – the longest-lived of China's dynasties and the only one to regain power – extended the reach of imperial government southward to control the coast as far as the Gulf of Tonkin, introduced Chinese civilization to Korea, and drove the nomads of the steppes back beyond the Gobi desert to take control of the caravan routes which brought China for the first time into contact with the west (*Map 13*). Political unity and improving communications – road and canal systems had been developing for centuries, more often for military and political than for commercial reasons, and had been greatly extended and systematized by the first Ch'in emperor shortly before 200 BC – stimulated trade, and created a cash economy and a wealthy merchant class. The Emperor Wu (*r.*140-86 BC) made minting and the distribution of salt state monopolies, and made part of the land tax payable in grain which could be stored for redistribution in times of famine, offsetting one of the commonest causes of revolt.

The vision of empire had been left to India by the Mauryas in the third century BC. It was most nearly realized by Candra Gupta (*c.*AD 320-35) and his successors. The Guptas ruled the densely populated Ganges valley directly, but their influence over much of the rest of the subcontinent was expressed through a network of tributaries and alliances reminiscent of the relations of the Chinese and Roman empires with the barbarian peoples beyond their boundaries (*see Map 16*). The ensuing stability contributed to a marked increase in the prosperity of the privileged classes, and with it an opulent flowering of sculpture, building and literature which made the fourth and fifth centuries AD the golden age of Hindu culture.

The drama of the rise and fall of empires tends to obscure their nature, which is more truthfully shown by their internal than by their external frontiers. *Map 10* shows how the Han Chinese people, who carried Chinese culture with them as they spread from their homeland in the Yellow River basin, advanced gradually through the most fertile and accessible country, while above them on the mountains and beyond them in the rain forests of the tropical south lived peoples who were very slowly – or never – assimilated into Chinese civilization. In India disease exacerbated and caste acknowledged the same failure of conquest to eradicate multiplicity, and in Europe the spectacular expansion of the Roman empire along its roads and through its cities conceals the reality of peoples of mountain and forest remaining effectively untouched by the march of Roman civilization.

The great empires rested on the ability to exploit the process of colonization, the formation of settlements to become agricultural centres. The expansion of the Han Chinese is paralleled by that of the Romans, who conquered the neighbourhood of Latium in 498-93 BC. Their progress was temporarily checked when the Celts sacked the city in 387 BC, but after regrouping their allies they launched the series of wars that made them masters of Italy south of the Po by 272 BC, and then of the Mediterranean and of western Europe (*see Map 8*). At each victory the Romans annexed territory and peopled it with colonists, at first as individual settlers and later in heavily fortified self-governing towns with the right to control the land (*territorium*) around them. Thus they provided land for Roman citizens, defence of the conquered territories, and bases for further expansion.

The process of conquest transformed the conquerors. The very precariousness of Rome's early existence helped to shape a society for which warfare was not an occasional expedient but a normal, even necessary, part of its life. Expansion confirmed the pattern. There were perhaps only four or five years in which Rome was not at war between 327 and 241 BC, and perhaps ten in the next century and a half. This was too great a burden for a peasant economy to bear. In the prolonged absence of their proprietors, small farms went unworked. The ruin of many was completed by the devastation of southern Italy in the war of 218-201 BC against Hannibal and perpetuated

13 China under the Early Empire
Under its longest-lived dynasty, the Han (206 BC-AD 9, AD 25-220), the economic, administrative and cultural foundations of Chinese unity were laid securely enough for it to survive the fragmentation of the third century and re-emerge under the leadership of the highly developed north.

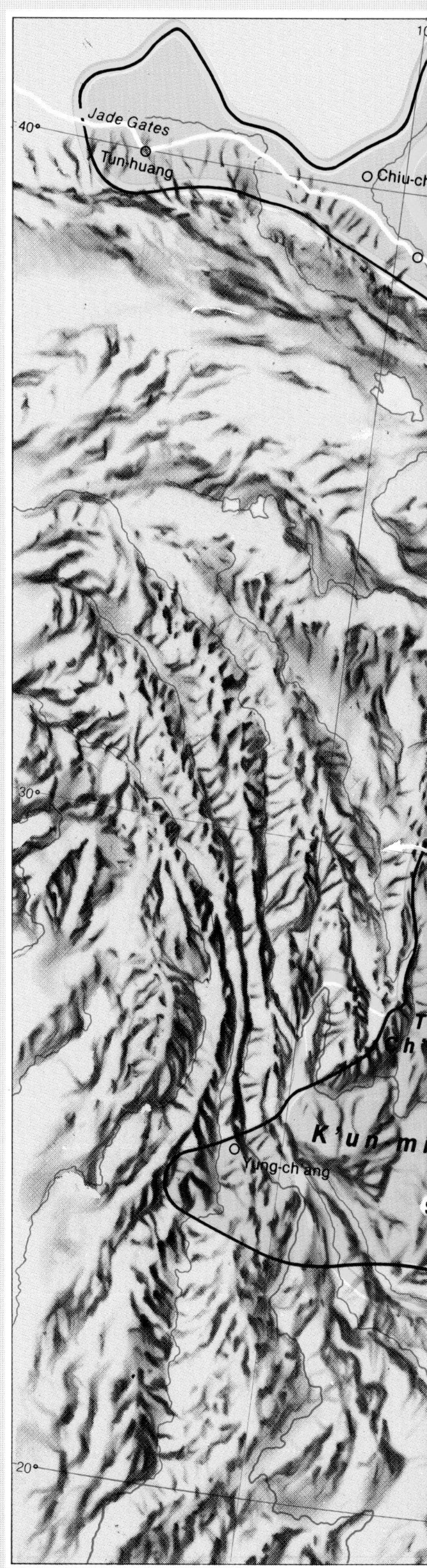

when expansion in the wake of that victory took Roman armies ever further from home and for ever longer periods (*see Map 8*). In the second century BC periods of conscription of ten to sixteen years were normal, to support an army which has been estimated at about one-eighth of all citizens, one of the highest proportions ever known.

The victories which ruined the peasantry brought immense gains to the generals. Vast fortunes were created by the spoils of war and the pillaging of the provinces which followed. Much of the loot was invested in land which the peasantry was being forced to abandon. It was stocked instead with slaves, of whom the wars created a plentiful supply; great factory farms (*latifundia*) were built up, producing specialized crops and large profits, owned by syndicates of shareholders who probably never set eyes on them. Such holdings soon dominated the agriculture of southern Italy and Sicily and became widespread throughout the western empire.

The republican constitution of early Rome could not stand the strain. The dispossessed drifted into the city to live off the public dole of corn, and provide in the mob a reservoir of discontent and instability. The professionalisation of the army followed the destruction of its citizen base – the property qualification for military service was abolished in 107 BC – and this created an even more tempting instrument for the ambitious. The immense fortunes of the few, renewed by conquest and dissipated in display and competition for office, fuelled political jobbery on a dizzying scale. The restoration of the peasantry through redistribution of land was the only solution, as Tiberius and Gaius Gracchus saw; their deaths, in 123 and 121 BC, showed that the oligarchy would not accept it. A century of bloody warfare across the Roman world followed, as the generals bid in turn

MAP 13 CHINA UNDER THE EARLY EMPIRE

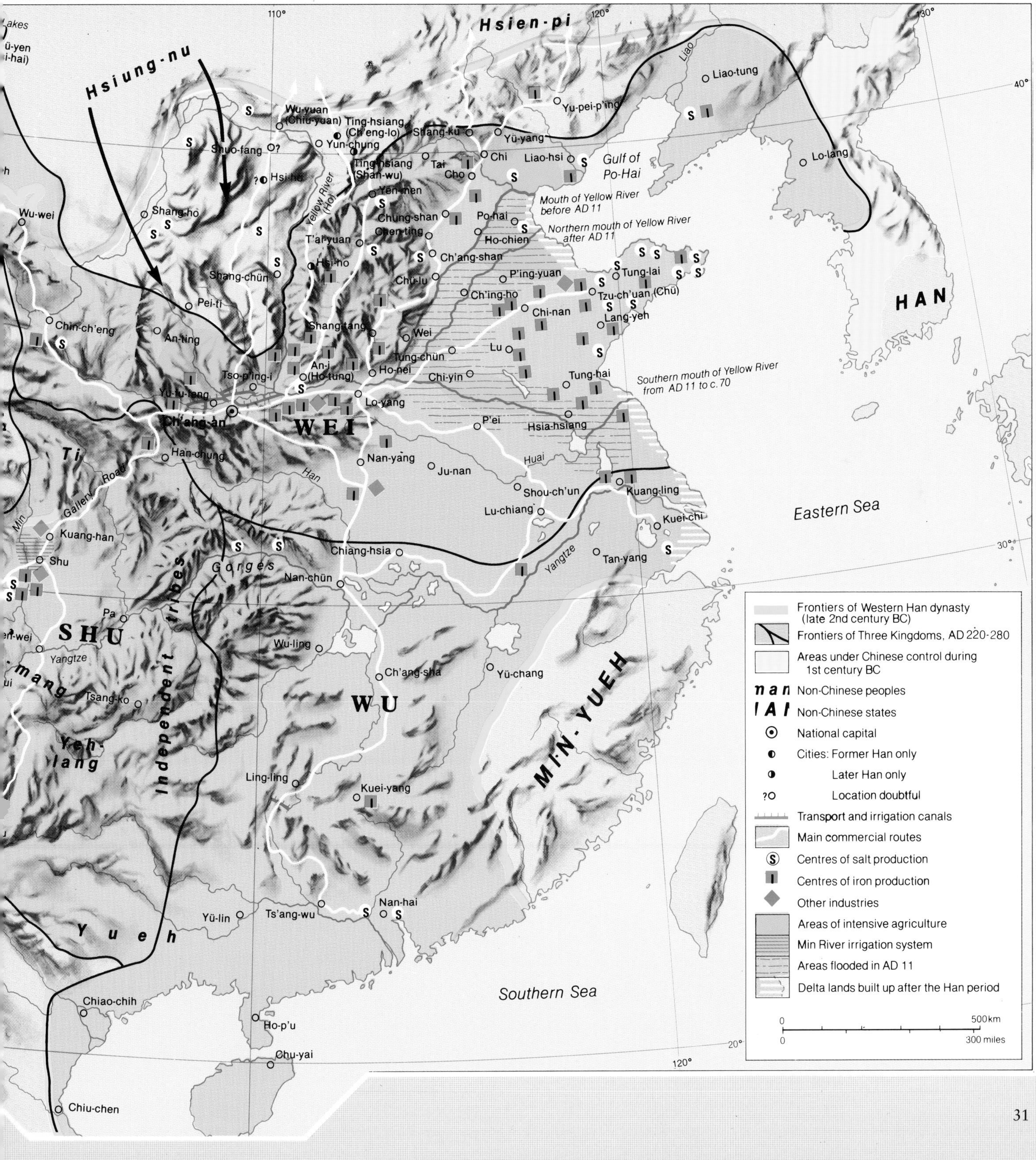

Frontiers of Western Han dynasty (late 2nd century BC)
Frontiers of Three Kingdoms, AD 220-280
Areas under Chinese control during 1st century BC
Non-Chinese peoples
Non-Chinese states
National capital
Cities: Former Han only
Later Han only
Location doubtful
Transport and irrigation canals
Main commercial routes
Centres of salt production
Centres of iron production
Other industries
Areas of intensive agriculture
Min River irrigation system
Areas flooded in AD 11
Delta lands built up after the Han period

0 500km
0 300 miles

for supreme power. It ended only with the overthrow of the republic, the brief dictatorship of Caesar, and the inauguration of the Empire and reorganization of its government during the long reign of Augustus (*r.*27 BC-AD 14).

The burden of military service affected the Chinese peasantry in much the same way as the Roman. The cost of raising and supplying huge armies precipitated the revolts and civil war in which the Ch'in dynasty failed. The defence of the great walls was a heavy drain on manpower, and the maintenance of the growing administration drained the taxes. The free peasant economy gave way to *latifundia* – in effect – in which merchants and officials invested their profits. The Emperor Wu, though, unlike the Gracchi, was strong enough to carry out extensive confiscations of land. These weakened the princes and created a reserve of land for granting to small proprietors, though in practice they were more often used to reward favourites and hangers-on. But Wu's northward expansion against the barbarian threat produced, as he feared, just the consequences that his land policy was designed to avert. By AD 9 famine, peasant revolt and aristocratic turbulence brought his dynasty down. It was restored, in AD 25, by a coalition of magnates, and under the Later Han the growth of great estates and the reduction of the peasantry to personal dependence on the proprietors again continued unchecked.

From the borders of Scotland to the Sinai desert, from Tangier to the Black Sea, the physical remains of the Roman Empire are more numerous, more massive and more durable by far than those of any other civilization. Their roads still carry traffic, their aqueducts water, their drains sewage. These are the visible fruits of the Augustan Peace and the end of the long struggle of the Romans to win their empire, and among them to control it. The piecemeal structure which left each province as it was won to be looted by its governor was replaced by a unitary administration (*compare Maps 8 and 12*). Cities were planted over the western Empire of a new size, with water supplies, baths, theatres and markets. Superb communications and internal order – the Mediterranean was freer of piracy in the first two centuries AD than it would be again before the nineteenth century – permitted a wide circulation of goods within the Empire. International trade was swollen as Rome exchanged its wines and pottery, its glass and precious metals, for the furs and amber of the northern barbarians, the spices, jewels, textiles and dancing girls of India, and, at times, the silks of China.

Since their imposing and intricately decorated buildings were of wood and their finest paintings on silk the physical remains of the Han are less imposing, although nothing Roman matched the magnificence of the Han tombs and their contents. In China too restoration was immediately successful. The Later Han recovered control of the northern frontier and the central Asian territories and routes, resumed the colonization of the south, and presided over an epoch of commercial expansion and cultural brilliance. In AD 166 the Emperor received men who claimed to be envoys of the western ruler An Tun (Marcus Aurelius Antoninus), though he suspected that they were only merchants trying to smooth their path.

At that moment it seemed that both empires had attained a secure height of splendid achievement. But their problems had been evaded, not solved. The maintenance of armies, the defence of the walls and the support of the bureaucracy still, in both empires, laid an insupportable burden on the peasantry. In both, land and power accumulated in the hands of magnates increasingly able to evade imperial control and taxation, thus transferring these burdens ever more relentlessly to the shoulders of the primary producers. The pressure of barbarians on the frontiers hastened the process of internal dissolution.

By the time a real envoy from Rome reached China in AD 226 the Han empire had fallen apart, prey to the now-familiar combination of peasant revolts, ambitious princes and invading barbarians. The permanence of Rome was also illusory. Expansion of the frontiers did not end with Augustus, as he had intended. There were still client states to be reduced, restless neighbours and outsiders to be subdued. The victories of Trajan (*r.*98-117) were as spectacular as those of any of his predecessors, and it took his successors another century to bring the frontier to natural limits and consolidate control within them in the fortress-empire of Septimius Severus (*Map 12*).

In 212, the year after his death, all free inhabi-

Above: The Pont du Gard, built in 19 BC to carry water from the River Eure to Nîmes

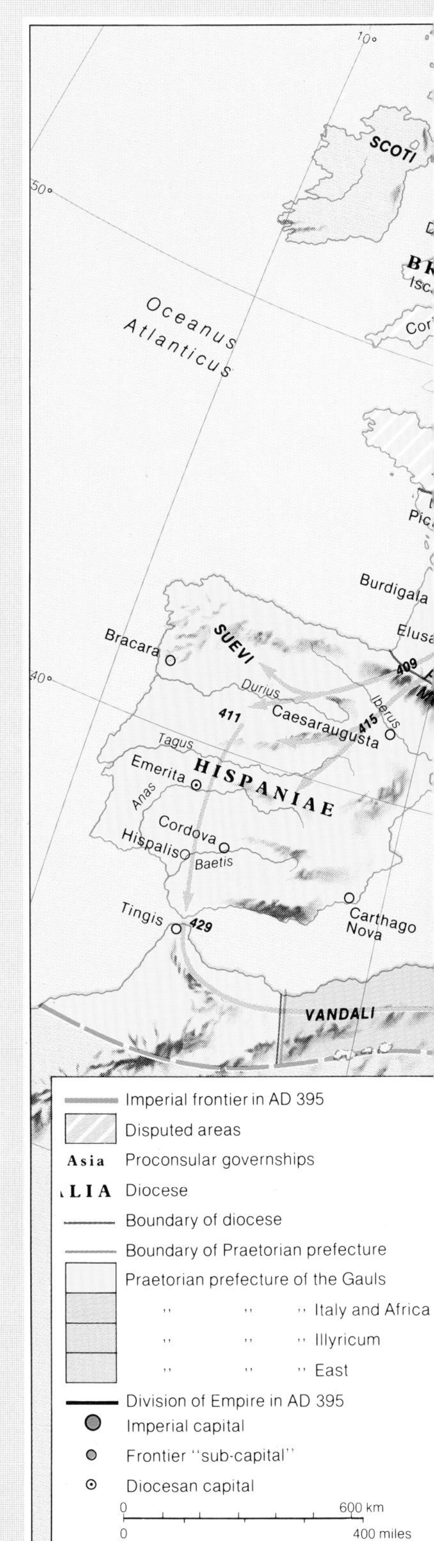

14 The later Roman Empire
The Emperors Diocletian (*r.* 284-30s) and Constantine (*r.* 312-337) overhauled the administration, and divided the Empire between East and West, but failed to make it either strong enough to prevent entry of peoples living beyond its frontiers or flexible enough to absorb them.

tants of the empire were granted citizenship. But in 251 the Emperor Decius was killed by Goths who had crossed the Danube, and in the next two decades every frontier collapsed, Persia under the newly established Sassanid dynasty again became a formidable threat (*see Map 15*), and raiders on sea and land penetrated the heart of the Empire. Rome was saved by military takeover. A succession of common soldiers culminating with Diocletian (*r*.284-305) seized the throne, excluded the aristocracy from military command, doubled the size of the army (to some 600,000 men), imposed a rigid and detailed direction of labour, and radically decentralized the government of the Empire (*Map 14*). These measures gained for it another century of life, one of the most brilliant and fascinating in its history, though increasingly based on the wealthier and more populous eastern part of the Empire and its new capital at Constantinople. But the fundamental problems were aggravated, especially in the west, where population declined, land went out of cultivation, trade declined and cities shrank. The Empire had not changed its nature, or made life bearable for those who bore it on their backs, and they showed no inclination to save it by resisting new invasions. 'What are kingdoms if not great robberies?' asked Augustine of Hippo, one of the ornaments of late antique culture. Writing a few years after the Visigoths had sacked Rome in AD 410, he knew that the answer was – nothing.

Further reading: J. Gernet, *A History of Chinese Civilization* (Cambridge U. P. 1982); A. Cotterell, *The First Emperor of China* (Macmillan 1981; Viking Penguin); R. Thapar, *A History of India*, vol. 1 (Penguin 1966); P. Garnsey and R. Saller, *The Roman Empire* (Duckworth 1987; University of California Press); K. Hopkins, *Conquerors and Slaves* (Cambridge U. P. 1978); R. N. Frye, *The Heritage of Persia* (Weidenfeld and Nicolson 1983)

MAP 14 THE LATER ROMAN EMPIRE

The ancient world 5

EMPIRES AND BARBARIANS

The Ottoman conquest of the Byzantine Empire in the fifteenth century and the Manchu of Ming China in the seventeenth (Maps 37 and 43) were the last of the barbarian invasions. Since then the backward peoples of the world have retreated before the advanced.

15 The Sassanid empire in Persia
The Sassanid revolution against the Parthian kings in AD 224 brought to power a dynasty which, seeing itself as successor to the Achaemenids, created a powerful and highly centralized state in Persia. It expanded to take over the Kushan empire to the east and present a growing threat to Rome in the west, especially after its reorganization by Khosrau I. The Hephthalites, or White Huns, were nomad invaders from the steppes.

16 The empire of the Guptas in India
The Gupta empire was the first native state to establish itself since the fall of the Mauryas – the extent of whose empire is indicated by the inscriptions of Ashoka – in 180 BC. It based its power on the Ganges valley and at its height exercised a hegemony over much of the sub-continent through a variety of links of which few were permanent.

Formerly, though the frontiers of civilization always tended to expand in the long run, they were always liable to collapse before the invader, and known to be so by those who lived within them. The decline of the great empires of antiquity was one of the most momentous and has remained one of the most discussed of these collapses. In AD 316 northern China was overrun by the Hsiung-nu, who divided it into several kingdoms. Between 375 and about 410 several peoples crossed the Roman frontiers, this time to stay (*see Maps 14 and 17*). Throughout the fifth century the Hephthalites (misleadingly called White Huns) launched campaigns against Bactria which eventually forced the reorganization of the Sassanid empire on a strictly military footing under Khosrau I (*Map 15*) and they are often credited with the collapse of the Indian empire of the Guptas.

It is easy to exaggerate. The Gupta emperors, whose influence outside the Ganges and Indus valleys was so indeterminate that its decline hardly requires explanation (*Map 16*), were already facing disaffection among their underlings, and had been forced to debase their coinage before the attacks became serious in the middle of the fifth century AD. The Sassanid empire, after spectacular expansion in the two centuries after its foundation in AD 226, was riven by disputed succession, aristocratic faction, bitter social division and religious animosity (*compare Map 11*). The fragmentation of northern China reflected Chinese social divisions as well as the rivalries of the barbarian tribes, who were thoroughly siniticised by contact and often by inclination. When one of them, the Toba, became strong enough to reunite the region and found the Northern Wei dynasty (439-535) they adopted Chinese ways in agriculture and administration, manners and dress, made Chinese the language of their court and moved their capital to Lo-yang (*see Map 13*). Throughout this period traditional education, literature and the arts flourished in China, as they did in India and Persia. Only in the western Roman world did the end of a political regime threaten that of the culture which had accompanied it.

The western barbarians admired the Romans. The Goths adopted the Arian form of Christianity, for example, not because it was anti-Roman but, on the contrary, because when their apostle Ulfilas was consecrated in 341, Arian teaching was that commended by the court and bishops of Constantinople. Later the Romans used the 'heresy' of the barbarians as a rationalization of the same aloofness that made them refuse to receive ambassadors from the Visigoths before the battle of Adrianople in 379 at which the Emperor Valens was killed, or to discuss food supplies with them outside the walls of Rome in 410 before the city was sacked. The barbarians set up their own kingdoms inside the western empire during the fifth century not from choice, but because they were denied assimilation.

When Justinian became emperor in Constantinople in 527 the west was the most hopeful spot on his horizon. Theodoric the Ostrogoth had ruled Italy as an imperia nominee from 493 to 526 in the spirit of his famous saying that 'Every Goth wants to be a Roman; only a poor Roman would want to be a Goth.' Gaul was dominated by the sons of Clovis, who had accepted baptism from Catholic bishops and a consular robe from the Emperor Anastasius (*see Map 17*). By contrast the Danube frontier was heavily pressed by Avars and Slavs and war had just broken out with the old enemy, Persia, formidably strong again under Khosrau I. Worst of all, generations of imperial incompetence had allowed great stretches of territory to fall under the unfettered domination of noble families, and through conceding or selling to the magnates the right to make appointments (the *suffragium*) seen the imperial bureaucracy itself become simply an expensive extension of their privilege.

Justinian's claim to greatness is that he tried to dismantle that privilege, his misfortune that his propaganda still disguises it. His quaestor Tribonian renewed the basis of imperial authority with a new, and as it turned out definitive, codification of Roman law, the *Corpus Juris Civilis*. His praetorian prefect, John the Cappadocian, overhauled the administration: Justinian's enemies said that he kept a torture chamber beneath the palace, to make the rich pay their taxes. His general, Belisarius, sustained imperial prestige and won rich rewards at little cost by reconquering the provinces of Africa (533-4) and Italy (535-40). It was a bold strategy which nearly worked. But in 540 Khosrau I attacked, breaking the 'eternal peace' for which he had been handsomely paid in 532, and the Slavs took the opportunity to cross the Danube. In 542 plague killed perhaps a quarter of the population of the Empire, and, recurring every few years, left armies devastated, land uncultivated and taxes unpayable. The struggle for survival destroyed Justinian's policy. While vast sums were raised to man and fortify the Persian and Danube frontiers the reconquered provinces rebelled and Italy became the Vietnam of the age; Slav incursions became ever deeper and more frequent, the Persian threat more ominous; and to resist them posts and power were once more mortgaged to the magnates, this time irredeemably.

Like many radical reformers Justinian pretended only devotion to the past, seeking the loyalty of his subjects by proclaiming his intention to restore the Roman Empire, and that of the bishops by professing a fervent concern for Catholic unity. In fact what he conquered was the old Greek world, soon to shrink almost to its ancient extent (*compare Maps 17, 5 and 20*). He gave it a law, a tradition of imperial absolutism in church and state, and, through the public and religious buildings which he everywhere erected or inspired, a uniform and magnificent art. He failed to rescue it from the rapacity of its aristocracy.

Background illustration: Tartars travelling on horseback. Attributed to Li Tsuan Hua, Chinese tenth century

17 The world of late antiquity
The distribution of population – though the figures given are highly conjectural – reflects a lasting division between the Greek, Roman and barbarian worlds which reappeared as the Roman Empire disintegrated and the struggle for political and cultural leadership intensified. The 'frontier of literacy' shows the northern limit in Gaul of inscriptions and other indications of secular literacy.

Further reading: Peter Brown, *The World of Late Antiquity* (second ed. Thames and Hudson, Norton 1989); Ramsey Macmullen, *Corruption and the Decline of Rome* (Yale U. P.); Patrick Geary, *Before France and Germany* (Oxford U. P. 1990); Edward Gibbon, *The Decline and Fall of the Roman Empire* (1776-88, many subsequent edns, including J. B. Bury, Macmillan 1909-13); T. Barfield, *The Perilous Frontier: Nomadic Empires and China* (Basil Blackwell 1989).

MAP 15 THE SASSANID EMPIRE IN PERSIA

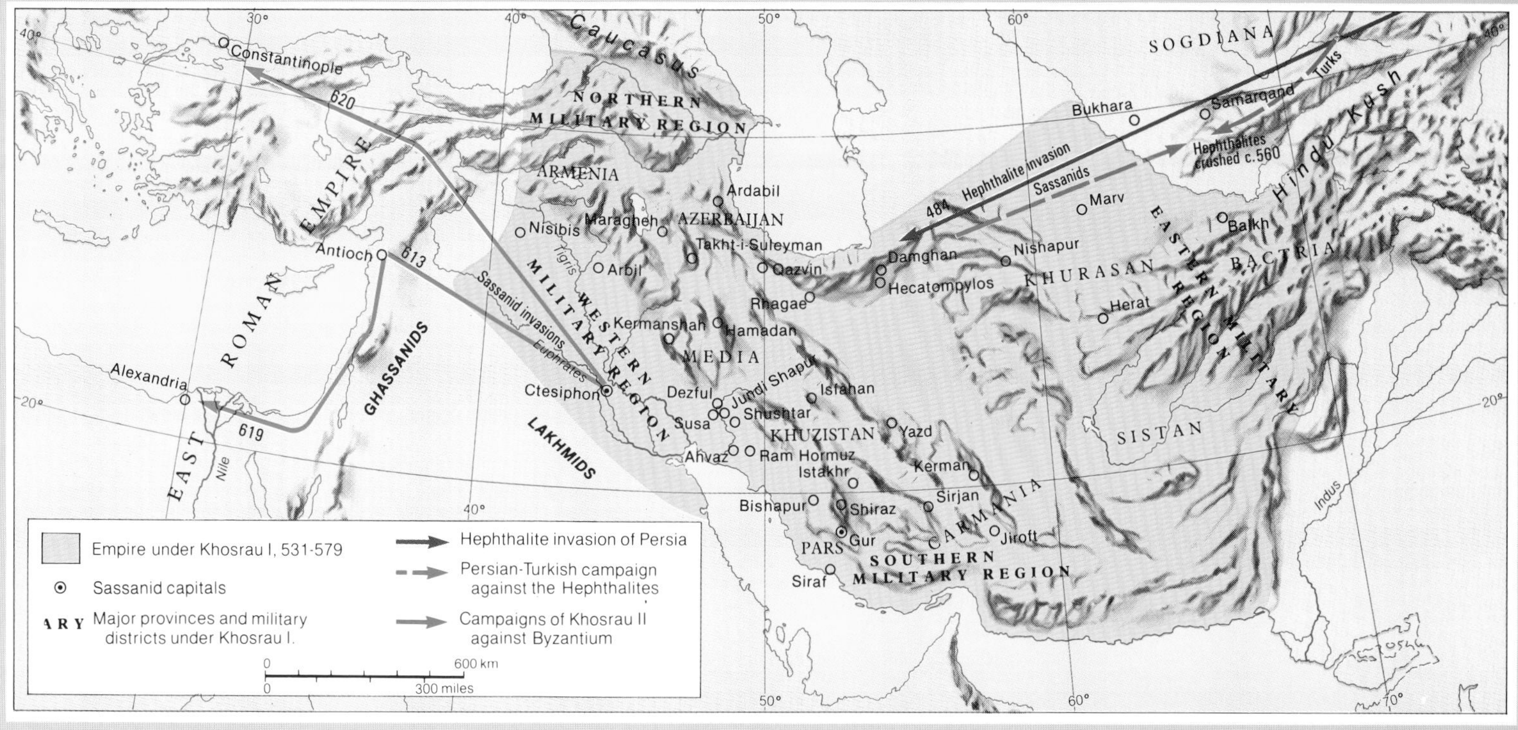

MAP 16 THE EMPIRE OF THE GUPTAS IN INDIA

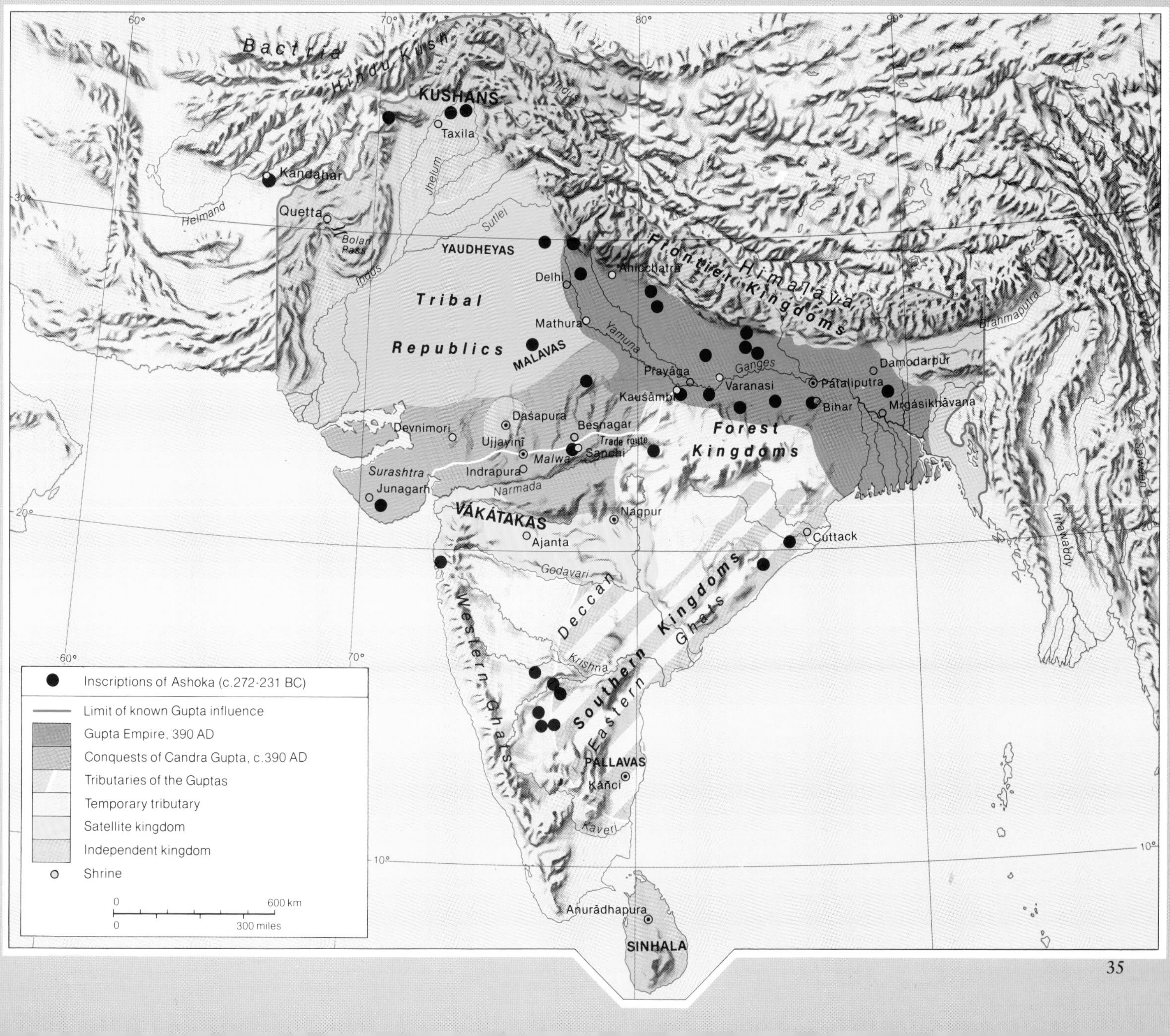

Bactria
Hindu Kush
KUSHANS
Taxila
Kandahar
Quetta
Bolan Pass
Helmand
Indus
Jhelum
Sutlej
YAUDHEYAS
Tribal Republics
MALAVAS
Delhi
Ahicchatra
Mathura
Yamuna
Frontier Kingdoms
Himalaya
Ganges
Prayāga
Kauśāmbī
Varanasi
Pātaliputra
Bihar
Damodarpur
Mṛgāsikhāvana
Brahmaputra
Forest Kingdoms
Devnimori
Daśapura
Besnagar
Ujjayinī
Trade route
Malwa
Sanchi
Surashtra
Junagarh
Indrapura
Narmada
VĀKĀTAKAS
Nagpur
Ajanta
Cuttack
Godavari
Deccan
Western Ghats
Southern Kingdoms
Eastern Ghats
Krishna
PALLAVAS
Kāñci
Kaveri
Anurādhapura
SINHALA
Irrawaddy

Inscriptions of Ashoka (c.272-231 BC)
Limit of known Gupta influence
Gupta Empire, 390 AD
Conquests of Candra Gupta, c.390 AD
Tributaries of the Guptas
Temporary tributary
Satellite kingdom
Independent kingdom
Shrine
600 km
300 miles

Atlantic Ocean
North Sea
Bay of Biscay
PICTS
Iona
Lindisfarne
Devenish
Armagh
Kells
Clonard
Whithorn
NORTHUMBRIANS
MERCIANS
EAST ANGLIANS
WEST SAXONS
KENT
Canterbury
St. Davids
Tintagel
c.540-560
c.460
KINGDOM OF THE FRANKS (481)
Rouen
Soissons
Reims
Paris
Rennes
Dol
Le Mans
Faremoutiers
Sens
Orléans
Auxerre
Tours
Poitiers
Vouillé
Bourges
Nevers
Clermont
Limoges
Bordeaux
Cahors
Toulouse
Narbonne
Cologne
c. 511-48
Trier
ALEMANIA
Luxeuil
Besançon
St. Gall
Bregenz
Chur
BURGUNDIAN KINGDOM (443-534)
Lyons
Vienne
Avignon
Arles
Marseille
Lerins
The Alps
LOMB
568
Monza
Milan
Pavia
Verona
Aquileia
Grado
Parenzo
Pola
Bobbio
Parma
Genoa
Luna
Ravenna
Rimini
Ancona
Auximium
KINGDOM OF THE OSTROGOTHS (489-555)
Perugia
Subiaco
Rome
Monte Cassino
Capua
Naples
Lucera
Salerno
Brindisi
Taranto
Otrant
Cosenza
Croton
Vivarium
Messina
Reggio
Palermo
Agrigento
Sicily
Syracuse
Salona
Corsica
Ajaccio
Sardinia
Forum Trajani
Cagliari
KINGDOM OF THE SUEVI (464-585)
Oviedo
Leon
Palencia
Braga
Burgos
Pamplona
Pyrenees
Ebro
VISGOTHIC KINGDOM (455-711)
Saragossa
Gerona
Reccopolis
Toledo
Tortosa
Tarragona
Merida
Valencia
Balearic Is.
Ibiza
Seville
Cadiz
Cartagena
Tingis
Septem
KINGDOM OF THE VANDALS (442-534)
MAURETANIA
Caesarea
Pomaria
Sitifis
Cirta
Hippo Regius
NUMIDIA
PROCONSULARIS
Carthage
Thagaste
Timgad
Thelepte
BYZACENA
Grasse
Hadrumetum
Caput Vada
Tacape
Sabrata
Leptis Magna
TRIPOLITANIA
Atlas Mts.
Medit
Rhine
Elbe
Oder
Danube
Rhône
Po
Balti
486
507
511
533-4
537
50°
40°
30°
10°
0°

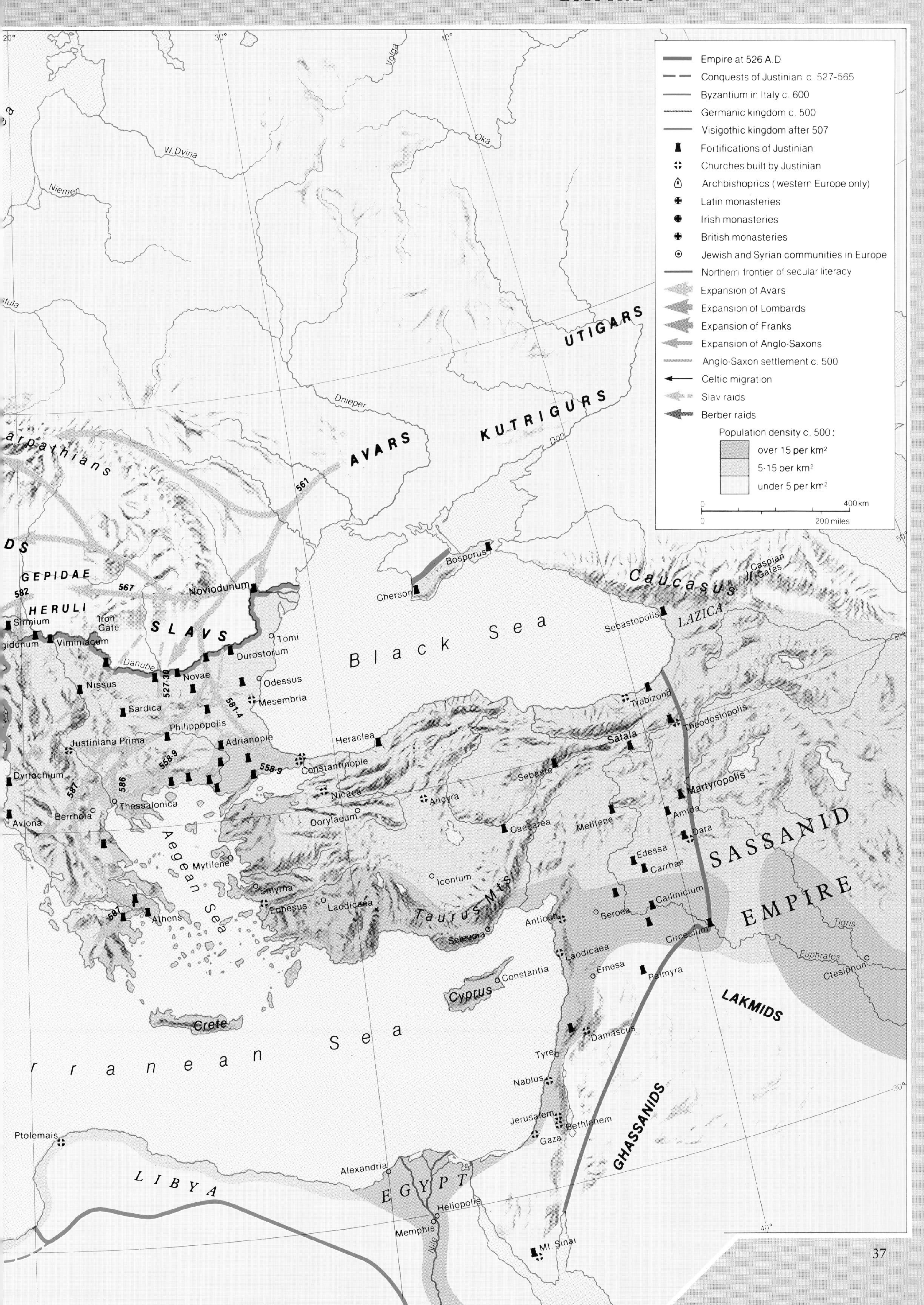

Empire at 526 A.D
Conquests of Justinian c. 527-565
Byzantium in Italy c. 600
Germanic kingdom c. 500
Visigothic kingdom after 507
Fortifications of Justinian
Churches built by Justinian
Archbishoprics (western Europe only)
Latin monasteries
Irish monasteries
British monasteries
Jewish and Syrian communities in Europe
Northern frontier of secular literacy
Expansion of Avars
Expansion of Lombards
Expansion of Franks
Expansion of Anglo-Saxons
Anglo-Saxon settlement c. 500
Celtic migration
Slav raids
Berber raids
Population density c. 500:
over 15 per km²
5-15 per km²
under 5 per km²
0 400 km
0 200 miles
UTIGARS
KUTRIGURS
AVARS
GEPIDAE
HERULI
SLAVS
W. Dvina
Niemen
Volga
Oka
Dnieper
Don
Carpathians
Danube
Iron Gate
Sirmium
Viminiacum
Noviodunum
Tomi
Durostorum
Novae
Odessus
Mesembria
Nissus
Sardica
Philippopolis
Justiniana Prima
Adrianople
Constantinople
Dyrrachium
Avlona
Berrhoia
Thessalonica
Athens
Aegean Sea
Mytilene
Smyrna
Ephesus
Laodicaea
Nicaea
Dorylaeum
Ancyra
Heraclea
Iconium
Taurus Mts
Seleucia
Caesarea
Sebaste
Satala
Melitene
Trebizond
Theodosiopolis
Martyropolis
Amida
Dara
Edessa
Carrhae
Callinicium
Circesium
Beroea
Antioch
Laodicaea
Emesa
Palmyra
Damascus
Tyre
Nablus
Jerusalem
Bethlehem
Gaza
Mt. Sinai
Black Sea
Bosporus
Cherson
Sebastopolis
LAZICA
Caucasus
Caspian Gates
SASSANID EMPIRE
Tigris
Euphrates
Ctesiphon
LAKMIDS
GHASSANIDS
Cyprus
Constantia
Crete
Mediterranean Sea
LIBYA
Ptolemais
Alexandria
EGYPT
Heliopolis
Memphis
Nile
561
567
582
527-30
581-4
558-9
586
587

Heirs to the ancient world 1

RELIGIONS AND CIVILIZATIONS

The bloody rivalry between Persia and Byzantium which had continued since the end of Justinian's reign in 565 was rudely interrupted when Arab armies seized the Byzantine provinces of Syria in AD 635, Palestine in 638 and Egypt in 642, and took the Persian capital of Ctesiphon in 636. In those years the ancient world gave way to the modern.

The conquests of Islam, which continued only slightly less rapidly until its armies seized Toledo, Samarqand and Multan in 711-13 (*see Map 19*), changed the course of world history. The Mediterranean basin, upon whose commercial and cultural unity classical civilization had been built, was divided for ever. The fragmentation of the Roman world which had become increasingly obvious in the preceding centuries (*Maps 14 and 17*) now became permanent, and each part was sent on its own distinctive path (*Maps 18, 21 and 22*). The world of Islam became a vast market linking all the economies of the known world to support a civilization of opulent splendour, whose hunger for manpower and raw materials stimulated the opening up of the forests and plains of central Europe and initiated the systematic plundering of Africa that has sustained the development of advanced economies ever since (*Map 27*). The pattern of the great religions of the world, and its principal cultural and political divisions, was completed (*Maps 11 and 20*).

The Arabian peninsula in the time of Muhammad (traditionally, *b.*570) combined violence with sophistication. The endemic feuding of both the pastoral Bedouin who occupied its rugged desert terrain and the merchant dynasties of the cities, and the incessant warfare between the two represented, but dissipated, immense military potential. Muhammad's uncompromising monotheism – 'There is no God but God, and Muhammad is the messenger of God' – provided the basis for the common purpose and common allegiance that would unleash it. His power was rooted in diplo-

18 The making of Byzantium
After administrative and military reorganization, Constantinople (Byzantium) and its hinterland, to which the eastern Roman Empire was reduced by the invasions of Slavs and Arabs in the seventh century, became the centre of fresh expansion and a vigorous civilization in the eighth and ninth centuries.

MAP 18 THE MAKING OF BYZANTIUM

macy. The *Koran*, revealed to him in a series of visions from about 610 onwards, contained the basis upon which, as his followers said, 'Allah has sent us a prophet who will make peace between us'; the message was largely one of repudiating the network of family obligation and social custom of traditional Arab society, with its ever-violent code of manliness, honour and revenge, in favour of a stark confrontation between the believer and his God, whose inexorable judgement would ask only whether the precepts of the *Koran* had been unflinchingly observed, regardless of worldly connection and reputation. Muhammad unified the peninsula by diplomacy, aided when necessary by the doctrine of holy war – 'It was not you who slew them, but Allah who slew them', as the prophet assured his followers when the slaughter of a Meccan caravan seemed momentarily to have flouted the Koran's prohibition of violence. He was planning the conquest of Syria when he died in 632.

His work was continued by the Caliphs (successors) Abu Bakr (*r.*632-4) and Omar (*r.*634-44). Their decree that the land of those who surrendered would remain inviolate while that of any who had actually to be conquered would be forfeit to the state, to be merely leased again to its former owners, facilitated the advance. It was a prudent policy, for the Arab armies, with no advantages save great speed of movement, the brilliance of their generals, and remarkable confidence in their own destiny, could probably not have overcome sustained resistance, despite their spectacular victories over numerically superior forces at Yarmuk (636) and Qadesiya (637). But the Roman hold on Africa and the Middle East was tenuous in the extreme, and the Sassanid empire on the point of collapse. These two powers had recently waged savage wars in which they alternately committed the most brutal atrocities upon the subject populations of the Middle East who repeatedly passed from the control of one to the other, with religious minorities, Christian and Jewish, suffering particularly heavily, being constantly vulnerable to accusations of treason and collaboration. These wars simply emphasized the weakness and the unpopularity of both their rules. The new Islamic masters demanded more modest taxes and services, and did not even inconvenience their new subjects to the extent of living in their towns, preferring to build new ones for themselves nearby; inevitably they were readily welcomed by exhausted and long-tyrannized communities. Like the fall of the Roman Empire in the west, the collapse of so much of the eastern Roman Empire and of its Persian counterpart rid their former lands of an expensive, cumbersome and blood-stained rule that had long outlived its vitality and its usefulness.

The established world religions also underwent fundamental changes in the early centuries of the Christian era. Hinduism now assumed greater coherence by concentrating its literature and religious activity upon three of the many gods whose worship the Vedic religion had embraced, Brahma (the creator), Vishnu (the preserver) and Shiva (the destroyer of the corrupt world). The myth and ceremony associated with the last two in particular, together with the Sanskrit language, were deliberately employed by various dynasties to disseminate Aryan culture from its strongholds in the north of the subcontinent. Hinduism, however, was not a missionary religion. To an even greater extent than Judaism, which was disseminated widely in the West through the travels of the Jews, but did not usually attempt to convert outsiders (*see Map 11*), Hinduism spread with but not beyond those who were born into it. Birth was indeed the only means of entry, and the absorption of new peoples by the creation of sub-castes – a technique which could not be applied to individuals – was necessarily a slow business. The process of rapid evangelisation in India was left to the Jains and to Buddhism, which, like Christianity in the West, was a religion of personal conviction and conversion.

The teaching of the Buddha was not written down for several centuries after his time, with the result that a large number of sects offered competing versions of it. Some held, despite his warning that he was not to be deified, that the historical Buddha was only one of a series of incarnations in which the divine being appeared, sacrificing the *nirvana* which he had earned by his perfection to secure the redemption of others through his own suffering. As such he could be represented and

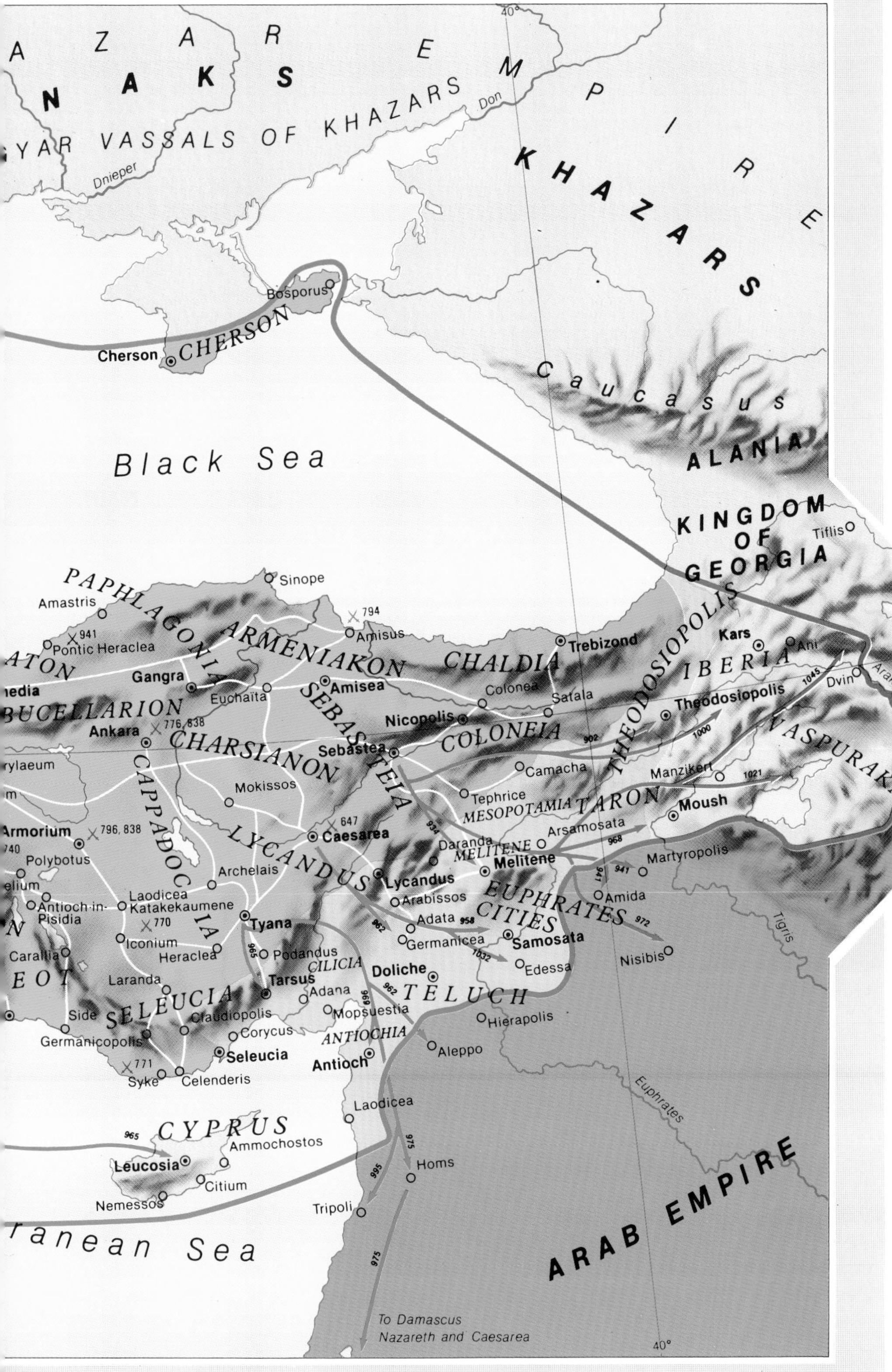

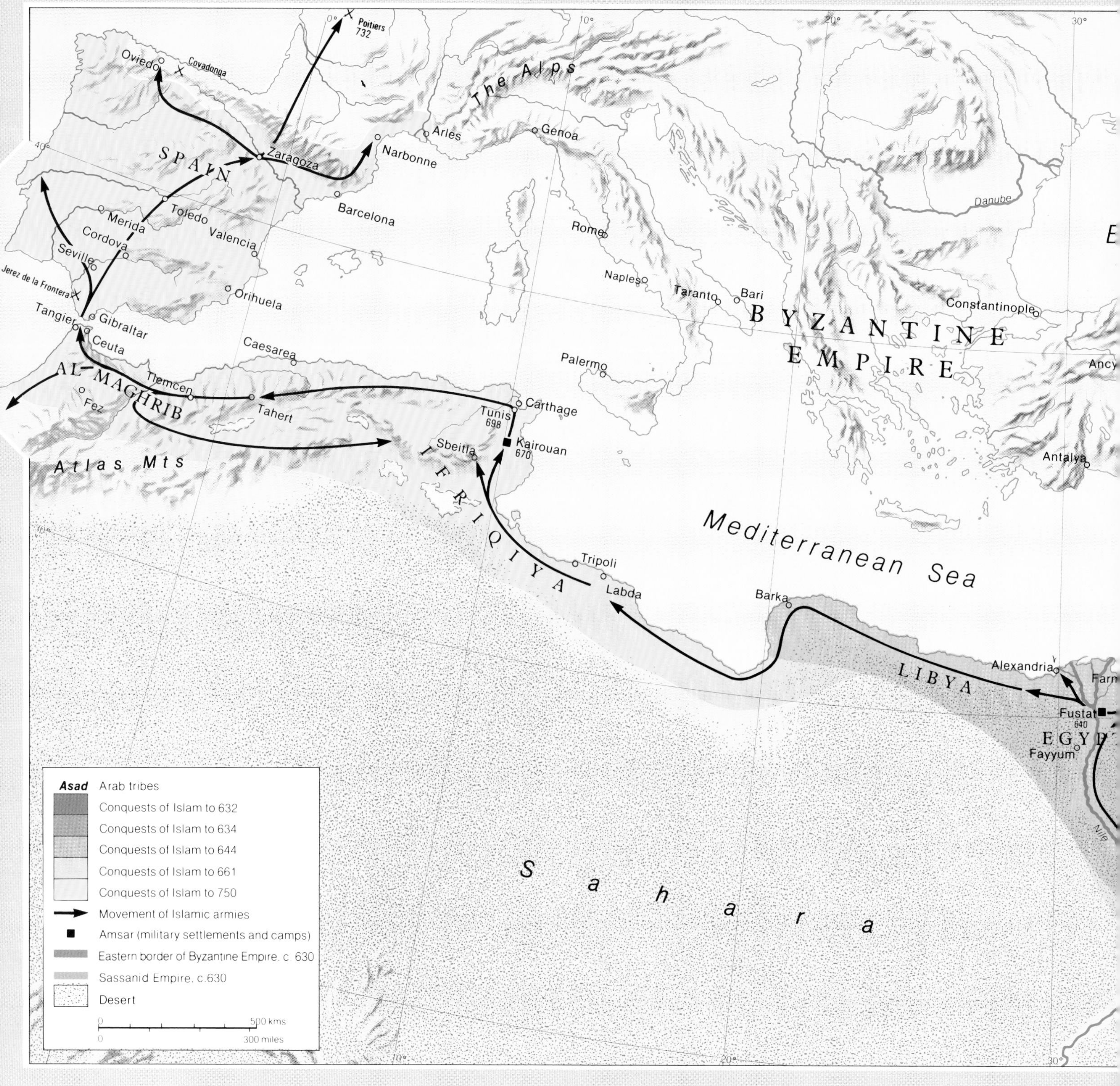

19 The conquests of Islam
Within ten years of the death of Muhammad in 632 the armies of Islam had conquered most of the old Roman Empire and occupied the Persian capital; within 70 they commanded territories stretching over 5000 miles, of which only Spain and Portugal are no longer predominantly Muslim.

worshipped in the *bodhisattvas*, the idealized stone images which now proliferated in the great monuments of Buddhist art. Early in the second century AD, those who held this belief, together with others who wished to incorporate new practices and philosophies into their faith, separated to follow their 'Greater Vehicle' (*Mahayana*) from those who clung to the 'Lesser Vehicle' (*Hinayana*) of the teaching of the historical Buddha, literally observed. As Buddhism spread the Mahayana system became predominant in China, Japan, Korea and Vietnam, while the Hinayana prevailed in Burma, Thailand, Cambodia and Ceylon.

Buddhism probably reached China along the central Asian trade routes in the early years of the Later Han dynasty; the traditional date is AD 65. Its early development there was slow, hindered both by philosophical difficulties – such as the flat contradiction between the Chinese veneration of family and the Buddhist renunciation of all family ties – and by practical ones such as the difficulty of translating the Sanskrit scriptures – which reached China haphazardly and piecemeal. The work was done by Chinese monks who made a number of pilgrimages to India for the purpose. By the fourth century, however, China was ruled by barbarians. The foreignness of Buddhism became a positive attraction, and many of the rulers adopted Buddhist monks as political advisers to offset the influence of the Confucian Chinese around them. The favour of the courts and the lavish patronage of the powerful stimulated the spread of Buddhism in northern China in the fourth and fifth centuries, accompanied by magnificent temples and sculptures. At the same time the noble Chinese families who had migrated to the south in large numbers found the Buddhist custom of withdrawal an attractive expedient in troubled times, and chose to

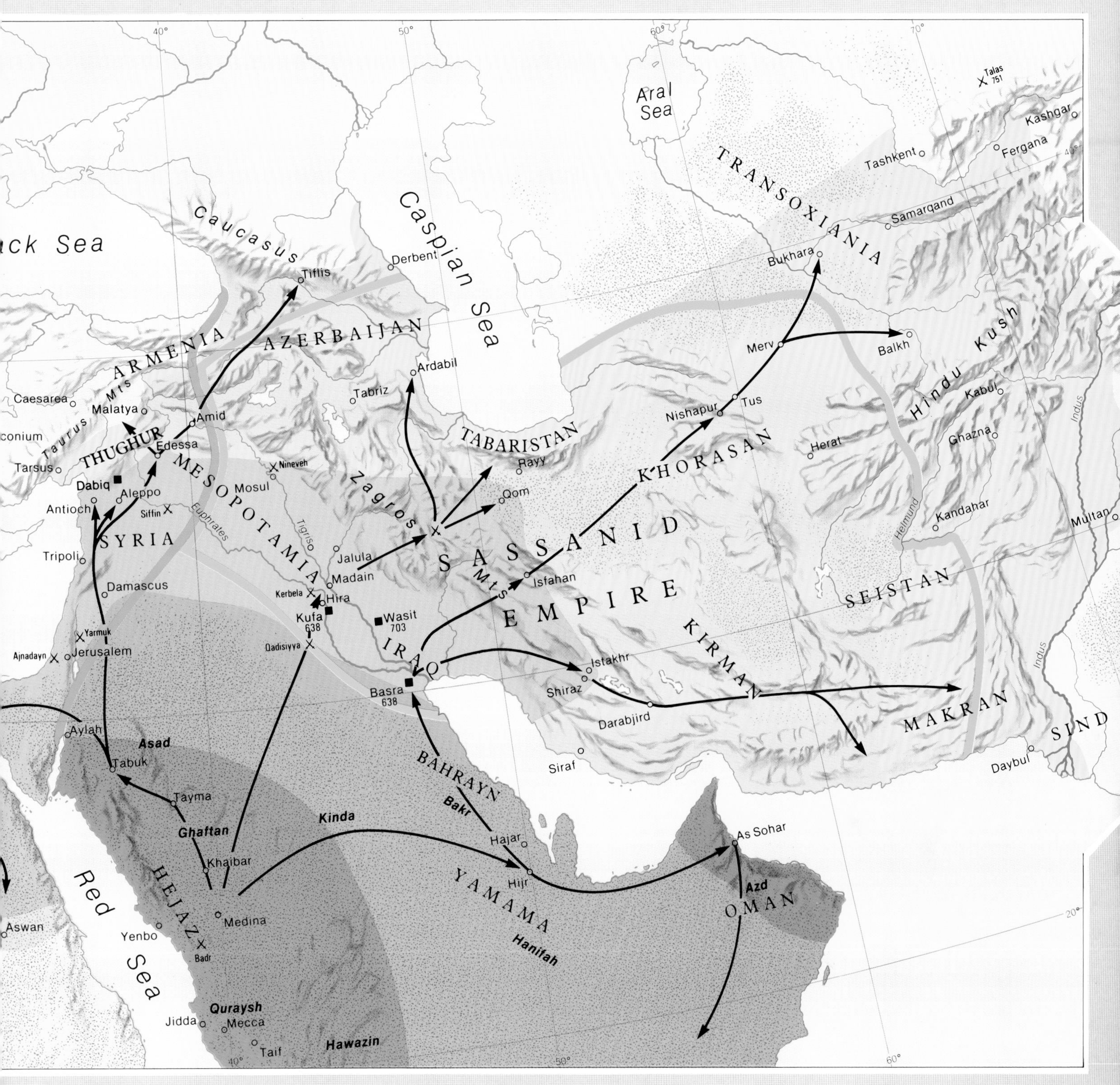

20 Religions of the medieval world
Between the eighth and fifteenth centuries, four universal religions (all with internal sects and divisions which are not shown here) came to dominate the civilized world, eradicating paganism from most areas. The social and cultural patterns which they created or reflected have endured.

make the monasteries, which they founded in large numbers, centres for the preservation of their own cultural traditions. Hence Buddhism contriyed to appeal both to the Taoist aspiration of withdrawal from the world, and to the Confucian veneration of tradition and scholarship, while in the north it won great influence among the non-Chinese. In consequence although it was occasionally subjected to persecution Buddhism became the third of China's religions. Conversely it is a notable proof of the essential stability and sophistication of Chinese culture that it was, until comparatively recent times, the only one in the civilized world which did not require to be underpinned by religious monopoly.

The early history of Christianity had a great deal in common with that of Buddhism. It too was founded essentially as a movement of reform within an older religion, by comparison with which it stressed personal spirituality rather than formal adherence to law, charity rather than ascetic prohibitions. It too repudiated political structures, social distinctions and, implicitly, the priority of kinship loyalties, renouncing violence and emphasising the brotherhood of mankind. Like the Buddha, Christ was regarded by his followers as a perfect being who redeemed the sins of mankind through his own suffering. In his case too the absence of a strictly contemporary record of his teaching encouraged the multiplication of sects among his devotees, most of whom came to attribute to him a divinity which he had not explicitly claimed. They drew upon the philosophical and cultural traditions of their time to evolve a universal theology to support their cult. Particularly important was the reconciliation of Christian theology with the neoplatonist system of philos-

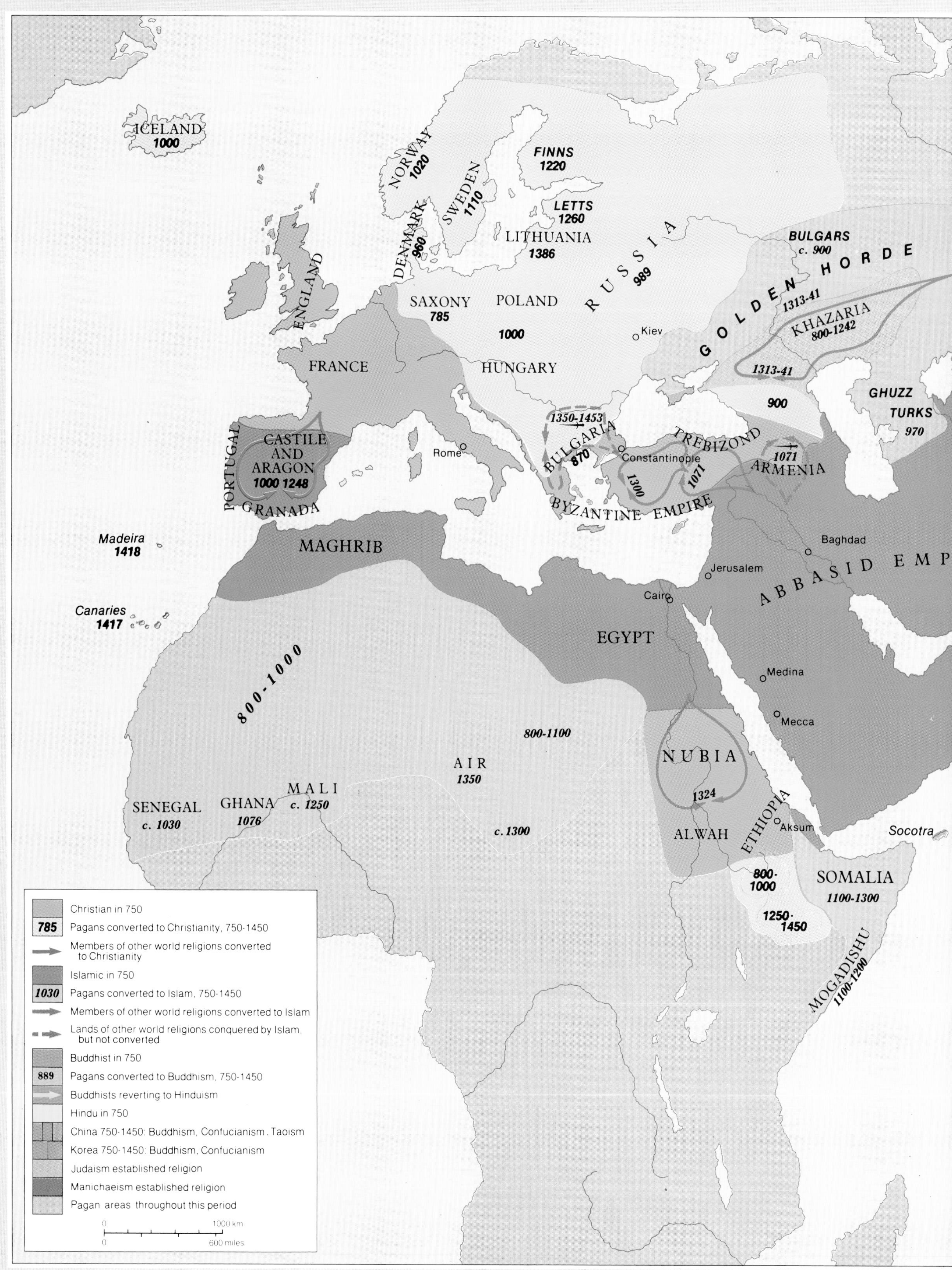

ICELAND
1000
NORWAY
1020
SWEDEN
1110
DENMARK
960
FINNS
1220
LETTS
1260
LITHUANIA
1386
ENGLAND
RUSSIA
989
BULGARS
c. 900
GOLDEN HORDE
1313-41
KHAZARIA
800-1242
1313-41
900
GHUZZ
TURKS
970
SAXONY
785
POLAND
1000
Kiev
FRANCE
HUNGARY
PORTUGAL
CASTILE AND ARAGON
1000 1248
GRANADA
Rome
1350-1453
BULGARIA
870
Constantinople
TREBIZOND
1071
1300
1071
ARMENIA
BYZANTINE EMPIRE
Madeira
1418
MAGHRIB
Baghdad
Jerusalem
ABBASID EMP
Cairo
Canaries
1417
EGYPT
800-1000
Medina
Mecca
800-1100
NUBIA
AIR
1350
MALI
c. 1250
SENEGAL
c. 1030
GHANA
1076
c. 1300
1324
ALWAH
ETHIOPIA
Aksum
Socotra
800-1000
SOMALIA
1100-1300
1250-1450
MOGADISHU
1100-1200
Christian in 750
785 Pagans converted to Christianity, 750-1450
Members of other world religions converted to Christianity
Islamic in 750
1030 Pagans converted to Islam, 750-1450
Members of other world religions converted to Islam
Lands of other world religions conquered by Islam, but not converted
Buddhist in 750
889 Pagans converted to Buddhism, 750-1450
Buddhists reverting to Hinduism
Hindu in 750
China 750-1450: Buddhism, Confucianism, Taoism
Korea 750-1450: Buddhism, Confucianism
Judaism established religion
Manichaeism established religion
Pagan areas throughout this period
0 1000 km
0 600 miles

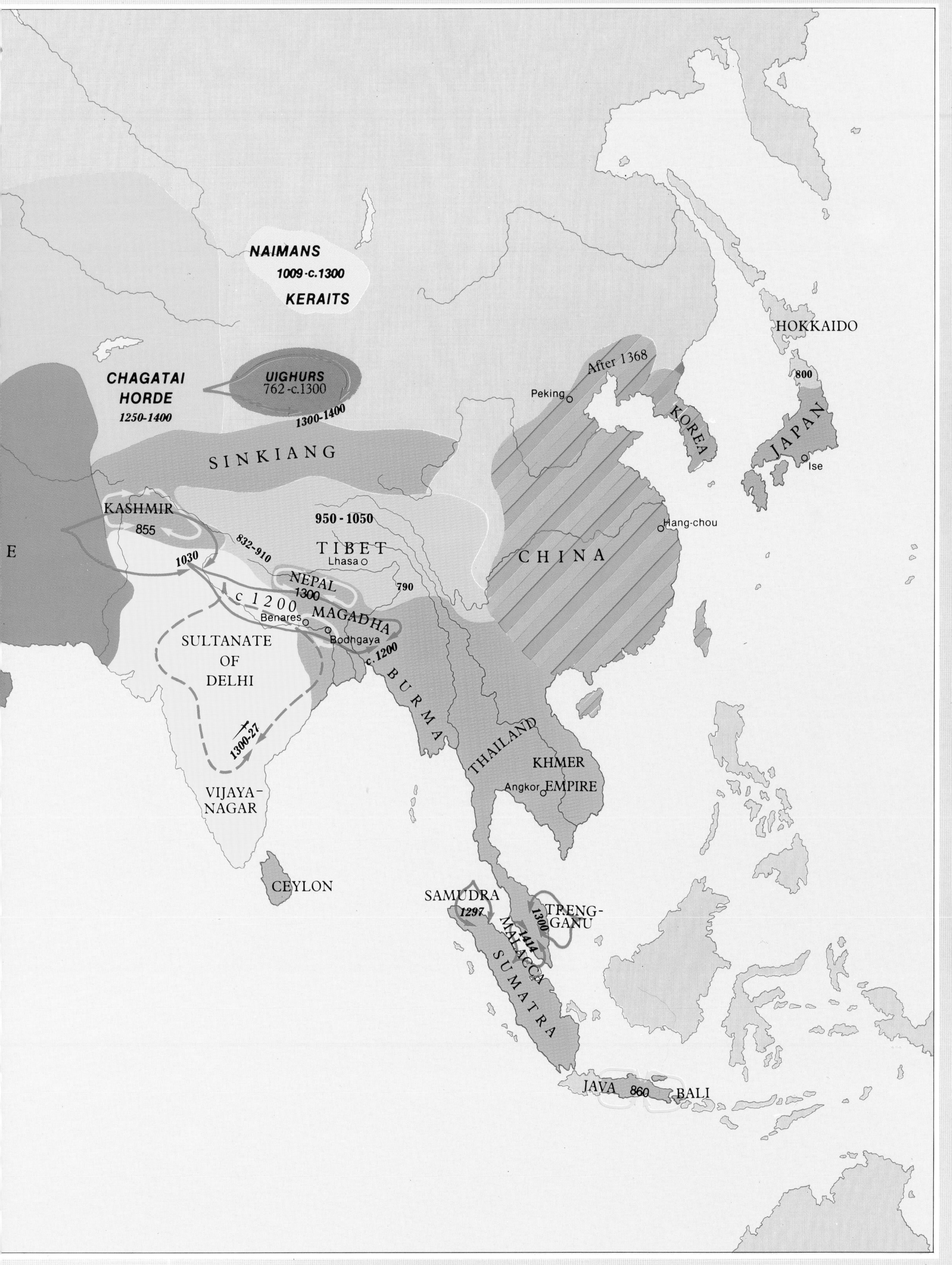
NAIMANS
1009-c.1300
KERAITS
CHAGATAI
HORDE
1250-1400
UIGHURS
762-c.1300
1300-1400
SINKIANG
KASHMIR
855
1030
832-910
950-1050
TIBET
Lhasa
NEPAL
1300
790
c 1200
MAGADHA
Benares
Bodhgaya
c.1200
SULTANATE
OF
DELHI
1300-27
VIJAYA-
NAGAR
CEYLON
BURMA
THAILAND
KHMER
EMPIRE
Angkor
CHINA
Peking
After 1368
Hang-chou
KOREA
JAPAN
Ise
800
HOKKAIDO
SAMUDRA
1297
1300
TRENG-
GANU
1414
MALACCA
SUMATRA
JAVA
860
BALI
E

ophy, based on the idea of the unity of creation, which also provided an idealist foundation for the pagan cults of the third and fourth centuries AD. Finally, like Buddhism, Christianity was assisted in its diffusion by the regular and far-flung communications of a great empire (*see Map 11*), but attained real social power and political influence by exploiting its decline.

The Christians of the Roman Empire were conceded freedom of worship by Constantine in 313, and the communities which were now found in most parts of the Roman world could come into the open. Christianity did not, however, immediately become the dominant religion of the Roman world. During the fourth century the legal disabilities which it had suffered were gradually transferred, by imperial decree, to the traditional pagan cults. In the east, where the cities in which Christianity flourished were most populous and the pagan aristocracy least influential, the order to close the temples and the prohibition of pagan worship in public were taken as licence for successful persecution. Monks and holy men from the deserts of Egypt and the mountains of Syria led bloodthirsty mobs in a reign of terror which destroyed the fabric of pagan life and culture. The worst excesses were the destruction of the shrine of Serapion at Alexandria, and with it the greatest library of antiquity, in 391 and in 415 the lynching of Hypatia, the virgin queen of the neoplatonist schools.

In the west, social leadership and public office remained in the hands of the Roman aristocracy. To its members paganism, which was now heavily impregnated with neoplatonist idealism, expressed the values and enshrined the traditions of their class, much as Confucianism did in China. The aristocracy did not hurry to implement the anti-pagan decrees of the upstart emperors they despised, and they were under little popular pressure to do so. A pagan attempt to recapture the Western Empire failed only through the chance of battle (or, as the winners said, a miracle) as late as 394. Christianity triumphed only when the Roman aristocracy came to see it as the means of preserving their culture from the collapse of the empire, and the church as the vehicle through which, under traditional leadership, Rome would recover its ancient pre-eminence. As the empire dissolved, the scions of the Roman aristocracy adopted episcopal mitres to resume the leadership that their forefathers had exercised in senatorial purple. They copied the manuscripts which contained their culture and collected them in monasteries, where literacy might, however precariously, be preserved. When these men began to come to terms with the invaders the foundations of a new age were laid. In Gaul Clovis, king of the Merovingian Franks, was converted in *c.*500, and made them the guides and mentors of a dynasty which brought Gaul under a single, if rapidly enfeebled, rule and inaugurated Europe's most important Catholic regime (*see Map 17*).

Thomas Hobbes described the Roman Church as 'the ghost of the Roman Empire sitting crowned upon the grave thereof'. So it was elsewhere. The world religions neither replaced nor transformed the ancient civilizations. They were the means by which the civilizations survived the ruin of their original political structures. Even Islam, the starkest and most uncompromising of the new faiths, was no different. The Abbasid revolution began in Khorasan in 750 to restore the fundamentals of Islam. The Umayyad dynasty which it replaced had treated conquest as a means of enriching the Arab aristocracy, and was led by the very families which had once driven the Prophet from Mecca. Under their rule Christian Arabs enjoyed high office, and the capital was moved from Medina to the Roman city of Damascus, where, like the Dome of the Rock in Jerusalem, the Great Mosque was decorated by Byzantine craftsmen, in Byzantine style. The Abbasid regime turned its back on the corrupting shores of the Mediterranean, to rule from Iran a central Asian empire of great wealth and magnificence. Its caliphs claimed over their subjects absolute powers which they exercised ruthlessly with the help of Persian officials. Their splendid courts observed the etiquette and ceremonial of the Sassanids, whose literature and art now experienced a revival. Their new capital was at Baghdad, 35 miles from the ruins of Ctesiphon.

21 The Byzantine commonwealth
The Slavs were converted to Christianity in the ninth century by Saints Cyril and Methodius. Although their work was largely destroyed within a century by Magyar invasions, the Orthodox Church, represented by Byzantine artists and builders as well as missionaries and monks, remained the greatest formative influence on eastern Europe.

Left: Royal Mosque in Isfahan, southern Iraq.

Below: The Dome of the Rock, Jerusalem, begun 687.

Further reading: Diana Eck, *Banaras, City of Light* (Princeton U. P. 1982); R. Lane Fox, *Pagans and Christians* (Allen Lane, 1986; Harper); Judith Herrin, *The Formation of Christendom* (Basil Blackwell 1987, Princeton U. P.); D. Obolensky, *The Byzantine Commonwealth* (Weidenfeld and Nicolson 1971; St. Vladimir's); M. Cook, *Muhammed* (OUP 1983); Ira M. Lapidus, *A History of Islamic Societies* (Cambridge U. P. 1988); R. Dawson, *The Chinese Experience* (Weidenfeld and Nicolson 1978).

L. Ladoga
Ladoga
1167
Beloozero
VIATKA
Khlynov
Birka
Reval
LETTS
NOVGOROD
c.1000
Novgorod the Great
Volga
Yaroslavl
Izborsk
Pskov
Rostov
c.1040
Kholm
Tver
SUZDAL
Suzdal
Nishni Novgorod
Grobina
Riga
1201
Apuole
LITHUANIANS
Baltic Sea
TEUTONIC ORDER
POLOTSK
Vladimir
1198
Dmitrovo
Great Bulgar
Moscow
Murom
c.1090
BULGARS
Bukhara
Polotsk
1105
SMOLENSK
Kolomna
RYAZAN
Wolin
c.1140
Koenigsberg
1254
Elbing
1237
PRUSSIANS
Smolensk
c.1136
Ryazan
c.1200
Elbe
WESTERN EMPIRE
Magdeburg
962
Oder
Vistula
Thorn
1234
Cherven
Gneizno
1000
Poznan
968
Plock
c.1075
Varangian
Bryansk
CHERNIGOV
Trubchevsk
Starodub
KINGDOM OF POLAND
Pinsk
VOLHYNIA
Novogorod Sevirsky
Kursk
Saracen Route
Breslau
c.1000
Turov
c.1120
KIEV
Chernigov
c.1066
Prague
975
BOHEMIA
Vladimir-in-Volhynia
1090
PEREJASLAV
Cracow
c.1000
Kiev
989
c.1040
Perejaslav
c.1000
Olmutz
1063
Przemysl
Galich
c.1160
MORAVIA
Belgorod
c.989
Dnieper
Salzburg
Danube
GALICIA
Route
Donets
Volga
The Alps
KINGDOM OF HUNGARY
Carpathians
Dniester
Esztergom
CUMANS
1091-1240
Sarkel
Bukhara
Itil
Baghdad
Aquileia
Venice
11th, 12th centuries
Kalocsa
c.1000
PATZINAKS
895-1091
Don
Zagreb
1093
Rijeka
Pazin
Krk
Senj
Alba Julia
c.1106
KHAZARS
Sea of Azov
Bosporos
STATES OF THE CHURCH
Ancona
Zadar
Sibenik
Spalato
CROATIA
Adriatic Sea
Sirmium
c.1252
Singidunum
Belgorod
CHERSON
Cherson
Alania
ALANIA
Caucasus
c.900
KINGDOM OF GEORGIA
Tiflis
Hvar
Milisevo
1230
Studenica
1200
Sopočani
1202-5
Ragusa
Pec
c.1200
Danube
Cherven
Pliska
Turnovo
1201
Preslav
SERBIA
BULGARIA
Sardica
Mesembria
870
Black Sea
Rome
Grottaferrata
Monte Cassino
1057-86
Capua
Naples
Amalfi
Melfi
Salerno
Bari
Dyrrachium
Nerizi
1164
Veles
Ochrida 1037-56
Kurbinovo
1150
Rila
Philippopolis
Adrianople
Constantinople
Brindisi
Taranto
Lecce
Prespa
Thessalonica
Trajanopolis
NORMAN KINGDOM OF SICILY
Rossano
Mt. Athos
Nicaea
11th cent
Claudiopolis
Neocaesarea
Coloneia
Trebizond
c.1250
Echmiadzin
ARMENIA
Araks
Ankara
Sebastea
Camacha
Palermo
1132-43
Cefalù
1148
Mileto
Larissa
1282-9
Arta
Aegean Sea
Cotyaeum
Monreale
1184-92
Messina
Troina
Hosios Lucas
c.1000
Lesbos
Mitylene
1042-54
Patras
Nea Moni
Chios
Smyrna
Antioch
Rock monasteries of Cappadocia
c.850-1200
Caesarea
Melitene
Syracuse
Daphne
11th cent
Athens
11th cent
Ephesus
Laodicea
Iconium
Taurus Mts
Malta
Patmos
Side
Seleucia
Rhodes
Myra
Black Mountain
Antioch
Euphrates
Tigris
Candia
Crete
Koutzivendi
1164
Constantia
Cyprus
ABBASID CALIPHATE
Tyre
Jerusalem
1048, 1170
St. Saba
Bethlehem
c.1167
Alexandria
Nile
Sinai
Mount Sinai
0 500 km
0 300 miles
Orthodox Christendom (Greek rite)
Orthodox Christendom (Slavonic rite)
Orthodox Christendom (Georgian rite)
Latin Christendom
Patriarchal sees
Metropolitan sees and archbishoprics*
Bishoprics*
Latin archdioceses and dioceses in which Glagolitic rite was used
Orthodox monasteries (Greek rite)
Orthodox monasteries (Slavonic rite)
Orthodox monasteries (Georgian rite)
Greek monasteries of the Latin obedience
Strongholds of the Teutonic Knights
Centres of Byzantine artistic activity with dates of prominence
Boundary of Byzantine Empire at its greatest extent c.1045
Boundary of the Norman Kingdom of Sicily
Creation of new provinces in the Orthodox Church
Creation of new provinces in the Latin Church
Principalities of Kievan Russia on the eve of the Mongol invasions
Main Viking routes
*Where appropriate, approximate dates of foundation are given

Heirs to the ancient world 2

LAND AND POWER

The differences between the eastern and western parts of the Roman Empire, still clearly visible in the modern world (compare Maps 14 and 84), were greatly accentuated when the Roman state itself, having disappeared from the west, emerged from its difficulties in the east with even more comprehensive pretensions than it had had before.

The Byzantine Empire came very close to destruction at the beginning of the seventh century. Persian armies reached the Nile and the Bosphorus for the first time since the Achaemenids (*Map 15*). The Slavs overran the Balkan peninsula and laid siege to Constantinople. When Heraklius became emperor in 610, he considered abandoning the city and setting up his capital at Carthage. Yet by 629 his armies had recaptured Jerusalem, and their approach to Ctesiphon had provoked a coup d'état there. The conquests of Heraklius were immediately nullified by those of Islam, which threw Byzantium desperately on the defensive again. In preparing for them, however, he renewed the foundations of a Byzantine state which re-established itself as the dominant power in the Balkans, the bulwark of Christendom against Islam and the peoples of Asia (*see Map 18*), and the evangelist of the Slavonic peoples (*Maps 20 and 21*).

Heraklius broke the sequence which led from military expansion to swollen bureaucracy and heavy taxation, the ruin of the peasantry and reliance on mercenary armies, and which had brought down the great empires of antiquity. Ordinary soldiers were given land in frontier regions in return for military service; otherwise they were exempt from taxation. Their sons inherited the obligation. The provinces were reorganized into *themes (see Map 18)* under the command of generals to whom the civilian administration was subordinated. Thus a cheap and effective defence force was created, needing neither complex administration nor long lines of supply, and the peasant class, the source of future recruitment, was strengthened. And these soldiers were not only less expensive than mercenaries but could be better trained, enabling the empire to recover military superiority over its barbarian neighbours. In the long run the

22 The empire of Charlemagne
The exploitation of land between the Seine and the Rhine brought power to the Carolingian family, enabling it to unite much of western Europe and create a common institutional and cultural heritage. But there was no apparatus of the state: the personal movements of the kings provide the best indication of their real power and their priorities.

MAP 22 THE EMPIRE OF CHARLEMAGNE

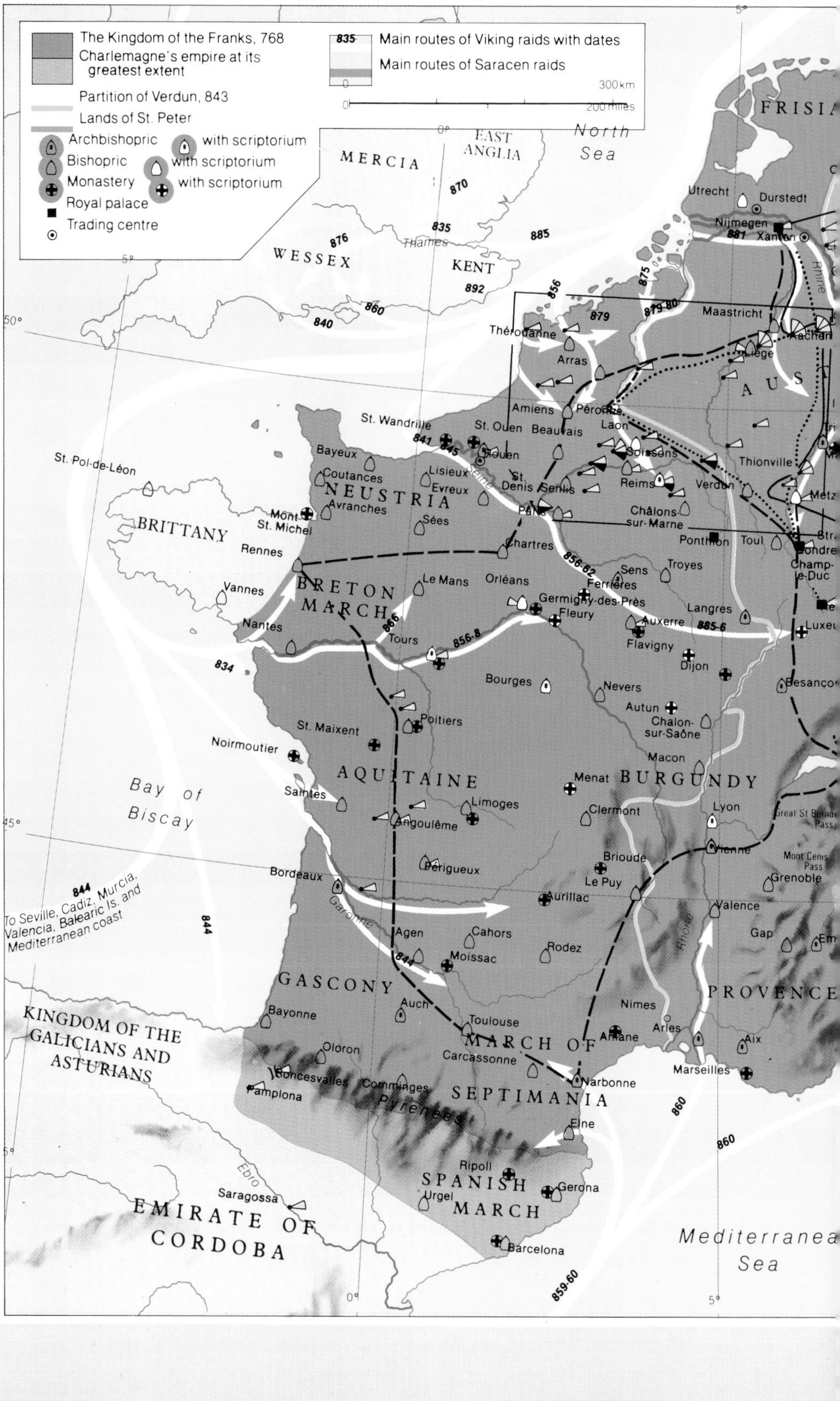

creation of provincial strongholds for military dynasties would inevitably cause trouble, but, until that happened, after the death of Basil II in 1025, the system of Heraklius sustained the most successful and creative period of Byzantium's history.

The Byzantine theme system has been compared with that which enabled the Sui (589-617) and T'ang (618-906) dynasties to reunify China and carry out governmental reform and territorial expansion. In 590 Emperor Wu of the Sui dynasty decreed that old soldiers were to be given land; it was distributed both to veterans and to those who remained as guards in frontier regions. As in Byzantium this created a trained peasant militia and strengthened the class from which soldiers were recruited, permitting significant advances in training and technique. At the same time a network of canals was built, using forced labour on a huge scale. Its masterpiece, the Grand Canal – forty paces wide – joined the north of China to the Yangtze basin, the most productive agricultural region (*Map 10*). This facilitated the supply of the armies, and permitted taxes in grain to be collected and redistributed more efficiently, an important insurance against famine and rebellion. The principle of recruitment to the imperial bureaucracy by examination was revived, and gradually became the sole means of entry. In these respects the reunified China repeated, more systematically and on a larger scale, the policies of the early emperors.

In the seventh and eighth centuries the T'ang emperors presided over one of the greatest periods of Chinese civilization. It was exceptionally open to contact with the west, welcoming missionaries of the Nestorians and the Manichees (*Map 20*), and giving refuge to the last Sassanid emperor, who died an exile in Chang-an. But the immense extension of the empire which stimulated these contacts required the creation of professional armies which, operating on distant frontiers, became effectively independent powers and the source of the revolts in which the dynasty failed.

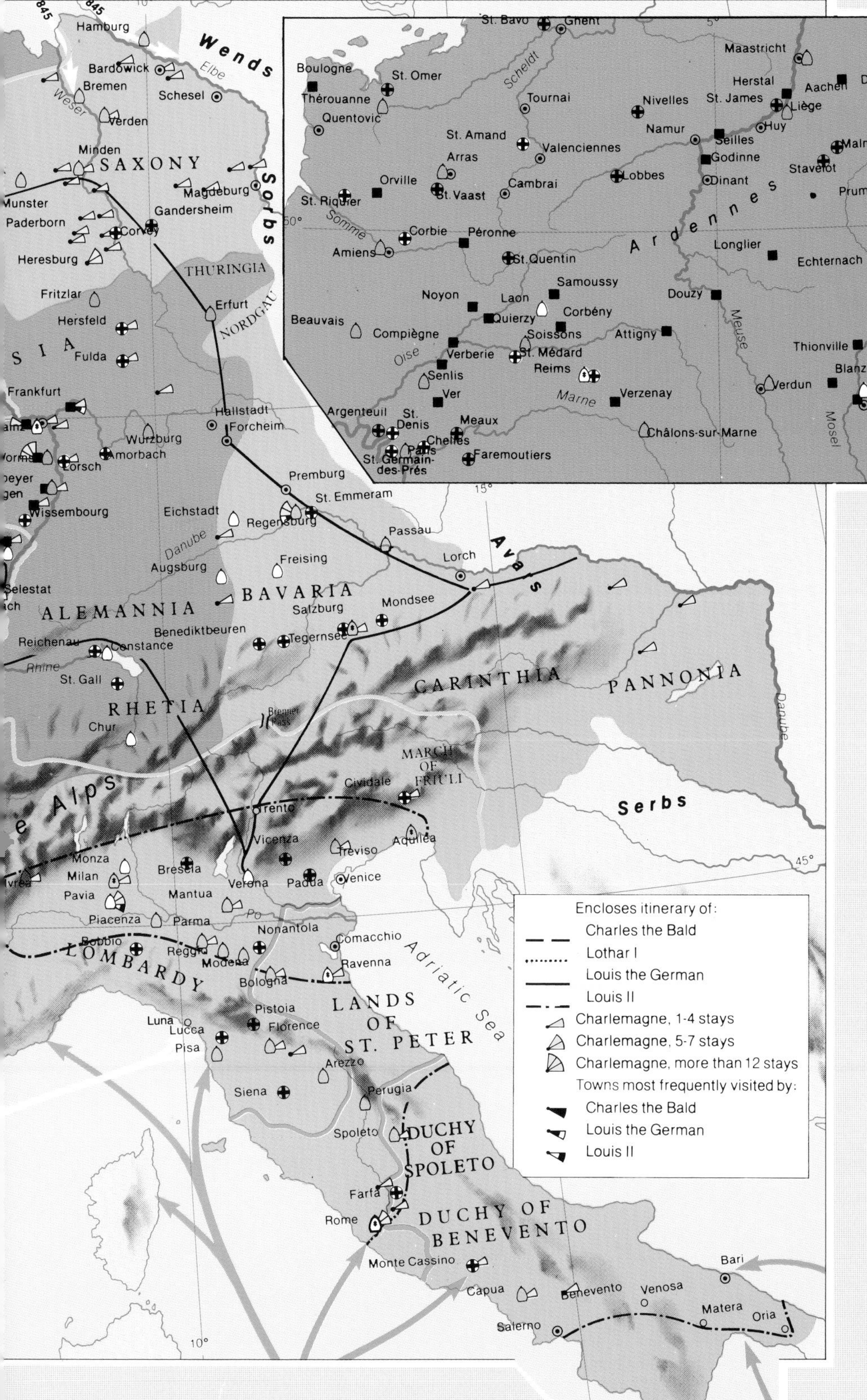

Byzantine influence was extended in a different way. The churches of Rome and Constantinople, already growing apart in doctrinal emphases, were further separated by the Lombard invasion of Italy in 568 (*Map 17*). Islam engulfed the patriarchal sees of Jerusalem, Antioch and Alexandria. Constantinople remained as the unchallenged arbiter of eastern Christendom. As its missionaries spread their faith in Asia Minor and among the Slavs (*see Map 20*) they disseminated the influence of the Byzantine state of which their church was, in effect, an arm, for it was under direct imperial control. Monks, scholars and artists carried Byzantine civilization in the wake of the missionaries, to form the culture and shape the destinies of the Slavonic peoples (*see Map 21*).

The Byzantine and Chinese empires were revived by vigorous assertion of the power of the state. The Carolingian empire was the product of its decay. As the Roman world declined its trade diminished, its cities shrank, its roads fell out of use and its institutions ceased to operate. Power resided exclusively in the possession of land. This meant that sooner or later power in Europe would move to the north, whose deep and rich soils were potentially far more fertile than those of the Mediterranean regions. The revolution began in the eighth century. With the assistance of the 'heavy' plough, whose mould-board turned the soil over instead of simply scratching its surface, land in the middle Rhine region, where it seems to have been introduced, began to be cleared and population to grow. The Carolingian family which controlled Austrasia seized the opportunity to endow an army of mounted warriors. Charles Martel conquered northern Gaul, vindicating his claim to supremacy by defeating an Arab army at Poitiers in 732. His son Pepin III overthrew the last Merovingian in 751, and got the Pope to legitimize his coup in return for support against the Lombards. Pepin's son Charlemagne (*r.*768-814) brought the emerging society of western Europe under a single rule for the first time (*Map 22*), and entered legend when Pope Leo III crowned him emperor at St Peter's in Rome on 25th December 800.

The coronation of Charlemagne was an echo of the past. In reality he was already spending most of his winters at his 'new Rome', Aachen, in the region which had already become, as it remains, the cockpit of Europe (*Map 22 inset; compare Map 57 and Map 75 inset*). The shift of wealth and power

was clearly displayed by the appearance of new centres of population (*portus*) where merchants stopped along the Rhine and its tributaries, while the Roman cities of the Mediterranean languished, and by the establishment of most of the *scriptoria* (writing offices) on what in the sixth century had been the barbarian side of the northern limit of surviving indications of literacy (*compare Maps 17 and 22*). By the middle of the ninth century the growing importance of the strongholds on the eastern frontier foreshadowed the rise of the Saxon empire when Otto I in his turn inaugurated a dynasty, secured a papal coronation at Rome in 962, and, succeeding where the Carolingians had failed, founded an enduring empire (*Map 24*).

The Carolingians conceived the responsibilities of kingship more broadly than their predecessors had. Charlemagne attempted, persistently and often successfully, to provide protection through his courts for *miserabiles personae* – the weak – against the tyrannies of the powerful, and, in a measure which led directly to the appearance of universities in the twelfth century, he commanded every bishop to provide elementary education in his diocese for those who could benefit from it. His enthusiasm for learning and patronage of scholars stimulated a renaissance in art and literature. So many of the earliest surviving manuscripts of classical works are written in the script invented by Carolingian scribes that Italian Renaissance scholars mistakenly dubbed it 'Roman', as we still do.

The Carolingian Empire was ruined by the force which raised it. Charlemagne's government barely extended beyond his personal presence, except so far as his will was understood and respected by the counts and bishops who governed the empire in his name. As a result, on *Maps 22 and 24*, his itinerary and those of his successors display the extent of their power more truthfully than largely notional boundaries. But just as, with literacy confined to a very few, there was no way to govern the empire except through the nobility, in a natural economy there was no way to reward them except by granting them benefices (presents) of land. This equation of landholding with service, the classic definition of feudalism, became effectively, though not yet legally, universal in Charlemagne's reign. It wrote the death warrant of his empire. Land was power; once transferred it might not easily be recovered. For a time the system had worked well. Charles Martel and Pepin III entrusted the government of their growing kingdom to fellow-members of the Austrasian nobility from which they sprang. Charlemagne tried to maintain the coherence of this ruling group by bringing up their sons at his court. But by the end of his reign corruption and rebellion already made it plain that control was gone. The feudatories took advantage of the rivalries of his successors to tear the empire apart, and the Vikings – though not strong enough to destroy well-governed kingdoms, as the Muslims in Spain and Alfred in Wessex (*d.*899) showed – took advantage of the disorder to plunder the towns and monasteries, spreading terror wherever they appeared.

The Merovingian kings had regarded public rights and duties as private property which might be given to favoured subjects, and especially to the Church. A grant of 'immunity' from taxation to a

MAP 23 THE WORLD OF THE VIKINGS

landlord entitled him to raise the taxes from the land involved for his own benefit, and by extension to demand the services which had formerly gone to the state, to do justice and keep for himself its considerable profits. As the Carolingian Empire disintegrated, the counts, most of whom already had immunities of this kind, kept for themselves the public rights which their office had conferred on them. Collectively referred to as the *ban* – the right to compel – these rights were exercised over all free men, and were therefore much more extensive, and potentially more lucrative, than those of landlordship. But by about 1001 the counts had suffered at the hands of their own retainers the usurpation which they had inflicted on the kings. Effective power was exercised from the castles which had appeared everywhere, over such an area as one man and his retinue could control by direct force. And over that area the castellan, unchecked by any superior power, claimed the *ban* for himself, and with it whatever 'customary' rights and payments he chose to demand. The powers that had once been the state's were now indistinguishable from those conferred by the ownership of private property.

This ruthless consolidation of seigneurial power was one consequence of the impoverishment suffered by the nobility in the tenth century. Another was the rush to bring new land into cultivation during the eleventh, increasing the revenues of its owners as well as supporting a rapid growth of population. It was caused not only by the extravagant lifestyle, but especially by the custom of dividing land between all the children of each generation. To preserve the integrity of the inheritance, male primogeniture was now introduced in northern France. This change produced the most characteristic figure of European medieval society, the younger son who, as the mounted knight bound to his aristocratic relations by a common code of chivalry, was condemned to wander far and wide until by his wits and his sword he could win a rich wife, or her price in combat. Political power would lie with whoever could assert control over his feudatories and attract these adventurers to his banner. The Duchy of Normandy, probably founded by some such process (although the Normans told a splendid tale that they were descended from Viking pirates who had been confirmed in the duchy by a Carolingian king), showed the way. Its younger sons and dispossessed wandered over Europe to play prominent parts in the reconquest of Spain, the foundation of the Kingdom of Sicily and the crusades (*Maps 21, 26 and 32*). Meanwhile its Duke William I (*r.*1033-87) subdued his inheritance and won himself a kingdom in England, which his successors plundered with ruthless brilliance to create an empire which dominated western Europe in the twelfth century (*see Map 25*). It was broken only by even greater exponents of feudal power, their rivals of the French royal house of Capet.

Opposite July from Les Tres Riches Heures Duc de Berry

23 The world of the Vikings
Settlement was a major objective of Viking activity, and by the tenth and eleventh centuries created a distinctive northern community, based on maritime communications, whose legacy is still apparent. The Vikings were quickly converted to Christianity in England, but elsewhere their pagan burial places provide abundant evidence of their presence.

24 Germans and Slavs 900-1200
The expansion of Christianity in Germany and central Europe encouraged the extension of agriculture and assisted the formation of territorial entities, both German and Slav, linked with varying degrees of intimacy in a common allegiance to the Empire of Otto I and his successors. This development brought the region increasingly into the mainstream of European affairs.

25 Normans, Angevins and Capetians
The Norman kingdom and then the Angevin empire dominated western Europe in the twelfth century, to be ousted by Capetian France in the thirteenth. The power of both monarchies rested on their control of castles, towns and the church, and on the exploitation and extension of their rights of justice over subjects.

Further reading: H. Pirenne, *Mahomet and Charlemagne* (Allen and Unwin 1937; Barnes and Noble); Richard Hodges and David Whitehouse, *Mohammed, Charlemagne and the Origins of Europe*, (Duckworth 1983; Cornell U. P.); Georges Duby, *The Early Growth of the European Economy* (Weidenfeld & Nicolson 1974; Cornell U. P.); Marc Bloch, *Feudal Society* (Routledge 1961; University of Chicago Press); Cyril Mango, *Byzantium* (Weidenfeld and Nicolson 1980); Ray Huang, *China: A Macro History*, (East Gate 1988); David Ludden, *Peasant History in South India* (Princeton U.P. 1985; OUP India 1989).

MAP 24 GERMANS AND SLAVS 900-1200

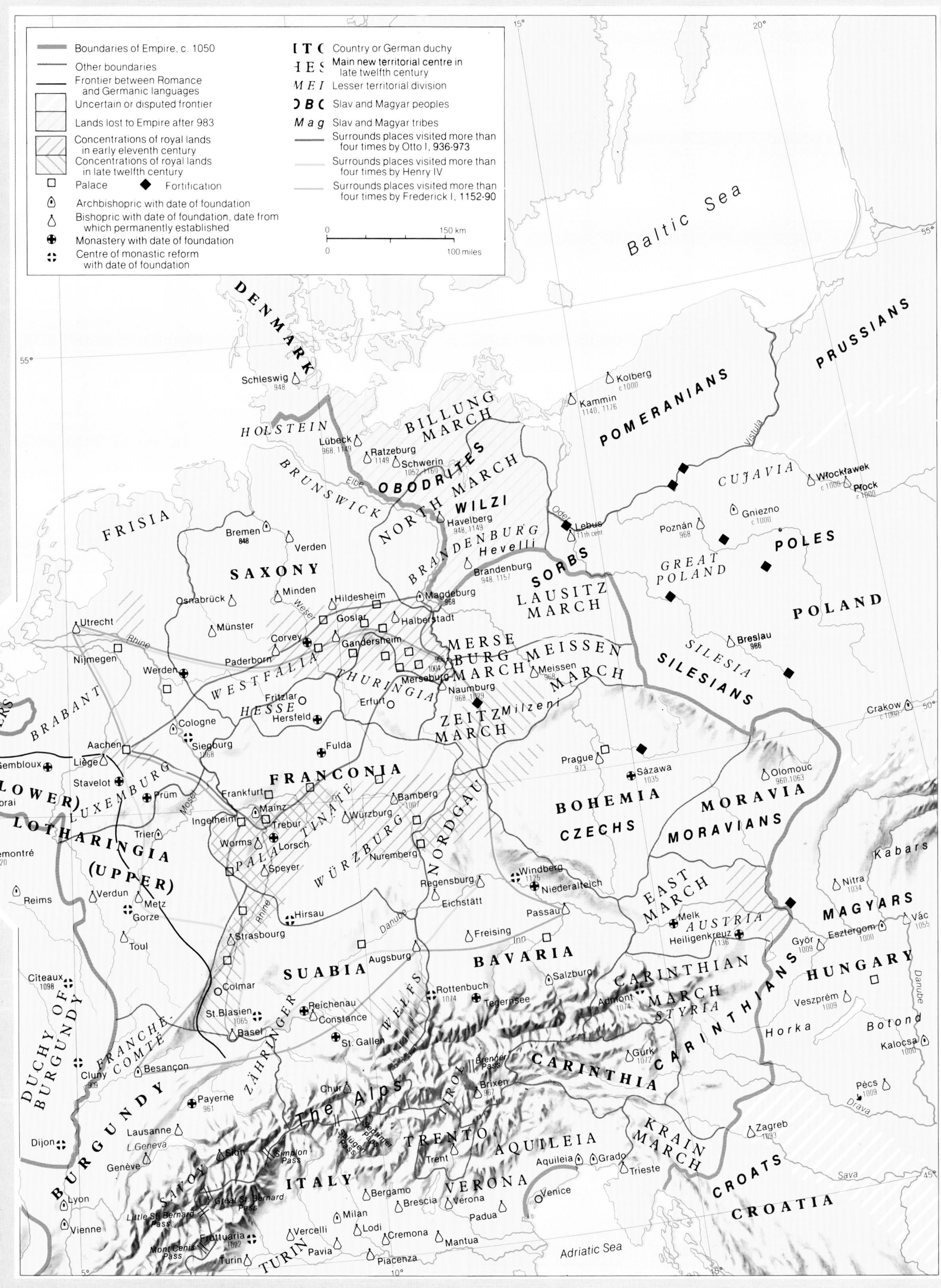

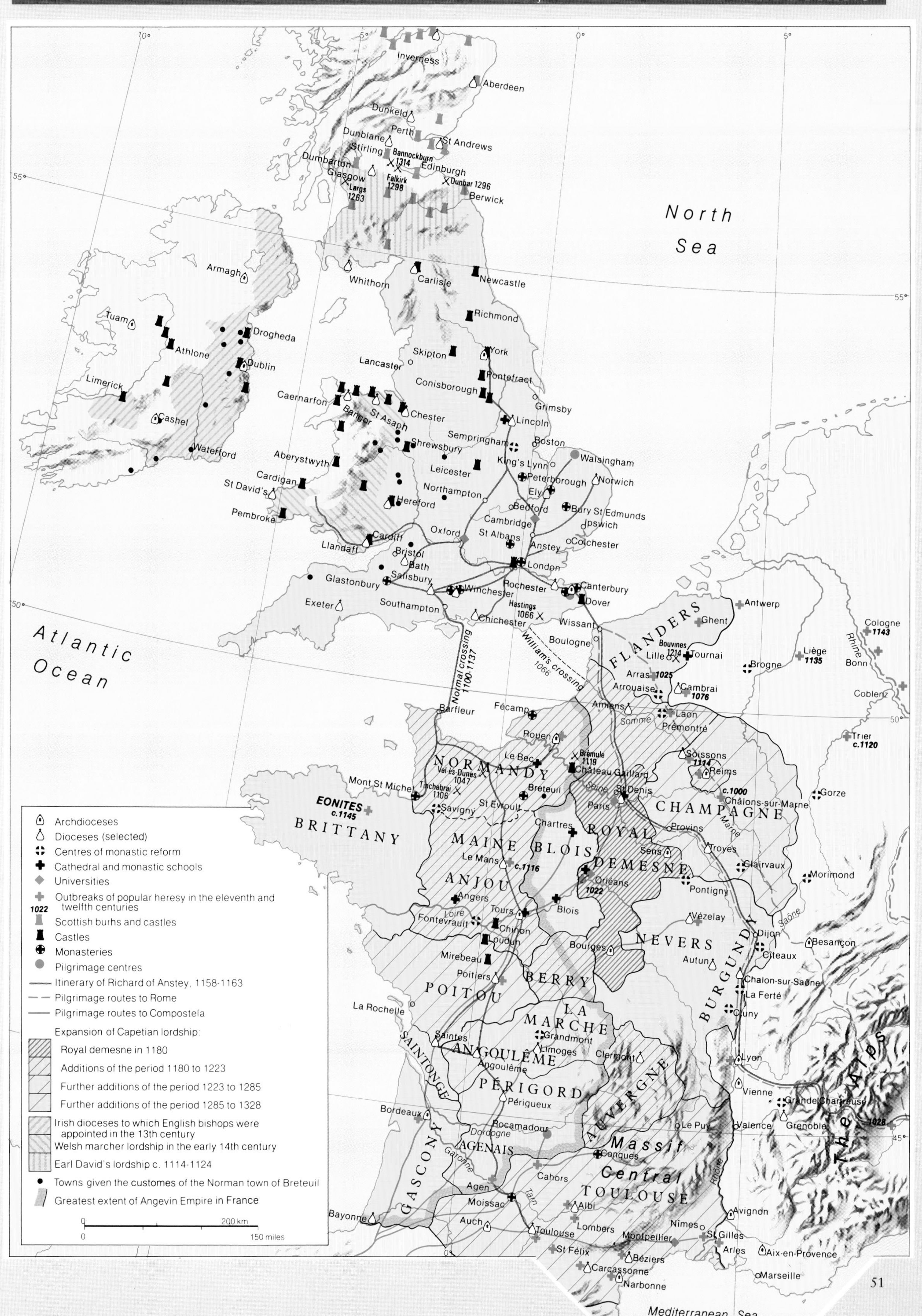
Archdioceses
Dioceses (selected)
Centres of monastic reform
Cathedral and monastic schools
Universities
Outbreaks of popular heresy in the eleventh and twelfth centuries
1022
Scottish burhs and castles
Castles
Monasteries
Pilgrimage centres
Itinerary of Richard of Anstey, 1158-1163
Pilgrimage routes to Rome
Pilgrimage routes to Compostela
Expansion of Capetian lordship:
Royal demesne in 1180
Additions of the period 1180 to 1223
Further additions of the period 1223 to 1285
Further additions of the period 1285 to 1328
Irish dioceses to which English bishops were appointed in the 13th century
Welsh marcher lordship in the early 14th century
Earl David's lordship c. 1114-1124
Towns given the customes of the Norman town of Breteuil
Greatest extent of Angevin Empire in France
0
200 km
0
150 miles
North Sea
Atlantic Ocean
Mediterranean Sea
Inverness
Aberdeen
Dunkeld
Perth
Dunblane
St Andrews
Stirling
Bannockburn 1314
Dumbarton
Edinburgh
Glasgow
Falkirk 1298
Dunbar 1296
Largs 1263
Berwick
Armagh
Whithorn
Carlisle
Newcastle
Tuam
Richmond
Drogheda
Athlone
Dublin
York
Skipton
Lancaster
Pontefract
Limerick
Conisborough
Caernarfon
Grimsby
Bangor
St Asaph
Chester
Cashel
Lincoln
Sempringham
Boston
Waterford
Shrewsbury
Aberystwyth
Walsingham
King's Lynn
Leicester
Peterborough
Norwich
Cardigan
Ely
St David's
Northampton
Hereford
Bedford
Bury St Edmunds
Pembroke
Cambridge
Ipswich
Oxford
St Albans
Anstey
Colchester
Llandaff
Cardiff
Bristol
Bath
London
Glastonbury
Salisbury
Rochester
Canterbury
Winchester
Exeter
Southampton
Dover
Hastings 1066
Chichester
Wissant
Antwerp
Boulogne
Ghent
FLANDERS
Bouvines 1214
Lille
Tournai
William's crossing 1066
Normal crossing 1100-1137
Arras 1025
Brogne
Liège 1135
Cologne 1143
Rhine
Bonn
Arrouaise
Cambrai 1076
Coblenz
Barfleur
Fécamp
Amiens
Somme
Laon
Prémontré
Trier c.1120
Rouen
Soissons 1114
Bremule 1119
Le Bec
Château Gaillard
Reims
NORMANDY
Val-ès-Dunes 1047
Tinchebrai 1106
Mont St Michel
St Denis
c.1000
Châlons-sur-Marne
Gorze
Breteuil
Seine
Paris
EONITES c.1145
Savigny
St Evroult
CHAMPAGNE
BRITTANY
Chartres
Provins
Marne
ROYAL
MAINE
BLOIS
Sens
Troyes
DEMESNE
Le Mans
c.1116
Clairvaux
Morimond
Orléans
1022
Pontigny
ANJOU
Angers
Blois
Loire
Tours
Fontevrault
Vézelay
Chinon
Loudun
Dijon
Saône
NEVERS
Bourges
Besançon
Cîteaux
Mirebeau
Autun
Poitiers
BERRY
Chalon-sur-Saône
POITOU
La Ferté
BURGUNDY
La Rochelle
LA MARCHE
Cluny
Grandmont
Saintes
Limoges
ANGOULÊME
Clermont
Angoulême
Lyon
SAINTONGE
AUVERGNE
The Alps
PÉRIGORD
Vienne
Grande Chartreuse
Périgueux
Bordeaux
Le Puy
Valence
Grenoble
1028
Rocamadour
Dordogne
Massif Central
AGENAIS
Conques
GASCONY
Garonne
Cahors
Agen
TOULOUSE
Moissac
Tarn
Rhône
Albi
Avignon
Bayonne
Auch
Lombers
Nîmes
Toulouse
Montpellier
St Gilles
St Félix
Arles
Aix-en-Provence
Béziers
Carcassonne
Narbonne
Marseille
10°
5°
0°
5°
55°
50°
45°

Heirs to the ancient world 3

TRADE AND AGGRESSION

26 The world of the Crusaders
Between the invasions of the Seljuk Turks in the eleventh century and the Mongols in the thirteenth the Byzantine and Arab worlds were subjected to successive attacks from both western Europe and central Asia. The Latins lost Constantinople in 1261 and Acre in 1291, but the empire of the Turkish Mamluks, like that of Byzantium, survived until the Ottoman conquests.

The politics and culture of the medieval civilizations deliberately imitated or unconsciously perpetuated those of the ancient world.

It was not in the first instance their achievements in those fields, impressive as they were, that enabled these civilizations to break out of the rhythms which had governed the rise and fall of civilizations for millennia. The crucial achievement both of China and western Europe was to transform economic life sufficiently to produce a sustained population growth which, although it was liable to prolonged recession such as that associated with the epidemics of the later middle ages (*see Map 35*) was, in the long run, irreversible. Recent estimates put the population of Europe at about 36 million in AD 1000, 79 million in 1300, and 81 million in 1500; of China at 66 million, 86 million and 110 million at the same dates; and of the Indian sub-continent at 79 million, 91 million, and 105 million. By contrast such evidence as there is – usually very little – suggests that the population of most other parts of the world remained stagnant. That of the world of Islam reached a peak during its golden age, between about 800 and 1000, and was generally somewhat in decline thereafter.

The agricultural advances of the early middle ages which sustained this growth were very similar in China and in Europe. The heavy plough was widely used in both regions by about 1000, and was increasingly assisted by other technical advances. In Europe there were iron tools, efficient harnessing for animals and wind- and water-mills, and similarly in China dams, dykes, waterwheels and other aids to irrigation. As Europe had an eastward frontier region, in addition to its great expanses of forest and marsh, so China had the ricegrowing region of the south to invite steady expansion and continuous growth over a very long period (*Maps 10, 23 and 34*). Finally, in large parts of both regions the partial freeing of slaves since ancient times combined with the widespread enserfment of free men by coercion had produced a manorial organization which could permit the direction of labour and the investment of capital in such land and tools as large projects might require. To sustain their growth, however, agricultural

MAP 26 THE WORLD OF THE CRUSADERS

Land lost by Crusaders in or before 1187
Land held or gained by Crusaders after 1187
Land held by Byzantines after 1204
Land acquired by Venice in 1204
Muslim land
Ayubbid Empire, 1170-1250
Muslim powers in 1096
Muslim powers in 1291
Crusader attacks on Moslem territory
Reconquests by Byzantines of Nicaea
Mongol attacks
Haj route from Damascus
Syrian campaigns of John II and Manuel I Comnenus
Crusader castles
Assassin castles
Latin metropolitan sees
Centres of Italian trade in Crusader States
Ports held by Venice after 1204
Battles
Boundary of Byzantine Empire in 1180

0 300 km
0 200 miles

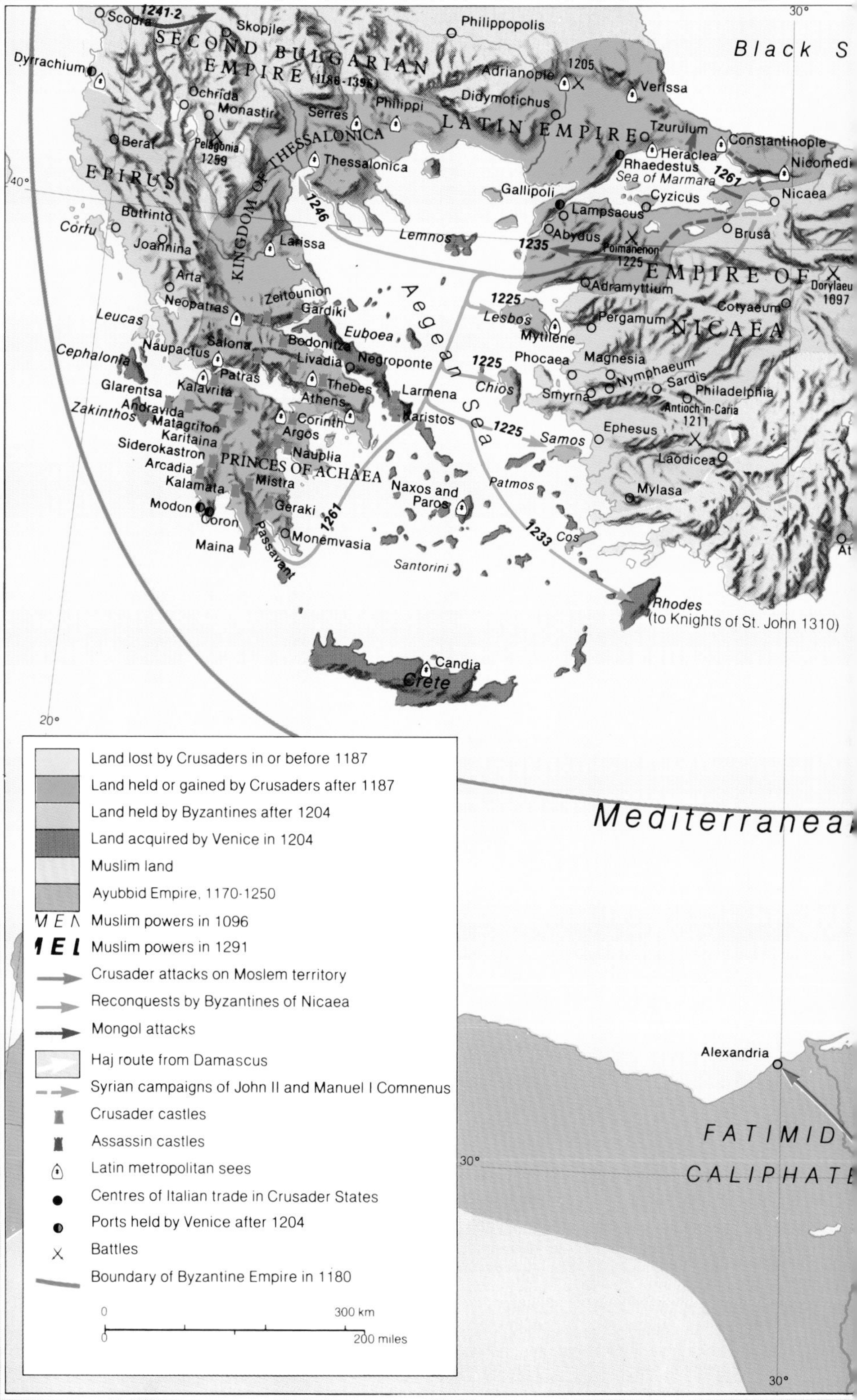

communities needed markets to reward them for producing beyond their immediate needs, and cities to drain off their surplus population and encourage its rapid replacement. The second part of the medieval economic revolution was the creation of world-wide markets, exchanging goods and services more regularly and in greater volume, across greater distances, and in particular providing a growing demand for manufactured goods.

The conquests of Islam united the economies of the Persian and much of the Roman worlds, between which there had previously been little exchange. They also implanted a way of life which demanded the creation of a massive international trade. The conquerors did not expect to demean their hands with labour, and were inhibited in the exploitation of their new subjects by the readiness of most of them to convert to Islam. They expected to live in cities – Baghdad was the largest city in the world, two million in population, within half a century of its foundation in 762 – and to enjoy the enormous variety of goods which could be collected from across their vast territories. Yet those territories, the home of the most ancient civilizations, were near exhaustion, their soils poor, their forests stripped bare, their population very low. So the world of Islam became a trading empire on a scale never seen before (*see Map 27*). At first the imports were paid for largely with the silver of the fabled mines of the Hindu Kush, inherited from the Sassanids, but after the Abbasid revolution the migration of Arabs and other dissidents from Persia began to open up the Islamic west. North Africa was brought more firmly under control, and ports were established on the Nile and new towns on the desert caravan routes to bring gold and ivory, as well as slaves, from the Africa interior, both east and west.

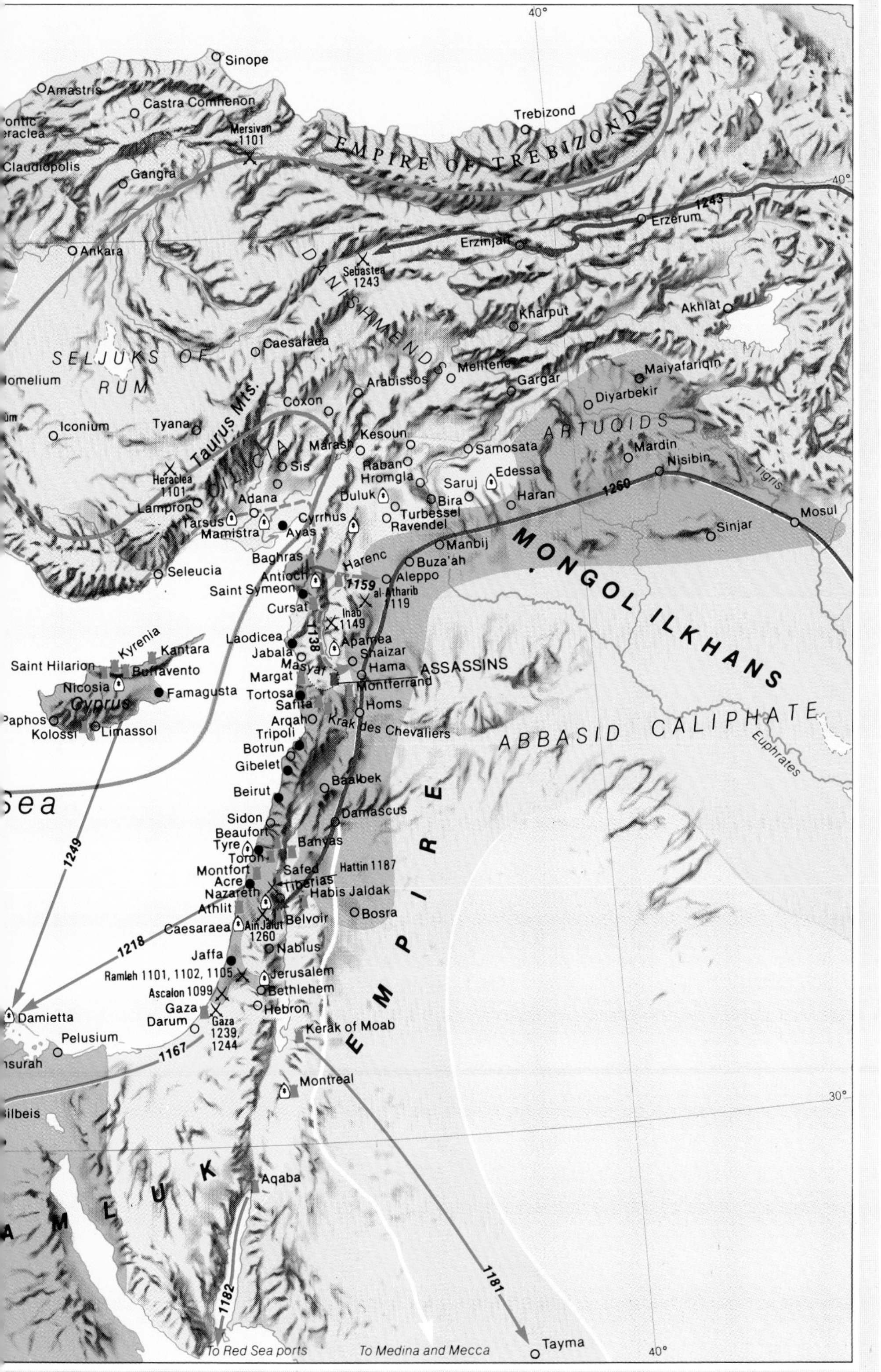

The needs of Islam had momentous consequences for Europe. In Carolingian times Metz and Verdun, junction between the German interior and the routes to Spain and Africa (*via* Marseilles), were important slave markets and Muslim wealth was a major, if distant, stimulus of the traffic along the Rhine and its tributaries (*Map 22*). Later the riches of the forests beyond the Elbe and in Bohemia and Carinthia made the more easterly route down the Adriatic the main thoroughfare to the Mediterranean leading to the rise of Venice, its mistress, and the Po valley, its link with western Europe. The revenue gained from those flows of Muslim wealth not only gave Otto the basis of an empire in the north, but drew him and his successors continually both eastwards and southwards (*Maps 24 and 33*).

The great pioneers of trade between the north and the advanced world were the Vikings. By the ninth century they were in touch with Muslim traders along the Volga, whose upper waters were easily accessible from the Baltic (*see Map 21*). For a century Persian silver poured into Scandinavian hoards (*Map 23*): more than sixty thousand Muslim coins have been found there, and as many more in northern Russia, Poland and Pomerania. By the end of the tenth century, when trade with Islam began to fall away, the Vikings – known as Varangians to the Greeks – had also reached the Black Sea by way of the Dnieper, down which the Rus people of Kiev had long brought their furs, honey and wax to Byzantium.

Along the rivers of Russia the Vikings forged permanent links between northern and eastern Europe (*compare Map 28*). Their voyages into the Atlantic, leading to the colonization of Iceland and settlement in Greenland and somewhere on the North American coast at Vinland, constituted the first extension of the known world since ancient times and, after their own conversion, a major expansion of Christendom (*see Map 20*).

Within the huge area which their ships and nautical talents opened to them the Vikings settled in many places, though seldom (most scholars now think) in large numbers. Colonies appeared in the ninth century at the mouths of many of the rivers along which they raided, including the Elbe and the Weser, the Rhine, the Seine and the Loire, but the most important were on the islands of the North Sea and around the British Isles, the nucleus of a great seaborne empire in the time of Cnut (*r.*1014-35), and still a region of distinctive cultural and political traditions (*Map 23*).

The history of the Vikings is a reminder that piracy is never far from trade, or trade from colonization. The raids on the accumulated treasures of the monasteries of Francia and England – almost

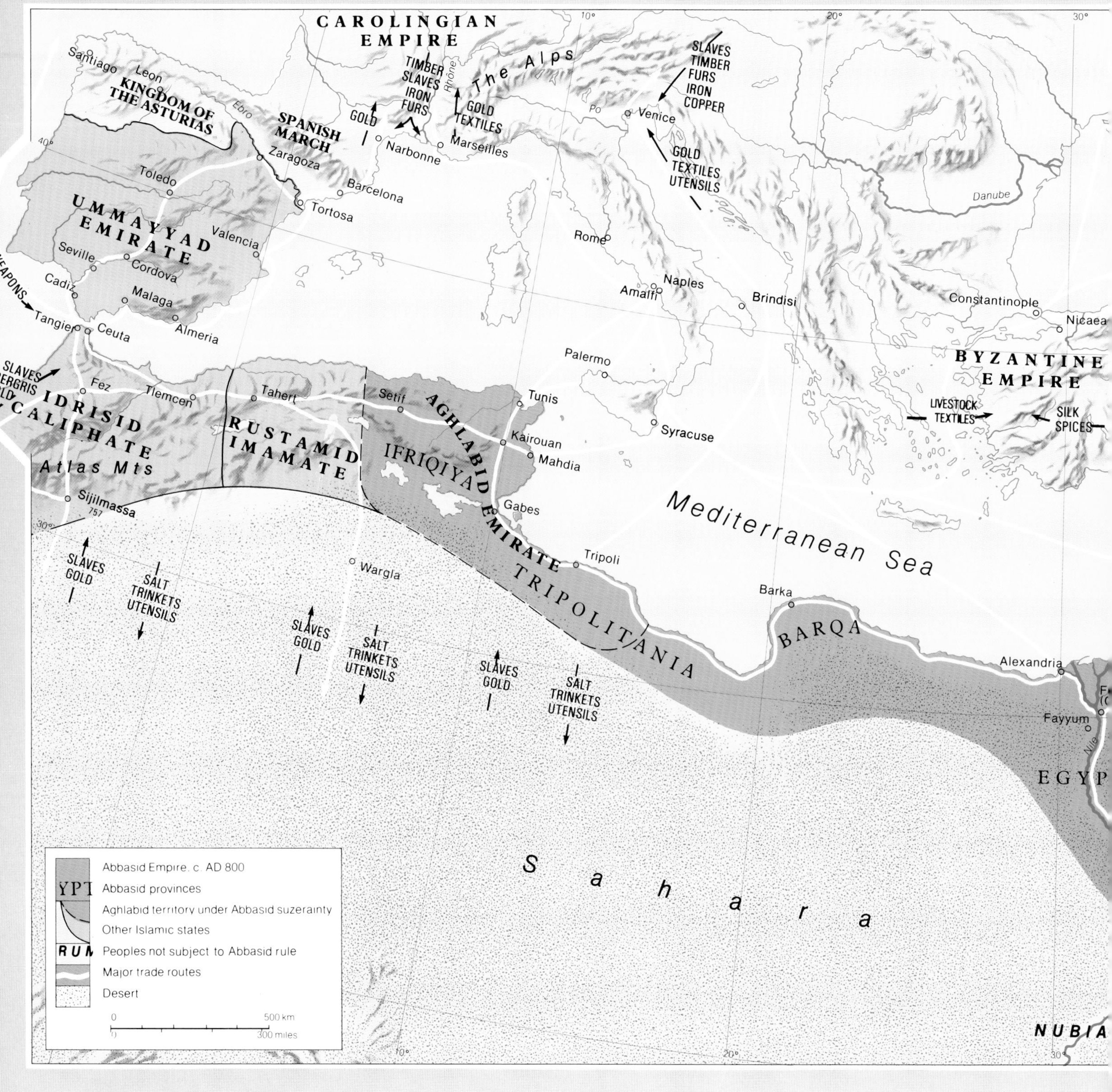

27 The golden age of Islam
The conquests of Islam joined the markets and trade routes of the known world. The wealth of its aristocracy stimulated a vast and varied trade which supported a brilliant civilization, although political fragmentation had already begun by the ninth century.

the only respect in which their activity differed from that of the warring nobles of Christian Europe – have given them the fearsome reputation of legend and exaggerated the importance of their destructive activity. Their voyages mark the beginning of the maritime unity of Europe, joining the coastal traffic of the Channel and the North Sea to that of the Atlantic and Mediterranean seaboards for the first time. Little of the tribute which they collected from the Franks and English found its way back to the Scandinavian hoards. It was most probably used to buy land for settlement, or to be recirculated as part of the trade which in their hands so clearly foreshadowed the medieval economy at its height (*see Map 28*).

Rather as the Vikings benefited from the disintegration of the Carolingian empire Europe as a whole profitted from the decline of Islam and Byzantium. The political unity of the Caliphate ended after the Abbasid revolution, when the leaders of provincial armies – emirs – became increasingly inclined to declare themselves independent of Baghdad. The process was accelerated by the growing habit of granting them the farm of taxes and revenues of the state in place of payment for their troops, and completed when Baghdad itself was seized by a Persian prince in 945, leaving the Caliph as a spiritual figurehead, bereft of real power. In the eleventh century the precipitous decline of its external trade, a series of rebellions and civil wars among the Muslim peoples, which saw the creation of a Berber empire in Africa and Spain, and the devastation of Libya and Tunisia by Bedouin tribesmen (it was now that the ancient agricultural prosperity of the region was destroyed), and, most important, the advance of the Seljuk Turks from central Asia (*Map 26*), – all laid the Muslim world open to Christian attack.

The dissolution of the Caliphate of Cordoba in

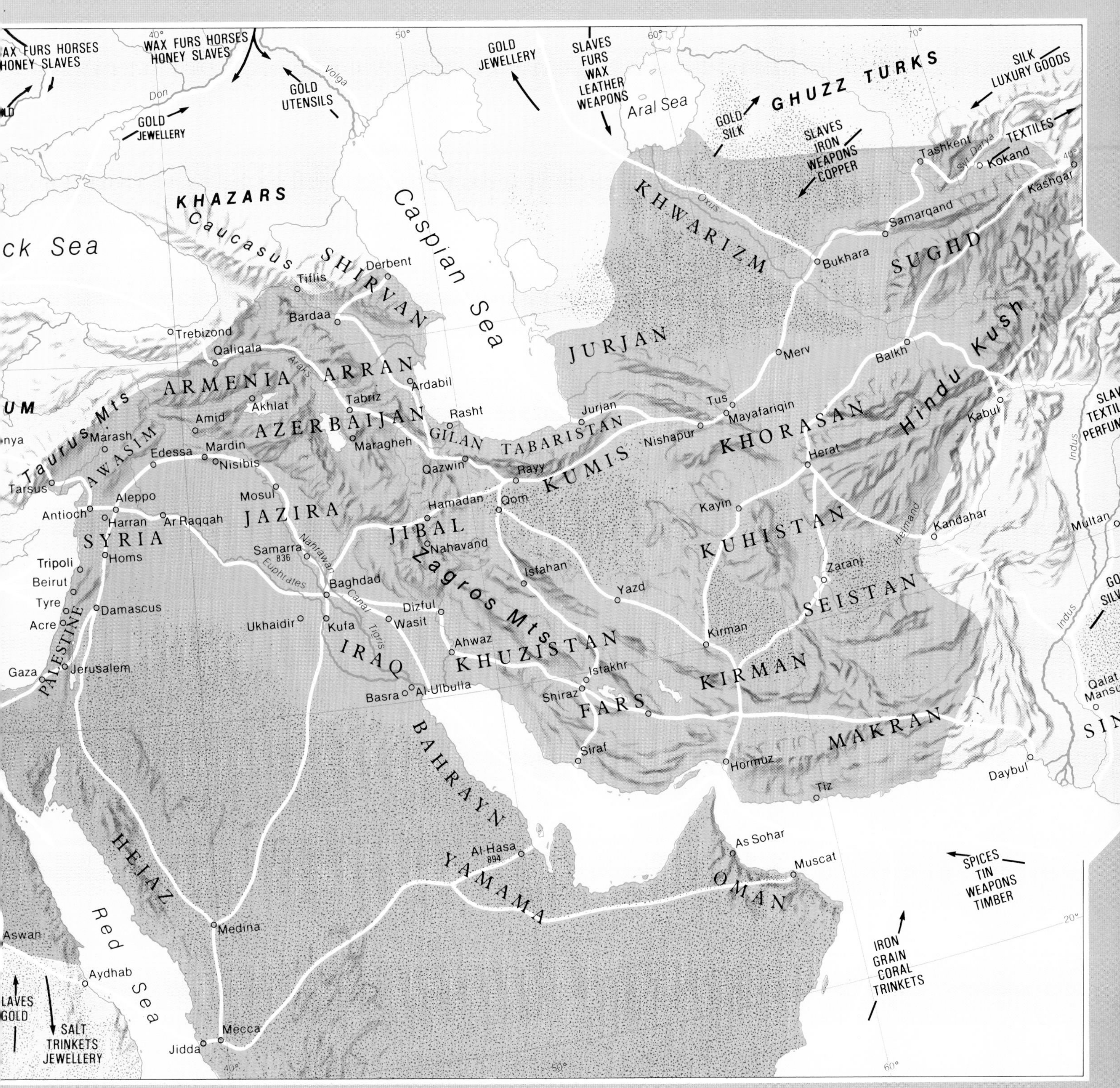

Spain in 1010 provided the Christian kings of León and Castile with an opportunity to enlarge their territories and to launch the reconquista which was to be the theme of Spanish medieval history (*see Map 32*). It rapidly became a European enterprise as the prospect of land and booty attracted knights from far and wide, and the monastic orders came behind them to bring spiritual comforts and Christian services in return for a handsome share of the spoils. Still richer pickings in southern Italy were available to the followers of the Norman adventurers who by 1048 had conquered most of Apulia and Calabria from the Byzantine Empire (*see Map 21*). They forced the Pope to recognize their conquests in 1059, and turned against Islam in 1072 when they captured Palermo, which their descendants would make the capital of the wealthiest and most sophisticated kingdom in the twelfth-century West.

The death of the Byzantine emperor Basil II in 1025 was followed by a period of prolonged conflict between the military dynasties of the provinces and the civilian aristocracy of Constantinople, during which the state was permanently weakened by the farming out of revenues and offices in bids for political support. Basil's annexation of Bulgaria and Armenia (which was implemented after his death, in 1043) removed what had been in effect buffer states against the Asiatic nomads. In 1065 Armenia fell to the Seljuk Turks and in 1071 they defeated the Emperor at Manzikert to take Anatolia, as the Arabs never had. In the same year Bari, his last stronghold in Italy, fell to the Normans.

The assault of Christian Europe on the Middle East and the Balkans (*Map 26*) was conducted, in principle, not by wandering adventurers but by its anointed leaders. The Pope issued the summons to

28 The medieval economy at its height
By the thirteenth century the traders and trade routes of Europe were well enough established to encourage increasing economic specialization, and the growing cities – though still very small by world standards – provided markets for luxuries from far afield as well as for the products of their own hinterlands.

MAP 28 THE MEDIEVAL ECONOMY AT ITS HEIGHT

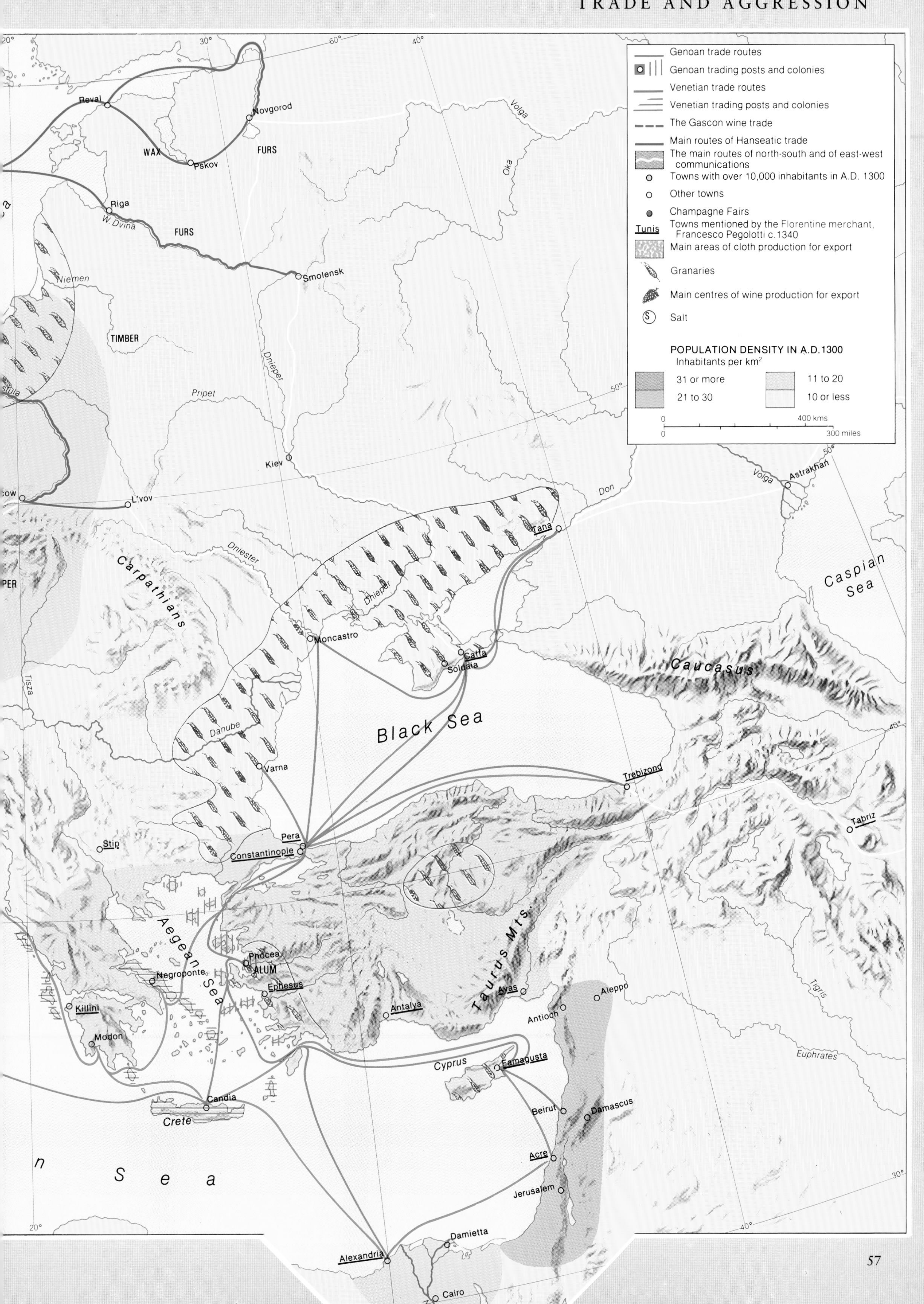
Genoan trade routes
Genoan trading posts and colonies
Venetian trade routes
Venetian trading posts and colonies
The Gascon wine trade
Main routes of Hanseatic trade
The main routes of north-south and of east-west communications
Towns with over 10,000 inhabitants in A.D. 1300
Other towns
Champagne Fairs
Tunis
Towns mentioned by the Florentine merchant, Francesco Pegolotti c.1340
Main areas of cloth production for export
Granaries
Main centres of wine production for export
Salt
POPULATION DENSITY IN A.D.1300
Inhabitants per km²
31 or more
21 to 30
11 to 20
10 or less
400 kms
300 miles
Reval
Novgorod
WAX
Pskov
FURS
Riga
W. Dvina
FURS
Smolensk
Niemen
TIMBER
Dnieper
Pripet
Kiev
L'vov
Volga
Oka
Volga
Astrakhan
Don
Tana
Dniester
Carpathians
Dnieper
Moncastro
Caffa
Soldaia
Caspian Sea
Caucasus
Black Sea
Danube
Varna
Tisza
Trebizond
Tabriz
Pera
Constantinople
Stip
Aegean Sea
Phocea
ALUM
Ephesus
Negroponte
Killini
Modon
Taurus Mts.
Ayas
Antalya
Aleppo
Antioch
Tigris
Euphrates
Cyprus
Famagusta
Candia
Crete
Beirut
Damascus
Acre
Jerusalem
Sea
Damietta
Alexandria
Cairo
Nile

the First Crusade at the Council of Clermont in 1095, and his successors always took the lead in marshalling the resources of the feudal west for future crusades. The Second Crusade (1147-49), preached by the spiritual leader of Christendom in his time, St Bernard of Clairvaux, was led by the Holy Roman Emperor and the King of France; the Third (1189-92) by the Kings of France and England. The ostensible origin of the crusading movement was the request of the Byzantine Emperor Alexius I for western mercenaries to help against the Turks; its ostensible goal the defence of the Holy Places against the infidel. Jerusalem was taken in 1099 and held until 1187, and western feudal kingdoms constructed in the Holy Land. But its most important consequence was the sack of Constantinople by crusaders in 1204 and the dismemberment of the Byzantine Empire.

The crusades are often described as part of the expansion of feudal Europe. But the fleets of the First Crusade were provided by the Genoans and the Pisans, and the Fourth Crusade was directed to Constantinople by its Venetian paymasters, whose interests in the Balkans had expanded rapidly since Alexius I had bought naval assistance from them in return for extensive trading privileges throughout his Empire. Genoa and Pisa had begun their rise to power late in the tenth century, on the profits of piracy upon Muslim vessels in the Mediterranean; Venice by exporting slaves to Egypt. Throughout the period of the crusades the Italian cities were the main paymasters and the chief beneficiaries. The fortunes of the crusading states fluctuated far more according to the extent to which Italian trading interests were threatened than with the attitudes of the feudal monarchs. Unlike the knights and their clerical brothers who devoted much energy (and much sincerity) to convincing themselves of the righteousness of the holy war, the cities felt no need to disguise their interest, and no ideology inhibited their pursuit of profit. 'The Venetians, the Genoese and the Pisans bring into Egypt choice products of the West, especially arms and war materials' wrote Saladin, the greatest of the Muslim leaders. 'This constitutes an advantage for Islam and an injury to Christianity.' In return for those goods, they brought to the West, which now offered a rapidly expanding market for luxuries, the spices, silks and perfumes of the Orient. Networks of trading posts were established and continued to flourish long after the crusading kingdoms had died (*Maps 26 and 28*) – as they did after the Mongol conquests diverted the Far Eastern trade routes towards the Black Sea ports (*see Map 31*), so that there was no longer any need for the Venetians and their compatriots to maintain outposts in the Holy Land.

The clash of values between the merchants and the knights which the crusades revealed so clearly was already transforming European society. Around 1000 society could be described as consisting of 'those who fight, those who pray and those who work (*agricultores*)'. The growth of population and diversification of economic activity brought new classes into being. Cities grew rapidly in what had been a wholly rural world (*see Map 28*). Their inhabitants clashed bitterly with each other as sharp divisions of wealth and power appeared between the weavers or seamen, often wretchedly poor, and the patricians, rapidly forming their own dynasties, who employed them; the cities themselves clashed with the secular and ecclesiastical aristocracy as they sought freedom to conduct their own affairs, protect their own interests, and eventually dominate the countryside around them (*see Map 33*). New tensions produced new institutions, new mentalities and a new culture, often sharply opposed to the chivalrous code of the aristocracy and the hierarchical conservatism of the church. The contrast was observed with distaste, but not with contempt, by Otto of Freising when he described the expedition of his nephew the Emperor Frederick Barbarossa to Italy in 1154. 'That they may not lack the means of subduing their neighbours' he wrote of the Milanese, 'they do not disdain to give the girdle of knighthood to young men of inferior status, and even some workers of the vile mechanical arts whom other peoples bar like the plague from respected and honourable pursuits. From this it has resulted that they surpass all other states of the world in wealth and power.'

Above: A street market at Soochow by Chang Tse-tuan, early twelfth century.

29 India under Muslim domination
The Sultanate of Delhi, founded in 1211 by Turks from Afghanistan, was the principal centre of Muslim power in India; but the fortunes of both Muslim and Hindu kingdoms fluctuated with the loyalties of the chiefs and officials commanding the military strongpoints which controlled the trade routes and the countryside. The invasions of Timur destroyed the hegemony of Delhi, and independent sultanates emerged in several regions.

Further reading: Janet Abu Lughod, *Before European Hegemony: The World System, AD 1250-1350* (OUP New York 1989): P. H. Sawyer, *Kings and Vikings* (Methuen 1982); Jacques le Goff, *Medieval Civilization* (Basil Blackwell 1988); J. R. S. Phillips, *The Medieval Expansion of Europe* (Oxford U.P. 1988); K. N. Chaudu-ri, *Asia before Europe* (Cambridge U.P. 1990); Mark Elvin, *Patterns of the Chinese Past* (Methuen 1973; Stanford U.P.); R. Latham (trans.), *The Travels of Marco Polo* (Penguin 1958).

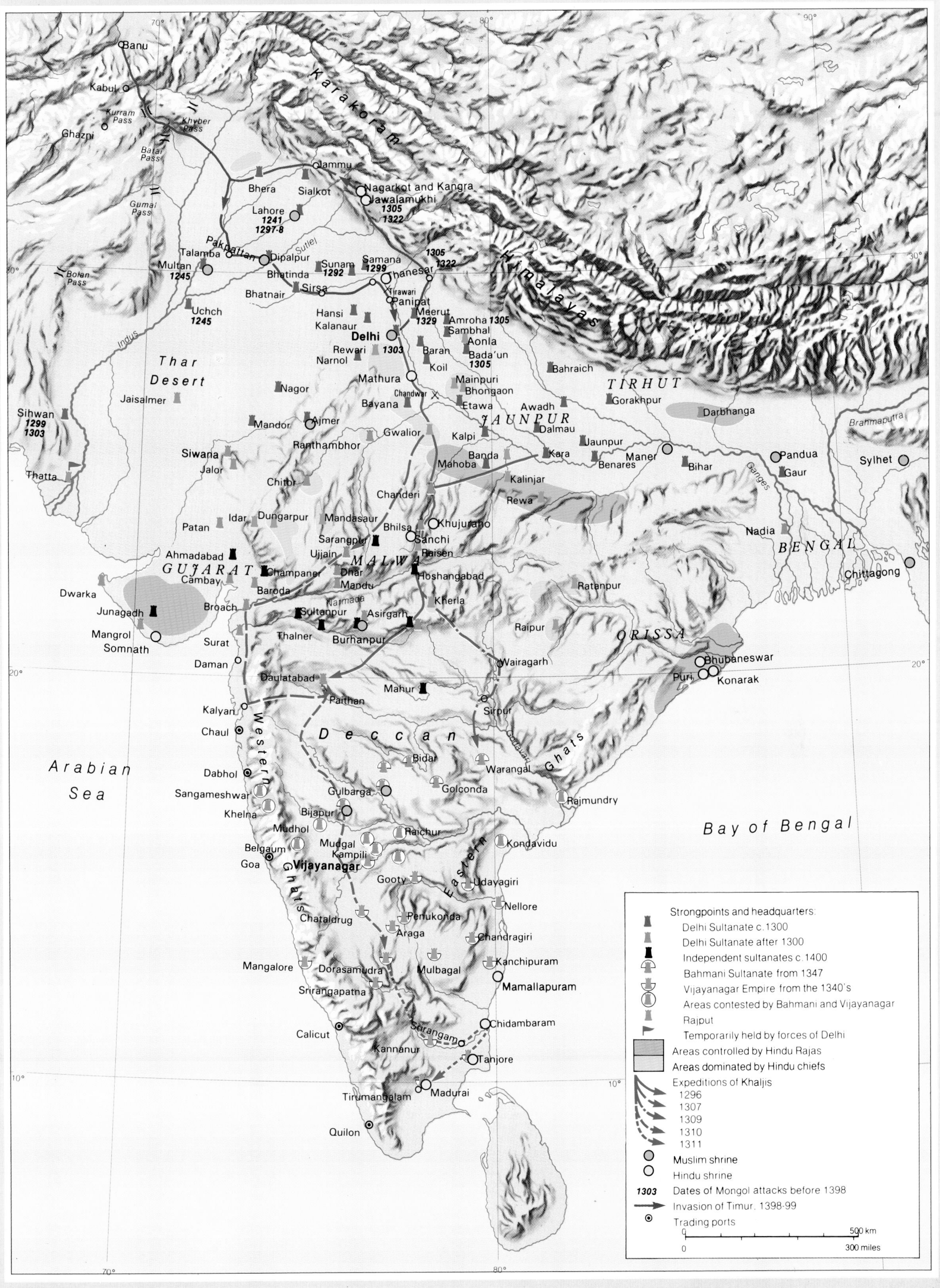
Banu
Kabul
Kurram Pass
Khyber Pass
Ghazni
Batai Pass
Gumal Pass
Bolan Pass
Karakoram
Jammu
Bhera
Sialkot
Nagarkot and Kangra
Jawalamukhi
1305
1322
Lahore
1241
1297-8
Pakpattan
Talamba
Dipalpur
Multan
1245
Sutlej
Sunam
1292
Samana
1299
Thanesar
1305
1322
Himalayas
Bhatinda
Sirsa
Tirawari
Panipat
Bhatnair
Uchch
1245
Indus
Hansi
Kalanaur
Delhi
1303
Meerut
1329
Amroha 1305
Sambhal
Aonla
Rewari
Narnol
Baran
Koil
Bada'un
1305
Thar
Desert
Jaisalmer
Nagor
Mathura
Chandwar
Mainpuri
Bhongaon
Etawa
Bahraich
TIRHUT
Gorakhpur
Sihwan
1299
1303
Mandor
Ajmer
Bayana
Gwalior
JAUNPUR
Awadh
Dalmau
Darbhanga
Brahmaputra
Ranthambhor
Kalpi
Jaunpur
Siwana
Jalor
Banda
Mahoba
Kara
Benares
Maner
Bihar
Pandua
Gaur
Sylhet
Thatta
Chitor
Kalinjar
Ganges
Chanderi
Rewa
Patan
Idar
Dungarpur
Mandasaur
Bhilsa
Khujuraho
Sarangpur
Sanchi
Nadia
BENGAL
Ahmadabad
Ujjain
Raisen
GUJARAT
MALWA
Champaner
Dhar
Hoshangabad
Chittagong
Cambay
Mandu
Baroda
Ratanpur
Dwarka
Narmada
Kherla
Junagadh
Broach
Sultanpur
Asirgarh
Mangrol
Somnath
Surat
Thalner
Burhanpur
Raipur
ORISSA
Daman
Wairagarh
Bhubaneswar
Puri
Konarak
Daulatabad
Mahur
Kalyan
Paithan
Sirpur
Chaul
Western
Deccan
Godavari
Ghats
Arabian Sea
Dabhol
Bidar
Warangal
Sangameshwar
Gulbarga
Golconda
Rajmundry
Khelna
Bijapur
Mudhol
Raichur
Bay of Bengal
Belgaum
Mudgal
Kampili
Kondavidu
Goa
Vijayanagar
Eastern
Ghats
Gooty
Udayagiri
Nellore
Chataldrug
Penukonda
Araga
Chandragiri
Mangalore
Dorasamudra
Mulbagal
Kanchipuram
Mamallapuram
Srirangapatna
Chidambaram
Calicut
Srirangam
Kannanur
Tanjore
Tirumangalam
Madurai
Quilon
70°
80°
90°
30°
20°
10°
Strongpoints and headquarters:
Delhi Sultanate c.1300
Delhi Sultanate after 1300
Independent sultanates c.1400
Bahmani Sultanate from 1347
Vijayanagar Empire from the 1340's
Areas contested by Bahmani and Vijayanagar
Rajput
Temporarily held by forces of Delhi
Areas controlled by Hindu Rajas
Areas dominated by Hindu chiefs
Expeditions of Khaljis
1296
1307
1309
1310
1311
Muslim shrine
Hindu shrine
1303 Dates of Mongol attacks before 1398
Invasion of Timur, 1398-99
Trading ports
0
500 km
0
300 miles

Heirs to the ancient world 4

TRADITION AND INNOVATION

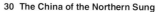

The conquests of Islam which had halted at the Indus in the eighth century (see Map 19) were carried into India by Mahmud of Ghazni (r. 999-1030), whose West Asian empire was based on Afghanistan, and more permanently by Muhammed Ghuri, who conquered the kingdom of Delhi in 1192. His successors failed to create an Indian empire but the Sultanate of Delhi became the dominant political power of northern and central India, and the principal force in the establishment of Islam and its culture in the sub-continent (see Map 29).

30 The China of the Northern Sung
About 1100 China probably excelled the rest of the world in economic development, literacy and numeracy. A far-flung trade and the presence on its boundaries of the relatively settled and civilized states of the Hsi-Hsia and the Liao made it more nearly part of a system of international relations than was the case under the Han or the Manchu.

Below: Merton College, Oxford, founded 1264 by Walter de Merton, Chancellor to Henry III.

31 The Mongols
The unification of the Mongol tribes under Chingiz Khan paved the way for the destruction of states and kingdoms throughout central Asia and eastern Europe, culminating in the conquest of China and the creation of the greatest land empire in history. It disintegrated rapidly, but Timur (*r.* 1360-1405), a descendant of Chingiz, threatened to renew it, and was planning to attack China at the time of his death.

Throughout the Islamic world conquest made a clear break with the past. The adoption of a new religion which accompanied it involved the explicit repudiation of the old cultures and traditions, even if in practice they remained deeply influential, and their literature and thought provided the foundation for the brilliant civilization of Islam's golden age. In Christendom and in China, on the other hand, the classical past and its traditions and values were cherished, and played a formative role in the civilizations' development. In both civilizations respect for tradition, as might be expected, acted as an inhibiting force, but by the end of the fifteenth century it was clear that the difference in the ways in which it had done so was to have momentous consequences.

By about 1100 the economic revolution had produced in China many of the features of an industrial society (*see Map 30*). Coal and iron were mined on a large scale, and the iron put to a great variety of uses for nails and chains and currency, in bridges and in buildings, for machinery, for the textile industries and agricultural tools, which were probably more widely available to the peasantry at this time than in the early twentieth century. Most of it, however, went to the state armaments factories, which every year turned out arrowheads by the million, swords and suits of armour by the tens of thousands, even armoured vehicles for use against cavalry. Other major industries included salt-processing, ship-building and printing, for a population in which both literacy and numeracy were widely diffused. Networks of roads and canals built and maintained by the state and elaborate arrangements for credit, including a paper currency, sustained a thriving internal trade. Ships with watertight bulkheads – unknown to Europeans until the nineteenth century – exchanged silk and porcelain for the luxuries of the civilized world in the Pacific, the Indian Ocean and the Persian Gulf.

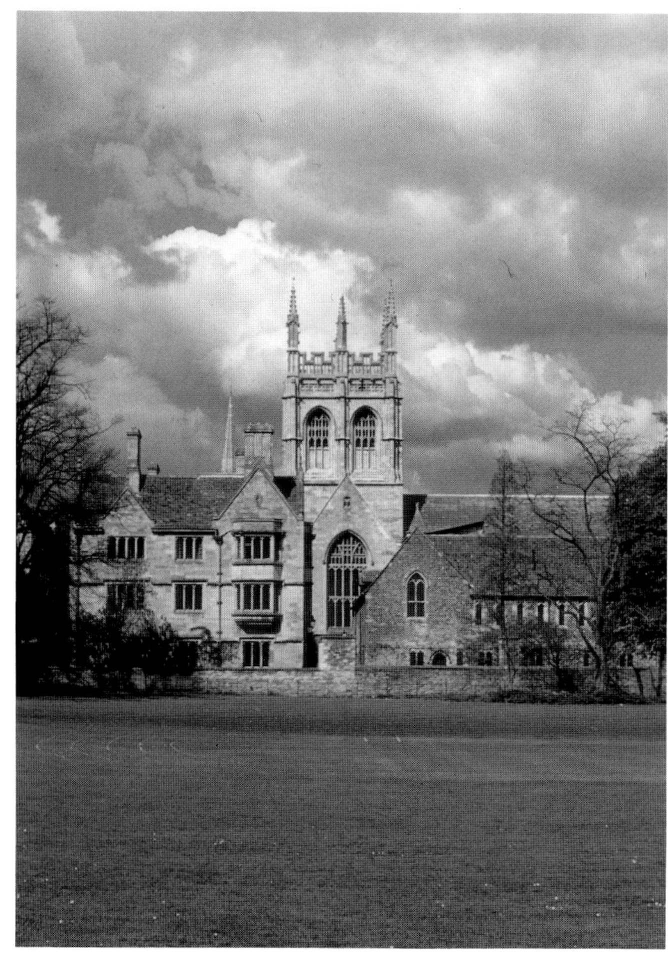

If the wealth of the Northern Sung period (960-1126) enabled China to sustain tremendous military strength it also made it an ever more tempting prey to its barbarian neighbours. The Liao and the Hsi-Hsia were relatively civilized states with which the Chinese had regular if not invariably cordial diplomatic and trading relations. But in 1125 the Liao fell to invaders, the Chin Tartars from Mongolia who went on to occupy much of northern China, including the capital Kai-feng. The immediate consequences were not catastrophic. The industrial north was lost but the Southern Sung dynasty retained the regions where agricultural wealth had been increasing rapidly and overseas trade was most naturally based. The new capital at Hangchou soon became the largest city in the world, the centre of a wealthy, sophisticated, more urban, and in many ways more ostentatious society than its predecessor.

In the long run the fall of Liao had graver consequences. The Chin state became a conduit through which Chinese iron weapons passed to the Mongols beyond, to provide – quite literally – the sharp edge of the most horrific and most dramatically successful of all the barbarian invasions. Temujin was declared Supreme Monarch – Chingiz Khan – of the Mongol tribes in 1206 after he had unified them in years of bitter warfare. By simple military superiority – they were usually greatly outnumbered by their civilized opponents – and unexampled ferocity, his armies conquered the greatest empire in history. *Map 31* suggests that their raids were designed to prepare the way, by systematically eliminating every possibility of rivalry elsewhere, for the invasion of China, the traditional objective of the inhabitants of the Mongolian steppes. Chingiz died in 1227, while completing his second and permanent occupation

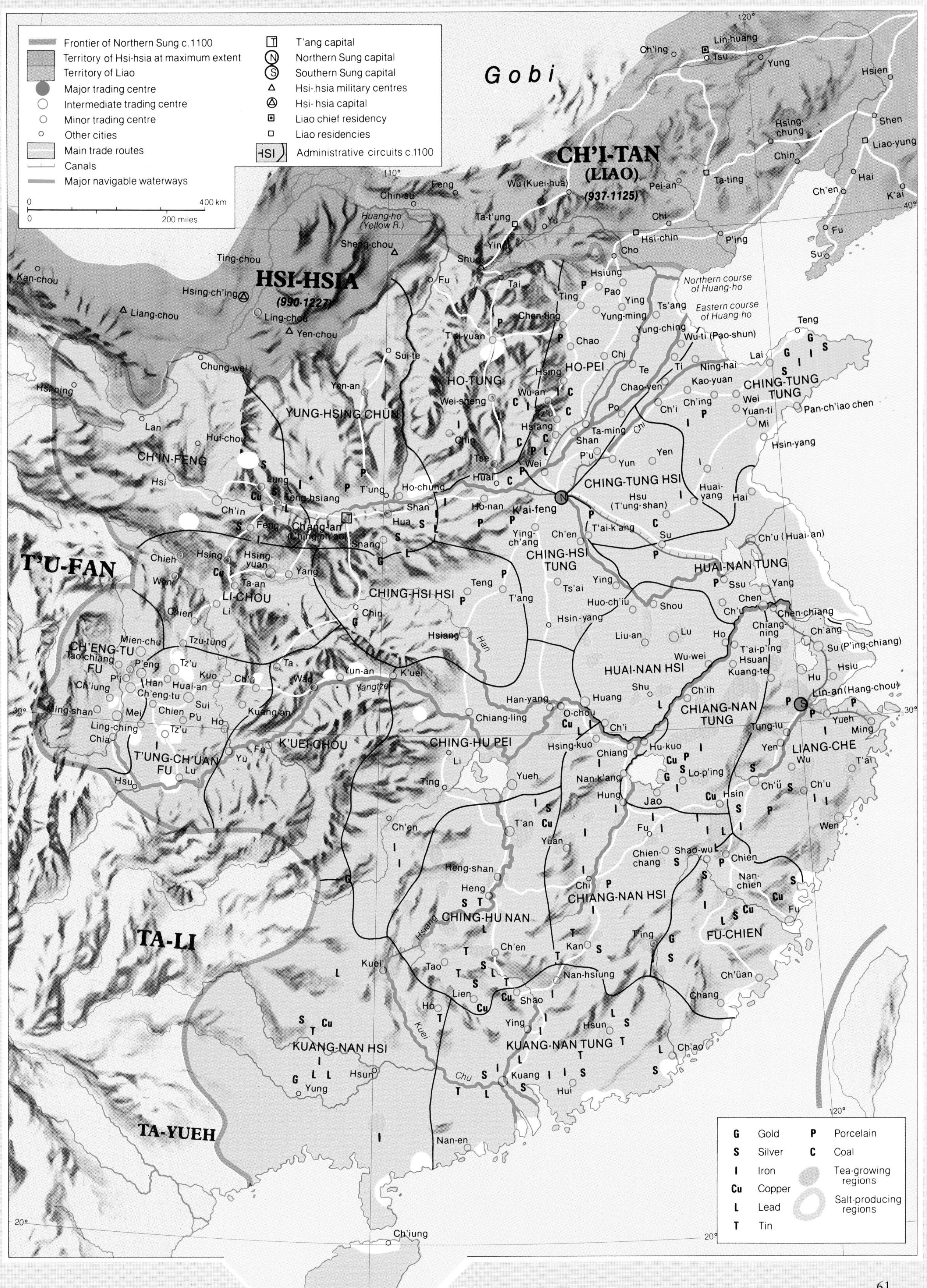

Frontier of Northern Sung c.1100
Territory of Hsi-hsia at maximum extent
Territory of Liao
Major trading centre
Intermediate trading centre
Minor trading centre
Other cities
Main trade routes
Canals
Major navigable waterways
T'ang capital
Northern Sung capital
Southern Sung capital
Hsi-hsia military centres
Hsi-hsia capital
Liao chief residency
Liao residencies
Administrative circuits c.1100
0 400 km
0 200 miles
Gobi
CH'I-TAN
(LIAO)
(937-1125)
HSI-HSIA
(990-1227)
T'U-FAN
TA-LI
TA-YUEH
Huang-ho
(Yellow R.)
Northern course of Huang-ho
Eastern course of Huang-ho
Yangtze
Han
Hsiang
Kuei
Chu
HO-TUNG
HO-PEI
YUNG-HSING CHÜN
CH'IN-FENG
CHING-TUNG HSI
CHING-TUNG TUNG
CHING-HSI TUNG
CHING-HSI HSI
LI-CHOU
CH'ENG-TU FU
T'UNG-CH'UAN FU
K'UEI-CHOU
HUAI-NAN TUNG
HUAI-NAN HSI
CHIANG-NAN TUNG
CHIANG-NAN HSI
LIANG-CHE
CHING-HU PEI
CHING-HU NAN
FU-CHIEN
KUANG-NAN HSI
KUANG-NAN TUNG
Lin-huang
Tsu
Ch'ing
Yung
Hsien
Shen
Hsing-chung
Liao-yung
Chin
Hai
Ch'en
K'ai
Ta-ting
Pei-an
Wu (Kuei-hua)
Feng
Chin-su
Ta-t'ung
Yü
Chi
Hsi-chin
P'ing
Fu
Su
Cho
Ying
Shuo
Sheng-chou
Ting-chou
Kan-chou
Hsing-ch'ing
Liang-chou
Ling-chou
Yen-chou
Chung-wei
Hsi-ning
Lan
Hui-chou
Hsi
Ch'in
Feng-hsiang
Lung
Feng
Ch'ang-an (Ching-chao)
Hua
Shang
Yang
Hsing-yuan
Hsing
Chieh
Wen
Ta-an
Chien
Li
Mien-chu
Tzu-t'ung
Tao-chiang
P'eng
P'i
Ch'iung
Han
Ch'eng-tu
Huai-an
Kuo
Tz'u
Sui
Ch'ü
P'u
Ho
Mei
Ming-shan
Ling-ching
Chia
Tz'u
Yü
Fu
Lu
Hsu
Ta
Wan
Yun-an
K'uei
Kuang-an
Chin
Hsiang
Teng
T'ang
Yen-an
Sui-te
T'ai-yuan
Tai
Hsiung
Pao
Ting
Chen-ting
Ying
Yung-ming
Ts'ang
Yung-ching
Wu-ti (Pao-shun)
Chao
Chi
Te
Hsing
Wu-an
Wei-sheng
Tz'u
Hsiang
Chao-yen
Ti
Ning-hai
Kao-yuan
Ch'i
Ch'ing
Po
Ta-ming
Shan
P'u
Yun
Yen
Wei
Tse
Huai
Ho-chung
T'ung
Shan
Ho-nan
K'ai-feng
Hsu (T'ung-shan)
Huai-yang
Hai
Su
T'ai-k'ang
Ying-ch'ang
Ch'en
Ts'ai
Ying
Huo-ch'iu
Shou
Hsin-yang
Liu-an
Lu
Ho
Wu-wei
Shu
Huang
Han-yang
Chiang-ling
O-chou
Ch'i
Ch'ih
Hsing-kuo
Chiang
Hu-kuo
Nan-k'ang
Lo-p'ing
Jao
Hsin
Hung
Lai
Wei
Yuan-ti
Mi
Pan-ch'iao chen
Hsin-yang
Teng
Ch'u (Huai-an)
Ssu
Yang
Chen
Ch'u
Chen-chiang
Chiang-ning
Ch'ang
Su (P'ing-chiang)
T'ai-p'ing
Hsuan
Kuang-te
Hsiu
Hu
Lin-an (Hang-chou)
Yueh
Ming
T'ai
Wu
Yen
Tung-lu
Ch'ü
Ch'u
Wen
Chien
Nan-chien
Fu
Chien-chang
Shao-wu
Fu
T'ing
Ch'üan
Chang
Ch'ao
Li
Ting
Yueh
T'an
Yuan
Heng-shan
Heng
Chi
Ch'en
Kan
Tao
Nan-hsiung
Lien
Shao
Ho
Ying
Hsun
Kuang
Hui
Kuei
Hsun
Yung
Nan-en
Ch'iung
Ch'en
30°
20°
40°
110°
120°
Gold
Silver
Iron
Copper
Lead
Tin
Porcelain
Coal
Tea-growing regions
Salt-producing regions

Cologne
Breslau
Prague
Cracow
Venice
Invasion of eastern Europe 1240-42
RUSSIAN PRINCIPALITIES
Kiev
1240
GOLDEN HORDE
Volga
CUMANS
Don
Danube
New Sarai
1224
1236
Tana
Constantinople
Black Sea
1223
Old Sarai
CHAGATAI
Ural Mts.
Ural
Ob
Caspian Sea
Caucasus
SELJUKS OF RUM
TREBIZOND
Konya
LESSER ARMENIA
Mediterranean Sea
Tiflis
1221
Aral Sea
KHWARAZM
Urgenj
Oxus
Otrar
1219
L. Balkhash
Balasaghun
QARA-KHITAI
Aleppo
AYYUBIDS
Tabriz
Maragheh
1220
CALIPH'S DOMINIONS
Euphrates
Acre
Jerusalem
Damascus
1260
MAMLUK EMPIRE (from 1250)
Nile
Sultaniyeh
1258
Baghdad
Tigris
Alamut
Rayy
Hamadan
KHWARAZM-SHAH'S EMPIRE
Nishapur
Bukhara
Samarqand (Timur's capital)
Kashgar
Marv
Balkh
Hindu Kush
1221
Herat
Isfahan
ILKHANATE
Kerman
Shiraz
Indus
Delhi
DELHI SU
Pre-Mongol conquest capitals
Capitals of Mongol Khanates
RDE Mongol Khanates within the Empire
IRE Pre-Mongol states
Approximate boundary of empire at death of Chingiz Khan 1227
Approximate boundary of Empire c.1280
Boundaries of Mongol Khanates
Campaigns under Chingiz Khan 1206-27
Later major Mongol campaigns
Route of Marco Polo
Route of the elder Polos
Route of John of Plano Carpini, 1245-7
Route of William of Rubruck, 1253-7
Empire of Timur (Tamberlane), c.1405
Principal directions of Timur's invasions outside his empire
0 1000 km
0 750 miles

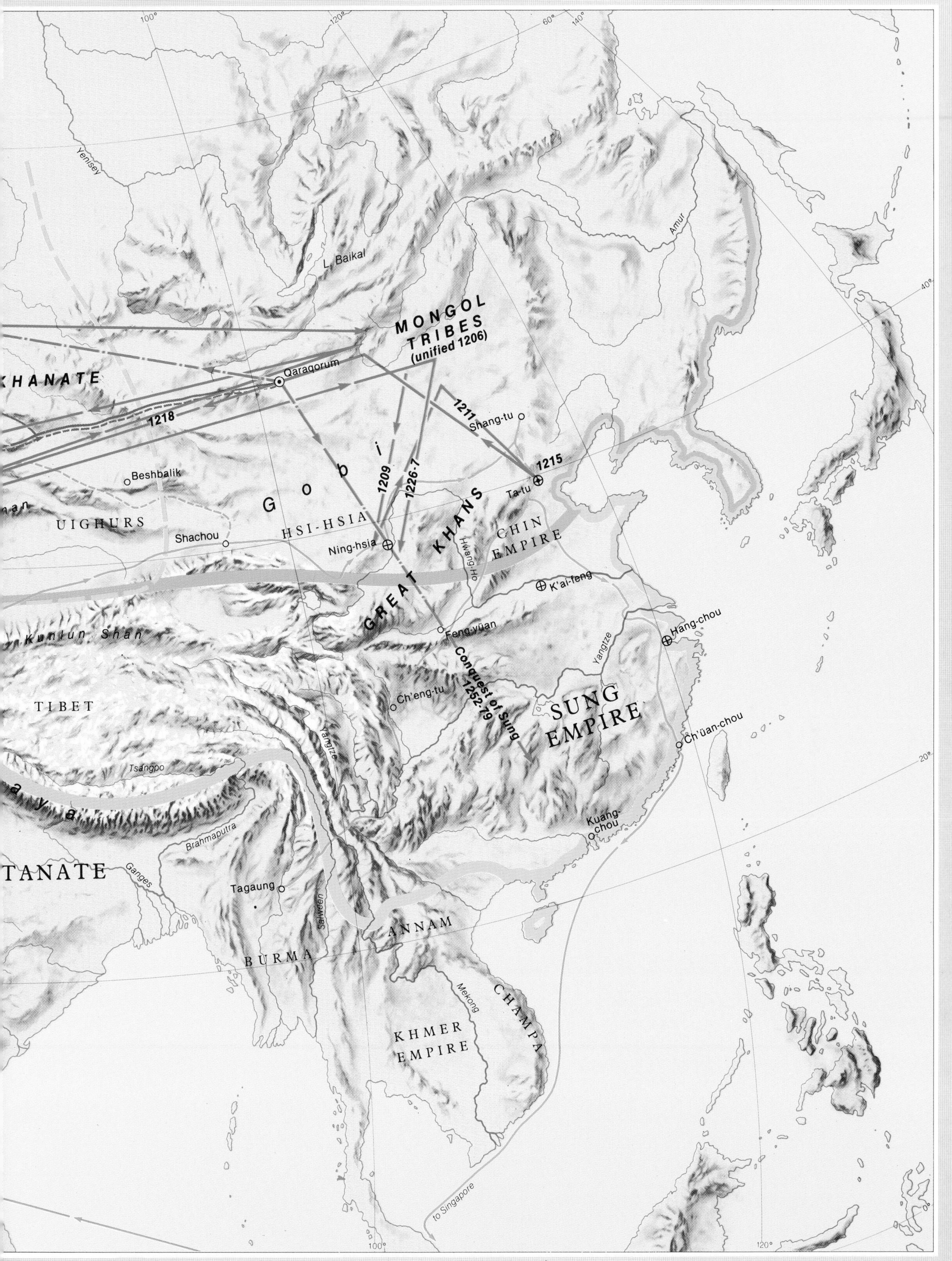
MONGOL
TRIBES
(unified 1206)
Qaraqorum
KHANATE
1218
1211
1215
1209
1226-7
Shang-tu
Ta-tu
L. Baikal
Amur
Yenisey
Beshbalik
Gobi
UIGHURS
HSI-HSIA
Shachou
Ning-hsia
GREAT KHANS
CHIN
EMPIRE
Hwang-Ho
K'ai-feng
Feng-yüan
Hang-chou
Yangtze
Kunlun Shan
TIBET
Ch'eng-tu
Conquest of Sung
1252-79
SUNG
EMPIRE
Ch'üan-chou
Tsangpo
Brahmaputra
Kuang-
chou
TANATE
Ganges
Tagaung
Salween
ANNAM
BURMA
Mekong
CHAMPA
KHMER
EMPIRE
to Singapore

of the Hsi-Hsia. The subjugation of China (which required the Mongols to learn new techniques of waterborne and siege warfare), as well as that of Russia and parts of the Middle East, was completed by his successors. They divided his empire between them, but always recognized the ruler of China as the Great Khan to whom the others remained subordinate in theory, and for some time in practice.

The Mongols drew a line across the history of Asia. Their savagery, no doubt exaggerated by legend, was quickly moderated as they realized the value of prosperous subjects. The Mongols lived on tribute and quickly saw how they could profit from trade, which they always encouraged. Italian merchants were prominent beneficiaries. Their bases in the Crimea and on the Black Sea became the great terminals of the overland trade which flourished as the routes to China and Qaraqorum became safer, and busier, than ever before. Correspondingly, the one successful defence against the Mongols, that of Egypt by its Mamluk rulers, severed Africa once again from the Middle East and made Mesopotamia a southern backwater of the empire of the steppes (*compare Maps 31 and 27*).

The political consequences of the Mongol conquests were less beneficial. Unlike most previous conquerors they did not govern their empire through existing administrations. They appointed in each region governors from some other part of the empire, or outside it altogether, whose sole function was to see that their tribute was paid and their dictates respected. Nothing less than total compliance was accepted from these officials, and no constraint was placed on the means by which they secured it. This system not only made Mongol rule detested but left a brutal and absolutist legacy. The Russian principalities, for example, which had emerged from the disintegration of the Kievan state (*Map 21*), had retained from their Byzantine inheritance a tradition that the ruler should consult the interests of his subjects and respect the restraints of Christian conduct. Their successor when the Mongol empire began to disintegrate was the Duchy of Moscow, whose effective founder Ivan I (*r.* 1328-40) secured his position by receiving from the Khan, for himself and his descendants, the right to collect the tribute in return for guaranteeing its payment (*see Map 43*). He got with it the right to exercise the Khan's absolute power over his new subjects. It was the beginning of a very different political tradition.

The Mongol conquest of north China was carried out with appalling ferocity. When it was completed the Chinese were treated as a subject people for the first time in their history. This followed the fall of a dynasty which had presided over unequalled peace and prosperity. The lesson was not lost. Chu Yuan-chang, the founder of Ming dynasty (1368-1644) left on his grave the words 'Rule like the T'ang and the Sung'. Action was suited to the words with a devotion that was, in the long run, self-defeating. The examination for the imperial bureaucracy, brought to a peak of scrupulous impartiality by the Sung (under whom scripts were recopied to protect the anonymity of the candidates) was restored. But its syllabus now demanded not only a minute knowledge of the great commentators on Confucius of the Sung period, but unquestioning adherence to their precepts. Even the form in which essays were to be written was soon exactly prescribed. The Sung had fallen not through any difficulty in maintaining their armies and military expenditures, such as had brought down their predecessors, but because Chinese weapons, knowledge and materials had been exported to the barbarians. The conquest had been assisted, perhaps decisively, by Chinese advisers. The Ming regime drew itself apart from the outer world. In spite of some notable achievements like the voyages of Cheng Ho to the African coast and East Indies between 1405 and 1433 the navy was run down, and trade and cultural contacts with outsiders increasingly discouraged. The accumulated wisdom and governmental expertise of the Chinese past was applied with devoted skill to the maintenance of the agricultural wealth of the interior and the development of internal trade and communications to produce a self-sufficient economy, maintaining relative prosperity and an advanced culture, without resort to the world beyond. It did so at the price of stagnation.

Compared with the territories which the Mongols ruled, western Europe was remarkably diverse in its economy and culture. This was due partly to its range of climate and terrain, and partly to the variety of influences to which it had been subjected. That it exhibited, nevertheless, a common culture and common attitudes and assumptions was the work of the Catholic Church. Ever since Pope Gregory I had organized the conversion of England just before 600, it had assumed responsibility for bringing new peoples within the orbit of civilization – with which indeed Christianity was synonymous among the western as it was among the eastern successors of the Roman Empire (*see Map 20*). In the middle of the eleventh century the Papacy began to shake the Church away from lay control, beginning a conflict with the German emperors which dominated European politics for centuries. The church gradually secured its freedom to elect its own popes, appoint its own bishops and other officers, and subject its clergy to its own (canon) law and machinery of government, centred on Rome, rather than those of the secular powers. In 1215 the Fourth Lateran Council, attended by more than 400 bishops from all over Europe, endorsed a programme of doctrinal, ritual and moral precepts to be observed by the faithful and administered and enforced by a clergy which was now clearly distinguished from the laity in dress, conduct (quite often in practice as well as in theory) and allegiance.

The clergy was Europe's equivalent to China's mandarins. No prince or magnate was without his clerical advisers, who often had very great influence. Since the clergy had a monopoly of literacy, except perhaps in Italy, from the ninth to the thirteenth centuries, the operations of government were necessarily in their hands. Great advances in administration were made in the twelfth century, through written instruments, the keeping of records and accounts, the making of surveys of land and resources (of which the English Domesday in 1087 was the most remarkable example); these were carried out by clerks (*clerici*) under the supervision of the bishops and abbots who were the monarch's closest advisers. While the clerks contributed indispensably to the development of royal power they also strove, with a good measure of success, to set limits to its use. Charlemagne had been encouraged, as a Christian prince, to conquer Saxony, but his clerical adviser Alcuin rebuked him

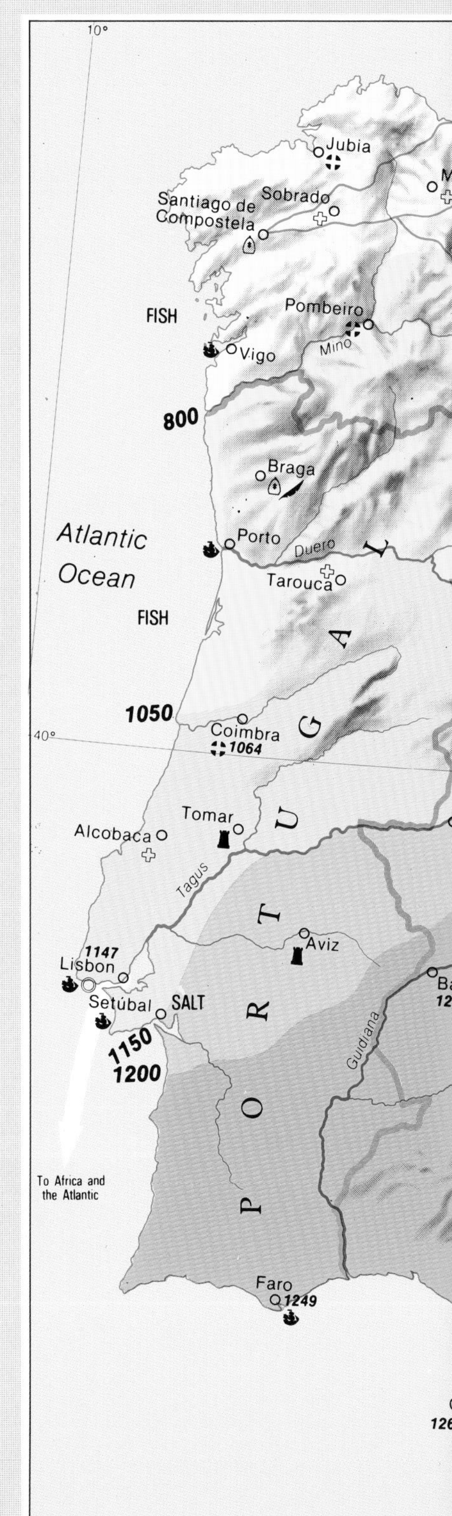

32 Spain in the middle ages

The gradual 'reconquest' of Spain by Christians – by no means an exclusively military process – left Muslim and Jewish communities in the Christian kingdoms. Their co-existence produced the most distinctive characteristics of Iberian history, providing the main channel through which Greek and Arabic philosophy and science reached the West in the twelfth century, and, later, a bitter legacy of intolerance and persecution.

for massacring its pagan inhabitants. The men who staffed the Treasury and Chancery which gave Angevin England the most powerful grip over its subjects of any government in the Latin world (*see Map 25*) wrote 'mirrors for princes' which portrayed royal virtue as lying in moderation, compassion for the weak and respect for the rights and interests of their subjects. And when the barons of England decided, in 1215, to protect their rights and interests by rebellion, the archbishop of Canterbury helped them to write their manifesto, which became Magna Carta.

Like the mandarins, the European clergy derived their own common standards and culture from the intensive study of a body of venerated writings and commentaries on them. Like the mandarins they strove in their best moments to preserve their caste from becoming a closed one, notably (from the eleventh century) by insisting on celibacy, so that it could not be hereditary. But here the analogy, however loose, breaks down. The clerks were too various a class, serving too many masters with an insufficiently sophisticated bureaucratic apparatus either to maintain the same degree of conformity among themselves as the mandarins could, or the same degree of control over the world around

33 Italy in the middle ages
The cities of northern Italy used their early prosperity to establish independence as self-governing communes and their control over the countryside around them. By the end of the thirteenth century they were beginning to surrender to despotism. Their population is shown here on the eve of the Black Death, *c.* 1340.

34 Germany and Central Europe in the later middle ages
The expansion of German settlement in central Europe continued until the fourteenth century. It provided the chief stimulus to economic and commercial development and assisted the continuing consolidation of the territorial principalities in the Empire and in the kingdoms of Poland, Bohemia and Hungary.

MAP 32 SPAIN IN THE MIDDLE AGES

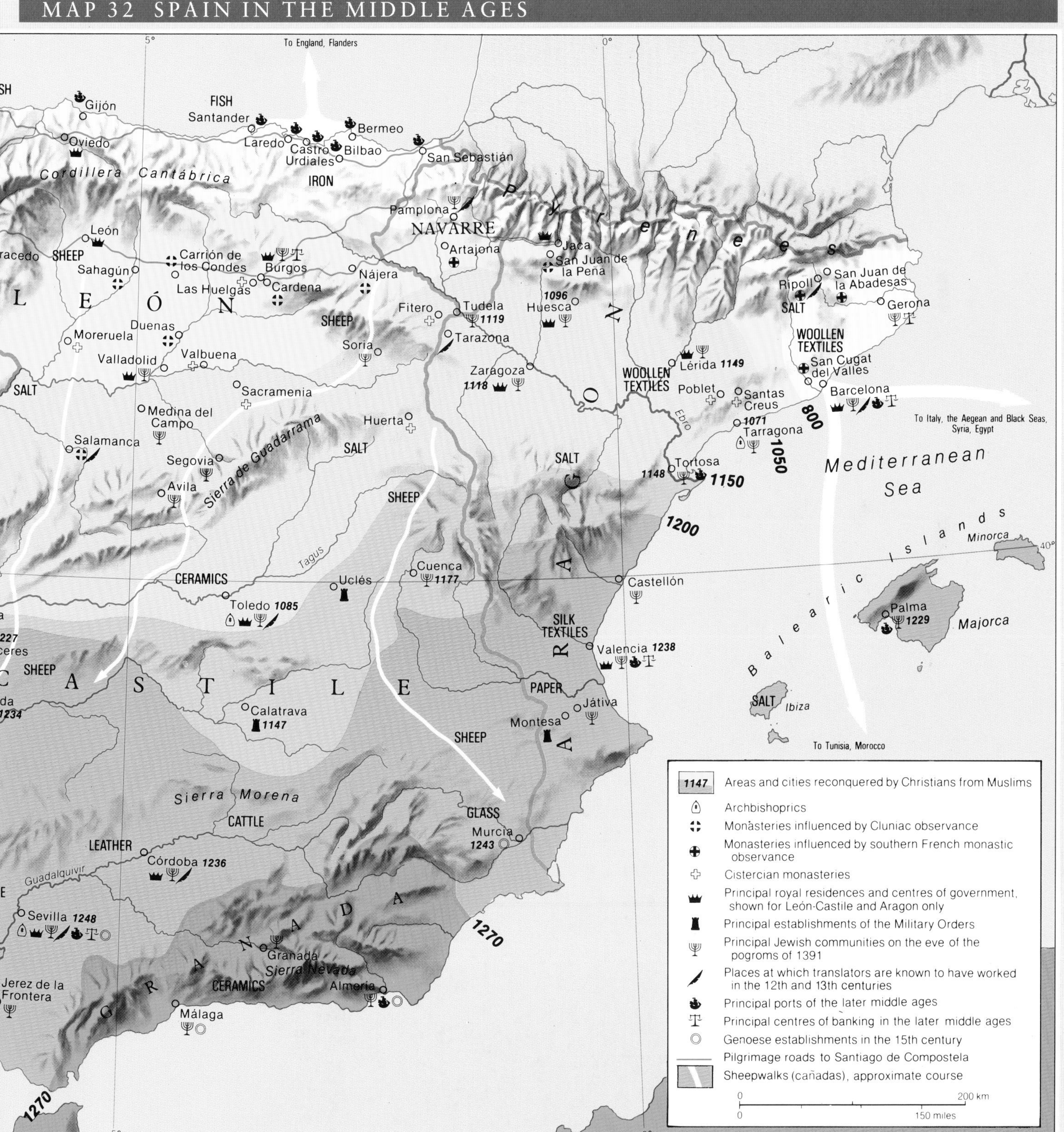

Roads
Battles
Archdioceses
Principal monasteries
Principal universities
Guelf alliance in Tuscany
Ghibelline alliance in Tuscany
Early communes
Town/city population over 50,000
c.50,000
20,000-40,000
c.10,000
Areas dominated by Rome, Milan, Genoa, Florence and Venice c.1100
Boundary of lordship 1450
Milan Centre of lordship 1450
0 200 km
0 150 miles
DUCHY OF MILAN
REPUBLIC OF VENICE
PAPAL STATES
KINGDOM OF NAPLES
KINGDOM OF SICILY
REP. OF FLORENCE
The Alps
Appennines
Ligurian Sea
Adriatic Sea
Tyrrhenian Sea
Mediterranean Sea
Gulf of Táranto
Straits of Messina
Corsica
Sardinia
Elba
Lipari Is.
Pantelleria
Malta
Tunis
St Gotthard
Brenner
Septimer
St Bernard
Mt Cenis
Pontebba
Villach
Drava
Sava
Como
Bergamo
Novara
Legnano 1167
Milan
Vercelli
Turin
Lodi
Crema
Pavia
Brescia
Vicenza
Verona
Padua
Treviso
Aquilèia
Grado
Venice
Chioggia 1381
Cremona
Mantua
Po
Piacenza
Asti
Alessándria
Parma
Ferrara
1244
Bobbio
Reggio nel'Emilia
Modena
Bocchetta
Cisa
Genoa
Via Aemilia
Bologna
Ravenna
Faenza
Forli
Rimini
Futa
Pistoia
San Godenzo
Camaldoli
Mandrioli
Lucca
Pisa
Arno
Florence
Vallombrosa
Meloria 1284
Arezzo
Ancona
Fonte Avellana
Siena
Perugia
Via Francigena
Orvieto
Via Flaminia
Viterbo
Tiber
Via Latina
Farfa
Tagliacozzo 1267
Subiaco
Rome
Civitate 1061
Manfredonia
Monte Cassino
Barletta
Trani
Bari
1071
Monopoli
Capua
1265
Benevento
Aversa
Naples
Conza di Campania
Via Appia
Acerenza
Brindisi
1283
Sorrento
Salerno
Amalfi
Táranto
Rossano
Cosenza
Santa Severina
Messina
Réggio Calabria
Palermo
1090
Trápani
Via Valeria
Catania
Cagliari
10°
15°
50°
40°

Town of over 20,000 population
Town of 10-20,000 population
Town of under 10,000 population
Archbishopric / bishopric with important territory
Archbishopric (with date of foundation)
Bishopric (with date of foundation)
University
Member of Hanseatic League
MAI Electoral territory
GELD Important territory
Boundaries of Empire in 1378
Boundaries of lands of Teutonic Order in 1378
Other boundaries
Important trade routes
Alpine passes
Hapsburg lands in 1378
Wittelsbach lands in 1378
Luxemburg lands in 1378
Lands of Swiss Confederation in 1378
Areas of German settlement
Areas of extensive use of German town law
0 150 km
0 100 miles
Baltic Sea
North Sea
DENMARK
TEUTONIC ORDER
HOLSTEIN
MECKLENBURG
POMERANIA
FRISIA
BRAUNSCHWEIG
BRANDENBURG
(GREAT) POLAND
(LITTLE) POLAND
SAXONY
LAUSITZ
BRESLAU
GALICIA
HESSE
THURINGIA
COLOGNE
TRIER
MAINZ
PALATINATE
BOHEMIA
MORAVIA
AUSTRIA
BAVARIA
WÜRTTEMBERG
HUNGARY
STYRIA
CARINTHIA
KRAIN
TYROL
SWISS CONFEDERATION
The Alps
SAVOY
DAUPHINÉ
FRANCHE-COMTÉ
BURGUNDY
LOTHARINGIA
LUXEMBURG
BRABANT
HOLLAND
ZEELAND
GELDERN
UTRECHT
MILAN
VERONA
Adriatic Sea
Königsberg
Frombork 1243
Danzig
Elbing
Marienwerder
Kulm
Thorn
DOBRZYN
Włockfawek
Płock
Warsaw
Lowicz
Gniezno
Poznan
Kalisz
Glogau
Breslau
Cracow
Königgratz
Leitomischl
Olmütz
Brno
Prague 1348
Cheb (Eger)
Pilsen
Schleswig
Stralsund
Greifswald
Kammin
Rostock
Lübeck
Ratzeburg
Schwerin
Stettin
Hamburg
Lüneburg
Havelberg
Lebus
Berlin
Brandenburg
Bremen
Verden
Minden
Braunschweig
Magdeburg
Halberstadt
Hildesheim
Goslar
Osnabrück
Münster
Paderborn
Kampen
Deventer
Haarlem
Amsterdam
Leiden
Hague
Delft
Dortmund
Soest
Westfalia
Berg
Cologne
Merseburg
Naumburg
Meissen
Bautzen
Erfurt
Fulda
Nassau
Jülich
Maastricht
Aachen
Antwerp
Mechelen
Brussels
Liège
Namur
Tournai
Hainault
Frankfurt
Mainz
Würzburg
Bamberg
Upper Palatinate
Nuremberg
Regensburg
Worms
Heidelberg
Speyer
Trier
Metz
Verdun
Reims
Toul
Strasbourg
Tübingen
Ulm
Nördlingen
Eichstätt
Passau
Augsburg
Freising
Munich
Chiemsee 1216
Salzburg
Vienna 1468
Wiener Neustadt 1468
Bratislava
Nitra
Esztergom
Vác
Eger
Győr
Pest
Veszprém
Kalocsa
Pécs
Seckau 1218
Gurk
Lavant 1228
Ljubljana 1462
Zagreb
Dakovo 1229
Aquileia
Trieste
Treviso
Venice
Padua
Vicenza
Verona
Mantua
Brescia
Bergamo
Cremona
Piacenza
Milan
Pavia 1361
Vercelli
Turin
Trent
Brixen
Brenner Pass
Septimer Pass
St Gotthard Pass
Lukmanier Pass
Splügen Pass
Great St Bernard Pass
Little St Bernard Pass
Mont Cenis Pass
Chur
Constance
Zürich
Zug
Basel 1460
Solothurn
Lucerne
Lausanne
Sion
Geneva
L. Geneva
Dijon
Lyon
Grenoble
Rhine
Weser
Elbe
Oder
Vistula
Danube
Meuse
Saône
Drava
Sava
Po
55°
45°
5°
10°
15°
20°

them. On the contrary, the relative autonomy of the European intelligentsia from the structures of both church and state was its most distinctive characteristic. It stemmed directly from the collapse of the Roman state in the west, which compelled the guardians of learning and culture to develop their own institutions (at first in the monasteries), find patrons and protectors wherever they could, and in doing so acquire a measure of independence which they never entirely lost.

The tremendous advance of thought and learning in the twelfth-century West both owed and contributed much to this independence. It was largely a by-product of the assault on Islam, and in the first place of the Spanish reconquest. Islamic civilization far excelled that of Europe; when the largest libraries of the West contained four or five hundred volumes that at Cordoba had four hundred thousand. Among them were the works of the Greek and Hellenistic philosophers and scientists, translated into Arabic after the conquests of Syria and Egypt, but for the most part unknown to readers of Latin. Now they were translated with the help of Christian Arabs and of the Jews who were well established all over Spain (*see Map 33*). Later Norman Sicily, the crusading kingdoms and Constantinople became centres of translation directly from Greek. The flood of new material, rising fast from about 1140 onwards, transformed every branch of knowledge and teaching. At the same time the transformation of Europe into an urban and bureaucratic society was creating an immense demand for education. In consequence the teachers in the great cities were able to establish their right to decide who should be of their number, and who and what they should teach. From the thirteenth century the universities of Europe, led by Paris and Bologna (*see Maps 25, 33 and 34*) were legally self-governing corporations, effectively independent of both Church and state.

Like the universities, the towns of Europe won their freedom in the high Middle Ages, successfully demanding from the end of the eleventh century charters which granted them exemption from the taxes and jurisdiction of their feudal lords. Northern Italy, its cities more numerous and much more populous than those of any other region, was Europe's urban region par excellence (*compare Maps 28 and 33*). To the profits of their far-flung trading colonies (*see also Map 26*) they were now adding those of the banking and insurance services, which they provided all over Europe, often playing a critical role in political events in consequence. The Bardi and Peruzzi banks had more branches and more capital at the beginning of the fourteenth century than the Medici bank (*see Map 35*) had a hundred years later, and had far more liquid wealth at their disposal than any monarch. In such a world the skills of literacy and numeracy were necessarily widely distributed. The intense competitiveness and rich opportunities of city life produced on the one hand continuous, often bitter and eventually self-destructive conflict both within and between the cities, and on the other a secular culture of immense vitality, the greatest masterpieces of European building, painting and literature, and a tradition of political and intellectual independence which survived the efforts of German emperors and papal agents alike to subdue it.

The agricultural expansion upon which economic growth and political development rested reached its limit in most places in the late thirteenth century. Falling crop yields and more frequent famine produced the Black Death which between 1347 and 1352 killed up to a third of the population in the worst affected regions (*see Map 35*). Recurrent epidemics delayed recovery until the end of the century and beyond. Prolonged and savage wars over much of Europe increased the consequent miseries, and swelled the taxes which monarchs extorted from their subjects. The peasant revolts which followed, severely frightening the governors of France and England in particular, were paralleled by the growing bitterness of civil conflict in the towns, and rising signs of popular discontent with the privileges and exactions of the clergy. All these elements were involved in the devastating and fateful wars which originated in criticism of clerical corruption by a distinguished scholar and teacher, John Hus (who died at the stake in 1415) and became a popular rebellion with aristocratic support, against the imperial domination of Bohemia (1419-36; *see Map 35*). This war foreshadowed the wars of the Reformation era in bloodiness and bitterness as well as in the issues involved.

The growth of government in the twelfth and thirteenth centuries and the miseries of the fourteenth contributed to the creation of a less open and less pluralistic society. The Church vindicated its claim to spiritual leadership by persecuting as heretics those who resisted it. They were especially numerous in the Low Countries, Lombardy and the Languedoc, where their presence provided the Capetian kings with an excuse for the brutal conquest of the County of Toulouse (1209-29; *see Map 25*) and the Pope for the creation of the Inquisition. The Church's demand for Christians to conform now also encouraged a rising tide of popular hostility towards the Jews, who were ordered to wear distinctive clothing by the Fourth Lateran Council. The withdrawal of royal protection (which was largely responsible for their unpopularity in the first place) as the rise of the Italian banks made their financial services superfluous and the debts owed to them an embarrassment led to their expulsion from England in 1290 and France in 1306; and they were driven from western Germany towards the new lands in the east when a succession of pogroms made them scapegoats for the Black Death. In Spain too, where three cultures had coexisted fruitfully for so long, tolerance broke down, and persecution of the Jews started in earnest in 1391; the Inquisition made up for its late arrival there, in 1480, by pursuing their descendants – particularly those who had converted to Christianity – with special ferocity. Secular monarchs did not hang back. In 1307 the king of France seized the lands of the Knights Templar in his dominion, justifying the action by torturing them until they confessed that they were part of an international satanist conspiracy. A century later the technique was being widely imitated by those who had grudges against their neighbours: accusations of witchcraft were pursued by inquisitors and magistrates with an enthusiasm which would bring scores of thousands to the stake all over early modern Europe.

Nevertheless these reverses did not undo the achievements of the twelfth and thirteenth centuries. Economic failure in some areas was offset by rapid development in others. The Hansa towns of northern Europe formed a political and trading

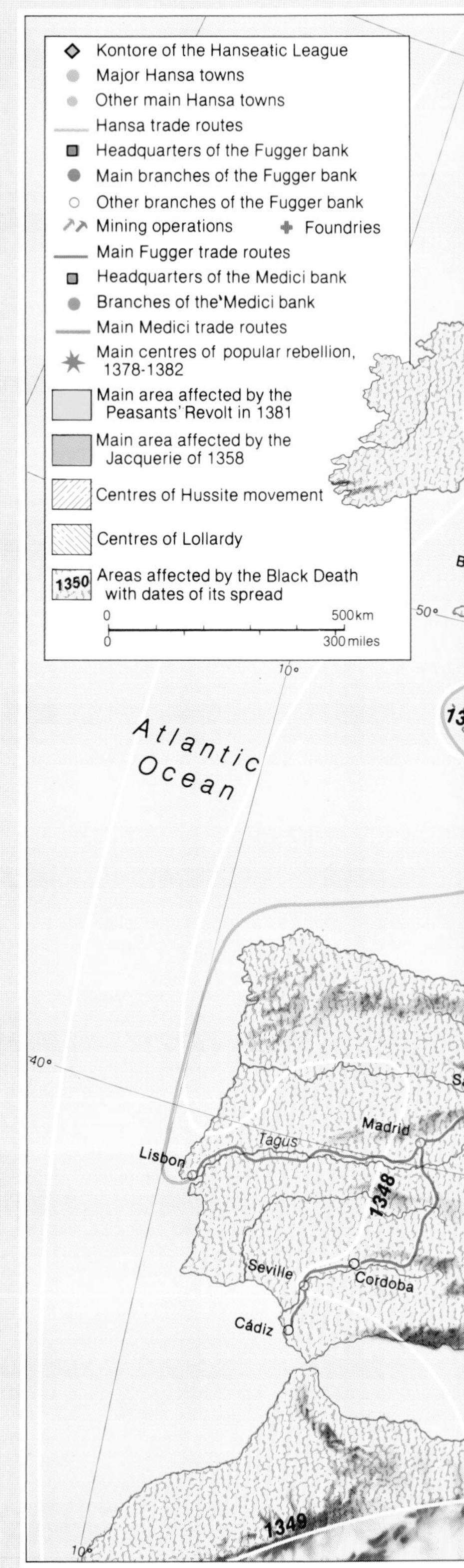

35 The economy of the later middle ages
In the fourteenth century Europe was seized by disease, famine and revolt. Nevertheless new trade routes were established and new centres of production and exchange opened up, especially in central and eastern Europe, to create a larger, more varied economy: compare with *Map 28* which this map complements, but does not supersede.

monopoly which dominated their area, and contributed greatly in the thirteenth and fourteenth centuries to the development of the Baltic and the eastern expansion of the Germans (*see Maps 34 and 35*); the extension of their routes through southern Germany to the Mediterranean and along the Atlantic coast helped to create a larger and more varied European trading community. If the Flemish cloth industry declined, Dutch shipping grew vigorous on the Baltic trade; and wars in the Iberian peninsula hastened the maritime expansion of Portugal. The tyrannical ambitions of the European rulers were also a sign of the limitations on their power, and of how little they controlled the vital forces of European society; the peasant revolts attacked political weakness as well as financial exaction, and the Inquisition could prevent neither the dissemination of religious disaffection among the people nor the increasing boldness of speculation among the intellectuals both inside and outside the Church. For many Europeans the fifteenth century was not a happy time or, as they saw themselves become the last heirs of antiquity when Constantinople fell to the Ottoman Turks in 1453, a secure one. Nevertheless, theirs was a fortunate inheritance.

Further reading: D. O. Morgan, *The Mongols* (Basil Blackwell, 1987); Morris Rossabi, *Khubilai Khan, His Life and Times* (University of California Press 1988); Joseph Needham, *The Grand Titration* (Allen and Unwin 1969; Books Demand UMI); R. Mottahedeh, *The Mantle of The Prophet: Religion and Politics in Iran* (Chatto and Windus 1985; Simon & Schuster Trade); R. I. Moore, *The Formation of a Persecuting Society: Power and Deviance in Western Europe, 950-1250* (Basil Blackwell 1987); George Holmes, *Europe: Hierarchy and Revolt, 1320-1450* (Collins 1975); Lauro Martines, *Power and Imagination* (Allen Lane 1980; Random House).

MAP 35 THE ECONOMY OF THE LATER MIDDLE AGES

The age of European supremacy 1

EUROPE AND A WIDER WORLD

At the end of the fifteenth century Europe was not evidently the most advanced civilization. Those of India, the Islamic world and, especially, China were richer and more sophisticated. Yet within three hundred years Europe had seized control of the oceans, destroyed the Aztecs, Incas and Mayas of South America (Map 36), conquered vast territories throughout the Americas and in India and Siberia, and organized a complex and immensely profitable worldwide commercial system (see Map 46).

Opposite page above: Columbus landing at San Salvador in the Bahamas, October 12 1492.

36 The European discovery of the world
Late in the fifteenth century the Europeans began to discover the oceans and the other advanced people of the world. The Portuguese established a maritime empire in the Far East from the base provided by their earlier exploration of the African coast, while the Spanish conquered a land empire in America from their base in the Caribbean.

Further reading: G. V. Scammell, *The World Encompassed* (Methuen, 1981; University of California Press); Eric Wolff, *Europe and the People Without History* (University of California Press, 1982); Philip D. Curtin, *Cross-cultural Trade in World History* (Cambridge U.P. 1984); C. R. Boxer, *The Portuguese Seaborne Empire* (Hutchinson 1969); J. H. Elliott, *The Old World and the New* (Cambridge U.P. 1970); J. Burckhardt, *The Civilization of the Renaissance in Italy* (1 ed., Penguin, 1860).

It seems surprising that China, with its huge land mass, large population and stable political organization under the Ming dynasty (1368-1644) did not 'discover' Europe. After 1400, sturdy Chinese junks traded extensively in the Pacific and Chinese paper currency circulated widely. In seven expeditions between 1405 and 1433 the Grand Eunuch Cheng Ho sailed to Borneo, the Philippines, Ceylon, Malacca and East Africa. The conservatism of China's governors stifled the initiative. The mandarins disliked Muslims, eunuchs and favourites – Cheng was all three – and regarded trade as exploitation, and the outside world with suspicion. Official records of Cheng's expeditions were destroyed within 30 years, monopolies discouraged commerce, the paper currency collapsed, and external influences were discouraged. The Ottoman Turks, who presented such a desperate threat to Europe (*see Map 39*) had similar inhibitions. The rich bankers of Constantinople in 1500 were foreigners, Greek Christians or (like the 'Fugger of the Orient', Joseph Nasi) Portuguese Jews, and the Ottomans dispatched no ambassadors to the west, translated none of its literature – much of it by now available in print – and relied on slaves in their army to provide new military technology.

The 'age of reconnaissance' was launched from the smallest and least-endowed of European principalities, Portugal. The capture of the North African Moorish city of Ceuta in 1415 was followed by nearly a century of patient exploration of the West African coast, frequently interrupted by war in the Iberian peninsula, and by Portugal's domestic concerns (*see Map 36*). At last Bartholomeu Diaz triumphantly rounded the Cape of Good Hope in 1487, and in 1498 Vasco da Gama reached India. Within a decade and a half the Portuguese, using Asian pilots, bribery, and extensive naval bombardment, established fortresses and trading stations at Goa, which became the spiritual, administrative, and commercial centre of the Portuguese empire, Malacca, the centre of the spice trade in the Orient, and the Moluccas. The port of Mozambique was founded in 1507, and Ormuz, the guardian port of the Persian Gulf, in 1515. In 1557 they made a base on the China coast at Macao. For a few years nearly all the spices for Europe were carried by the Portuguese, but they never established a monopoly of the trade. They were dependent upon a delicate commercial system, always subject to disruption, in which the gold from the Zambeze area bought spices in the Indies, which paid for the expedition on its return.

Discovery begat imitation. The rivalry between Portugal and Castile spread down the West African coast with Castile's capture of the Canary Islands in the 1470s. Portugal (like the crusading powers of the thirteenth and fourteenth centuries) appealed in vain to the Pope to protect the monopoly granted in Papal Bulls of 1454 and 1456. In 1493, five years after Diaz returned from the Cape of Good Hope, Christopher Columbus' ship the *Nina* put into Lisbon, having returned across the Atlantic in a Spanish-sponsored expedition which claimed that it had discovered Cathay (Asia). Columbus, descended from a family of Genoese cartographers, was a careful and accurate navigator. The route of his first voyage to the 'West Indies' became that used by Spanish shipping to and from the New World, and his speed of crossing was rarely beaten in the sixteenth century. Castile claimed, and received, Papal protection for this new route to 'Asia', and an important line of demarcation between Portuguese and Castilian 'Asia' was achieved in the Treaty of Tordesillas (1494), although its precise geographical position was still disputed.

The purpose of Columbus' three subsequent voyages was rather different from that of the Portuguese explorers. He took with him not trading goods, but farmers, artisans, priests, tools, seeds and animals, to establish a new community across the Atlantic. Colonies were established at Española, and Santo Domingo (*see Map 43*). Increasingly, after 1500, as explorers' reports were digested, the suspicion hardened that this was not Asia but a new world. The conviction was strengthened by John Cabot, Amérigo Vespucci and others and confirmed in 1519, when Ferñao Magalhaes (Magellan) sailed round the tip of southern America. His captain, del Cano, became the first man to sail round the world (*Map 36*). In less than 30 years the map of the main islands of the Caribbean was established, but that was twice as long as it had taken the Portuguese, with the aid of their Asian pilots, to chart the East Indies.

The early settlements in the Caribbean proved disappointing. They were vulnerable, quarrelsome and economically insecure. European diseases and ill-treatment cut down the native Carib population. Partly to escape the quarrels, various expeditions were sent through the Gulf of Mexico. On the basis of their intelligence a new colony was established in Panama in 1519 and a larger expedition set out for Mexico under the command of the first and greatest of the *conquistadores*, Hernan Cortès (*Map 44*). His letters and four other eyewitness reports of his conquest of Mexico give a uniquely detailed account of their aims and methods. They reveal Cortès trying to prevent unnecessary bloodshed amongst the Aztecs he was conquering, aware of his difficulties in controlling the ill-disciplined forces under him, fascinated by the new culture before his eyes, constantly alive to the classical precedents for the conquest of primitive peoples (such as Julius Caesar's), and persistent in his attempts to maintain the chivalric and knightly values of his native southern Spain. But Cortès could not prevent the destruction of the capital of the Aztecs, Tenochtitlán, (where, subsequently, he founded Mexico City), and to reward the extravagant aspirations of his followers he distributed Aztec villages amongst them in *encomienda*, a system of quasi-manorial tribute.

With the Mexican example before them, other *conquistadores*, with less sympathy and more greed, carved out similar empires for themselves. Guatemala (1523-42), New Granada (1536-9), and central Chile (1540-58) were all conquered, but they never rivalled Mexico and Cuba. *Conquistadores* like Francisco de Pizarro and Nuño de Guzmán bloodily subdued the Incas and Mayas. Wherever there were Indians, the *encomienda* system was established, and the parasitic Spaniards lived off the tribute in the cities which they founded in the New World – Panama, Darien, Santiago, Lima, Santa Fé de Bogotá. The finest fruits of conquest, the first productive silver mines, were discovered at Potosí in central Peru in 1545, which remained the biggest single source of silver in the world for a hundred years (*see Map 43*).

The age of the *conquistadores* was troublesome and brief. They had undertaken great hardships and risked their lives and fortunes, and some had great rewards. Others were overwhelmed by the unexploitable, untapped reserves of space in America. Hernando de Soto, whose expedition reached the Appalachians and the Mississippi, or Coronado who crossed the Rio Grande and reached the Prairies, could make nothing of the vast expanse of lands, nomadic peoples and roving herds of cattle (*see Map 36*). Francisco de Orellana, who sailed down the Amazon after crossing the Andes, despaired of the dense tropical forests of the Amazon basin. Even those who were successful attracted the suspicions of the Crown, and if they escaped the knives of their rivals were soon replaced by an effective royal administration. Some settled as ranchers and miners. Others, like Cortès, returned to Spain to a bored and litigious retirement.

The motives of the Portuguese seamen and the Castilian *conquistadores* were mixed, powerful and long-established. Memories of crusade were still powerful in the Iberian peninsula. The last province of Castile was captured from the Moors in the same year that Columbus set out for America (*see Map 32*). None of the early explorers would have repudiated the motive which was attributed to Prince Henry the Navigator (master-mind of the Portuguese explorations in the middle of the fifteenth century) by his contemporary biographer: the conversion of the natives to Christianity and the defeat of the Infidel. But Prince Henry was also interested ('as was natural') in profit. The pace of Portuguese discoveries increased once they had reached the gold, slaves, and spices along the Guinea coast. More gold was discovered in the kingdoms of East Africa, and with the spices of the East Indies provided the basic staples of the Portuguese empire. Two powerful legends symbolized the motives of the early explorers: that there was a powerful Christian ruler somewhere to the East (*Prester John*), and a powerful and rich city of gold somewhere in the Orient (*Cathay*).

The first thing that distinguished Europe from

other civilizations and enabled it to discover the world was its ability to imitate, especially in technical developments. The fifteenth century saw, for instance, a fruitful combination of the Arabic type of Mediterranean ship with Atlantic vessels, to produce a craft which could go anywhere and get back again. The combination of lateen and square-rigged sails, developed by Portuguese shipbuilders in the caravel, could be worked by a small crew (shortage of water and food was the main hazard of long voyages) and could sail closely to the wind. Other advances in hull design produced ships which could sail their course more accurately. Few expeditions were mounted in first-class ships, but even fewer suffered from defects in their sailing craft. Mounted with guns, they proved capable of protecting oceans as well as discovering them. The other tradition alive in the Spanish peninsula was that of mathematics and astronomy, in the hands of Jews. Jewish mathematicians produced traverse tables to indicate approximate journey times and Jewish astronomers produced manuals for the declination of the sun at various latitudes. In Portugal, unlike Spain, Jews were tolerated.

Secondly, Europe did not despise merchants and mercantile wealth. The towns of northern Italy had grown rich upon the trade of the Mediterranean; Italian merchants traded in the bulk-cargoes of grain, salt and fish and, more importantly, with the Arabs in silks, spices and precious metals (*see Maps 28 and 35*). In their manner of conducting their business, sharing their risks, accounting for their profits, and facilitating credit, they were admired and copied in the cities of the southern Netherlands and southern Germany. The Portuguese crown, after initial reluctance, encouraged the participation of merchants in its ventures, and the great fleet which sailed from Lisbon in 1505 was largely financed by foreigners – Genoese, Florentine and German. In later expeditions the Crown undertook the voyages, but sold the entire cargoes, frequently in advance, to merchant syndicates. Once the colonies of the New World were established, it was the merchants of Antwerp who provided the colonists with the goods of the Old World, and the bankers of the Spanish crown in Genoa and Augsburg (like the Fuggers) who distributed the silver from the mines of Potosí across Europe.

Above all, the 'age of reconnaissance' was also the 'age of renaissance'. One of the most brilliant chapters of Jacob Burckhardt's famous book, *The Civilization of the Renaissance*, was entitled 'The Discovery of the World and of Men'. In it he discussed the delicate relationship between two forms of exploration, that of the inner world and the senses, and that of the physical world. He compared the accounts of medieval travellers outside Europe with those of the Renaissance explorers and concluded that the medieval travellers took what they found for granted, neither criticising it nor comparing it with their own experiences. The Renaissance explorer was different. Having gained a sense of historical perspective from the rediscovery of the different culture and civilization of the ancient world, he was more receptive, intellectually readier to appreciate, without rejecting, the different cultures and civilizations around him. Yet this is difficult to apply to most of the *conquistadores.* And it took two centuries for Europe to absorb the impact of the initial discoveries of the sixteenth century. Only by 1600 were the flora and fauna of the New World adequately described and categorized; it took longer for its carbohydrates (potato, sugar and maize) and vitamins to change the European diet. Only by 1700 was the New World in North America and Brazil beginning to be settled (*Map 44*). Only in the seventeenth century did the Dutch and English develop effective commercial and colonial empires along the lines of the Portuguese or Castilian. When the fruits of discovery had been absorbed, the process could begin again – this time in Siberia, India, Australia and on the margins of America.

Arc
Spitzbergen
Bylot-Baffin 1616
Eskimos
North-West Indians
Eskimos
Baffin Island
Davis 1585/87
Hudson Straits
Hudson Bay
Frobisher 1576
Hudson 1610
Button 1612
Algonquins
S. Cabot 1517
Cabot 1497
Davis 1587
Bristol
Eu
Drake 1579
Cabrillo 1542
Drake
Cartier 1534
John Cabot 1497
John Cabot 1498
Cabot 1498
Drake
Californians
American Indians
Verrazano 1523-4
Atlantic Ocean
Lisbon
Cadiz
John Cabot 1498
Westerlies
Azores
Diego de Sevilla 1432
de Soto 1539
Gomez 1524
Ulloa 1539
Ponce de Leon 1515
Canary Islanders 1312?/1336
Texans
Urdaneta 1565
Becerra 1533
Cortes 1519
Bahamas Is.
Columbus 1492
Gonçalo Velho 1416
Nomads of the Sahara
Mexico City (Tenochtitlan)
Caribs
Cuba
Drake
Cordoba 1517
Columbus 1502-4
Aztecs
Mayas
Montejo 1527-8
Española
Columbus 1493-4
N.E. Trades
Nuno de Tristão 1441/43
Saavedra 1527
Spanish Main
Diniz Diaz 1443-4
Cape Verde Is.
Cadamosto de Noli. 1456/8
Timbuctoo
Columbus 1502-4
N.E. Trades
Nuno de Tristão 1446
West Sudanese
SONGHAI
East Sudane
HAUSA
Dávila 1514
Balboa 1513
Ehinger 1529
Bastidas 1500
Columbus 1498
Vespucci 1499
Niani
MOSSI
A. Fernandez 1446
Pedro de Evora 1483
Caribs
A. de Hojeda 1498-9
S. da Costa 1461/70
Guinea coast peoples
BENIN
João de Santarem 1471
Peo
Pacific Ocean
Isthmus of Panama
Pizarro and Almagro 1524/26
Magellan 1519
Fernando Po 1472
Sequeira 1472
Afr
Ruiz de Estrada 1526
Equator
Mendaña and Quiros 1595-6
Pizarro 1528
Brazilian Indians
Pinzon 1499-1500
Fernão Noronha 1501/2
S.E. Trades
KON
Diego Cã 1485-6
Terra de Vera Cruz
Mendaña 1567-69
America (name first used in 1507)
Incas
João da Nova 1501
Treaty of Tordesillas 1494
Drake 1577/80
Gê-Botecudos
João da Nova 1502
Saint Helena Bay
Bantu
Drake
Chilean Indians
Chaco Indians
Brazilian Indians
Walfish Bay
Bartholemeu D 1486-88
PORTUGAL
SPAIN
Hunter-gathering cultures
Nomads and stock-raisers
Primitive cultures
Advanced cultures
Literate civilisations
Routes for voyages of discovery
Drake Explorers
Spanish expeditions
Portuguese ..
French ..
English ..
Dutch ..
Political lines of demarcation between Spanish and Portuguese exploration
The world known to Europeans, c. 1450
The world known of by Europeans, c. 1450
Mayas Peoples
Approximate prevailing winds (shown for the first quarter of the year)
Magellan 1519-20
Dias de Solis 1516
Patagonians
Valdivia 1540
Tristan da Cunha c. 1510
Vasco da Gama 1497
Cabral 1500
Westerlies
Roaring Forties
Port Saint Julian 1520
Falkland Is.
Hawkins 1594
Magellan's Straits
Tierra del Fuego
F. de Hocues 1526

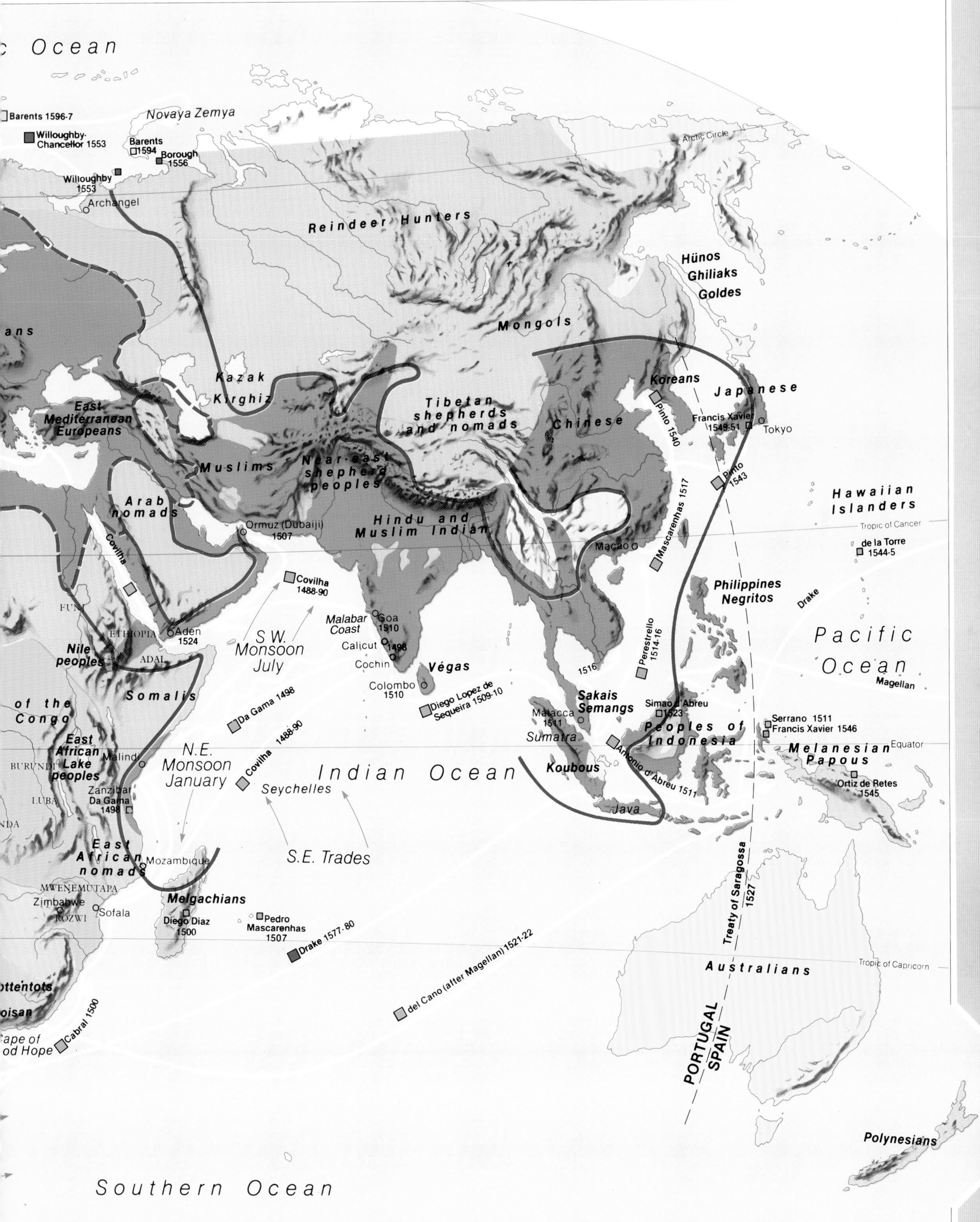

Ocean
Barents 1596-7
Willoughby-Chancellor 1553
Novaya Zemya
Barents 1594
Borough 1556
Willoughby 1553
Archangel
Reindeer Hunters
Hünos
Ghiliaks
Goldes
Mongols
Kazak
Kirghiz
East Mediterranean Europeans
Tibetan shepherds and nomads
Koreans
Japanese
Chinese
Pinto 1540
Francis Xavier 1549-51
Tokyo
Muslims
Near-east shepherd peoples
Pinto 1543
Hawaiian Islanders
Arab nomads
Hindu and Muslim Indian
Mascarenhas 1517
Tropic of Cancer
Ormuz (Dubaiji) 1507
Macao
de la Torre 1544-5
Covilha
Covilha 1488-90
Philippines Negritos
Drake
Malabar Coast
Goa 1510
Aden 1524
S.W. Monsoon July
Calicut
1498
Perestrello 1514-16
Pacific Ocean
Nile peoples
Cochin
Végas
Magellan
Somalis
Colombo 1510
Diego Lopez de Sequeira 1509-10
1516
Sakais Semangs
Simao d'Abreu 1523
of the Congo
Da Gama 1498
Malacca 1511
Serrano 1511
Francis Xavier 1546
Sumatra
Peoples of Indonesia
East African Lake peoples
Malindi
N.E. Monsoon January
Covilha 1488-90
Indian Ocean
Melanesian Papous
Equator
Koubous
Antonio d'Abreu 1511
Zanzibar
Da Gama 1498
Seychelles
Ortiz de Retes 1545
Java
East African nomads
Mozambique
S.E. Trades
Treaty of Saragossa 1527
Zimbabwe
Sofala
Melgachians
Diego Diaz 1500
Pedro Mascarenhas 1507
Drake 1577-80
del Cano (after Magellan) 1521-22
Australians
Tropic of Capricorn
ttentots
oisan
Cabral 1500
ape of od Hope
PORTUGAL
SPAIN
Polynesians
Southern Ocean
Arctic Circle

The age of European supremacy 2

THE EURASIAN LAND EMPIRES

Both China and Japan looked back to the philosophy of Confucius and developed it in different ways into a powerful ideology serving the practical needs of empire.

Above: The Taj Mahal.

37 The Far East in the seventeenth century
The Manchu occupation of China after the fall of the Ming dynasty in 1644, and the establishment of the Tokugawa shogunate in Japan in 1603, installed strong regimes. Both now achieved internal order and prosperity though with social rigidity and deep suspicion of the westerners who were now beginning to appear in the Far East.

38 The Manchu empire at its height
The enormous extension of the Chinese empire under the Manchu dynasty brought an end to the millennial conflict between urban and agrarian China proper and the peoples of the steppes, mountains and forests beyond. A dual political entity came into being: the older (Ming) empire remained under bureaucratic rule while most of the new acquisitions were ruled by the Court of Colonial Affairs (Li-fan-yuan) working through local rulers and chiefs.

In China, Confucianism stood for benevolent and patriarchal bureaucracy with a mildly conservative, conformist and inward-looking stamp. In Japan, by contrast, it was a newer ideology, only officially adopted by the Tokugawa dynasty in the early seventeenth century, expressly imported upon a Chinese model to uphold a warrior aristocracy (turned bureaucracy) and an autocratic emperor (*see Maps 37 and 38*).

Ming China was an impersonal empire. An ambitious, forceful emperor could act decisively but the weight of tradition guarded by the mandarins of the largest and most impressive bureaucracy of the early modern world limited his power. Central government was located in the planned capital of Peking after 1421, and its six ministries supervised major areas of imperial life through a carefully organized provincial administration which extended to the borders of old Han China. Mandarins were recruited nationally through rigorous examinations. Incompetence and corruption were checked by the Office of Censors, to which young bureaucrats were seconded to censure their elders and advance themselves through their zeal and integrity.

The military power of the empire (by contrast) was separate and subordinate. Positions in the army were hereditary, and the quality of the armed forces gradually deteriorated. Troops were stationed defensively along the (partially) reconstructed Great Wall. Although the Tartars advanced to the gates of Peking in 1556, the Ming dynasty was largely spared heavy pressure on its landward frontiers.

The prosperity of the Chinese empire in the sixteenth century reflected its political stability. It was first disrupted by the Japanese invasion of Korea in 1592 and 1597 (*Map 37*). The Japanese were repulsed, but the economic stagnation of many regions in the next century increased the relative cost of the administration, and peasant rebellions enfeebled the central government. The emperor, surrounded by up to 10,000 eunuchs, withdrew to the seclusion of his court, and left power entirely in the hands of a divided bureaucracy. These weaknesses were exploited by the Manchu, militarily formidable neighbours on the north-east border who, partly under Mongol influence, rejected Chinese overlordship about 1609. They took Peking in 1644 and in another four decades had firm control over the whole of China and Taiwan. Whereas the Mongol Yuan dynasty had ruled China through foreigners, the Manchu relied on the established machinery of imperial government to control the former empire, while their vast new territories were ruled by a newly-created Court of Colonial Affairs that worked through local rulers and chiefs (*see Map 38*).

Sixteenth-century Japan was an island kingdom, with no real central government, political stability or civilian rule. In theory sovereignty resided in the emperor, in the court at Kyoto, but in practice power had passed through civil war from the hands of his hereditary military commander (the *shogun*) to local overlords (*daimyos*) who commanded a hereditary caste of warriors (the *samurai*). Under the *daimyos* Japan suffered a century of fierce warfare and shifting allegiances. Powerful Buddhist monasteries and merchant guilds added to the forces of fragmentation, while self-governing leagues of farmers and landowners were formed to resist the *daimyos*.

From this confusion a series of military leaders emerged to attempt, often with great cruelty, to impose their authority upon Japan. Odo Nobunaga took Kyoto in 1568 and destroyed the Buddhist temples, massacring 20,000 monks. His lieutenant and successor Hideyoshi eliminated the remaining opposition, appointed himself chief minister and legalised the position of the *samurai* as an exclusive nobility of the sword. Hideyoshi's ambitious and unsuccessful invasions of Korea failed to consolidate his rule and it was left to his former councillor, Tokugawa Ieyasu (appointed *shogun* in 1603) to complete the work of his predecessors by imitating rather than irritating the Chinese empire. He founded a bureaucracy, imported Confucianism, established a new imperial capital at Edo (Tokyo) and provided the basis for the *Pax Tokugawa* that lasted for two hundred years.

The *Pax Tokugawa* was, like the Manchu dynasty in China, an oriental *ancien regime*. The rigid caste system exploited the peasantry and allowed no social mobility. 'The offspring of a toad is a toad; the offspring of a merchant is a merchant' was the saying in Japan. Japanese towns and merchants benefited particularly from peace. By 1691 Edo, with its population of over half a million, became one of the largest cities in the world. Here, as in other Japanese cities, the wealth of merchant townsmen supported a refined patrician culture, similar to that in the towns of China.

In both China and Japan, the Confucian *ancien regime* excluded Europeans. Portuguese overtures at Canton were rebuffed and only allowed to return to China at Macao in 1557 (*see Maps 36 and 46*). The Dutch operated from Taiwan from 1626 until they were expelled in 1662. Only the Spanish maintained a regular presence for trade at four open coastal ports, and only the Jesuits were allowed into Peking, where they accepted Chinese customs and dressed their Christianity in Confucian disguise until they too were expelled, in the eighteenth century. But their missionary efforts (like Europe's trading ventures) remained superficial. In Japan, the Europeans were initially more successful. From 1540 the Portuguese (exploiting political uncertainty and the dislike of Buddhist monks) established a lucrative trade monopoly based on Nagasaki, and fostered Christian churches and seminaries. Under Tokugawa rule official tolerance quickly diminished; persecution began in 1629. By 1650 some 2000 Christians (including 70 European priests) had been killed. From 1639 trade with outsiders was forbidden except that Chinese and Dutch traders were allowed to call at Nagasaki once a year. China and Japan remained almost closed to the wider world until the nineteenth century, when the impetus of western imperialism destroyed their isolation (*see Map 64*).

The great Islamic powers in the sixteenth and

MAP 37 THE FAR EAST IN THE SEVENTEENTH CENTURY

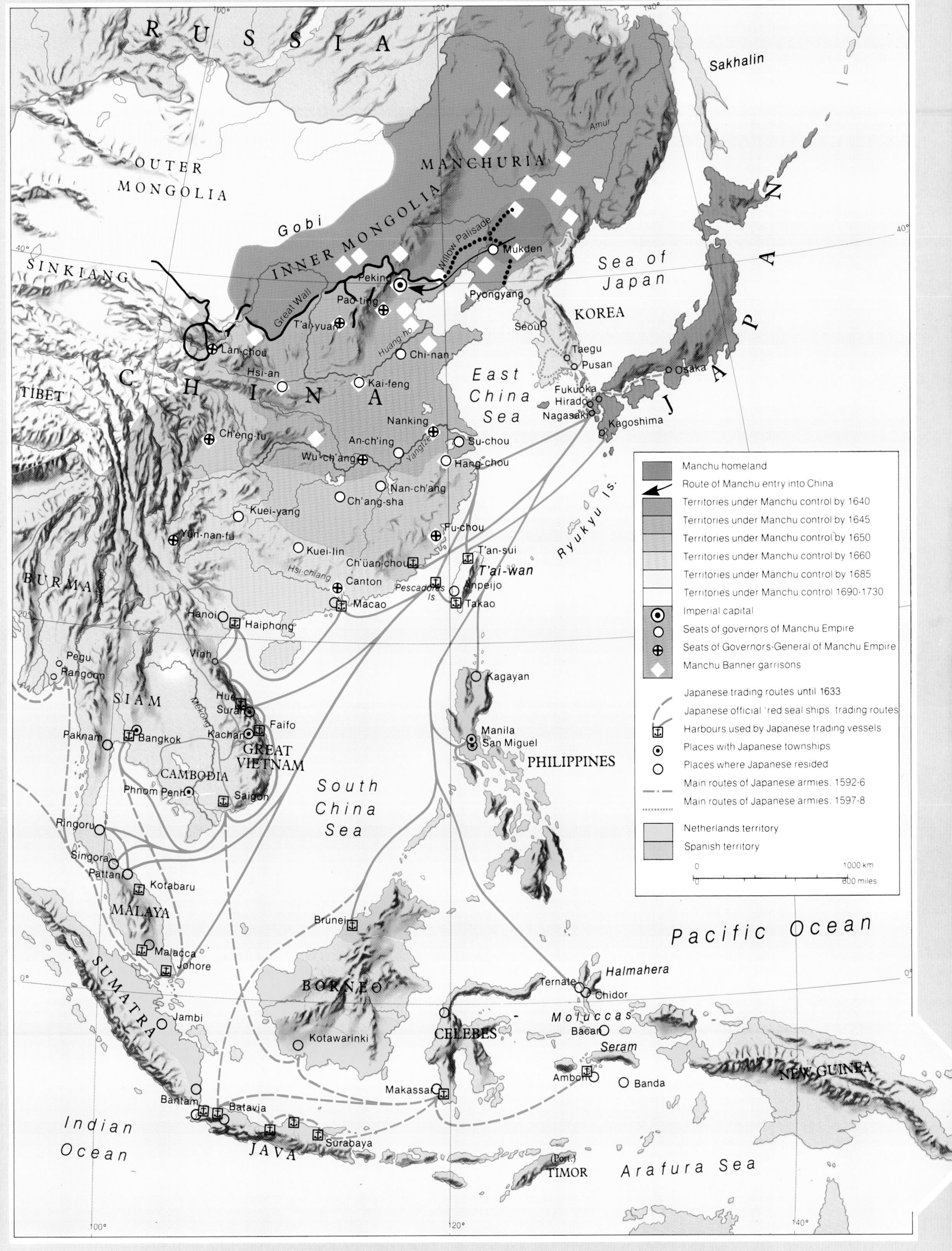

SINO-RUSSIAN TRA
(TEA COTTON CLOTH ETC
FOR FURS ETC.)
L. Balkhash
Tarbagatai
Kobdo
Uliassutai
ZUNGHARIA
(1757)
(MILITARY ADMINISTRATION)
MONGOLIA
(FEUDAL)
Ili
(Hui-yuan)
(Kulja)
Urumchi
Tien Shan
Aqsu
Turfan
Hami
Tarim
Kashgar
EASTERN TURKESTAN
(1759)
(MILITARY ADMINISTRATION)
Yarkand
An-hsi
Etsina
Khotan
Su-chou
Kan-chou
Kunlun Shan
LADAKH
Leh
Tsaidam
Ch'ing-Hai
(Koko Nor)
Hsi-ning
Lan-chou
Indus
TIBET
(1720 to 1751)
(PROTECTORATE)
Ya-lung
Min
Himalayas
Chamdo
Shigatse
Lhasa
Ch'eng-
NEPAL
Katmandu
Ta-chien-lu
SIKKIM
BHUTAN
Darjeeling
Lu-ch
Ganges
Brahmaputra
Ta-li
Teng-yueh
K'un-ming
MIEN-TIEN
(BURMA)
Red
Salween
Mekong
Ava
HSIEN-LO
(SIAM)
Chiao-chou
YEH-NA
(ANNAM)
Provinces included in main economic regions
1 CHIH-LI, SHAN-TUNG, HO-NAN, AN-HUI (partly), CHIANG-SU (partly)
2 SHAN-HSI, SHAAN-HSI (SHENSI), KAN-SU
3 CHIANG-SU (partly), CHE-CHIANG (partly), AN-HUI (partly)
4 CHIANG-HSI, HU-PEI, HU-NAN
5 SSU-CH'UAN
6 CHE'CHIANG (partly), FU-CHIEN, KUANG-TUNG (partly)
7 KUEI-CHOU, YUN-NAN
8 KUANG-TUNG (partly) KUANG-HSI

The Ming Empire c.1600
Regions of the Manchu Empire administered by the Court of Colonial Affairs
Regions acquired by the Manchu, administered by imperial bureaucracy
(1683) Date of establishment of Manchu rule
Tributary states of Manchu Empire
Tributary states of Lhasa
Wall rebuilt late 14th century
Wall rebuilt 15th-16th centuries
Wall rebuilt 16th century
Major imperial courier routes
Maximum time in weeks permitted for mounted courier from Peking
Other courier and trading routes
Willow Palisades (northern limit of legal migration by Han Chinese)
Economic regions: core areas
Economic regions: peripheral areas
Major trading centre
Port open to western trade after 1757
Grand Canal
Desert
500 km
300 miles
I Ironware exporting centre
W Wine exporting centre
P Porcelain exporting centre
S Silk exporting centre
C Cotton exporting centre
SC Silk and cotton exporting centre
MANCHURIA
CHAO-HSIEN (KOREA)
JAPAN
L'IU-CH'IU ISLANDS
T'AI-WAN (1683) (Civil administration)
HAI-NAN
Ördös
PEKING
Nerchinsk
Aigun
Amur
Tsitsihar
Sungari
Chi-lin
Liao
Mukden (Sheng-ching)
Nui-chuang
Yalu
P'ing-jang
Ching-ch'eng
Nagasaki
Je-ho
Kalgan
Sui-yuan
Kuei-hua
T'ien-chin
Pao-ting
Mouth of Huang-ho after 1853
Teng-chou
Cheng-ting
Te-chou
T'ai-yuan
Lin-ch'ing
Chi-nan
Huang-ho
Mouth of Huang-ho before 1853
YANGTZE-MANCHURIA TRADE (COTTON CLOTH AND TEA FOR SOYA BEANS ETC.)
K'ai-feng
Hsu-chou
Huai-an
Hsi-an
Wei
Yang-chou
Han
Nanking
Chen-chiang
Shang-hai
Su-chou
L. T'ai
Sung-chiang
Ho-fei
Hsiang-yang
Hu-chou
Hang-chou
Yangtze
Han-k'ou
An-ch'ing
Chiang-ling
Han-yang
Wu-ch'ang
Shao-hsing
Ning-po
SINO-JAPANESE TRADE (SILKS, SUGAR, DRUGS ETC., FOR COPPER ETC.)
Chiu-chiang
Yo-chou
L. Po-yang
Ching-te-chen
Ch'ang-te
L. Tung-ting
Nan-ch'ang
Wen-chou
Ch'ang-sha
Hsiang-t'an
Kan
Heng-yang
Fu-chou
Ting-chou
Kan-chou
T'AI-WAN – MAINLAND COAL EXPORT TRADE
T'an-sui
Ch'üan-chou
Amoy
Kuei-lin
Hsi-chiang
Chang-chou
Ch'ao-chou
Swatow
Wu-chou
Canton
Hui-chou
Fo-shan
Nan-ning
Macao (Portuguese)
SINO-S.E. ASIAN TRADE (FABRICS, METAL GOODS, PORCELAIN ETC., FOR WOODS, RICE, RAW COTTON ETC.)
SINO-WESTERN TRADE (SILVER OPIUM (ILLEGALLY) ETC., FOR TEAS, SILKS, PORCELAIN)
Chiung-chou

seventeenth centuries were Ottoman Turkey, Safavid Persia and Mughal India (*see Maps 39 and 40*). They had much in common. Each was centred about a great capital city: Istanbul, Isfahan and Delhi. For each, Islam was not only a religion but a social and political code, essentially urban, worn lightly by some of its adherents and subject to some internal dissension, but still a common bond. Each city throughout the Islamic world had its mosque, built on an axis oriented on the heavenly city, Mecca, to which all Muslims turn in prayer. Arabic was a *lingua franca* for religion, government and law.

For all three empires, the sixteenth century was one of creation, growth and consolidation. The Mughal dynasty was founded by Babur (*d.*1530), a military adventurer who saw himself as the heir to the Mongol empire of Chingiz Khan. In 1522, he seized Qandahar, the key to northern India, and took Lahore. Mughal authority was established throughout northern India within four years (*see Map 40*), and reached its height under Akbar (*r.*1556-1605). Similarly, the Ottoman Turks had established themselves in Anatolia, captured Constantinople in 1453 and continued to expand their empire, until it reached its height under Süleyman the Magnificent (*r.*1520-66) (*see Map 39*). He alarmed Christian Europe by capturing Belgrade in 1521 and the island of Rhodes in 1522, arriving at the gates of Vienna in 1529 and 1532. Persia, too, had its Akbar or Süleyman, in Shah Abbas I, known as the Great (*r.*1587-1629), whose reign dominated the memory of Persia through the seventeenth century.

In each case, the easy talent for the absorption of different cultures and racial and ethnic groups characterized these regimes in their early period of expansion (*Map 40*). Akbar I declared himself, in 1572, sole arbiter of religious matters in his realms

MAP 39 THE OTTOMAN TURKS

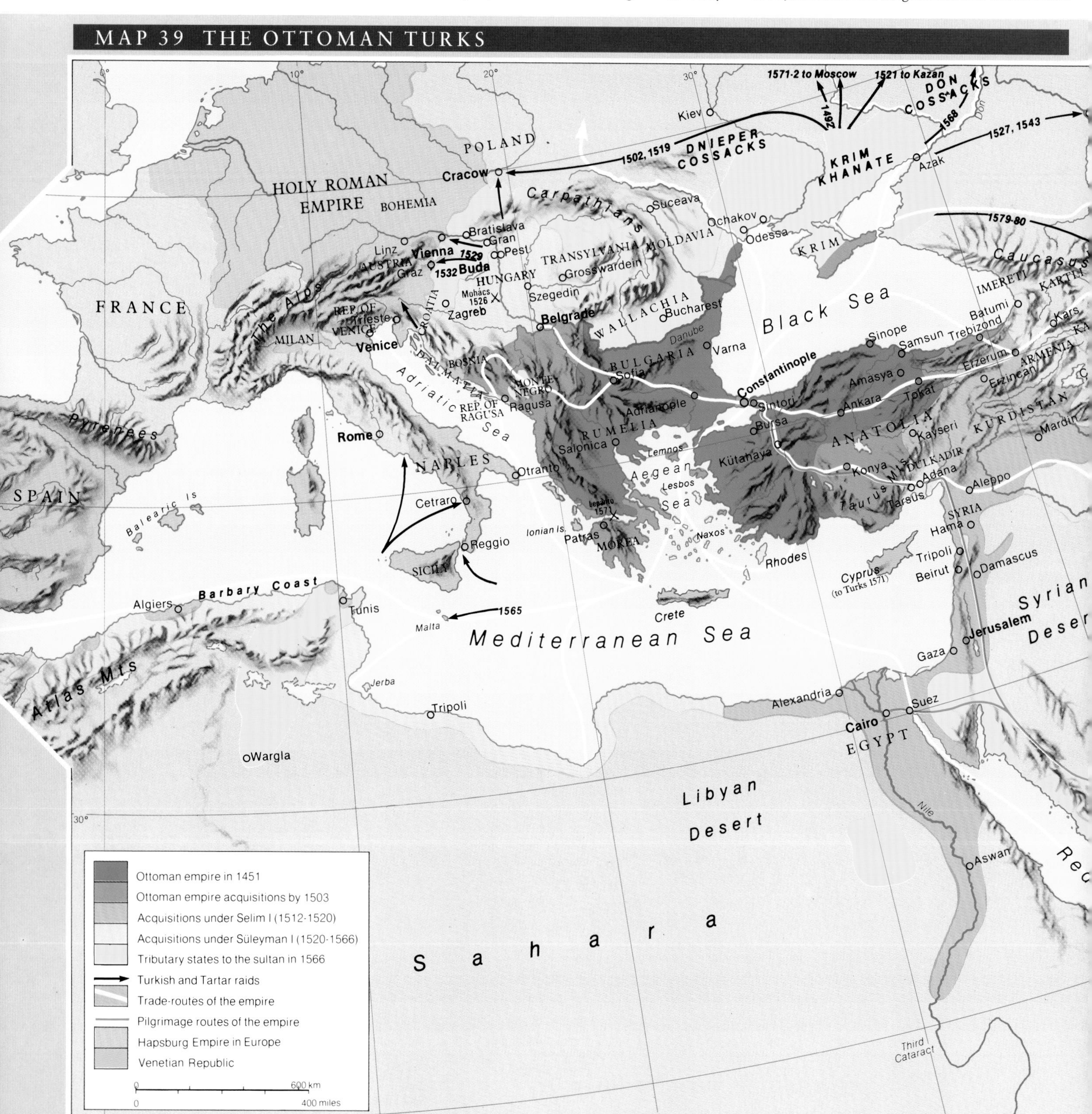

and repealed all discriminatory taxes on racial and religious minorities within the empire. Avowing a policy of toleration, he embarked upon discussions with various religions, including the Portuguese Jesuits, and finally devised a new universal faith. Ottoman Turkey gave the Catholic peasantry of Hungary and the orthodox inhabitants of Greece a welcome release from the seigneurial burdens and intolerance of Reformation Europe. Christians, Muslims and Jews served in the famous slave-based Janissary *corps* of the Ottomans.

Their achievements brought the Muslim powers wealth and sophistication, but also created a burden of empire which could not be indefinitely sustained. Each, in turn, ended its expansion in the seventeenth century with enormous internal problems. Feeding and fuelling their inflated capitals became a major problem in itself when the decline in economic activity in the seventeenth century affected the Islamic empires, as it had done, to a lesser extent, the Oriental ones. Frontiers and the long lines of communication with them were an enduring problem. The Mughal Jahangir sent his armies into the Deccan, which all Mughal emperors aspired to conquer, and which became the obsession of his successor in the decade 1670-80 (*see Map 40*). The Mughals also struggled with military potentates in irrepressible Bengal and worried over the frontier city of Qandahar. In Persia Shah Abbas was forced into offensive war in Khorasan. Even Süleyman the Magnificent admitted defeat outside Vienna and for the most part in the western Mediterranean. His Ottoman successors were forced to loosen their grip on Algiers and Tunis, suffered rebuffs from the Muscovites on the Steppes, saw Cossack oarsmen in the Bosphorus and were troubled by insubordinate tributary princes in Transylvania.

In the face of these problems, each empire in its turn looked to autocracy, centralization and militarism as the immediate solution. But structural change did not come easily. In the Ottoman empire, the Janissaries rebelled frequently (the outbursts were customarily announced by the overturning of the barrack-room soup-cauldron). In Persia, Shah Abbas' standing army of Christians from Georgia and the Caucasus also rebelled. Centralization caused provincial rebellions, such as those in Wallachia, Moldavia and Turkestan in the Ottoman empire and Bengal in the Mughal empire. These revolts were serious because provincial governors exploited them to influence the imperial succession. Across the Islamic world, court intrigue surrounding the succession of the shah, sultan or emperor was a constant danger. There was no formal law of succession in any of the empires. Emperors existed by right of conquest and survived by their ability to eliminate rivals. The harems of the ruler ensured a regular supply of pretenders, and brutal practices were adopted to limit them. The Ottomans had law which allowed successful

Above right: The Khân of Khurâsân on his return to Persia after being defeated by Shah Jehan, whose Taj Mahal at Agra (completed in 1648) can be seen in the background.

39 The Ottoman Turks
The Ottoman challenge to Christendom began in the early fourteenth century. The capture of Constantinople in 1553 was followed by increasingly rapid expansion until the empire reached its strategic limits under Süleyman the Magnificent (*r.* 1520-66).

40 The India of the Mughals
Between 1526 and 1636 the Mughals, from a base in Afghanistan, acquired control over most of the Indian subcontinent by seizing military and administrative centres along the main trade routes. Until the reign of Aurangzeb (*r.* 1668-1707) a balance between its various peoples was maintained in their administration; thereafter growing disunity and disaffection among the ruling élites undermined Mughal control, to the benefit of the intruding European powers.

41 The rise of Muscovy
Moscow's position at the intersection of the great trade routes and the ruthless determination of its Grand Dukes to subordinate every resource and institution to their power, suppress their fellow princes and shake off the rule of the Mongols (to whom Ivan III stopped paying tribute in 1480) made Moscow the unchallenged centre of the emergent Russian empire.

The ethnic composition of the Mughal service elite (mansabdars)
1595
1656
1678-1707
Hindu
Muslim
Turanis
Iranis
Rajputs
Marathas
Other Hindus
Other Muslims
Indian Muslims
Afghans
Arabian Sea
Bay of Bengal
Hindu Kush
Himalayas
Western Ghats
Eastern Ghats
Rise of the Mughals
Mughal centres with date of annexation:
Administrative, military and economic
Administrative and military
Strongholds of Deccan sultanates:
Bijapur
Bijapur, acquired from Vijayanagar, 1638-50
Golkonda
Golkonda, acquired from Vijayanagar, 1642-52
Annexed by Mughals with dates
Other Vijayanagar centres after 1565
Decline of the Mughals
Marathas, c. 1680
Marathas, c. 1750
Autonomous by c. 1765 under Nawwabs
Autonomous by c. 1765 under non-Muslim chiefs
BIHAR Mughal provinces lost to central control by c. 1750
European trading settlements
Principal trade routes
Places of industrial or commercial importance
0 500 km
0 300 miles
C Calico
Ch Chintz
Co Cottons
D Diamonds
I Indigo
Me Metalcraft
Mu Muslins
P Pepper
S Saltpetre
Sa Satin
Si Silk
Sp Spices
Su Sugar
T Tapestries
Te Textiles
W Weaving

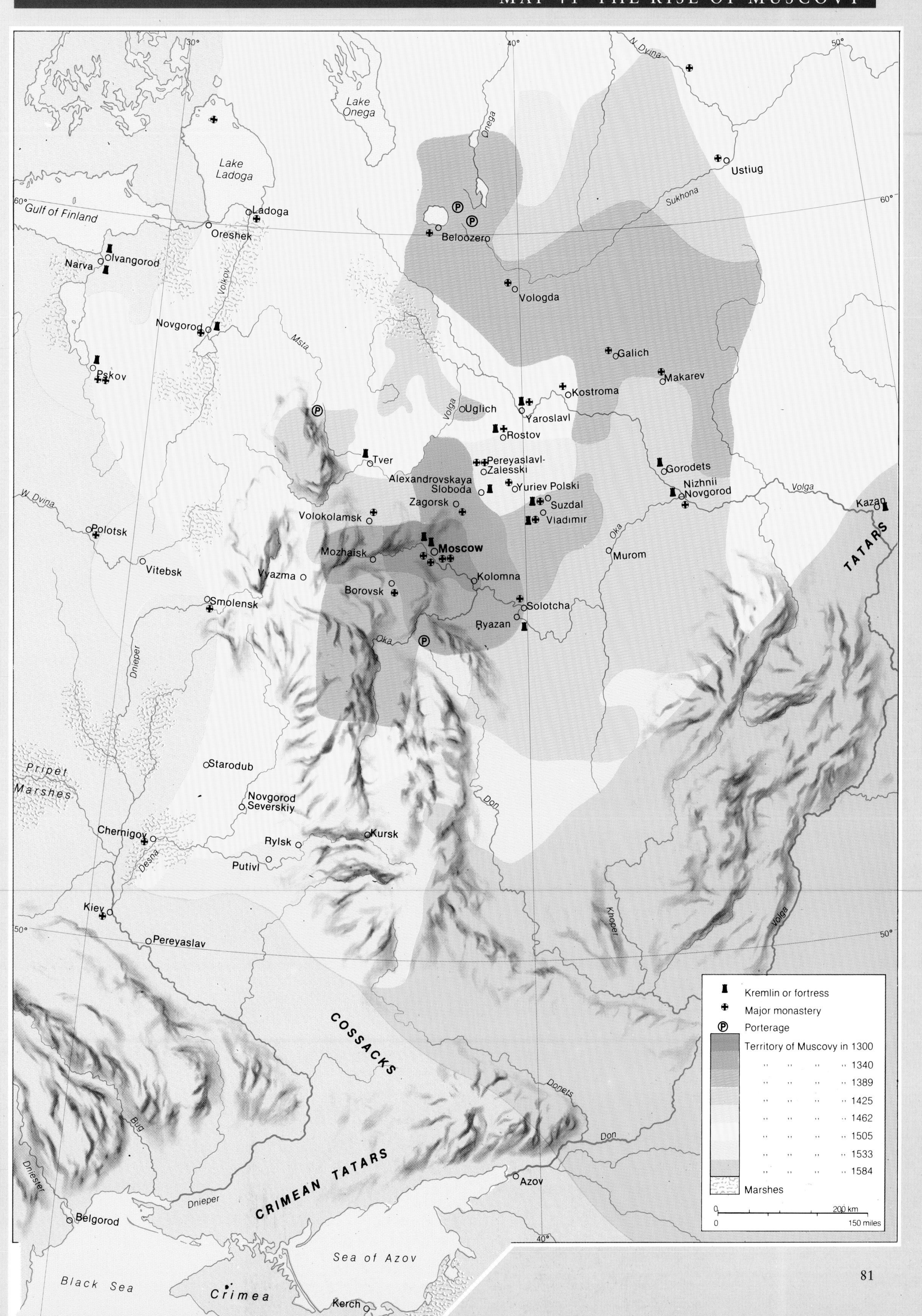
Lake Onega
Lake Ladoga
Gulf of Finland
Ladoga
Oreshek
Ivangorod
Narva
Novgorod
Pskov
Beloozero
Vologda
Ustiug
Sukhona
N. Dvina
Onega
Volkov
Msta
Galich
Makarev
Kostroma
Uglich
Yaroslavl
Rostov
Tver
Pereyaslavl-Zalesski
Alexandrovskaya Sloboda
Yuriev Polski
Gorodets
Nizhnii Novgorod
Suzdal
Vladimir
Zagorsk
Volokolamsk
Kazan
TATARS
Volga
W. Dvina
Polotsk
Mozhaisk
Moscow
Vitebsk
Vyazma
Kolomna
Murom
Oka
Smolensk
Borovsk
Solotcha
Ryazan
Dnieper
Starodub
Pripet Marshes
Novgorod Severskiy
Don
Chernigov
Desna
Rylsk
Kursk
Putivl
Kiev
Pereyaslav
Khoper
COSSACKS
Donets
Bug
Dniester
CRIMEAN TATARS
Azov
Belgorod
Sea of Azov
Black Sea
Crimea
Kerch
Kremlin or fortress
Major monastery
Porterage
Territory of Muscovy in 1300
1340
1389
1425
1462
1505
1533
1584
Marshes
200 km
150 miles

emperors to put their rival to death by strangulation with a silken bow-string. The Mughals tried to ensure a clear succession by nomination, but their efforts were ruined by ambition or bad blood. In Persia the practice of blinding royal princes who were potential contenders grew up from the end of the sixteenth century, and later both Persia and Turkey adopted the formal imprisonment of every heir to the throne. Enforced seclusion and incarceration led to a observable decline in the quality of their rulers.

The Islamic empires began to quarrel amongst themselves. War between Persia and the Ottomans, intermittent from 1502 onwards, became more violent in the seventeenth century. In the process the Islamic state adopted more exclusive ideologies; the Sunnite faith was preferred by the Ottomans and Shi'ite orthodoxy by the Persians. Both became less inclined to tolerate Christian and Jewish minorities. A rebellion among the Christians of Greece brought the European fleet (against orders) to Lepanto, where it won the sixteenth century's greatest offensive victory against the Ottomans. European merchants could not be excluded from the Islamic capitals, whose lavish tastes demanded fine cloth and precious metals. In their wake, later in the seventeenth century, came the rising military and naval power of Europe, whose colonial expansion the Islamic powers would find difficult to resist.

Despite the absorption of many Slavs into the Ottoman and Hapsburg empires, and the subjection of others to the Tartars, two separate Slav empires existed in the early modern world. On the borders of Europe Poland stretched from the Baltic to the Black Sea, while under Ivan III (*r. 1462-1505*) the Grand Duchy of Muscovy threw off the Tartar yoke and made Moscow the centre of a Russian empire (*see Maps 41 and 50*). Both states

MAP 42 THE HAPSBURG EMPIRE

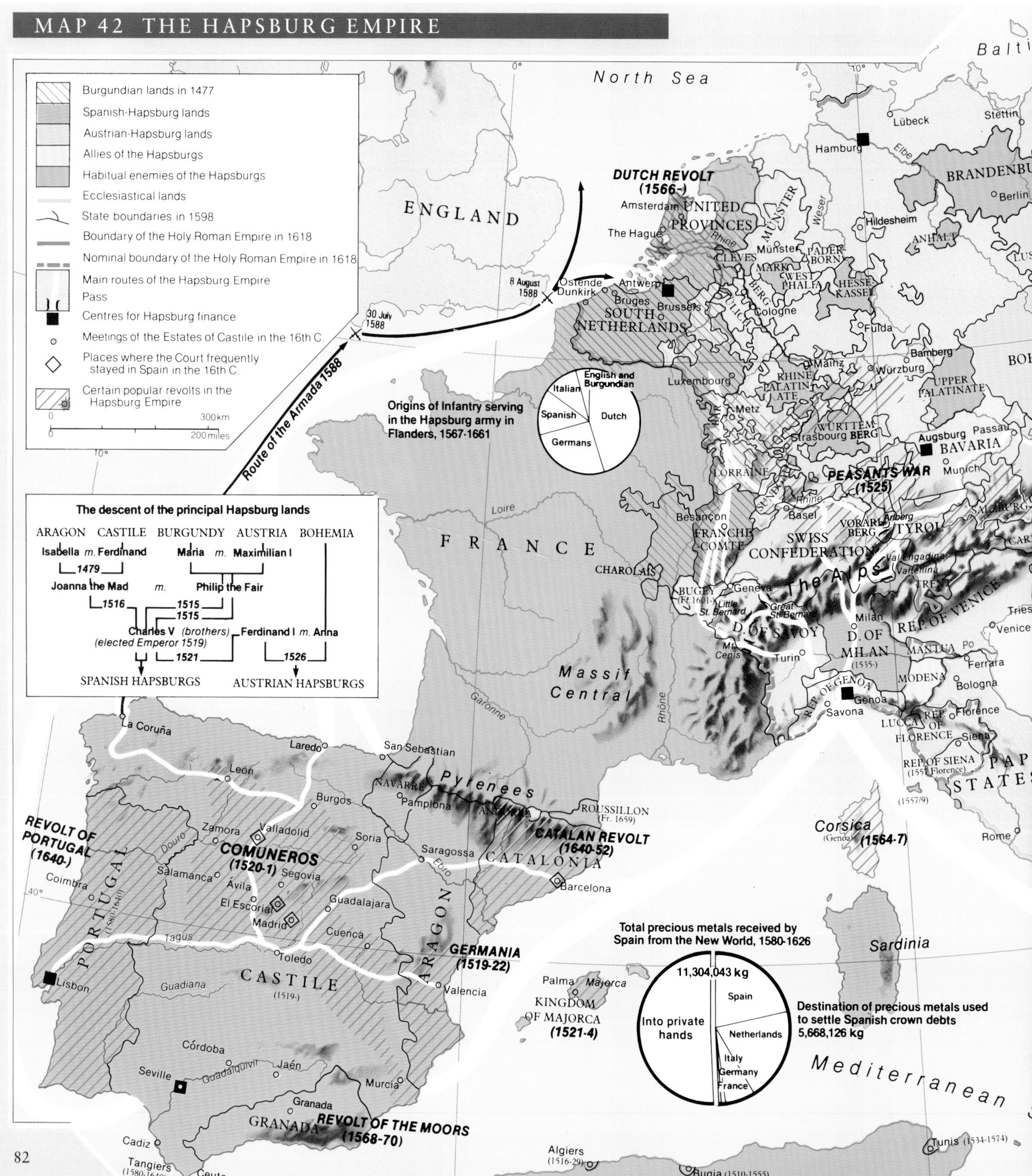

expanded during the sixteenth century. In 1569 the kingdom of Poland, endowed with strong representative institutions, a vigorous aristocracy and (until 1572) a hereditary monarchy of the European kind, joined in a condominium with the Grand Duchy of Lithuania, to which it had been driven closer by the common threat from Muscovy. The expansion of Muscovy was far more remarkable. The whole area around the independent city of Novgorod was subjugated in 1478, the Kazan Khanate in 1552, and Astrakhan in 1556. From the accession of Ivan IV in 1553 the realm of Muscovy expanded in each year by an area equal to the size of Holland until, by 1600, it was as large as the whole of Europe.

Prosperity encouraged expansion. Russia gained the route across the Urals to Siberia and control of the Volga and the routes to the Caspian Sea, and would have liked a port on the Baltic. Russian fur-trappers moved easily across Siberia and by the middle of the seventeenth century reached the Pacific Coast and the borders of China (*see Map 70*). New towns were established on the Volga and Belaya as visible signs of the wealth of the silk, rug and precious metals trade with Persia. Meanwhile Poland extended its authority over the old Hanseatic ports of the Baltic, Danzig and Riga, (*Map 50*) and the resulting prosperity was demonstrated in newly founded universities, churches and printing presses.

The foundations of Russia were entirely different from those of Poland. The essence of the Russian state lay in its patrimonialism. The tsars (as the grand dukes styled themselves officially from 1547, to emphasize their legendary descent from a brother of the Emperor Augustus) stressed that, on their hereditary lands, they were *gosudar*, supreme lord, ruler, autocrat. The land stewards of the patrimony (the *votchina*) provided the basis for the expanded and from the 1550s reorganized state officialdom (the *prikazi*). Trade in the Duchy had always been the private possession of the grand dukes and the tsars extended this monopoly over wholesale commerce and the manufacturing and mining industries of Russia at large.

Outside the domain of the grand dukes of Muscovy were the lands of the *boyars* (the aristocracy) and the Church. Since feudalism had never been established in Russia there was no vassalage or conditional land tenure to provide a law common to the aristocracy and the tsar. As Moscow extended its influence the *boyars* were gradually subjected to the will of the tsar, beginning in the 1470s when Ivan III denied their freedom to serve another prince. In the sixteenth century the tsars created new nobles and rewarded loyal service. In 1564 Ivan IV (the 'Terrible') divided the country clearly between his domain (*oprichnina*) and the rest (*zenichina*) so that in the former he could enforce his authority more vigorously. *Oprichniki*, a group of tsar's bailiffs, were permitted to abuse or kill the *boyars* in the domain with impunity, and to loot their properties. Although the *oprichniki* were withdrawn in 1572 the power of the *boyars* was destroyed and private land in secular hands no longer played a significant role in Muscovite Russia. The Church retained its wealth, and the monasteries and kremlins (some of which were designed by German military engineers) of the duchy of Moscow provided a solid base for the government and internal security of the tsars. The Russian Orthodox church, with its own patriarchal structure, fitted well with the tsars' pretensions, and each reinforced the authority of the other.

Conquered territories were treated as the tsar's patrimony. Independent cities such as Novgorod lost their privileges, and mass deportations, which became common in the expansion of Russia, emphasized that, as a German traveller remarked in the middle of the sixteenth century, 'All the people consider themselves *kholops*, that is slaves of their Prince'. Serfdom also spread outwards from the patrimony of the tsar, where no peasant considered himself the owner of land or property. As peasants seized the opportunities which expansion offered to abandon the domain and colonize the new territories of the Kazan and Astrakhan the tsars abandoned the custom which had given peasants freedom to leave their masters on one day in each year, began to keep a close watch on their debts and dues, made systematic enquiries of their own rights and finally, in 1592, introduced serfdom. Most Russian peasants had become serfs by 1650.

By prodigious efforts and at great cost the tsars transformed Russia into a gigantic royal domain. The costs were highest in the seventeenth century. Dynastic uncertainties, peasant rebellions, revolts of the Cossacks to the south and of Lithuanians to the west, produced civil disturbance beside which that of Europe at the same time pales into insignificance. In the long run the autocratic system of the tsars emerged victorious, and under Peter 'the Great' (*r.*1682-1725) the Russian *ancien regime* began.

Not so in Poland. The Lithuanian-Polish condominium collapsed three years after it was established. With the extinction of the Jagiellonian dynasty, Poland adopted an elective kingship (in form rather like that of the neighbouring Holy Roman Empire) but without a strong, well-endowed dynasty like the Hapsburgs to give it direction and muscle (*compare Map 42*). In the elections of the following centuries members of the European ruling dynasties were chosen as kings and pursued their own dynastic interests to the detriment of Polish peace and security. Poland's magnates (unlike the *boyars*) successfully defended their individual patrimonies and held the great offices of state. In a state racially, culturally, religiously, ethnically and politically divided, the monarch's authority rapidly gave way to the creeping political paralysis (disguised by the weaknesses common to all states in the seventeenth century and by a certain tolerance born of potential anarchy) which became evident in the eighteenth century and would make Poland the despair of the *philosophes* and the prey of the autocrats.

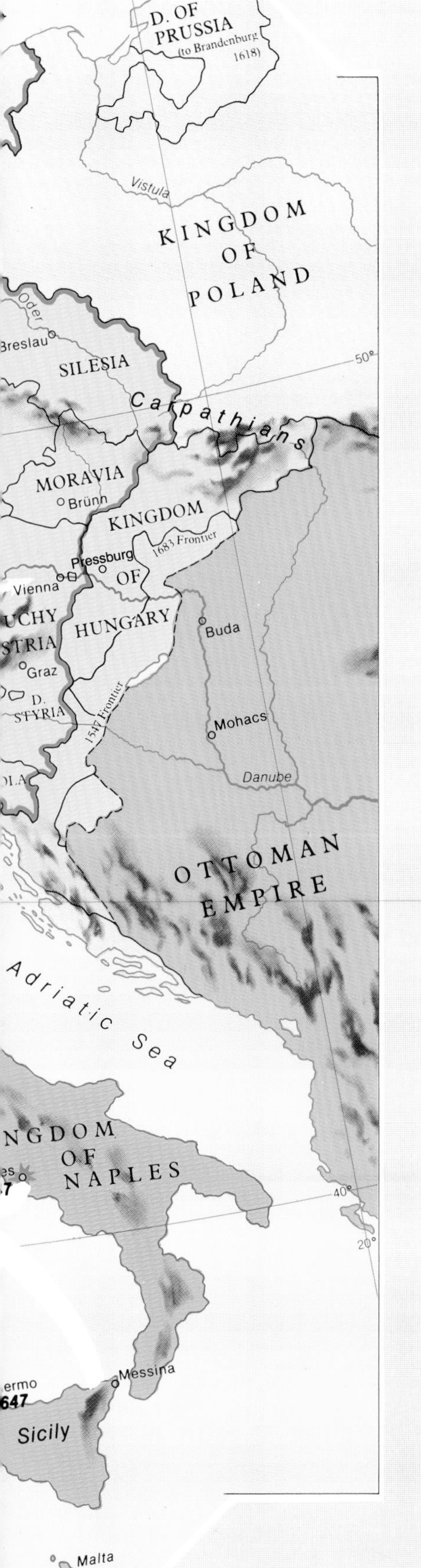

42 The Hapsburg empire
The devolution of the succession to four royal houses on Charles of Hapsburg between 1515 and 1519 and his election as Holy Roman Emperor in 1519 created a unique empire. Its territorial extent, claim to absolute rulership and championship of Catholicism threatened almost every interest and made it the focus of European politics for the next two hundred years.

Further reading: Jonathan Spence, *Emperor of China* (Cape, 1974; Random House); Susan Naquin and Evelyn S. Rawski, *Chinese Society in the Eighteenth Century* (Yale U.P. 1987); Conrad Totman, *Japan Before Perry* (University of California Press 1981); Francis S. Robinson, *Atlas of the Islamic World since 1500* (Phaidon 1982; Facts on File); Richard E. Pipes, *Russia under the Old Regime* (Weidenfeld and Nicolson 1974; Scribner); F. Braudel, *The Mediterranean and the Mediterranean World in the Age of Phillip II* (2 vols, Collins 1972-3; Harper Collins).

The age of European supremacy 3

COLONIES AND COMMERCE

43 Colonization and settlement in South America
The Americas continued to offer apparently limitless land for colonization until the end of the nineteenth century, and in the Amazon basin until the present day. This map shows the start of the process, under Europe's first colonial powers. The diagram indicating populations refers to the Indian population of North and South America combined.

44 Colonization and settlement in North America
The colonization of North America began later than that of South, and more powers participated in it. The Caribbean became the centre of the most intensive competition between them; England was the main beneficiary and Spain, the original colonizing power in central America, the main loser.

45 Slave economies of the Western Hemisphere
Reliance on imported slave labour was reflected in the changing patterns of crops and industries in the New World, each shown here at its period of greatest activity as well as in regional variation. The early closure of the trade to the United States deprived its slave population of the unsubdued reinforcements from Africa who contributed significantly to the revolts endemic elsewhere.

46 Trade and dominion
The major European powers had established their colonial spheres of influence by 1750, and the colonies were returning substantial profits. Sugar, slaves and spices were among the most lucrative commodities, and North America, the Caribbean and India the principal theatres of wars to control them.

The first European colonial empire was that of Spain. By 1600 it was the largest and the most populous and productive.

Theoretically, the Spanish crown claimed sovereignty over the Americas west of the line laid down by the treaty of Tordesillas in 1494 (*see Map 36*). In practice, wealth was concentrated in the fertile areas in central and southern America where the ranching of cattle and the cutting of woodland provided the basic necessities for the colonies. Except by the Jesuits, there was little settlement northwards from Mexico or eastwards from Peru. The ranch (or *hacienda*) became the chief productive unit. The other industry was silver, mined by Spaniards and Indians and requiring extensive initial investment. Neither *hacienda* nor mine employed Indians as slaves. A debate amongst theologians at Salamanca in 1550 had decreed that American Indians were not (the term was borrowed from Aristotle's *Politics*) 'slaves', although African natives were.

By 1700, the Spanish empire had suffered infringements. Portuguese smugglers had established themselves at the mouth of the Río de la Plata, a vital trade route through southern America to upper Peru. With Spanish encouragement the Jesuits colonized the wild Indian country in central southern America and reduced Uruguay to an ordered buffer-state. In the Caribbean, Dutch, English and French buccaneers plundered Spanish trade from Curaçao (which itself became Dutch from 1634), Jamaica (English from 1655) and Santo Domingo (French from 1665). But territorial losses were trifling and the Spanish remained the masters of the trade in the Pacific throughout the eighteenth century (*see Map 46*).

The problems of Spain's colonies were not territorial but structural and economic. Spanish trade across the Atlantic became depressed in the decade 1610 to 1620, and remained acutely so for the rest of the century. The interlocking economy of ranches, mines and plantations went into a severe recession, partly as a result of the depletion of the Indian population through plagues and a resulting acute shortage of labour (*Map 43*). The cost of mining and transporting silver outweighed the profit, so that the volume of silver produced reached its peak in the 1580s and dropped to its lowest point for a century in the 1650s. The colonies imported less from the Old World as they became self-sufficient. What trade there was ceased to benefit the merchants of Seville, who found themselves paying heavily for protection against piracy, attacked by the Inquisition for their suspect religious (or racial) background, and required to advance large sums of money to a rapacious Spanish monarchy, to keep its Catholic court solvent and its wars with the heretics active. The profits of the Spanish empire passed to smugglers who paid no duties and who were not obsessed by bullion, being prepared to take their returns in bulk cargoes such as sugar, hides and tallow.

The Portuguese overseas empire suffered the territorial depredations that the Spanish empire largely escaped. From 1580 to 1640, Portugal was politically united with Spain and, under the union, Portugal gained little and lost much (*Map 42*). Her colonies were able to trade only to a limited extent with those of Spain. Portuguese merchants found themselves harassed by the Inquisition, and taxed to pay for the Hapsburg's dynastic ambitions while her colonies, fair game to Spain's enemies, enjoyed no effective protection. Ceylon and Malacca were captured by the Dutch (*Map 37*); Goa declined to insignificance; African Guinea and Angola were conquered and a profitable strip of northern Brazil was also annexed by the Dutch.

But, unlike those of the Spanish empire, the merchants of Lisbon (in collaboration with the new, independent House of Braganza) adapted, developed and strengthened what was left to them after 1640. They quickly regained Angola and expelled the Dutch from Brazil (*Map 43*). There, in the northern captaincies of Bahía and Pernambuco, João IV, the first Braganza king, established sugar cane. Northern Europe in particular was sugar-starved and in the seventeenth century the plantations of Brazil, equipped with elaborate mechanical gins and refineries, supplied Europe with enough sugar to turn the product from an aristocratic delicacy into something of popular consumption. Sugar became the first trans-oceanic bulk cargo.

To operate the mills and tend and cut the cane required slave-labour. Sugar and slavery were, from the beginning, intimately associated (*Map*

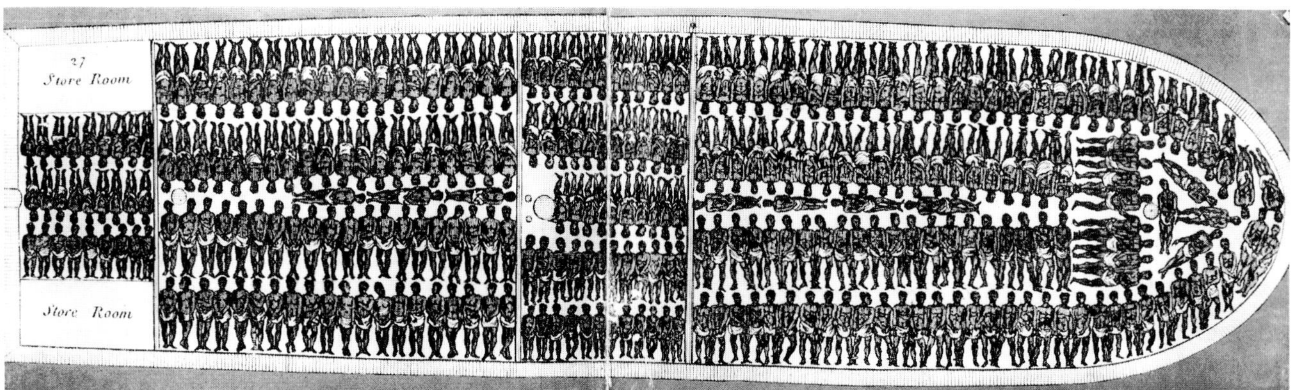

Left: A plan for a slave ship (*c.*1790). A well-designed slaver could carry as many as six hundred people, with virtually every inch of the hold filled with the living cargo.

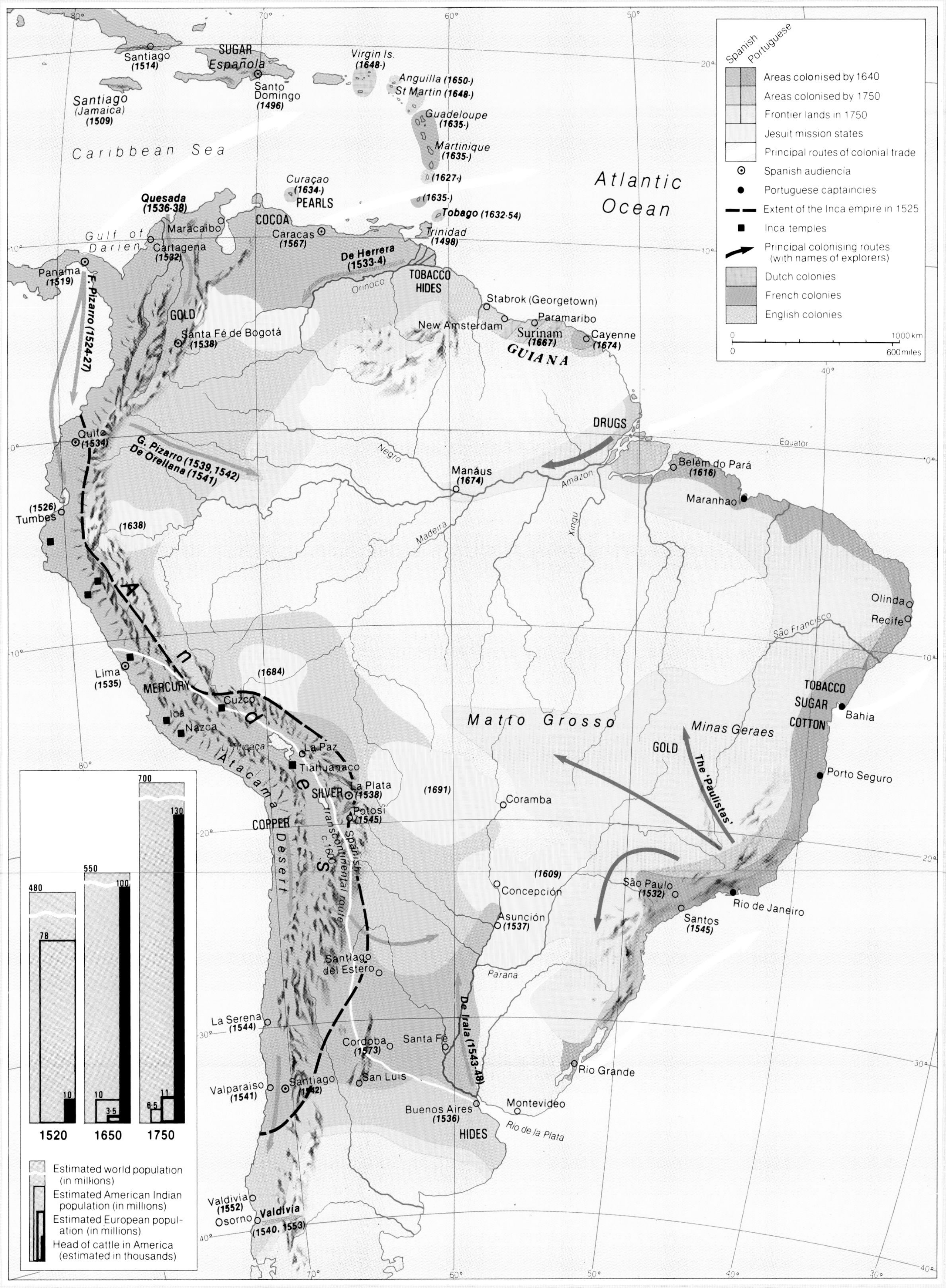

Areas colonised by 1640
Areas colonised by 1750
Frontier lands in 1750
Jesuit mission states
Principal routes of colonial trade
Spanish audiencia
Portuguese captaincies
Extent of the Inca empire in 1525
Inca temples
Principal colonising routes (with names of explorers)
Dutch colonies
French colonies
English colonies
Spanish
Portuguese
Caribbean Sea
Atlantic Ocean
Santiago (1514)
SUGAR
Española
Santo Domingo (1496)
Santiago (Jamaica) (1509)
Virgin Is. (1648-)
Anguilla (1650-)
St Martin (1648-)
Guadeloupe (1635-)
Martinique (1635-)
Curaçao (1634-)
PEARLS
Tobago (1632-54)
Trinidad (1498)
Quesada (1536-38)
Maracaibo
COCOA
Caracas (1567)
Gulf of Darien
Cartagena (1532)
Panama (1519)
De Herrera (1533-4)
TOBACCO
HIDES
Orinoco
Stabrok (Georgetown)
Paramaribo
New Amsterdam
Surinam (1667)
Cayenne (1674)
GUIANA
F. Pizarro (1524-27)
GOLD
Santa Fé de Bogotá (1538)
DRUGS
Quito (1534)
G. Pizarro (1539, 1542)
De Orellana (1541)
Negro
Manáus (1674)
Amazon
Belém do Pará (1616)
Maranhão
Equator
Tumbes (1526)
(1638)
Madeira
Xingu
Olinda
Recife
São Francisco
Andes
Lima (1535)
MERCURY
(1684)
Cuzco
Ica
Nazca
Titicaca
La Paz
Tiahuanaco
Atacama Desert
La Plata (1538)
SILVER
Potosí (1545)
COPPER
Spanish transcontinental route c.1600
(1691)
Matto Grosso
Minas Geraes
GOLD
The 'Paulistas'
TOBACCO
SUGAR
COTTON
Bahia
Porto Seguro
Coramba
(1609)
Concepción
Asunción (1537)
São Paulo (1532)
Santos (1545)
Rio de Janeiro
Santiago del Estero
Parana
La Serena (1544)
Cordoba (1573)
Santa Fé
De Irala (1543-48)
San Luis
Valparaiso (1541)
Santiago (1542)
Rio Grande
Montevideo
Buenos Aires (1536)
HIDES
Rio de la Plata
Valdivia (1552)
Osorno
Valdivia (1540, 1553)
480
78
10
550
100
10
3·5
700
130
6·5
11
1520
1650
1750
Estimated world population (in millions)
Estimated American Indian population (in millions)
Estimated European population (in millions)
Head of cattle in America (estimated in thousands)

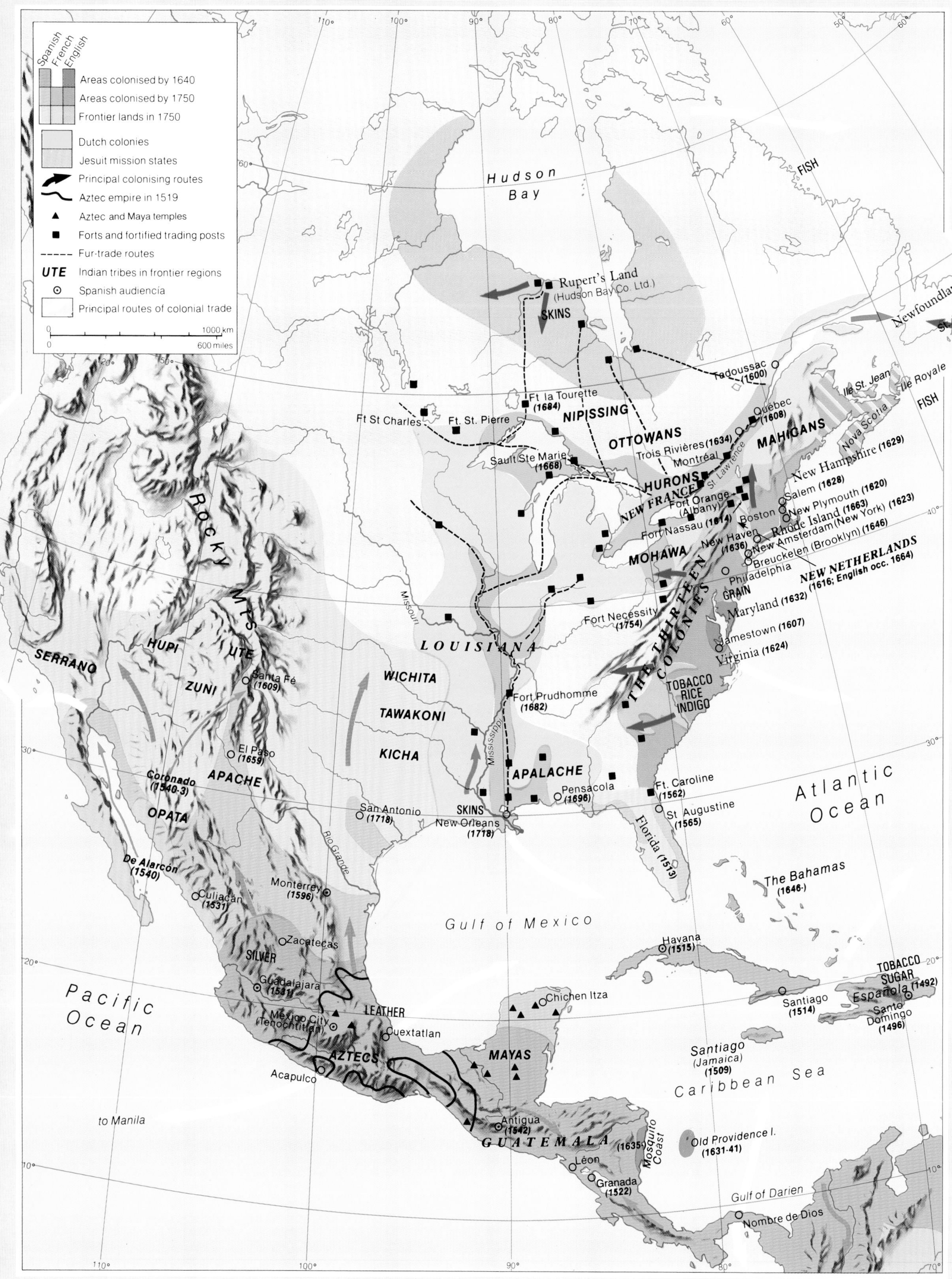
Spanish
French
English
Areas colonised by 1640
Areas colonised by 1750
Frontier lands in 1750
Dutch colonies
Jesuit mission states
Principal colonising routes
Aztec empire in 1519
Aztec and Maya temples
Forts and fortified trading posts
Fur-trade routes
UTE Indian tribes in frontier regions
Spanish audiencia
Principal routes of colonial trade
0 1000 km
0 600 miles
Hudson Bay
Rupert's Land (Hudson Bay Co. Ltd.)
SKINS
FISH
Newfoundland
St. John
Tadoussac (1600)
Ile St. Jean
Ile Royale
Nova Scotia
Québec (1608)
Trois Rivières (1634)
Montréal
St. Lawrence
MAHICANS
New Hampshire (1629)
Salem (1628)
New Plymouth (1620)
Boston
Rhode Island (1663)
New Amsterdam (New York) (1623)
Breuckelen (Brooklyn) (1646)
New Haven (1636)
NEW NETHERLANDS (1616; English occ. 1664)
Philadelphia
GRAIN
Maryland (1632)
Jamestown (1607)
Virginia (1624)
TOBACCO RICE INDIGO
THE THIRTEEN COLONIES
Ft la Tourette (1684)
NIPISSING
OTTOWANS
Ft St Charles
Ft. St. Pierre
Sault Ste Marie (1668)
HURONS
NEW FRANCE
Fort Orange (Albany)
Fort Nassau (1614)
MOHAWA
Fort Necessity (1754)
Rocky Mts
Missouri
LOUISIANA
WICHITA
TAWAKONI
KICHA
Fort Prudhomme (1682)
Mississippi
APALACHE
Pensacola (1696)
Ft. Caroline (1562)
St Augustine (1565)
Florida (1513)
Atlantic Ocean
SKINS
New Orleans (1718)
San Antonio (1718)
Rio Grande
SERRANO
HUPI
UTE
ZUNI
Santa Fé (1609)
El Paso (1659)
Coronado (1540-3)
APACHE
OPATA
De Alarcón (1540)
Monterrey (1596)
Culiacán (1531)
Gulf of Mexico
The Bahamas (1646-)
Zacatecas
SILVER
Havana (1515)
TOBACCO SUGAR
Española (1492)
Santo Domingo (1496)
Santiago (1514)
Pacific Ocean
Guadalajara (1531)
LEATHER
Mexico City (Tenochtitlan)
Cuextatlan
Chichen Itza
MAYAS
AZTECS
Acapulco
Santiago (Jamaica) (1509)
Caribbean Sea
to Manila
Antigua (1542)
GUATEMALA
(1635)
Mosquito Coast
Old Providence I. (1631-41)
Léon
Granada (1522)
Gulf of Darien
Nombre de Dios

MAP 45 SLAVE ECONOMIES OF THE WESTERN HEMISPHERE

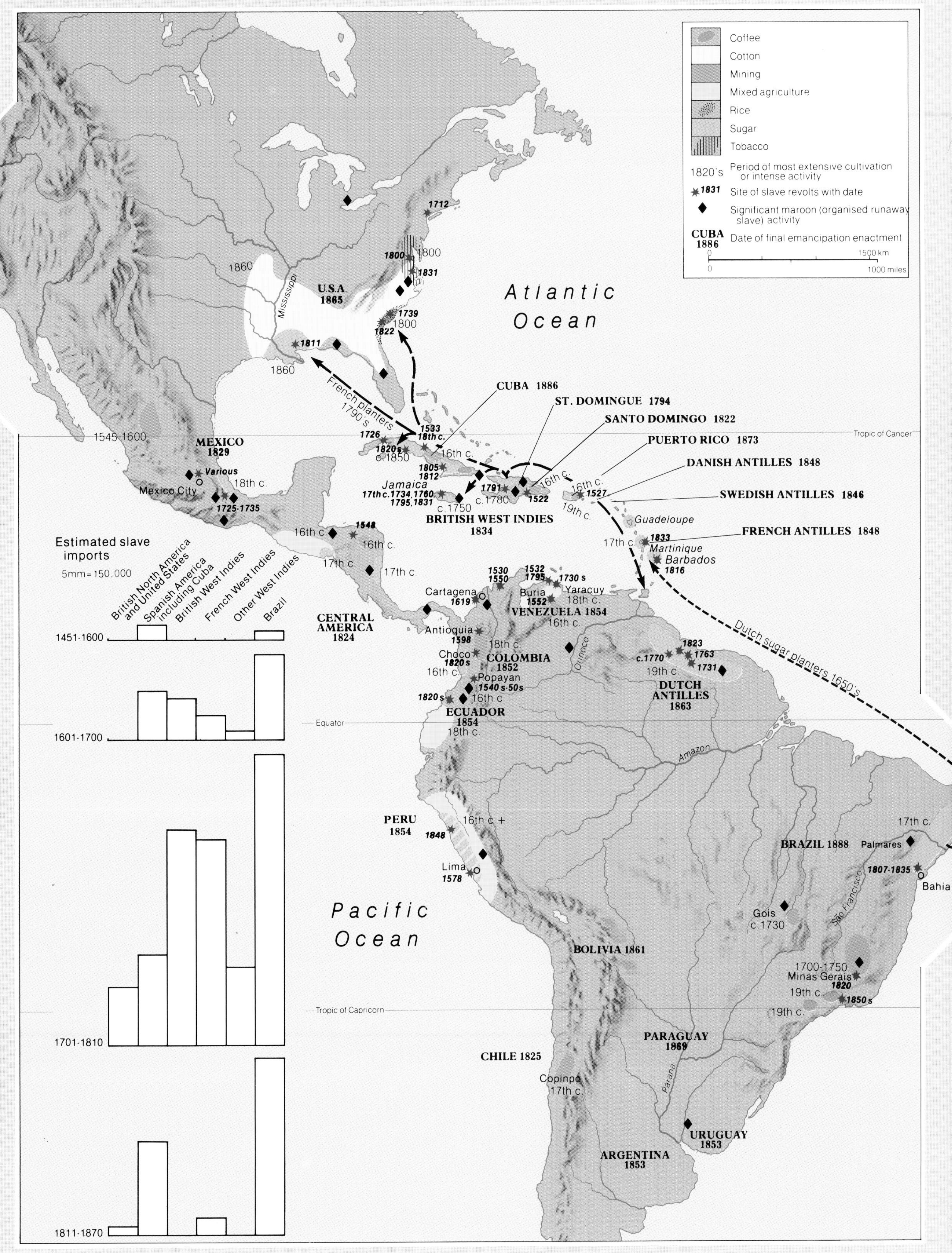

Coffee
Cotton
Mining
Mixed agriculture
Rice
Sugar
Tobacco
1820's Period of most extensive cultivation or intense activity
1831 Site of slave revolts with date
Significant maroon (organised runaway slave) activity
CUBA 1886 Date of final emancipation enactment
1500 km
1000 miles
Atlantic Ocean
Pacific Ocean
Tropic of Cancer
Equator
Tropic of Capricorn
U.S.A. 1865
Mississippi
1860
1712
1800
1831
1739
1822
1811
French planters 1790's
CUBA 1886
ST. DOMINGUE 1794
SANTO DOMINGO 1822
PUERTO RICO 1873
DANISH ANTILLES 1848
SWEDISH ANTILLES 1846
FRENCH ANTILLES 1848
Guadeloupe
Martinique
Barbados
1816
1833
1527
19th c.
16th c.
1533
18th c.
1726
1820s
c.1850
1805
1812
Jamaica
17th c.1734,1760,
1795,1831
c.1750
1791
c.1780
1522
BRITISH WEST INDIES 1834
MEXICO 1829
Mexico City
Various
1545-1600
18th c.
1725-1735
1548
17th c.
CENTRAL AMERICA 1824
Cartagena
1619
1530
1550
1532
1795
1730 s
Buria
1552
Yaracuy
VENEZUELA 1854
Antioquia
1598
Choco
1820s
COLOMBIA 1852
Popayan
1540 s-50s
Orinoco
ECUADOR 1854
c.1770
1823
1763
1731
DUTCH ANTILLES 1863
Dutch sugar planters 1650's
Amazon
PERU 1854
16th c.+
1848
Lima
1578
BRAZIL 1888
Palmares
1807-1835
Bahia
São Francisco
Gois
c.1730
1700-1750
Minas Gerais
1850 s
BOLIVIA 1861
PARAGUAY 1869
Parana
CHILE 1825
Copinpo
URUGUAY 1853
ARGENTINA 1853
Estimated slave imports
5mm = 150,000
British North America and United States
Spanish America including Cuba
British West Indies
French West Indies
Other West Indies
Brazil
1451-1600
1601-1700
1701-1810
1811-1870

Arctic
GREENLAND
(Denmark)
Iceland
(Denmark)
RUPERT'S LAND
CANADA
LOUISIANA
Indian Reserve
Quebec
Montreal
St. Pierre & Miquelon
Nova Scotia
Newfoundland
Boston
New York
Philadelphia
Jamestown
THIRTEEN COLONIES
GEORGIA
FLORIDA
(Br. 1763-83)
New Orleans
Bermuda
VICE-ROYALTY OF NEW SPAIN
Bahama Is.
Cuba
Santiago
Vera Cruz
Jamaica
Haiti
Santo Domingo
Belize
Acapulco
To Manila
Mosquito Coast
St. Thomas (Denmark)
St. Croix (Denmark)
Leeward Is. (Br. and Dutch)
Guadaloupe (Fr.)
Lesser Antilles
(Fr. and Br.)
Curaçao
Trinidad
Porto Bello
Middle Passage
Pacific Ocean
VICE-ROYALTY OF NEW GRANADA
ESSEQUIBO
SURINAM
Cayenne
VICE-ROYALTY OF BRAZIL
DUTCH BRAZIL
(1630-54)
Recife
Bahia
VICE-ROYALTY OF PERU
Spanish transcontinental route
VICE-ROYALTY OF RIO DE LA PLATA
Rio de Janeiro
Buenos Aires
Falkland Is.
(Fr. 1763-5, Br. 1765-70, Sp. 1770)
Canada £·12m
American Colonies 29 £2·6m
Bahamas £2·6m
£2·9m
TOBACCO
RICE
FURS
INDIGO
MEAT
TIMBER
GRAIN
SUGAR
COFFEE
£5m
Antilles 85
SUGAR
COFFEE
INDIGO
COTTON
French Antilles and St. Domingo
SUGAR
GOLD
HIDES
COFFEE
DIAMONDS
CALICO
TAXES
Azores
Brazil 42 £1·8m
Canary Is.
New Spain 65 £4·5m
SUGAR
COCHINEAL
INDIGO
HIDES
TAXES
75
Spanish South America
SILK
SPICES
Cape Verde Is.
St. Louis
Gorée
Fort James
Atlantic
Ocean
SLAVES
30
SLAVES
GREAT BRITAIN
DENMARK
SWEI
Bristol
St. Malo
FRANCE
(Emancipated 1789)
AUSTR
Bordeaux
PORTUGAL
SPAIN
Lisbon
Seville
Cadiz
SEGU
ASHANTI
Accra
DAHOMEY
OYO
NUPA
Lagos
BENIN
Fernando Poo
São Paulo de Loanda
ANGOLA
PEPPER
SPICES
SILK
COFFEE
St. Helena
SPICES
£2m
SILK
CALICO
£1·5m
£1·5m
165-215
Cape
Indonesia
Malaysia
£1·4m
China
SILK
CALICO
COFFEE
PEPPER
INDIGO
DRUGS
170-225
Ind
Southern
(1741)
British c.1770
French "
Dutch "
Portuguese "
Spanish "
Outward trade
Homeward trade
Indications of colonial rivalry
Trading factories in the Far East
Russian Empire in 1763
Boundaries of French Louisiana before 1763
22 Average number of days in sea-crossing
£1·8m Value of trade in decade 1760-1770
Areas of Europe with free peasantry
Areas of Europe where peasantry were subjected to very light seigneurial dues
Areas of Europe whose emancipation was undertaken, or commenced in the late eighteenth century
Areas of unfree peasantry

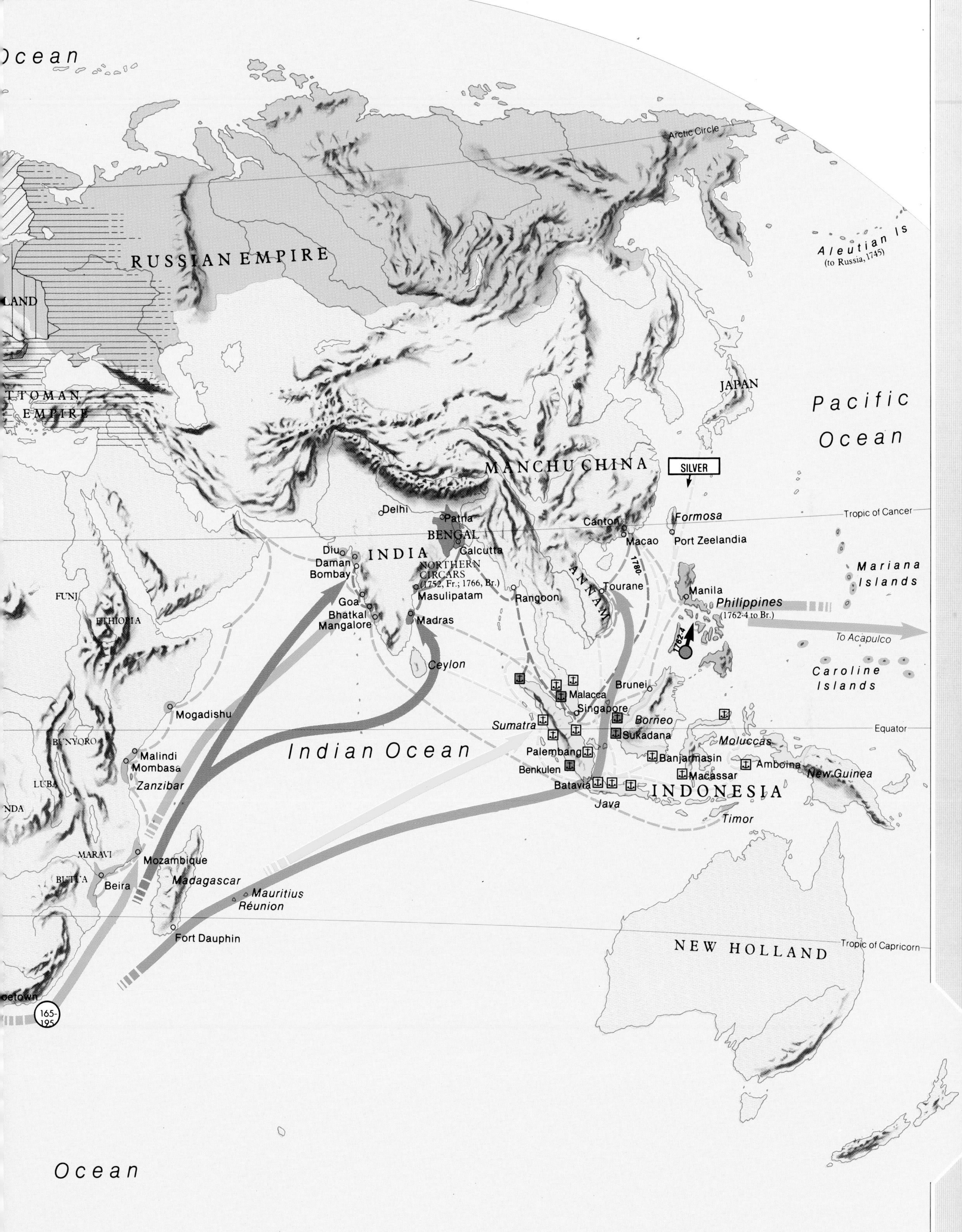
Ocean
RUSSIAN EMPIRE
Arctic Circle
Aleutian Is
(to Russia, 1745)
OTTOMAN EMPIRE
JAPAN
Pacific Ocean
MANCHU CHINA
SILVER
Delhi
Patna
BENGAL
Calcutta
Formosa
Tropic of Cancer
Canton
Macao
Port Zeelandia
Diu
Daman
Bombay
INDIA
NORTHERN CIRCARS
(1752, Fr.; 1766, Br.)
Masulipatam
ANNAM
1780-
Tourane
Mariana Islands
Manila
Philippines
(1762-4 to Br.)
1762-4
To Acapulco
FUNJ
ETHIOPIA
Goa
Bhatkal
Mangalore
Madras
Rangoon
Ceylon
Caroline Islands
Brunei
Malacca
Singapore
Mogadishu
Sumatra
Borneo
Sukadana
Equator
Moluccas
BUNYORO
Malindi
Mombasa
Indian Ocean
Palembang
Banjarmasin
Amboina
Benkulen
Macassar
New Guinea
Zanzibar
LUBA
Batavia
INDONESIA
Java
Timor
MARAVI
Mozambique
Beira
Madagascar
Mauritius
Réunion
Fort Dauphin
NEW HOLLAND
Tropic of Capricorn
Ocean

45). In Brazil the natives were nomadic, shy and primitive and their enslavement was forbidden. There were no such problems with African negroes, and the inland slave markets in the Black Monarchies of Angola provided a suitable source (*Map 46*). Boats on an outward voyage from Lisbon shipped slaves at Louanda, sailed to Bahía on the trade winds, and returned to Portugal, again with the wind behind them, filled with refined sugar. It was an ideal navigational and trading pattern.

The Dutch copied the Portuguese with larger mercantile resources, and with speed and success. The Portuguese eastern empire had been gained quickly by piracy and force. It was equally quickly dismembered by the Dutch in the early seventeenth century, using the same methods (*Map 46*). Muslim traders – even Portuguese trading stations – did not hesitate to trade with the new rivals. In some respects, though, the Dutch were different. Their merchants operated as a single trading company. A national charter of privileges guaranteed their monopoly status, organized such administration, jurisdiction and defence as were necessary, and enabled their risks to be shared. As a result, the Dutch operation in the East Indies never suffered from a shortage of capital and it was able to expand the range of goods shipped from the east. Not content with spices, peppers, tea, chinaware and gruff-goods (saltpetre and cottons), the Dutch governor-general introduced coffee-beans into Java and the first small shipment of Javanese coffee reached Amsterdam in 1712. It was a marketing triumph and soon coffee was one of the most profitable items of Dutch trade.

Secondly, the Dutch used the active bullion market in Amsterdam – developed during the days of shipments of Spanish silver to the Netherlands (*Map 42*) – to buy precious metals with which to pay cash for the goods of the East. Because there was no commodity that Europe could readily sell to the Orient the commerce of the East Indies remained, even for the Dutch, vulnerable to changes in the price of bullion in Europe.

Thirdly, the Dutch exploited the 'country' trades, the port-to-port conveyance through the Indian Ocean and towards the China Sea, of pilgrims to Jidda, of piecegoods to the Red Sea and the Persian Gulf from Surat and Bombay; from Madras to the many ports of the Moluccas. Other European nations established rival East India Companies. The English Company prospered during the seventeenth and eighteenth centuries and a French *Compagnie des Indes orientales* was founded by Colbert in 1664. But they suffered from government interference, interloping, and the indolence and petty corruption natural to great corporations. None had such a wide basis for the barter of spices and such a well-established mercantile position in the east as the Dutch (*Map 37*).

The Dutch also attempted to establish a commercial presence in the West Indies from the middle of the seventeenth century. But they never secured a firm footing against the English and the French, who were vigorously backed by their respective governments. By 1713 the days of the pirates were over and the pattern of control of the Caribbean islands was clear, governed by a treaty (the Peace of Utrecht in 1713), fully recognized and guarded by naval forces. The West Indies became part of the regular pattern of European diplomacy, and in particular of the rivalry between England and France, both of whom became accustomed to send fleets to the Caribbean at the beginning of any European war. All the colonies of English North America put together were still of less value in 1750 than a dozen sugar islands. The West Indies supplied more English imports and accounted for more English exports both in value and quantity than the American colonies (*Map 46*).

By 1700 the eleven English colonies of the North American mainland occupied a continuous strip of coastal territory (*Map 44*). Two days' travel inland brought one to untouched Indian country. Boston, the largest town, had only 7000-8000 inhabitants. Economic activity was on a small scale. The largest enterprises were those of the tobacco planters of Virginia and Maryland (*Map 45*). If their winters had been warmer they would have grown sugar. As it was they were tied to a product that exhausted the land quickly, required heavy labour, and declined steadily in price throughout the eighteenth century. Only the enormous size of their holdings and their slave labour enabled the Virginian planters to maintain their position. The other colonies were, from a commercial point of view, thoroughly unsatisfactory. Pennsylvania, Delaware, and Philadelphia were modest *émigré*-settled states of self-sufficient farming communities. New York traded with pirates and privateers and was a constant nuisance to the English government. The New England farmers worked small estates and frustrated the English government's attempts to monopolize the area's wood for ships.

The English colonists of the mainland did not only fail to live up to expectations. They also broke laws. In 1651 and again in 1667, the English Navigation Acts had established the basis of a network of rules designed artificially to direct the flow of English colonial commerce. Colonists were to trade only with their mother country. They were encouraged (by bounties) to produce the goods which England lacked and discouraged (by duties) from rivalling home industries. Goods were to be transported, in English ships, direct to the 'mother' country. In practice the legislation was regularly ignored. New England colonists exploited the country trades with both French and English islands of the Caribbean. They sold provisions to the French sugar-islands in time of war and traded directly with continental Europe.

The burden of defending the colonies grew greater in the eighteenth century. French colonization reflected the absolutism of its founders. From the beginning it was regimented by the state, with the result that the French settled far more of northern America than the British and began to constitute a threat both to the fur trade in the north and to English settlements along the Mississippi. The European war of 1756 to 1763 was also fought in America, between Britain and France. It was natural that the English government should wish to tax its colonists to defray the cost of defence. But by their charters the colonies possessed elected assemblies which, in practice, could neither be dislodged nor ignored. When pressed by the English government, they revolted and won their independence from the Crown in 1776 (*Map 53*).

The success of the rebellion appeared to be a disaster for British colonial expectations. But subsequent developments emphasized what liberal economists like Adam Smith were already preaching – that trade did not depend upon colonial dominion but upon economic power. The Industrial Revolution in Britain, founded in part on the wealth generated by the old colonies, provided the dynamic for a new imperialism. England's reaction to the disaster was to explore new areas for dominion. James Cook explored the remainder of the oceans, discovering Australia in 1775, Mungo Park set off from the Gambia in search of the Niger twenty years later, and the British East India Company expanded its territorial hold on mainland India.

Another form of liberalism also changed the nature of colonialism at the end of the eighteenth century. During four centuries of the European slave trade, ten million Africans were exported to slavery, of whom some 60% were transported between 1720 and 1820. At this time, the English, French and Portuguese handled 90% of the trade and the English share in most years was equal to the combined total of the others. Public opinion among the educated in Europe had never accepted slavery entirely, but moral unease and rational disquiet had stopped well short of wholesale condemnation. From the late eighteenth century abolitionists in America and England rejected all distinctions. The Quakers in America and the Evangelicals (known as the 'Saints') in England mounted an unprecedented campaign as a result of which slavery was abolished in most of the states of North America north of Pennsylvania (1780) and England abolished the slave trade in its own commerce (1807) – *see Map 45*. By 1824, slaving was declared piracy on the high seas and the efforts of the British navy to enforce the legislation were a tribute to its pre-eminence in the oceans. By 1820 Britain, alone of the colonists of Europe, possessed the self-confidence, righteous arrogance and naval force to infuse its commercial dominance with a sense of didactic responsibility which disguised its imperialism as the establishment of a guardianship over the less-developed world.

47 The rise of the Atlantic economies
In 1500 the Mediterranean was still the commercial, industrial and financial heart of Europe. In the years of economic crisis which began about 1610 the 'Atlantic economies' of England and Holland advanced at the expense of Spain and Italy through technical innovation, colonial expansion and the exploitation of the resources of the Baltic.

Further reading: F. Braudel, *Civilization and Capitalism* (3 vols. Collins 1981-4; Harper Collins); G. V. Scammell, *The First Imperial Age* (Unwin Hyman 1989); E. L. Jones *The European Miracle* (2 ed., Cambridge U.P. 1988); Philip D. Curtin, *The Rise and Fall of the Plantation Complex* (Cambridge U.P. 1990); Edmund S. Morgan, *American Slavery, American Freedom* (Norton 1975).

MAP 47 THE RISE OF THE ATLANTIC ECONOMIES

Atlantic Ocean
North Sea
Baltic Sea
Bay of Biscay
Mediterranean Sea
Adriatic Sea
FISH
FISH
FISH
FISH
GRAIN
SWEDEN
DENMARK
POLAND
UNITED PROVINCES
HOLY ROMAN EMPIRE
FRANCE
SPAIN
OTTOMAN EMPIRE
Stockholm
Copenhagen
Danzig
(Guilders)
Edinburgh
Whitby
York
Hatfield Chase
Holland Fen
Norwich
Great Yarmouth
Malvern Close
(Pound Sterling)
London
Canvey Is
Bristol
Southampton
Romney Marsh
Plymouth
Haarlem
Amsterdam
Leiden
(Guilders)
Bruges
Antwerp
Ghent
Dunkirk
Cologne
Louvain
Lübeck
Hamburg
Berlin
Magdeburg
Breslau
Cracow
Prague
Nuremberg
(Florins)
Oder
Elbe
Weser
Rhine
Vistula
Dieppe
Amiens
Rouen
Seine
Paris
(Ecus)
Strasbourg
Augsburg
Vienna
Danube
Tatra Mts.
Graz
Loire
Tours
Drava
Udine
Trieste
The Alps
Geneva
Lyon
Milan
Brescia
Verona
Venice
Cremona
Padua
Turin
Po
Bologna
(Ducats)
Genoa
Florence
Bordeaux
Garonne
Toulouse
Rhône
Nimes
Avignon
Marseilles
Leghorn
Ancona
Pyrenees
Valladolid
Ebro
Barcelona
Madrid
Toledo
(Cruzados)
Lisbon
Valencia
Rome
Naples
Cordoba
Seville
Granada
Alicante
Cadiz
Palermo
Messina
Syracuse
Algiers
Tunis
To and from the New World
60°
10°
0°
10°
20°
60°
50°
50°
40°
40°
20°
POPULATION OF SELECTED TOWNS 1600
over 250,000
80-120,000
50-70,000
30-40.000
other towns
0 400 km
0 200 miles
POPULATION DENSITIES c.1620 (per sq. km.)
rising population
static population
declining population
Over 40 inhabitants
20-40 "
5-20 "
Under 5 "
Areas of cloth production
Areas of metal production
Areas drained by Dutch engineers in the seventeenth century
Trade routes
Movement of exchange rates of major European currencies against the Dutch guilders on the Amsterdam market across the century, 1609-1700/9. For France and Portugal, the base year is 1619.
devaluation
evaluation

The age of European supremacy 4

EUROPE DIVIDED

The decisive event of the early sixteenth century was the Protestant Reformation. It split Europe into two camps. Like all powerful ideologies, Protestantism had a distinct message which divided families, cities and states.

48 Reformation and Counter-Reformation in Europe
The spread of Protestantism and the development of a variety of sects within it provided Europe with a range of ideologies to match the profusion of its courts and the increasing complexity of its social structure. The Catholic Reformation assisted the traditional powers to counter it with new vigour.

49 The Thirty Years War
The 'Thirty Years War' was in reality a series of conflicts between a succession of contenders for supremacy in post-Reformation Europe, among which France emerged victorious. The scale, duration and bitterness of warfare led to a degree of depopulation which crippled the empire for generations, although its extent cannot be measured with precision.

50 The Baltic under Swedish hegemony
In 1523 Sweden declared itself independent of the Union of Kalmar (Denmark, Norway and Sweden), adopted Lutheranism and developed its army, navy and economy. Its Baltic empire reached its height under Gustavus Adolphus (*r.* 1611-32) and was confirmed by the Peace of Roskilde in 1660. The erosion of the Polish-Lithuanian state culminated in successive partitions and its dissolution (1772-95).

At first it was fostered in the fast-expanding universities. Later, Protestants would establish their own academies in Strasbourg, Geneva and elsewhere to teach their vigorous analysis, refine their own theology, and attack that of their opponents. The cities of Europe were also growing rapidly (*Map 47*), and in them the new ideology found an interested literate laity. Persuasive Protestant preachers and theologians – Martin Luther in Wittenberg, Ulrich Zwingli in Zurich, Jean Calvin in Geneva, Jacob Sturm in Strasbourg – aided by the enormous diffusive power of the new printing press, could compel attention, create controversy and capture converts.

Ideologies are seldom fully developed in their first generation. Lutheranism spread from Wittenberg in Germany from 1517. During its first decade it had a liberating effect in much of western Europe, but it became the official religion only in German-influenced areas, spreading with the support of princes and their courts (*Map 48*). It offered no new view of society; when groups of Anabaptists, who did so, emerged in Lutheran areas preaching indifference towards constituted authority, and even sometimes a sharing of worldly possessions, they were always as firmly repressed as they were by the Catholic Charles V at Munster in 1535.

The second generation reform – Calvinism – spread from Geneva from 1536. It was ideologically more compelling. It offered a new model for society without the inherent anarchy of Anabaptism. Calvin created a new model Church with committees of pastors and elders to enforce its hard, clear, effective moral discipline. Refugees from Catholic persecution throughout Europe came to Geneva. They were sent out again as an élite – the Saints – to conquer, destroy and replace the 'great worldly Babylon'.

The seed of the Calvinist Church was found in the blood of martyrs. Initially, official persecution created refugees. Later, in the second half of the sixteenth century, sectarian conflict dominated the politics of Europe. Calvinists held up to ridicule, menace and abuse the Catholic images, crosses, shrines, feast-day processions, burials and marriage services. The Dutch religious wars started in this way with the 'iconoclastic' riots of 1566. Catholics retaliated against the defiling of their sacred things by taking the blood of Protestants. The massacre of St Bartholomew in France in 1572 began as a government-inspired attempt to eliminate Protestants but became, under popular Catholic enthusiasm, a season of pogroms in major French cities, and a climax to the forty years of religious wars.

At first, Calvin had tried to convert peacefully; but under the pressure of persecution, his successor in Geneva, Beza, openly advocated the deposition of the persecutors. And faced with persecution, Calvinism was forced back on to a narrow social base. It became the religion of urban republics, sometimes reaching out for support from other social groups – lesser princes, turbulent magnates, backwoods gentry or the urban poor – but always retaining its urban and semi-republican ethos.

By the 1560s, the Roman Church seemed everywhere on the defensive. All Europe north of the Alps and the Pyrenees was lost or endangered; the princes were uncertain, the nobility heavily Protestant, the clergy converting. But Roman Catholicism developed a powerful authoritarian counter-ideology. The formal statement of this came in the decrees of the Council of Trent, which concluded its sessions in 1563. When it had first met, summoned by the Emperor in 1545, its purpose had been to reunite and purify the Church and to reverse the 'Monarchical' tendencies of the Papacy. Its effect was otherwise; instead of restoring authority to the bishops, it confirmed their subjection to the Papacy, and presented in hardened form the doctrine of the absolute obedience of both laity and clergy to the Papal See.

Thenceforth Rome became like one of the courts of the great European princes. The Hapsburgs – whose own swelling courts were the envy of the rest of Europe – fought their wars, centralized their government, increased taxes, sold offices, sent out permanent ambassadors to Europe and elsewhere and planned their capitals (*Map 42*). The popes did likewise, and with Spanish-Hapsburg strength behind them, Catholicism triumphed in Europe and America (*Map 43*). Spanish power even protected Italy against the Turks (*Map 39*).

The Catholicism of the Counter-Reformation became the religion of princely courts and bureaucratic and hierarchical societies. Its spiritual force came with the Jesuits. Their powerful casuistry was disseminated through educational institutions in Europe and in the New World. Their political influence grew, and gradually they became linked to the Spanish court. Thanks to the Portuguese Jesuits, Philip II gained the crown in Portugal in 1580. The Jesuits promised him the crowns of England and France too. Spanish interests lurked behind the Jesuits who penetrated Lutheran Sweden and Orthodox Russia. It was as Spanish agents that they were expelled from Japan in 1640.

The Catholic Counter-Reformation reached its climax in 1630. Bavaria, Poland, Austria, France and the southern half of the Netherlands had been recovered by preaching and by force. In 1621 Rome had celebrated the destruction of Protestantism in Bohemia. In 1629, La Rochelle, the last Huguenot citadel of France, had been reduced (*Map 51*). In the same year, the Jesuits were advancing northwards to the Baltic. To the east they attached a part of the Greek Orthodox church to their cause, and Catholic missionaries counted the Red Indians of Canada, the war-like *daimyos* of Japan and even they liked to think the Confucian Mandarins of China among the souls they had saved. But in one major respect, Catholic victories were pyrrhic ones. In the decades of persecution the Catholic princes of Europe expelled the Calvinists and with them their financial reserves and mercantile and manufacturing skills. The industrial heart of Europe was displaced. After the iconoclastic riots the Protestants persecuted in the Spanish Netherlands moved north and east across the Rhine. The massacre of Saint Bartholomew sent French silk workers from Lyons across the Jura. In the seventeenth century, the Catholic reconquests scattered Calvinists from Bohemia, the Palatinate and the Baltic to Protestant regions. As a result, the towns of Holland and Zealand – Amsterdam,

Right: Huguenots massacred on St Bartholomew's day.

Haarlem, Delft – inherited the prosperity of Catholic Antwerp, and the cloth industry of Hondschoote (*Map 47*). The North Sea cities – Bremen, Hamburg and Emden – were enriched from the shattered urban life of the Catholic southern Netherlands. The cities of the Rhineland – the Palatinate and Alsace – benefited from the Calvinists expelled from France and from the prince-bishoprics of the Empire. France, Germany and Italy drained its refugees into Switzerland. On the Atlantic coast, tolerant, Anglican England was a refuge for Huguenot weavers.

The economic consequences would have been less serious if Europe's economy had continued to expand. In the sixteenth century – particularly in the first 50 years – the population of Europe was growing, its cities were more wealthy, its economic activity increasing. The merchants of Antwerp, Venice and Seville traded further and deeper across the Baltic, through Germany, into the Levant, into Brazil and across to America (*Maps 35 and 46*). But this pace and confidence could not be sustained at an even rate. Shortly after 1600 it halted or slowed down. First here, then there, the economy of the European states trembled mysteriously. What was the cause of this 'decay of trade'? Was it purely economic? There certainly were weaknesses in the economic system of Europe: it was vulnerable to plagues and disease; its transport remained cripplingly limited; technological change was slow; markets for manufactured goods were relatively small. Was it purely financial? Certainly the decline in the amount of silver imported from the New World (and still the main material for coinage) went hand in hand with the general contraction. Was it the climate? Europe was indeed colder and wetter in this century than in the sixteenth and some historians have spoken of a 'mini ice-age'. Or was it the result of the growing burden of administrative centralization, particularly in Catholic states? We do not know precisely. What is clear is that the effects of stagnation were felt unevenly in Europe.

Spain, despite its overseas wealth and its military power, felt the European-wide dearth of resources most keenly. It had ceased to be able to feed itself. Disastrous plagues in the 1590s decimated its inland population; its coins depreciated to become shadows of their former sovereign glory (*Map 47*). Italy and the Mediterranean felt the same process less severely. Further north, Holland escaped these ravages. Financial constriction was avoided and capital introduced by *emigrés* was put to good use in modest technological endeavours. The Dutch became drainage engineers across the whole of northern Europe, thus releasing new land for cultivation. Their famous fly-boats brought a revolution in bulk-carrying cargoes at sea. Their industries produced products which were saleable across a broad European market – cheap, durable cloth, mass-produced Delft tiles, sugar-enriched wines, salted fish. In the wake of the Dutch Wars, which reached a truce in 1609, Amsterdam became the successor of Antwerp as Europe's mercantile centre. Its Protestant neighbours also found their currencies and their economies more stable, their cities growing. This new strength enabled the Dutch to break into the oceans of the world and establish themselves at the centre of an East Asiatic empire which lasted until the twentieth century (*Maps 46 and 67*).

Economic crisis and European war came together. From 1618, the energies of Europe were turned inwards to be consumed in the long, destructive contest of the Thirty Years War (*Map 49*). This was a complex of wars, a pattern of rival imperialism amongst the European land empires. Spanish ambitions in the Netherlands and the Baltic, Saxon ambitions in Germany, Swedish ambitions in the Baltic, all encouraged the fears and hopes of their various satellite powers. At the beginning, it was also a war of ideologies, of the Counter-Reformation against Calvinism. As such it flowed across boundaries and was never a purely German affair. The war began in Bohemia with the mobilization by the Elector Palatine of his Protestant allies in England, Holland, and other minorities elsewhere to support his election as King of Bohemia. It could have started earlier, perhaps when the conversion to Protestantism of the elector of Cologne had caused the Cologne war in 1583, or when the death of the duke of Cleves in 1609 could have plunged Europe into war but for the timely assassination of King Henry IV of France. Ranged against the Elector Palatine was the Hapsburg empire. For the Hapsburgs it was a parasitic war. Economically bankrupt (as they admitted) after expelling their productive subjects, war seemed the only way of nourishing their court and the privileged society which regularly consumed more than it generated. It enabled them to suck from the heretics the sustenance they could not create themselves. The Austrian Hapsburgs devoured Bohemia, Bavaria, the Upper Palatinate, just as the Lutheran princes – Denmark, Sweden and Saxony – absorbed Lusatia and the German coastal littoral as the reward of supporting fellow Protestants.

But the Thirty Years War marked the end of religious ideology. In their imperialism, the European monarchs took up strange alliances across the ideological divide. Protestant Sweden intervened in Germany in 1631, funded by Catholic France. Catholic Bavaria joined the Protestant princes in Europe against the Hapsburgs. Albrecht von Wallenstein, of doubtful personal religious conviction, fought the Emperor's wars for him as a mercenary and used Protestant bankers. The material destruction which caused the depopulation of swathes of Germany (especially the Elbe and lower Rhine regions) and the devastation of its cities, discredited the ideologies that had permitted such savagery. The peace of Westphalia, which ended the wars in 1648, was not attended by a representative of the Papacy or ratified by the Pope.

When all was over, who had gained and who lost? Politically, it is clear. The Spanish empire in Europe was broken, the Hapsburg empire was shaken. Saxony and Bavaria had demonstrated their independence; Brandenburg followed where they led (*Map 52*). Above all France had a firm government, clearly defined boundaries, and boundless influence in Germany (*Map 51*). But the Thirty Years War destroyed far more than Spanish hegemony. It destroyed a whole system. In the cataclysm, the hierarchical courts of the Counter-Reformation, with their patronage, their swollen officialdom, and parasitic economies, were broken. Even some Protestant countries with courts – such as England – suffered the same fate. The international churches were broken too; the Roman Catholic church destroyed the international effectiveness of the Calvinists only to weaken itself fatally in facing the challenge of scepticism in the next century. The new forms of government – sober republics and mercantilist minded absolutist states based on rationalized privileges – which had recently germinated, began to show themselves after 1660. The European *ancien régime* was beginning.

Further reading: John Bossy, *Christianity in the West 1400-1700*, (Oxford U.P. 1985); Euan Cameron, *The European Reformation* (Oxford U.P. 1991); Mark Greengrass, *France in the Age of Henri IV: The Struggle for Stability* (Longman 1984); Simon Schama, *The Embarrassment of Riches* (Collins 1987; University of California Press); Geoffrey Parker, *The Military Revolution* (Cambridge U.P. 1988).

NORWAY (1539)□
Confessio Augustana, 1536/1607□
FINLAND □(1528)
Uppsala
ESTONIA (1542)□
LIVONIA (1542)□
Riga
COURLAND (1561)□
SWEDEN (1527)□
Confessio Augustana, 1593□
Skagerrak
SCOTLAND
Scottish Mission (1653/94)
Confessio Scotica, 1560□
Saint Andrews
Glasgow
North Sea
DENMARK
Confessio Hafnica, 1530□
(Northern Mission) (1673/78/88)
Lund
Baltic Sea
Königsberg
TEUTONIC ORDER PRUSSIA (1530)□
(under Polish Suzerainty from 1466)
IRELAND (1536)□
Dublin
York
SCHLESWIG (1542)□
HOLSTEIN (1542)□
Lübeck
MECKLENBURG (1548-9)□
POMERANIA (1534)□
Danzig
Vistula
Stettin
Oder
ENGLAND
English Mission (1623/88)
Norwich
EMDEN □(1526) □(1542)
Ac. BREMEN
Elbe
Hamburg
Bremen
Groningen
BRANDENBURG (1539)□
KINGDOM OF POLAND
Warsaw (-1572)
Act of Supremacy, 1534
□Act of Uniformity, 1549
□Act of Uniformity, 1552
Recatholicisation, 1554
□Act of Uniformity, 1559
Canterbury
Confessio Augustana, 1530□
Berlin
Amsterdam
Leiden
Utrecht
Münster
Bc. MÜNSTER
Magdeburg (1525)
Wittenberg (1524)
(ELECTORATE,) (1539)□
Consensus Poloniae, 1570/1595
Middleburg
Breda
Dortmund
Mühlhausen
SAXONY
Dresden
Leipzig
SILESIA
Breslau
Ghent
Antwerp
Confessio Belgica, □1559/61
(1594/97)
Cologne
Rhine
HESSE-KASSEL
(DUCHY,) (1526)□
Zwickau
English Channel
Lille
Tournai
Maastricht
Wetzlar
FULDA
Prague (1576-1612)
BOHEMIA
Confessio Bohemica, 1575
Confessio Pentapolitana, 1545□
NASSAU □(1528)
Frankfurt (1530)
B. BAMBURG
Ac. TRIER
RHINE PALATINATE □(1546) □(1559)
Ac. MAINZ
B. WÜRZBURG
Worms
UPPER PALATINATE
Nuremberg
Rouen
ANSBACH (1528)□
MORAVIA
Confessio Hungarica, 1562□
Meaux
Alençon
Paris (1500)
Heilbronn
Hall
Donauwörth
Regensburg (1538)
WÜRTTEMBERG □(1534)
BAVARIA
Troyes
Confessio Gallicana, □1559
Strasbourg
Ulm
Augsburg (1573/83)
Vienna (1524)
Münster
Munich (1573/83)
Salzburg
Angers
FRANCE
Loire
Saumur
Basel (1529)
Zurich
(French Congr
Marmoutiers
Innsbruck
Graz (1581-1621)
Danube

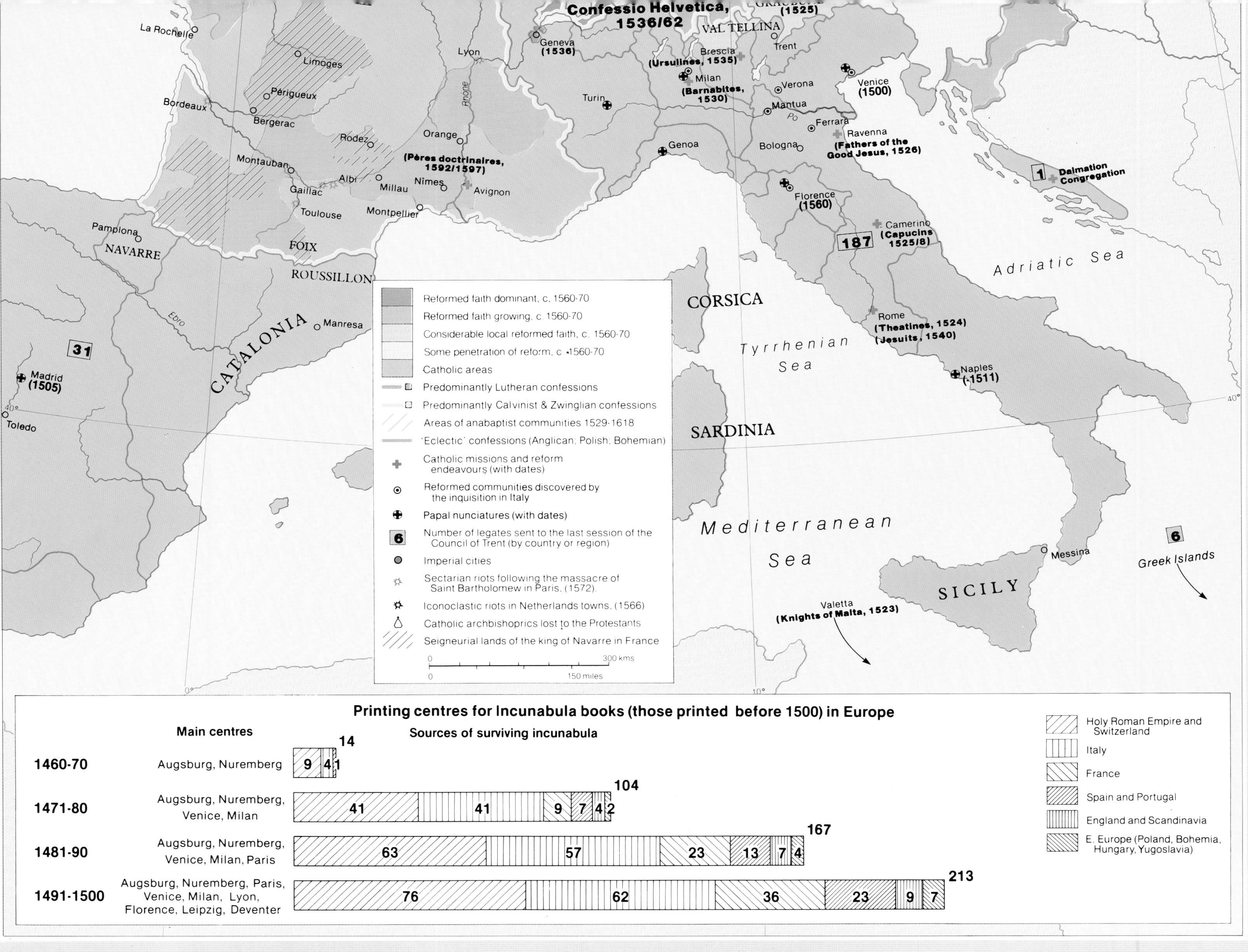
Confessio Helvetica, 1536/62
(1525)
VAL TELLINA
La Rochelle
Limoges
Périgueux
Bordeaux
Bergerac
Lyon
Rhone
Geneva (1536)
Turin
Brescia
(Ursulines, 1535)
Milan
(Barnabites, 1530)
Trent
Verona
Mantua
Po
Venice (1500)
Ferrara
Ravenna
(Fathers of the Good Jesus, 1526)
Bologna
Genoa
Orange
Rodez
Montauban
(Pères doctrinaires, 1592/1597)
Albi
Millau
Nimes
Avignon
Gaillac
Toulouse
Montpellier
Pamplona
NAVARRE
FOIX
ROUSSILLON
Ebro
CATALONIA
Manresa
31
Madrid (1505)
Toledo
Dalmation Congregation
1
Florence (1560)
Camerino (Capucins 1525/8)
187
Adriatic Sea
CORSICA
Rome (Theatines, 1524) (Jesuits, 1540)
Tyrrhenian Sea
Naples (-1511)
SARDINIA
Mediterranean Sea
Messina
SICILY
6
Greek Islands
Valetta (Knights of Malta, 1523)
Reformed faith dominant, c. 1560-70
Reformed faith growing, c. 1560-70
Considerable local reformed faith, c. 1560-70
Some penetration of reform, c. 1560-70
Catholic areas
Predominantly Lutheran confessions
Predominantly Calvinist & Zwinglian confessions
Areas of anabaptist communities 1529-1618
'Eclectic' confessions (Anglican; Polish; Bohemian)
Catholic missions and reform endeavours (with dates)
Reformed communities discovered by the inquisition in Italy
Papal nunciatures (with dates)
Number of legates sent to the last session of the Council of Trent (by country or region)
Imperial cities
Sectarian riots following the massacre of Saint Bartholomew in Paris, (1572).
Iconoclastic riots in Netherlands towns, (1566)
Catholic archbishoprics lost to the Protestants
Seigneurial lands of the king of Navarre in France
0 300 kms
0 150 miles
Printing centres for Incunabula books (those printed before 1500) in Europe
Main centres
Sources of surviving incunabula
1460-70 Augsburg, Nuremberg 9 4 1 14
1471-80 Augsburg, Nuremberg, Venice, Milan 41 41 9 7 4 2 104
1481-90 Augsburg, Nuremberg, Venice, Milan, Paris 63 57 23 13 7 4 167
1491-1500 Augsburg, Nuremberg, Paris, Venice, Milan, Lyon, Florence, Leipzig, Deventer 76 62 36 23 9 7 213
Holy Roman Empire and Switzerland
Italy
France
Spain and Portugal
England and Scandinavia
E. Europe (Poland, Bohemia, Hungary, Yugoslavia)

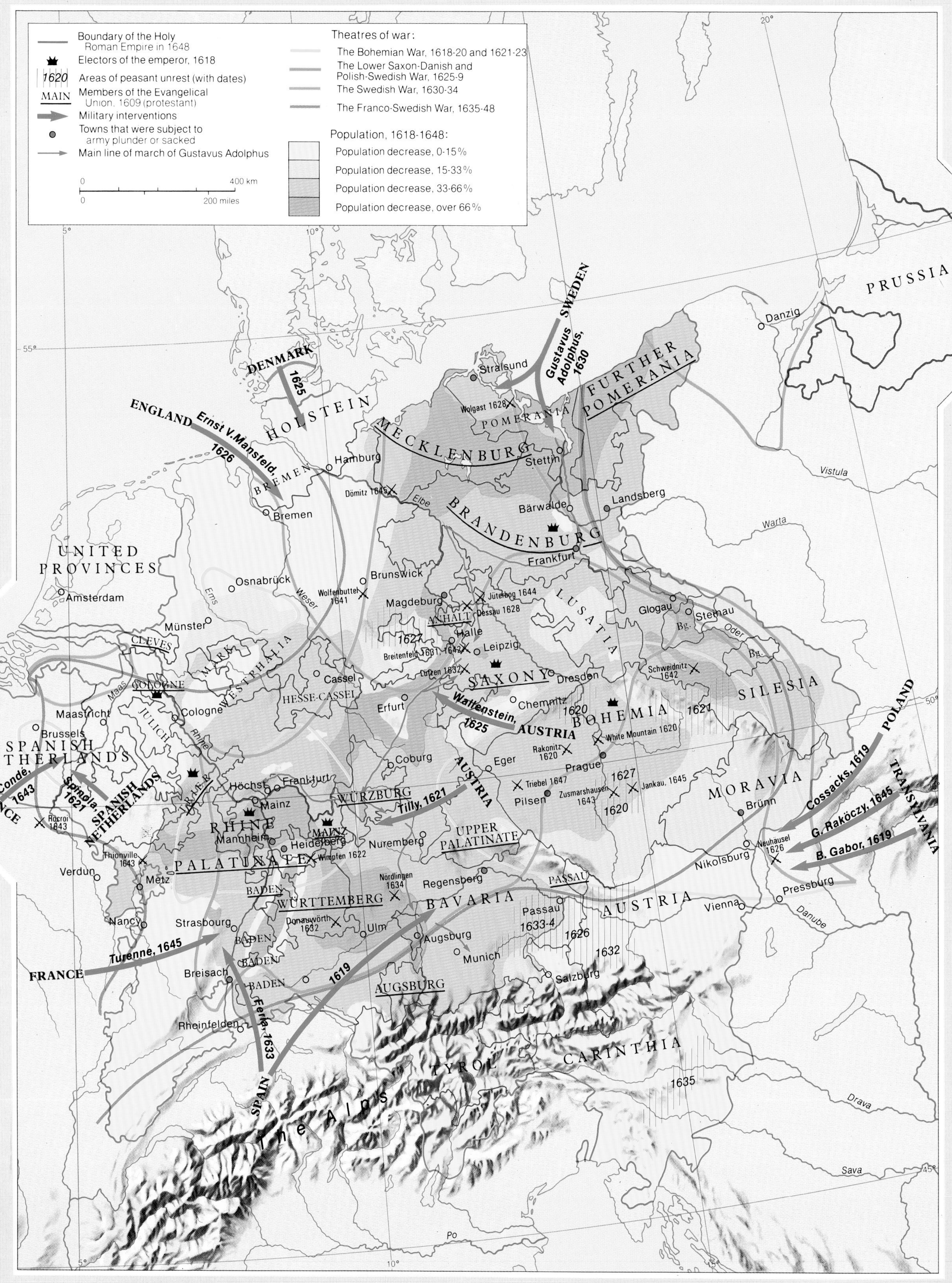
Boundary of the Holy Roman Empire in 1648
Electors of the emperor, 1618
1620 Areas of peasant unrest (with dates)
MAIN Members of the Evangelical Union, 1609 (protestant)
Military interventions
Towns that were subject to army plunder or sacked
Main line of march of Gustavus Adolphus
0 400 km
0 200 miles
Theatres of war:
The Bohemian War, 1618-20 and 1621-23
The Lower Saxon-Danish and Polish-Swedish War, 1625-9
The Swedish War, 1630-34
The Franco-Swedish War, 1635-48
Population, 1618-1648:
Population decrease, 0-15%
Population decrease, 15-33%
Population decrease, 33-66%
Population decrease, over 66%
PRUSSIA
Danzig
SWEDEN
Gustavus Adolphus, 1630
DENMARK
1625
HOLSTEIN
Stralsund
Wolgast 1628
POMERANIA
FURTHER POMERANIA
MECKLENBURG
Stettin
Hamburg
ENGLAND
Ernst V.Mansfeld, 1626
BREMEN
Bremen
Dömitz 1645
Elbe
Bärwalde
Landsberg
BRANDENBURG
Frankfurt
Vistula
Warta
UNITED PROVINCES
Amsterdam
Osnabrück
Brunswick
Wolfenbuttel 1641
Magdeburg
Jüterbog 1644
Dessau 1628
LUSATIA
Glogau
Steinau
Oder
Ems
Weser
Münster
ANHALT
Halle
1627
Breitenfeld 1631, 1642
Leipzig
CLEVES
MARK
WESTPHALIA
Cassel
Lützen 1632
SAXONY
Dresden
Schweidnitz 1642
SILESIA
COLOGNE
Maas
HESSE-CASSEL
Maastricht
Cologne
Erfurt
Wallenstein, 1625
Chemnitz
1620
BOHEMIA
1621
POLAND
Brussels
JULICH
AUSTRIA
White Mountain 1620
SPANISH NETHERLANDS
Rhine
Coburg
Eger
Rakonitz 1620
Prague
Condé, 1643
FRANCE
Spinola, 1621
TRIER
Höchst
Frankfurt
AUSTRIA
Triebel 1647
1627
Jankau, 1645
MORAVIA
Cossacks, 1619
Mainz
WÜRZBURG
Tilly, 1621
Pilsen
Zusmarshausen 1648
1620
Brünn
TRANSYLVANIA
G. Rakóczy, 1645
Rocroi 1643
RHINE
Mannheim
MAINZ
Heidelberg
Nuremberg
UPPER PALATINATE
Neuhausel 1626
B. Gabor, 1619
Thionville 1643
PALATINATE
Wimpfen 1622
Nikolsburg
Verdun
Metz
Nördlingen 1634
Regensburg
PASSAU
Pressburg
BADEN
WÜRTTEMBERG
BAVARIA
Passau
AUSTRIA
Vienna
Danube
Nancy
Strasbourg
Donauwörth 1632
Ulm
1633-4
1626
BADEN
Augsburg
FRANCE
Turenne, 1645
BADEN
Munich
1632
Breisach
BADEN
1619
Salzburg
AUGSBURG
Rheinfelden
Feria, 1633
CARINTHIA
TYROL
SPAIN
1635
The Alps
Drava
Sava
Po

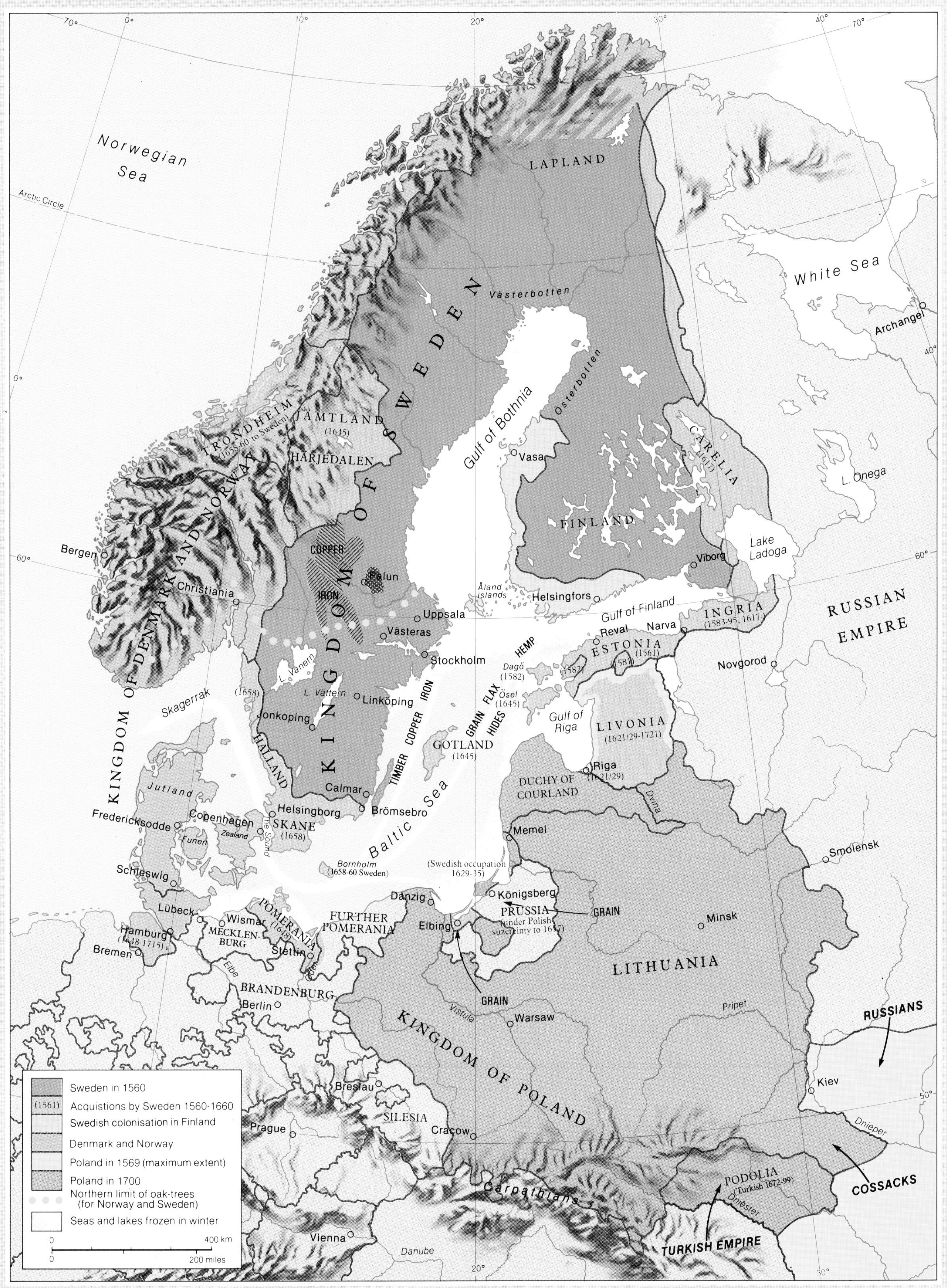
Norwegian Sea
Arctic Circle
LAPLAND
White Sea
Archangel
Västerbotten
KINGDOM OF SWEDEN
Österbotten
Gulf of Bothnia
TRONDHEIM (1658-60 to Sweden)
JÄMTLAND (1645)
HÄRJEDALEN
Vasa
CARELIA (1617)
L. Onega
FINLAND
KINGDOM OF DENMARK AND NORWAY
Bergen
COPPER
IRON
Falun
Viborg
Lake Ladoga
Christiania
Åland Islands
Helsingfors
Uppsala
Gulf of Finland
INGRIA (1583-95, 1617-)
RUSSIAN EMPIRE
Västeras
Reval
Narva
ESTONIA (1561)
HEMP
Stockholm
Novgorod
L. Vanern
Dagö (1582)
Skagerrak
(1658)
L. Vättern
Linköping
Ösel (1645)
Gulf of Riga
LIVONIA (1621/29-1721)
Jonkoping
TIMBER
COPPER
IRON
GRAIN
FLAX
HIDES
GOTLAND (1645)
HALLAND
Riga (1621/29)
Jutland
Calmar
DUCHY OF COURLAND
Dvina
Helsingborg
Brömsebro
Baltic Sea
Fredericksodde
Copenhagen
SKANE (1658)
The Sound
Funen
Zealand
Memel
Smolensk
Schleswig
Bornholm (1658-60 Sweden)
(Swedish occupation 1629-35)
Danzig
Königsberg
PRUSSIA (under Polish suzerainty to 1657)
GRAIN
Lübeck
FURTHER POMERANIA
POMERANIA (1648)
Wismar
Elbing
Minsk
Hamburg (1648-1715)
MECKLEN-BURG
Stettin
Bremen
Elbe
LITHUANIA
BRANDENBURG
Berlin
GRAIN
Vistula
Warsaw
Pripet
RUSSIANS
KINGDOM OF POLAND
Breslau
Kiev
SILESIA
Prague
Cracow
Dnieper
PODOLIA (Turkish 1672-99)
COSSACKS
Carpathians
Dniester
Vienna
Danube
TURKISH EMPIRE
Sweden in 1560
(1561) Acquistions by Sweden 1560-1660
Swedish colonisation in Finland
Denmark and Norway
Poland in 1569 (maximum extent)
Poland in 1700
Northern limit of oak-trees (for Norway and Sweden)
Seas and lakes frozen in winter
0 400 km
0 200 miles

The age of European supremacy 5

THE ANCIEN RÉGIME

In 1660, Europe emerged from a half-century of violent convulsions. The whole continent was at peace for the first time in over a generation.

51 The *ancien régime* in France
The gradual absorption of the great fiefs by the French crown and the decay of regional institutions permitted the creation of a centralized bureaucratic government which, despite widespread and often prolonged local resistance, laid the foundations of absolute monarchy and territorial expansion.

The last 'great rebellion' ended with the restoration of Charles II in England. Descartes' logical philosophical method enthroned human reason and seemed capable of resolving every intellectual problem. Demographic stagnation and areas of economic depression would persist into the eighteenth century, but this in its way was a facet of the social and political stability which was not radically disturbed for more than a century.

The basis of this stability was the pre-eminence of rich, hereditary landed oligarchies, most of which enjoyed nobility. Every state in Europe (except certain Swiss cantons) recognized the existence of a nobility. The French revolutionaries identified the principle of noble privilege as the essential component of the *'ancien régime'* to whose destruction they were committed.

The doomed nobility of France was the prime example of European nobility. France was held to comprise three orders or estates – clergy, nobility and the third estate. This originated in the medieval division of society into those who prayed, those who fought, and those who worked. The noble order had a complex hierarchy of titles and enjoyed substantial precedence and privileges, notably personal exemption from taxation. By 1660, it not only fought but prayed (the overwhelming proportion of Louis XIV's bishops were old nobles) and worked for the state (his ministers were also old nobles). It enjoyed a certain lifestyle in which manual work, which included the retail trades, was forbidden and which, in practice, required the possession and cultivation of land. Perhaps a third of France was owned by the nobility, and this proportion was about average for Europe. In Denmark, by comparison, 85% of the land was owned by the nobility. In England, four hundred noble families owned a quarter of the soil.

The attributes of the nobleman were universally agreed upon. 'Persons of Quality' (like the Englishman, Dr Burney) roamed across Europe, armed with a sheaf of letters of recommendation which opened up the polite society of metropolis and court along their route (*see Map 52*). The allurements of town and court life were irresistible and European nobles were divided between those who could afford them and the 'mere' squires who could not. In France, where residence in the royal palace of Versailles was the ultimate privilege, establishments had to be maintained in Paris, at court and in the country. Most ostentatious of all were the magnates of the Hapsburg empire, who not only resided at court in their Viennese palaces, but also built impressive country seats, of which the Esterhaz ('the Hungarian Versailles') was the most famous. With the European nobility went a European language (French), a cosmopolitan entertainment (music) and a common cultural attitude subsequently called 'Enlightenment'.

The central political problem for the nobility was to obtain a stable, firm government to maintain their privileges without at the same time encouraging despotism, or breeding democracy. In his *Leviathan* (1651), Thomas Hobbes, defending all forms of strong government, had argued that a sovereign power was the only source of authority, law and morality. 'The sovereign power . . . is as great as men can be imagined to make it. And although of so unlimited a power, men may fancy many evil consequences, yet the consequences of the want of it, which is perpetual war of every man against his neighbour, are much worse'. Tyranny, he said, was only a pejorative term for monarchy.

Hobbes' justification for the absolute power of the prince was used in France by Louis XIV's apologist, Bishop Bossuet, to construct a coherent theory of absolutism. The activity of Louis XIV enthralled Europe for fifty years and the memory of it haunted the eighteenth century (*see Map 51*). In many respects Louis XIV built upon the achievements of the Cardinal ministers Richelieu and Mazarin, who had introduced the bureaucratic mechanism of provincial government in the *intendants*, initiated an expansionist foreign policy, chastened the rebellious nobles in the *Frondes* (1648-53) and increased taxation. In other ways, Louis XIV's baroque taste for glory and sense of theatre led contemporaries to overestimate his absolutism. Nonetheless, he did dramatically expand the borders of France at the expense of the Hapsburgs, expel the Huguenots from his realm in 1685, and maintain a huge standing army and a developed navy. As a result, there was a reaction after his death since he had seriously undermined the privileges of the nobility, encountered peasant uprisings and resistance within the Catholic establishment, and built up a colossal debt which was stabilized only by multiple bankruptcies in the succeeding reign.

Nevertheless, others in eighteenth-century Europe followed Louis XIV's taste for glory. Prussia became a kingdom when the Elector Frederick III of Brandenburg was given a royal dignity in 1701 and crowned 'King in Prussia'. His military reforms created a standing army which his son used to make Prussia one of the leading powers in Europe (*see Map 52*). In Austria, Maria Theresa (*r.* 1740-80) compensated for the loss of Silesia by imitating Louis XIV in her hereditary lands of Austria, Bohemia and Hungary. Even countries with a strong tradition of representative institutions established painfully in the wars of the seventeenth century, such as Sweden and the Netherlands, faced autocratic monarchs like Gustavus III (*r.*1772-92) and Wilhelm V (*r.*1766-1806). They constructed their pastiche Versailles, where royal, imperial, or ducal courts could enjoy the delicate interplay between ruler, minister, courtier, mistress and financier. Imitations stretched from Naples to Madrid, from Vienna to St Petersburg. But, significantly, the only miniature Versailles on English soil – Blenheim Palace – was constructed not for a monarch but for a general in retirement from the last of Louis XIV's wars.

As armies grew, the profession of arms took on a new meaning. Higher standards of discipline were exacted from officers. For the rank and file, developments included impressment, parade-ground drill and execution by firing squad. Other continental autocrats undertook expansionist wars with the same thread-bare justifications as Louis XIV's mixture of strategic, commercial and dynastic motives, but they added a pseudo--scientific jargon of the 'balance of power' to justify the Peace of Utrecht in 1713 or the first partition of Poland in 1773. Some have spoken of a century of limited warfare, but when reason of state demanded it there was brutality and extensive war.

Royal domain in 1477
Fiefs which fell to the Crown in 1477-1527
Patrimony of Charles, Duke of Bourbon, escheating to the crown in 1527
Other fiefs still outstanding in 1550
Ven Region with estates (provincial assemblies) in the sixteenth century
Art Region with estates surviving to 1661
Siège of a parlement
1643 Intendency centres in c. 1716 (with dates of first permanent intendants)
Généralités in c 1716
Certain peasant revolts and town revolts
Acquisitions in 1552, confirmed in 1648 (Metz, Toul and Verdun)
Acquisitions 1643-1661
Acquisitions 1662-1715
Areas "reunited" with the French Crown by Louis XIV 1684-1697
Duchy of Lorraine (occupied by France 1634-59 and 1670-1697)
Ten Imperial cities in Alsace over which France acquired jurisdiction in 1648 and which were annexed in 1672
Fortresses constructed or strengthened by Vauban
Linguistic eastern frontier of France
French border in 1715
0
200 km
0
100 miles
SPANISH NETHERLANDS
HOLY ROMAN EMPIRE
SWISS CONFEDERATION
DUCHY OF SAVOY
The Alps
Pyrenees
Massif Central
C. of Flanders
Artois
Picardy
Normandy
D. of Brittany
1491
Ile de France
Champagne
Lorraine
D. of Bar
1634
Alsace
Franche-Comté
1674
D. of Burgundy
1477/82
C. of Nivernais
Bourbonnais
C. of Charolais
1684
Lyonnais
Bresse
Dauphiné
C. of Provence
1481
C. of Venaissin
Languedoc
Guyenne
Albret
Armagnac
Navarre
V-C. of Béarn
1620
Bigorre
Comminges
C. of Foix
1589
Rouergue
C. of Périgord
Limousin
La Marche
Auvergne
Forez
Angoumois
Saintonge
Aunis
Poitou
Touraine
Anjou
1525
C. of Maine
1489
Perche
1474-83
Alençon
1525
Orléanais
1498
D. of Vendôme
D. of Nemours
D. of Valois
1515
C. of Eu
C. of Rethel
LUSTUCRU
1662
NU-PIEDS
1639
TORRÉBEN
1675
SABOTIERS
1658
TARD-AVISÉS, CROQUANTS
1593-4, 1636, 1637
TARDANIZATS
1655-6
CROQUANTS
1593-4, 1637
TARD-AVISÉS
1707
CROQUANTS
1643
ROURE
1670
CAMISARDS
1702-7
AUDIJOS
1663
CROQUANTS
1642
CROQUANTS
1594
FLEMISH
WALLOON
FRENCH
GERMAN
ITALIAN
PROVENÇAL
Dunkirk
Calais
Gravelines
Ardres
St Omer
1678
Aire
Lille
Tournai
Condé
Arras
Bouchain
1659
Valenciennes
Cambrai
Avesnes
Maubeuge
Charleroi
Doullens
Amiens
1633
1628, 1638, 1642
St. Quentin
1477
Landrécies
Rocroi
Guise
Mézières
Sedan
1678
La Fère
Montmédy
Longwy
Luxemburg
Thionville
Verdun
Metz
Toul
Bonn
Arenberg
Mont Royal
Oberstein
Lautrecken
Sarrelouis
Phillipsburg
Landau
Wissembourg
Haguenau
1681/4
Strasbourg
1643
Kehl
Schlettstadt
Colmar
Münster
Freiburg
Breisach
1643
Hüningen
Belfort
1648
Cherbourg
Le Havre
Rouen
1630
1631, 1634, 1636, 1639
Caen
1630
1631, 1639
Soissons
1634
Reims
Vertus
1633
1636
Paris
1634
1631, 1648-9, 1653
Troyes
1630, 1641, 1642
Auxerre
Nemours
Orléans
1638
Brest
St Malo
Rennes
1634
1636, 1639
Le Mans
Alençon
1638
Angers
1556
Nantes
Belle Isle
Tours
1630
Bourges
1641
1639
Nevers
1639
Dijon
1635
1630
Besançon
Dôle
1678/9
Châlons
Poitiers
1633
1631-2, 1639, 1641
Ile de Ré
La Rochelle
Moulin
1634
1633, 1636, 1640
1684
Riom
Clermont Ferrand
1636-7, 1640, 1641-3
Lyon
1597
1632, 1641-2
Grenoble
1638
Limoges
1632
Angoulême
Blaye
Périgueux
1637
Bordeaux
1630
1631, 1635, 1649, 1651-3, 1675
Dordogne
Garonne
Loire
Seine
Marne
Meuse
Moselle
Rhine
Rhône
Saône
Montauban
1643
Orange
1713
Avignon
Nîmes
Montpellier
1613
1639, 1644-5
Toulouse
1613
Auch
Pau
Tarbes
Bayonne
Narbonne
1635
Aix
1629
1630, 1649, 1659
Marseille
1631, 1649, 1650, 1658
Toulon
1642
1642
0°
5°
45°

Louis XIV's armies devastated the Palatinate. Frederick II's laid waste Silesia. To pay for the wars, the autocrats established bureaucracies and increased indirect taxation on goods, windows, documents and stamps.

Like Louis XIV the eighteenth-century autocrats encountered opposition from philosophers, provincial nobles, peasants and the bourgeoisie. The philosophic Enlightenment is not easy to dissect. Philosophers, moralists, historians and political thinkers in eighteenth-century France, England and Germany gradually developed an optimistic faith in the power of human reason to reach a composite truth encompassing man and nature. They saw themselves engaged in a common battle against tyranny in politics, dogma in religion, superstition in science, prejudice in morals and hypocrisy in manners. The movement spread from England, where opposition to Louis XIV's absolutism was articulated in the works of John Locke, who set out to prove that absolutism was inconvenient, dangerous, unnatural and a threat to property. But Voltaire was, through his long life and prodigious output, the most formidable *philosophe*. His greatest works were composed during the last years of his life at his Swiss retreat, les Délices. His wit made the *ancien régime* ridiculous; his moral fervour made it hateful throughout the courts and salons of Europe. The philosophers created a climate of opinion in which change was seen as necessary and good. In their stress upon Truth, Equality and Liberty they laid the foundations for the ideology of the revolutions.

The most divisive issues were the position of established religion and tolerance for minorities. Everywhere the established Church was closely interlocked with the state and the aristocracy. Initially autocrats supported the Church and repressed religious extremists, whether Huguenots,

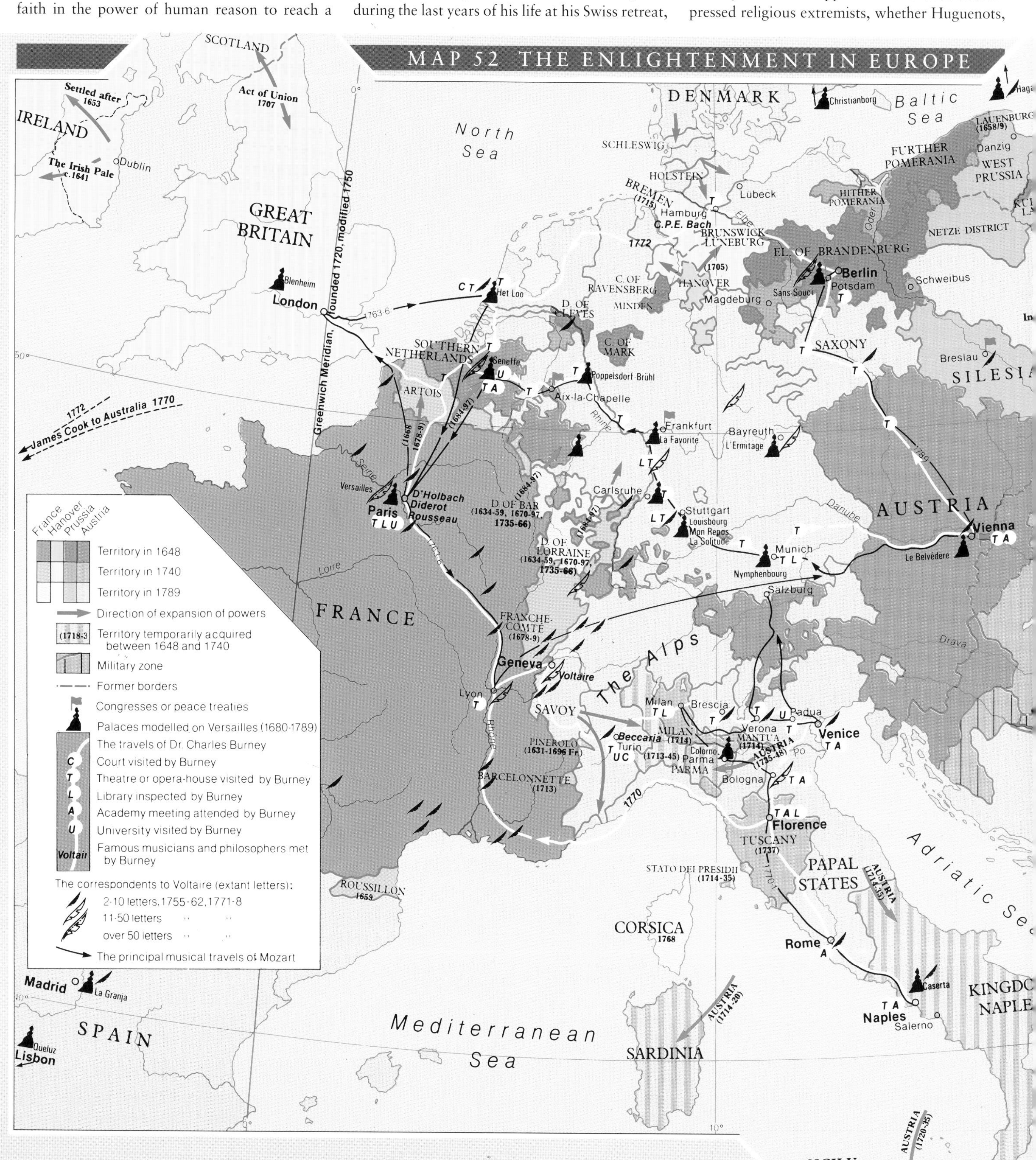

Jansenists or Quakers. But increasingly the 'enlightened' despots sought approval from the *philosophe*-inspired aristocrats and began to tolerate minorities. The expulsion of the Jesuits (who had once been the confessors and advisers of the princes) proved universally popular. Their wealth and power had made them envied, particularly for their trading companies to the New World. They were expelled from Portugal in 1759 and the order was dissolved twenty-five years later. Austria tolerated Jews from 1781; the Huguenots were officially tolerated in France from 1787. Everywhere the exclusive religion of freemasonry appealed to aristocrats for whom an embattled and obscurantist church held no attractions. Under the influence of the *philosophes* the monarchs and aristocrats of Europe rendered the established churches vulnerable in the coming revolutions.The opposition of provincial nobilities to the autocrats was patchy and sporadic. In Prussia the nobility was so involved with the army and administration that it obediently followed where the kings led. In Russia, Catherine the Great (*r.*1762-46) took care not to offend the nobility. But elsewhere in Europe, the provincial nobilities – in Ireland, Belgium, Hungary – felt that the powers of government should be reduced (*see Maps 53 and 54*).

Peasant revolts were, likewise, sporadic. These were serious in Hungary in 1678-81, 1703-11, 1735, 1751, 1755, 1763-4, 1765-6 and 1784. They were provoked by increases in seigneurial dues but extended to complaints about taxes and tithes. Twenty thousand peasants were involved in the revolt of 1755, and in the Transylvanian rising of 1784, 30,000 rebels butchered hundreds of nobles and their families. Similar revolts occurred in Russia. Further west, there was no serious peasant uprising after those at the end of Louis XIV's reign until the *Grande Peur* (Great Fear) of July 1789 (*Map 54*). The reasons lie in agricultural prosperity and the diminishing frequency of crisis years in which famine, plague, war and heavier taxation struck simultaneously and left the peasant with nothing to lose but his life.

The cornerstones of this economic growth, particularly towards the middle of the eighteenth century, were the towns, and a non-noble élite – the bourgeoisie – dominated the towns as the nobles dominated the countryside. Many continental towns had a legally defined group of burghers (bourgeois), enjoying privileges and qualifying for the status through heredity, favouritism and great wealth. They were not a new group in the eighteenth century, but they grew both in numbers and wealth. By 1800, they easily outnumbered the titled nobility in western Europe, being about 10% of the population, though no more than 3% in Hungary or Russia. Their wealth rapidly increased through trade, the professions, government investment and contracts, and prudent industrial ventures. Merchants in Marseilles, Bristol, Nantes, Cadiz, Cork, Hamburg; manufacturers in Manchester, Lyons and Barcelona; lawyers in the capital cities and judicial centres of Europe – all contributed to the expanding bourgeoisie.

It would be premature to speak of a bourgeois 'class-consciousness' anywhere before 1815 in sufficient strength to threaten the nobility or the autocrats. Only in particular circumstances did the bourgeois make use of their increased preponderance. When the forces of order failed to repress sedition, riots were sparked off by strikes, fears of bread shortage, taxation and religion. Riots in Geneva in 1781, in the towns of Holland in 1787, and in Paris in 1789 heightened the political awareness of the bourgeoisie. Religious dissent also separated some bourgeois from the common assumptions of their age sufficiently to articulate alternative ones. Baptist, Congregationalist, and Quaker merchants in England, Presbyterian manufacturers in Cork, Protestant financiers in Nîmes, Montpellier and Montauban, Jewish bankers in Berlin, Frankfort or Hamburg were all apart from or opposed to the values of the *ancien régime* despite its palsied attempts at toleration towards the end of the eighteenth century. It is not a coincidence that the most outspoken leaders in England, America and France in the age of revolutions came from religious minorities.

In the hands of far-sighted autocrats structural change in the *ancien régime* would not have been impossible. But here lay the congenital weakness of absolutism. The painters of the eighteenth century leave nothing to the imagination. From their canvases rulers and their consorts stare out, pop-eyed and pompous, their bewigged vacuous expressions revealing the emptiness of their minds. By the end of the eighteenth century western Europe lay in the hands of mad old George III in England, booby Wilhelm V in the Netherlands, erratic Joseph II in Austria and inadequate Louis XVI in France. Dominated by their diseases, their wives and their families, they present a picture not of individual misfortune, but of the generic and ineradicable disease of the *ancien régime.*

Voltaire

52 The Enlightenment in Europe
The Europe of the *ancien regime* was an agglomerate of vested interests – churches, guilds, corporations, aristocrats – whose members shared a cosmopolitan culture, increasing luxury and the excitement of the philosophical Enlightenment in their courts and salons. Some monarchs imitated the absolutism of Louis XIV, their ambitions demonstrated in their new palaces.

Further reading: Ernest Gellner, *Reason and Culture* (Basil Blackwell 1991); Pierre Goubert, *Louis XIV and Twenty Million Frenchmen* (Viking 1970); Norbert Elias, *The Court Society* (Basil Blackwell 1983); Marc Raeff, *The Well-Ordered Police State* (Yale U.P. 1983); James Casey, *The History of the Family* (Basil Blackwell 1989); Henry S. Commager, *The Empire of Reason* (Weidenfeld and Nicolson 1978; OUP New York).

The age of European supremacy 6

THE AGE OF REVOLUTIONS

When Alexis de Tocqueville published his work, The Ancien Régime and the Revolution *in 1856, he showed how much of the French Revolution was foreshadowed in the* ancien régime *(see Map 51).*

Its revolutionary principles were born of the *philosophes*; centralization of power in the state had already been achieved by the Bourbons; the peasantry was already emancipated; the process of reducing society to an aggregate of individuals, each purged of the bonds of blood, guild or corporation, had already begun. Above all, the French Revolution had been anticipated elsewhere, once with success (in the American War of Independence, 1775-83) and elsewhere in Europe with failure (notably in Geneva, 1780-82; the Netherlands, 1787-9; and Belgium, 1789).

These revolutions have been called 'democratic'. Some turned out that way, but they were not begun by democrats, and were not the result of a revolutionary movement. The collapse of the *ancien régime* came from conflicts between the ruling nobilities and autocrats. Leadership came, initially, not from the street, but from the provincial nobility – the outraged, but sober and conservative gentry. Among their leaders were George Washington, a successful soldier, a landowner, and a conscientious representative of the House of Burgesses in his state, Jan van der Capellen, the radical noble who urged the Dutch to resist their prince and govern the state themselves, and a clutch of noble radicals in the French estates general, such as the vicomte de Noailles or the affable marquis de Condorcet.

The nobility allowed the revolts to happen, but the bourgeoisie rapidly became the standard-bearers. Outraged lawyers and notables organized themselves across the east coast of America, following the example of Boston, into Sons of Liberty from 1763 (*see Map 53*). In Holland, the Patriot party grew up among the regent patricians (who ruled the towns) and their supporters so that, by 1784, they numbered 28,000 volunteers and held their first national convention. In Belgium, urban oligarchs who opposed the absolutism of Joseph II joined the clergy in a revolutionary society 'for altar and hearth' in June 1789. In France the resistance of the law-courts (the issue, as in America, was a stamp duty) encouraged the calling of an estates general in May 1789. Amongst the delegates, two-thirds were from the 'third estate', which was dominated by royal officials and lawyers from the professional bourgeoisie. Their self-confidence and their involvement in the machinery of state encouraged them to undertake a structural reform unparalleled in any other European state.

The successful revolutions reveal their ideology clearly. In the ringing terms of the American *Declaration of Independence* (1776) or the French *Declaration of the Rights of Man and Citizens* (1789) lie the manifestoes against privilege and for liberty and nationhood, blueprints for every nineteenth-century liberation movement. Liberty was a marvellous battle-cry, corrosive of all frontiers, classes, governments, boundless in its application. In the glorious dawn of 1789, when trees of liberty were being planted in France, some even dreamt of 'the possibility of a single Nation and the facility with which the Universal Assembly sitting in Paris will conduct the whole human race'. Subsequently, the National Assembly in France would grant citizenship to the great champions of liberty, Washington, Wilberforce, Schiller and Pestalozzi.

Nationalism was as corrosive as liberty but more exclusive in its impact. In August 1789, the Estates General in France transformed themselves into the National Assembly. They destroyed privilege because it damaged national integrity. A new mythology of patriotism was hastily fostered, to encourage a sense of invincible unity. Stones from the demolished Bastille were carried as souvenirs to all corners of France. In July 1793, the new nation's apparatus of flags, anthems, and identity cards was completed by an order to erect an altar of the fatherland, on which would be engraved the *Declaration of Rights* with the inscription 'The citizen is born, lives and dies for the Fatherland'.

When the Estates General referred to 'the people' in, for instance, the French *Declaration*, they meant 'the nation', sounding more democratic than, in practice, they intended to be. This impression was reinforced because their first sessions were accompanied by the enormous popular unrest in Paris which led to the fall of the Bastille on July 4 1789 and the *Grande Peur* (Great Fear) of the peasantry which destroyed seigneurial charters

53 The American Revolution
Much of the thirteen colonies area remained unaffected by the war, but the concentration of British power along the coast hampered attempts to suppress the revolution. As it gained ground the predominantly bourgeois leadership showed preference for 'Whiggish' rather than 'democratic' principles – for example, for appointive rather than elective office, and a narrow, property-based franchise – in the forms of government which were adopted.

Below: Congress approves the Declaration of Independence, July 4 1776.

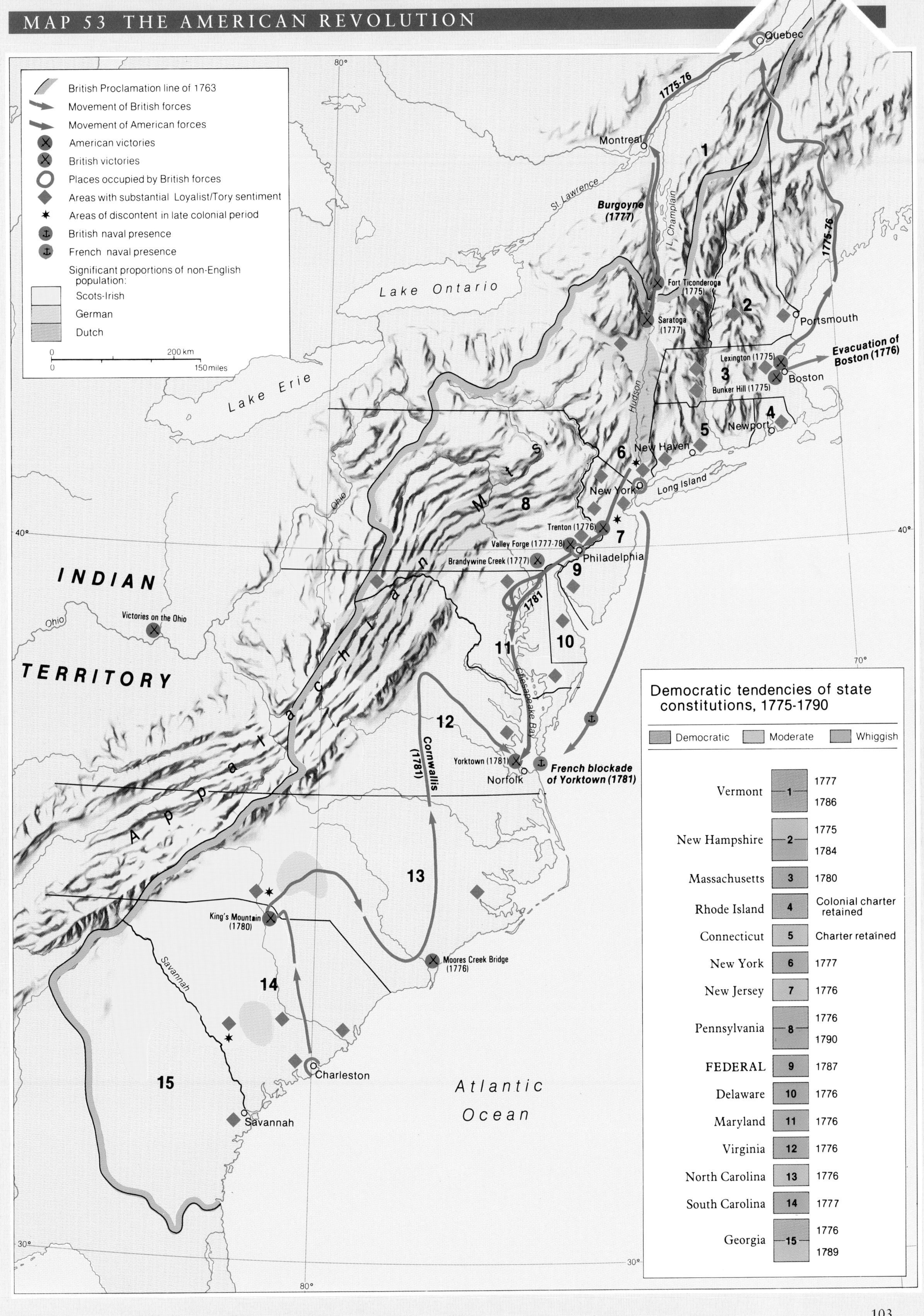

Democratic tendencies of state constitutions, 1775-1790

Democratic | Moderate | Whiggish

State	No.	Year
Vermont	1	1777, 1786
New Hampshire	2	1775, 1784
Massachusetts	3	1780
Rhode Island	4	Colonial charter retained
Connecticut	5	Charter retained
New York	6	1777
New Jersey	7	1776
Pennsylvania	8	1776, 1790
FEDERAL	9	1787
Delaware	10	1776
Maryland	11	1776
Virginia	12	1776
North Carolina	13	1776
South Carolina	14	1777
Georgia	15	1776, 1789

and documents and lent a mobbish atmosphere to their opening deliberations.

Since their independence could only be achieved through armed rebellion the American revolutionaries had no opportunity to put their ideology into practice in normal conditions. In France, on the contrary, the National (or 'Constituent') Assembly had three years to reconstruct every aspect of French life until, exploited by revolutionary exiles from England, Holland and Belgium, enthusiasm for attacking the *ancien régime* in all its manifestations caused France to declare war on Austria in 1792. The principles of this reconstruction were legal equality, representative government (with wide, but not universal, suffrage), the complete sovereignty of the state and a centralized administration. They were expressed by the reorganization of local government into eighty-three departments established on rational lines; a national system of weights and measures (in metric units) and a national system of education. Torture was abolished; privileged guilds were dismantled; the Jews were emancipated; customs dues abandoned; seigneurial obligations suppressed. The property of the French Church was nationalized and assigned to repay government debts. In a proposed constitution for the clergy, all clerics were to be chosen on democratic principles, the religious orders dissolved and the papacy excluded from influence in the French national Church. By the outbreak of war, old France had been destroyed and the most lasting institutional achievements of the age of revolutions established.

Changes on this scale bred reaction, and this changed the nature of the revolution. Louis XVI, encouraged by *emigré* royalists and the indignation of crowned heads across Europe, took flight to the frontier, only to be stopped at La Varenne. His trial and execution excited republican fervour in the National Assembly, Paris and elsewhere, and confirmed counter-revolutionary fears. Clerical opposition to the civil constitution of the clergy also divided France bitterly. Militant revolutionaries in the cities (which were already anti-clerical) became open enemies of the Church and religion, and made the priests the scapegoats for the revolution's own shortcomings. Rural France remained stubbornly Catholic and rural insurrection after 1790 in the Vende and the south of France was uniformly against the revolution. The old army and navy did not remain loyal to the new regime; its senior officers provided the bulk of the *emigrés*. From the barracks in the cities, the new National Guard, with its distinctive *sans-culottes* trousers spread the openly democratic force of Jacobinism throughout France.

Republicanism, atheism and Jacobinism inspired the language and euphoria of the revolution after 1792. They also excited streetfighters, spies, police and the dictatorial zealots of the committees of Public Safety. At the heart of 'the Terror' (as contemporaries referred to it) lay Paris itself. The way to securing the loyalty of Paris lay in the provision of its food supplies and in winning the confidence of the street-revolutionaries. The Directory (the effective successor of the National Assembly) which ruled France after 1795, failed in both tasks. Food supplies were consistently scarce and the Paris revolutionaries (like the Jacobins in the army) were bitterly divided between factions supporting various politicians of the Terror – Robespierristes, Dantonistes, etc. Nationally, the Directory became increasingly troubled both by those who feared reaction and by those who feared fresh popular violence. It depended increasingly upon force. Generals began to loom larger in its affairs and one of them, Napoleon Bonaparte, accepted the role offered him by some of the disenchanted. A *coup d'état* in November 1799 (Brumaire, year VIII, in the new calendar) made him First Consul of the Republic. Five years later, he inaugurated a hereditary empire, completing the transformation from revolution to dictatorship.

Napoleon was, in many ways, the incarnation of an eighteenth-century enlightened despot (*see Map 55*). Like his hero, Frederick the Great, he codified, rationalized, centralized, and militarized, without an *ancien regime* to cramp his style either at home or abroad. Napoleon's achievement was to define how much of the revolution should survive. In France, his *Code Napoléon* distilled the decisions of the Constituent Assembly into a readily understood and easily imposed constitutional settlement administered through departmental prefects. But he anaesthetized France against the republicanism, atheism and democratic Jacobinism of the Terror. His police harried one-time liberals and Jacobins in cities and in the army. The empire proclaimed the death of republicanism. His concordat with the Papacy in 1801 added to the widespread reaction against the excesses of the previous decade. Napoleon was so successful in reconciling the former nobles and oligarchs to his empire that there was little obstacle to the revival of traditional titles and the reintegration of the old French ruling-class and its monarchy in 1815. If the French Revolution had been a 'democratic' revolution, then Napoleon ensured its failure .

Napoleon's greatest achievement was outside France in the wider empire (*Map 55*). Here, too, he built upon revolutionary antecedents. The ideology of the French Revolution had crossed national frontiers in the 1790s, particularly affecting the areas where revolts had previously failed. Groups of social and political dissenters – 'Jacobins' – appeared in clubs and taverns in every city in Europe. They prepared the way for the French revolutionary armies which established themselves in the 1790s in Holland, Belgium, Switzerland and most of Italy.

Initially, France respected the self-determination of these 'allies' in revolution. Subsequently the Directory was less tolerant. In Belgium (which, as the Republic of the United Belgian Provinces, had seceded from the Hapsburg empire in 1790) a rigged plebiscite was held; property belonging to the 'accomplices' of tyranny was confiscated and an enfeebled French currency introduced. By 1795 Belgium had become once more a mere geographical expression, having been divided into nine French departments ruled from Paris. The Rhineland and north-western Italy were similarly treated, without the tiresome pretence of a plebiscite. The Dutch Provinces, Switzerland, Lombardy and Dalmatia were permitted the semblance of separate identity as the Batavian, Helvetian, Cisalpine and Illyrian republics. The inner collapse of the Directory and the European reaction against domination dressed as liberation left only Belgium secure in French hands by 1799.

Napoleon could rebuild the French continental empire because the memory of the revolutionary wars was still green in Europe. This time, the armies exported the code, the prefects, police, and conscription (over half the army at Moscow in 1812 was non-French) and imported the treasures of Florence, Venice and the Near East. Even countries like Prussia, which remained independent, could not avoid the influence of Bonapartism. Prussian reformers began to look to the destruction of serfdom, to open the army (cautiously) to non-nobles, and to preach a distinctive nationalism.

There was remarkably little popular resistance within the Napoleonic empire to this extension of French power. Where popular risings did occur, they were the product of traditional rivalries (the Tyrolese in 1808 against the Bavarians) or religious affiliations (in Spain in 1808 and Russia in 1812). In Italy, apart from the extreme Francophobe *Carbonari*, who pledged themselves to counter-revolution after 1809 (*see Map 60*), the French constructed national institutions which would form the basis of Italian movements for unification in the nineteenth century. In Germany too, Napoleon's rationalization of frontiers, emancipation of serfs and Jews, and abolition of restrictions on commerce, earned him support from men including Metternich, Hegel, Goethe and Beethoven.

Only in the great land empires of Ottoman Turkey and tsarist Russia, and the maritime empire of England, did Napoleon fail to leave any lasting monument. When these powers were finally victorious after the battle of Waterloo (1815) against Bonaparte, it was believed that the subsequent Congress of Vienna would recreate the *ancien regime*. In fact in France as throughout most of continental Europe this proved impossible. Boundaries, administrations, armies, laws and patterns of thought had all been irreversibly changed by the revolutionary experience. And one of the guarantors of the Congress of Vienna was England which, following its own distinctive path, undertook by peaceful means the changes that the men of 1789 had accomplished by force and emerged as the champion in nineteenth-century Europe of their liberal and nationalist principles.

54 The French Revolution
Under the pressure of internal opposition and external attack (which by autumn 1793 threatened to extinguish the revolution) the National Assembly, which had dismantled the *ancien regime* in France, gave way to the growing chaos of the Terror and the Directorate. But its main achievement was permanent. As Goethe said, 'Here begins a new age in the history of the world.'

Further reading: Alexis de Tocqueville, *The Old Regime and the French Revolution* tr. S. Gilbert (Anchor 1955); Edward Countryman, *The American Revolution* (I. B. Tauris 1986; Hill & Wang); T. C. Blanning, *The Origins of the French Revolutionary Wars* (Longman 1986); D. M. G. Sutherland, *France 1789-1815: Revolution and Counterrevolution* (Collins 1985; OUP. New York); C. A. Bayly, *Imperial Meridian: The British Empire and the World, 1780-1830* (Longman 1989).

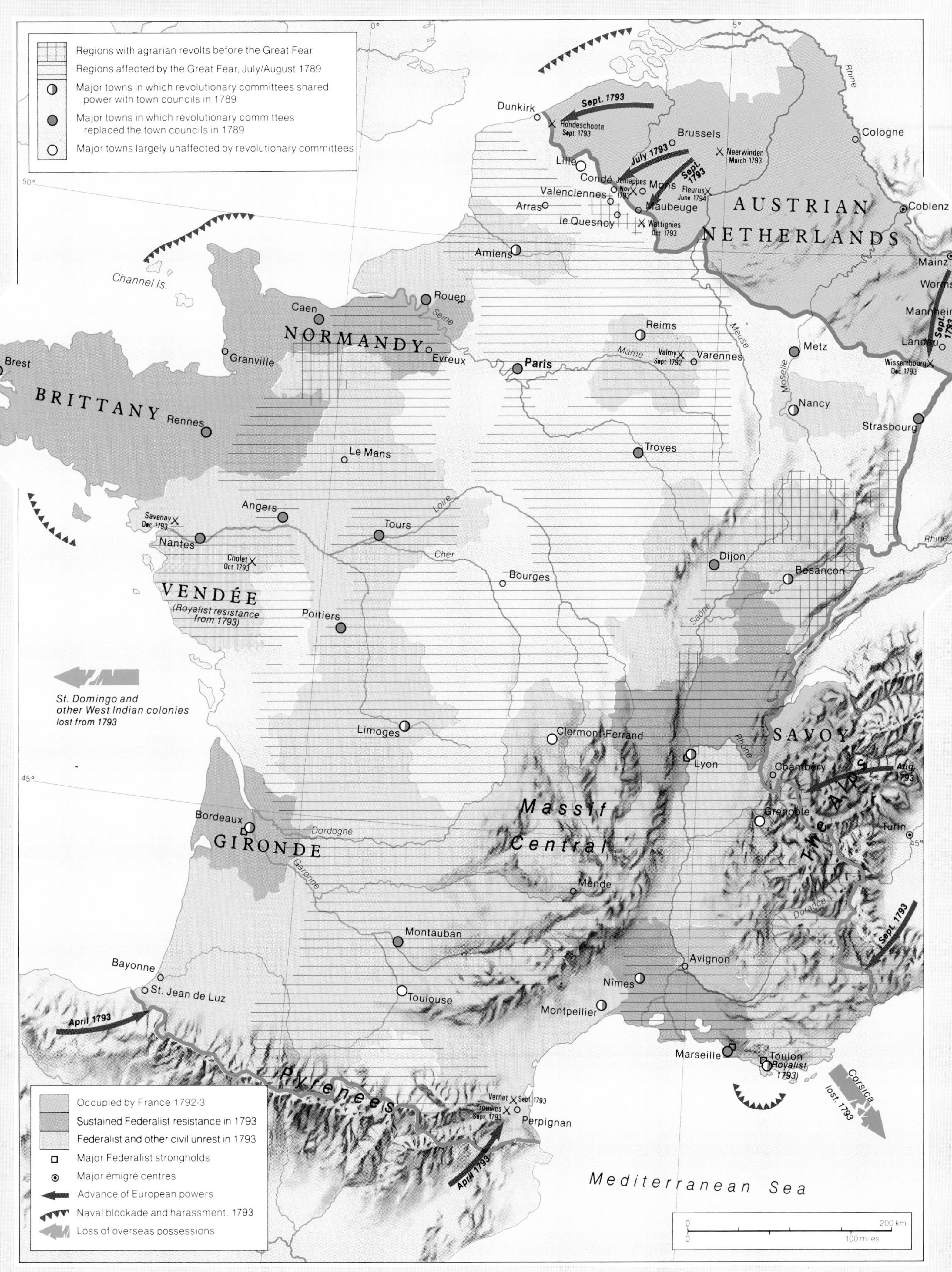

Regions with agrarian revolts before the Great Fear
Regions affected by the Great Fear, July/August 1789
Major towns in which revolutionary committees shared power with town councils in 1789
Major towns in which revolutionary committees replaced the town councils in 1789
Major towns largely unaffected by revolutionary committees
Occupied by France 1792-3
Sustained Federalist resistance in 1793
Federalist and other civil unrest in 1793
Major Federalist strongholds
Major émigré centres
Advance of European powers
Naval blockade and harassment, 1793
Loss of overseas possessions
AUSTRIAN NETHERLANDS
NORMANDY
BRITTANY
VENDÉE
(Royalist resistance from 1793)
GIRONDE
SAVOY
Massif Central
The Alps
Pyrenees
Mediterranean Sea
Channel Is.
St. Domingo and other West Indian colonies lost from 1793
Corsica lost, 1793
Dunkirk
Hondeschoote Sept. 1793
Sept. 1793
Brussels
Neerwinden March 1793
July 1793
Cologne
Lille
Condé
Jemappes Nov 1792
Mons
Fleurus June 1794
Valenciennes
Arras
Maubeuge
le Quesnoy
Wattignies Oct 1793
Coblenz
Amiens
Mainz
Worms
Mannheim
Landau
Rouen
Caen
Seine
Reims
Granville
Evreux
Paris
Marne
Valmy Sept. 1792
Varennes
Meuse
Metz
Moselle
Wissembourg Dec. 1793
Brest
Rennes
Nancy
Strasbourg
Le Mans
Troyes
Angers
Savenay Dec. 1793
Loire
Tours
Nantes
Cholet Oct 1793
Cher
Dijon
Rhine
Bourges
Besançon
Poitiers
Saône
Limoges
Clermont-Ferrand
Lyon
Rhône
Chambery
Aug. 1793
Grenoble
Turin
Bordeaux
Dordogne
Garonne
Mende
Durance
Montauban
Avignon
Bayonne
St. Jean de Luz
Nimes
Toulouse
Montpellier
April 1793
Marseille
Toulon (Royalist 1793)
Vernet Sept. 1793
Trouilles Sept. 1793
Perpignan
0° 5° 50° 45°
0 200 km
0 100 miles

The age of European supremacy 7

THE INDUSTRIAL REVOLUTION

As France was the progenitor of political revolution in the nineteenth century, England was the home of the industrial revolution. Industrial innovation was not new in itself, but the series of self-perpetuating and apparently unstoppable developments which were set in motion by the advances made in eighteenth-century Britain transformed the life of man and the nature of human society more profoundly and more rapidly than anything that had happened since the appearance of agriculture (see Map 2).

The industrial revolution originated in new methods for the exploitation of coal, iron and steam-power, which complemented and stimulated one another to create a massive increase in production, wealth and population. 'Carboniferous capitalism' (as it has been christened) had advanced far enough in Britain by 1815 to enable her to take a decisive lead in post-Napoleonic Europe (*Map 56*). Belgium followed the same course (under British influence) after its independence in 1830, and parts of Germany and France had experienced the same changes by 1870 (*see Map 57*).

Coal, already mined on an unprecedented scale in England in the seventeenth century, was transported from the coalfields of Northumberland and Durham by sea to provide the capital with domestic fuel. In the eighteenth century, it provided a source of energy which ended the domination of wind and water. By 1800, Britain was using 11 million tons of coal a year; by 1870, 100 million tons. The mines of the Newcastle area attracted civil and mechanical engineers as well as surveyors and managers of a higher calibre than anywhere else in Europe.

By the end of the seventeenth century iron too was worked on a large scale in England. But the vital process of producing pig iron by using coal (reduced to the form of smelting coke) established by Abraham Darby at Coalbrookdale in 1709

55 The Europe of Napoleon
The conquests of the French revolutionary armies were accompanied everywhere by the collapse of the *ancien régime*, to be replaced by the prefectoral system of government and the legal code which Napoleon had devised for France; despite the victory of 'legitimacy' in 1815 the *Code civil* continued to provide a basis for liberal regimes in Europe throughout the nineteenth century.

MAP 55 THE EUROPE OF NAPOLEON

Main campaigns of revolutionary and Napoleonic armies
Frontiers after 1815
German Confederation, 1815
Areas under direct French rule during revolutionary and Napoleonic periods:
for more than 10 years
5-10 years
less than 5 years
Main satellite regimes with date of establishment
Departmental administration introduced
Code civil remained in force after 1815
Later adoption of a legal code based on *Code civil*
(1873) Date of adoption of code
Departmental boundaries

increased the supply and reduced the cost. Iron freed the engineer from dependence upon wood and expensive soft metals. Its uses seemed endless. Pig iron output in Britain rose from about 20,000 tons in 1720 to 250,000 tons in 1806. By 1830 Britain produced more iron than continental Europe and America combined.

The steam engine used the new source of energy and the new material. Atmospheric engines were already used in England in the early eighteenth century to drain water from mines. In the 1760s, James Watt (1736-1819) produced a genuine steam engine. In the 1770s, he went into partnership with a metal manufacturer from Birmingham, Matthew Boulton, and their manufactory marketed a stationary steam engine which could force draught to blast furnaces, drain mines and power factories. As Boulton wrote in 1781, 'The people in London, Manchester and Birmingham are steam-mill mad'.

The application of steam-power to transport followed. Eighteenth-century turnpike trusts had improved English roads but the canal boom of the 1780s, which completed the improvement of river navigation undertaken since the seventeenth century, was vital for the transporting of bulk cargo such as iron ore and coal in the early industrial revolution (*Map 56*). While there were some steam-powered barges in the early nineteenth century, railways united the forces of iron, coal and steam-power. The first regular working railway – from Stockton to Darlington – was completed in 1825. By 1840, there were 1500 miles of trunk route in operation and many more under construction. By 1870 the English network was complete with over 15,000 miles of 'iron road'.

Britain also developed the first sizeable factory industry in cotton products, which were soon being exported throughout the world. The cloth industry in England flourished in the eighteenth century, producing woollens and worsteds, linens and, on a smaller scale, cottons. Everywhere in Europe the fabrication of these cloths was farmed out to rural spinners and weavers and finishing undertaken in the towns by the merchant entrepreneurs. Capacity was low and price was high because up to eight spinners were required to keep one weaver at work. The famous spinning jenny which was invented in 1770 by James Hargreaves replaced the old spinning wheel in the hands of rural workers. Cheaper cloth and the delays and expense of transport made industrial concentration an attractive prospect. Samuel Crompton (1753-1817) produced a hybrid jenny which could easily be steampowered and arranged in factories. Cartwright's powered loom, introduced after 1800, offered the same advantages. By the turn of the century, there were cotton mills on the Lancashire Plain. Less than two million pounds weight was imported through Liverpool in 1700; over fifty million pounds by 1800.

The industrial revolution wrought enormous changes. The construction of the railways, for instance, brought work to armies of navvies, transformed the value of land and stimulated unprecedented financial speculation. Their operation changed the meaning of time and distance. London, a capital city which (like every capital in Europe) had grown prodigiously in the eighteenth century, was the focus for many of these changes. But it was the new industrial towns of the Black Country and Lancashire Plain, mushrooming out to meet each other in conurbations, which experienced most keenly the first industrial revolution. Manchester, its population rising from 75,000 in 1800 to 400,000 in 1850, was surrounded by industrial towns expanding around their factories, workshops, blast furnaces and coke ovens. In them, change was untrammelled by institutions. Plans and regulations came too late. Streets of terraced houses were thrown up cheaply, often without sewerage and water. Poverty and insanitary conditions had been dispersed in the countryside, but concentrated in towns they reached horrifying proportions. Typhoid and cholera epidemics broke out throughout Europe in 1832 and again in 1848 and 1849 (*Map 58*). Because of the inadequate sewers, the water-borne germ was spread by polluted rivers. Many other diseases – notably scarlet fever and small-pox – were endemic and dangerous killers. The problem was an intensely serious one in England because by 1851 more than half the population was living in cities.

Migration to, and mobility within, these new industrial cities emphasized the chasm between rich and poor. Housing, income, living standards,

life-expectancy, education, geography, all reinforced the distinction. Every nineteenth-century industrial city had its West End and its East End, later its inner-city slum and its outer-city suburb. Amongst some contemporaries, it aroused guilty feelings which spilled over into early socialism. Others turned sour and escapist, reacting (like Wordsworth) to 'Industry's command' by retreating to a romantic nature and idealized past. Friedrich Engels was inspired to radical politics after seeing the industrial unrest around Manchester; his friend, Karl Marx, an exile from the European Revolutions of 1848, used the industrial cities of England as his model for a class struggle in which the industrial proletariat would shortly triumph.

Marx was proved wrong in Europe in the generation after 1848, partly because prosperity increased and was not confined to a narrow oligarchy. Real income per head rose substantially in Britain after 1850, for this was a century of falling prices in food as well as clothing and housing. Agricultural changes enabled England to meet the increased demand for food for its rapidly expanding population until the 1870s. These changes had already made the English countryside physically, economically and socially different from the rest of Europe by 1800. Open fields, where the absence of hedges between neighbouring plots preserved customary agricultural techniques, stretched across all the plains of Europe with the exception of the Po Valley, Flanders and England. There in the course of the seventeenth and eighteenth centuries, enclosed fields, farmed with all the intensity of a cottage garden, dramatically broke with traditional communal practices and made innovation possible in crops and methods. Economically, the English countryside was less isolated from its markets than that of the rest of Europe. Socially, no other country had such a large class of tenant farmers, capable of investing so much in agricultural expansion, new machinery, stock and seed. As a result, Britain avoided T. R. Malthus' law of population, that in history population always expanded beyond the means to sustain it.

Marx was also proved wrong because state legislation and new technology alleviated the problems of the industrial city. The state intervened in factory safety, public health and education in Britain in the later nineteenth century. The technology of conveying fresh water in iron pipes and sewerage in glazed pottery pipes reduced the dangers of water-borne infection; western Europe was clear of cholera by 1911. Cleaner gas heating, electric lighting, electric trams and underground railways all improved urban life dramatically by 1900. Co-operative shops and chain stores improved marketing and distribution in towns. As a result, it was the philosophy of infinite material progress rather than Marxism which appeared to be confirmed at every turn to urban man in the late nineteenth century.

The benefits and wealth generated by the industrial revolution were not confined to Britain. In 1850, Britain was the manufacturer, clothier, banker, shipper, insurer and transporter to the world, a pre-eminence demonstrated at the Great Exhibition of 1851. London invited the whole world to its shop-window, confident that its wares would outstrip all comers. But the pre-eminence did not last for long. Flanders began its industrial revolution in the 1830s; the Rhur in the 1850s and 1860s imitated British technology, frequently used British capital and engineers and sometimes avoided British mistakes. By the 1870s, the second phase of the industrial revolution (as it is now commonly called) had begun in Germany and the United States (*see Maps 57 and 69*). In this second phase, a new trinity of steel, electricity and petrochemicals dominated the industrial world. By 1900, Germany and the United States produced more steel than Britain. The United States developed – with its natural resources and tycoons – the technology of the internal combustion engine. Germany, with the help of state intervention and adventurous bankers, exploited electrical technology for power, transport and communications. After the turn of the century, the exploitation of hydro-electric power in the Alps helped France and Italy at last to increase the pace of their progress towards industrialization. English manufacturers, secure in their belief in progress, the continued primacy of coal and their imperial self-sufficiency, fitted snugly into a liberal society where tradition and innovation had been reconciled, and met competition with complacency. They were inevitably less conspicuous in the Great Exhibitions in Paris in 1867, Chicago in 1880 and Melbourne in 1891 than they had been in 1851. In Europe, as in Britain, food prices fell, spreading the benefits of industrial change amongst the citizens of the new industrial towns and compelling change amongst the peasantry of Europe which felt the demands from the new markets.

In another important respect, the industrial revolution was a 'Prometheus Unbound'. In 1846 the abolition of tariffs on corn imported into England was, in retrospect, a sign that the days of British self-sufficiency were numbered. The opening-up of the prairies in the 1870s and 1880s in America (*Map 68*), the application of mechanized farming methods there, and the impact of railways and steamships on transport, resulted in the large-scale importation of American wheat to Europe. A similar pattern was established with the imports of butter, cheese and Canterbury lamb from New Zealand (using refrigerated shipping) in the 1880s. The canned meat trade also developed from South America to Europe. The export of European capital across the world and the migration of Europeans which followed it, emphasized European predominance in the nineteenth century (*see Map 67*). But it also, with the development of world communications by telegraph and telephone, and the new patterns of trade established in the wake of the industrial revolutions, created the basis for a world community in the twentieth century.

Above left: The first large Iron Bridge, built across the River Severn at Colebrookdale, England, in 1777.

56 The Industrial Revolution in Great Britain
The complementary exploitation of coal, iron and steam power produced the rapid diversification of economic activity and huge increases in production which made Britain the first industrial society, rapidly becoming wealthier, more populous and more urban, in the first half of the nineteenth century.

57 The Industrial Revolution in Europe
Except in Belgium, industrialization did not gather pace in continental Europe until the second half of the nineteenth century. Its 'second phase', dominated by steel, chemicals and electricity, was led by Germany. In the most backward regions industrialization was far too late to absorb an explosion of rural population which created acute social tensions and rising emigration.

58 Cholera 1817-1952
The growth of world-wide communications with colonialism and of concentrated urban populations with industrialization made western man terrifyingly vulnerable to infectious diseases until they could be checked by the advances in medical knowledge, sanitation and public health.

Further reading: E. A. Wrigley, *Continuity, Chance and Change* (Cambridge U.P. 1988); David S. Landes, *The Unbound Prometheus* (Cambridge U.P. 1969); E. L. Jones, *Growth Recurring* (Oxford U.P. 1989); Eric Hobsbawm, *The Age of Capital* (Weidenfeld & Nicolson 1975; Scribner); Richard J. Evans, *Death in Hamburg: Society and Politics in the Cholera Years, 1830-1910* (Oxford U.P. 1987).

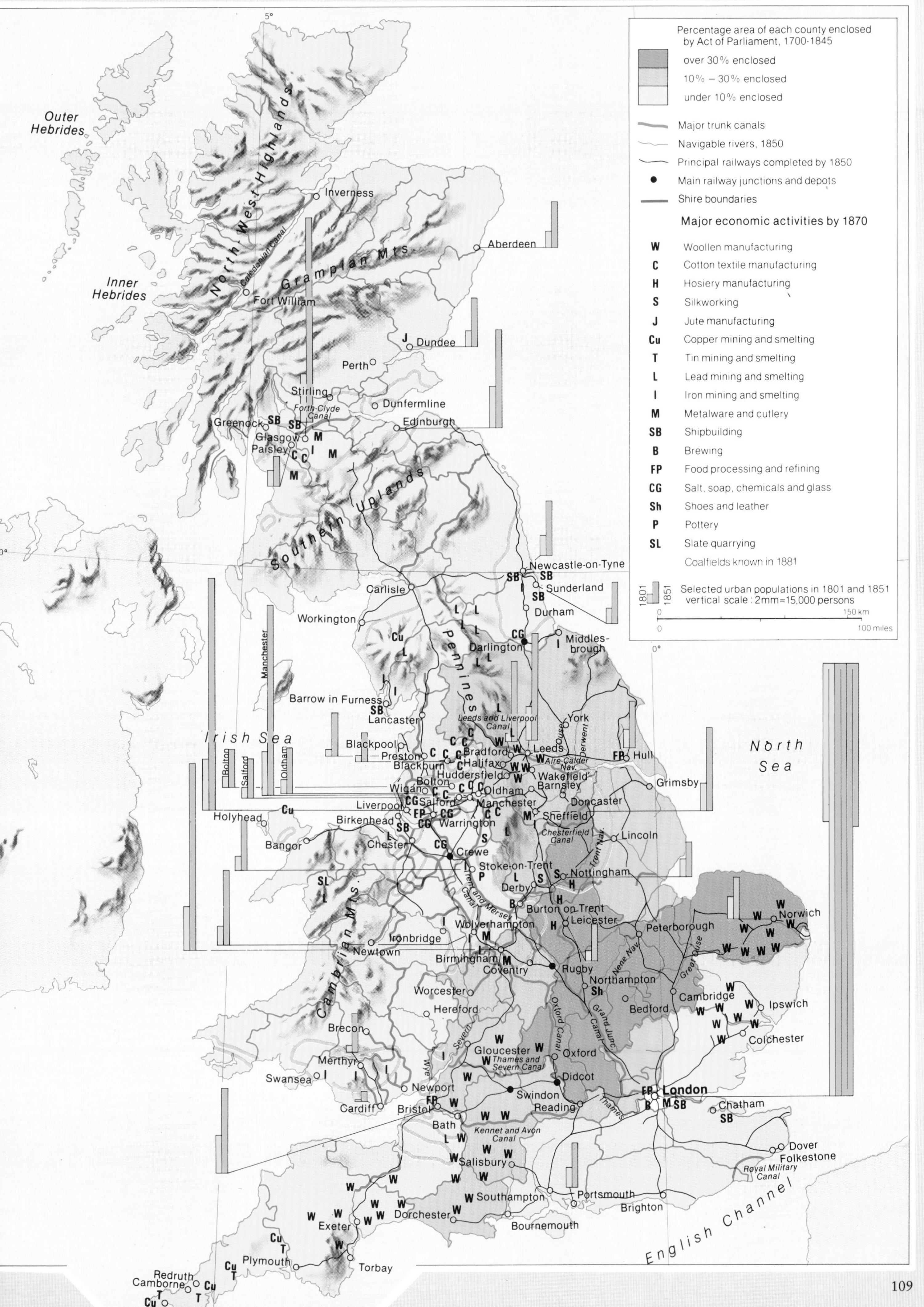

Percentage area of each county enclosed by Act of Parliament, 1700-1845
over 30% enclosed
10% – 30% enclosed
under 10% enclosed
Major trunk canals
Navigable rivers, 1850
Principal railways completed by 1850
Main railway junctions and depots
Shire boundaries
Major economic activities by 1870
W Woollen manufacturing
C Cotton textile manufacturing
H Hosiery manufacturing
S Silkworking
J Jute manufacturing
Cu Copper mining and smelting
T Tin mining and smelting
L Lead mining and smelting
I Iron mining and smelting
M Metalware and cutlery
SB Shipbuilding
B Brewing
FP Food processing and refining
CG Salt, soap, chemicals and glass
Sh Shoes and leather
P Pottery
SL Slate quarrying
Coalfields known in 1881
1801 1851 Selected urban populations in 1801 and 1851 vertical scale: 2mm=15,000 persons
0 150 km
0 100 miles
Outer Hebrides
Inner Hebrides
North West Highlands
Grampian Mts.
Southern Uplands
Pennines
Cambrian Mts.
Irish Sea
North Sea
English Channel
Inverness
Aberdeen
Fort William
Caledonian Canal
Dundee
Perth
Stirling
Forth-Clyde Canal
Dunfermline
Edinburgh
Greenock
Glasgow
Paisley
Newcastle-on-Tyne
Sunderland
Durham
Carlisle
Workington
Darlington
Middles-brough
Manchester
Barrow in Furness
Lancaster
Leeds and Liverpool Canal
York
Blackpool
Preston
Blackburn
Bradford
Leeds
Halifax
Aire-Calder Nav.
Huddersfield
Wakefield
Barnsley
Hull
Grimsby
Bolton
Salford
Oldham
Wigan
Liverpool
Manchester
Doncaster
Holyhead
Birkenhead
Warrington
Sheffield
Chesterfield Canal
Lincoln
Bangor
Chester
Crewe
Stoke-on-Trent
Trent and Mersey Canal
Trent Nav.
Nottingham
Derby
Burton on Trent
Leicester
Wolverhampton
Peterborough
Norwich
Ironbridge
Newtown
Birmingham
Coventry
Rugby
Nene Nav.
Great Ouse
Northampton
Cambridge
Ipswich
Worcester
Hereford
Bedford
Oxford Canal
Grand Junc. Canal
Brecon
Severn
Gloucester
Thames and Severn Canal
Oxford
Colchester
Merthyr
Wye
Swansea
Newport
Didcot
Swindon
Reading
Thames
London
Cardiff
Bristol
Chatham
Bath
Kennet and Avon Canal
Dover
Folkestone
Royal Military Canal
Salisbury
Southampton
Portsmouth
Brighton
Dorchester
Exeter
Bournemouth
Plymouth
Torbay
Redruth
Camborne
Penzance
50°
5°
0°

Population, 1850-1910:
Declining
Stable
Increase up to 50%
Increase 50% - 100%
Increase more than 100%
Selected urban populations in 1850 and 1910:
under 100,000
100,000 - 500,000
500,000 - 1,000,000
over 1,000,000
Emigrants from Europe, 1881-1910, with principal destinations
Alsace-Lorraine, ceded to Germany, 1870
Area within which the main rail network was complete by 1870
Lines constructed by 1848
Other major lines constructed, 1848-1870
Other major lines constructed, 1870-1914
Industry, c.1870:
Areas of coal mining, c.1870
Areas of iron working, c.1870
Areas of textile production, c.1870
Industry, c.1914:
S Steel
E Engineering
Sb Shipbuilding
C Chemicals
El Electrical industry
O Oil production
0 500 kms
0 300 miles
North Sea
Mediterranean Sea
to N. America from Scandinavia 1,535,000
to U.S.A. from Ireland 1,414,000
to N. America, S. Africa and Australasia from Great Britain 7,144,000
to N. and S. America from Germany 2,143,000
to U.S.A. from Low Countries 171,000
to Central and S. America from France 223,000
to S. America from Portugal 775,000
to Central and S. America and N. Africa from Spain 1,472,000
to N. and S. America from Austria-Hungary 1,799,000
to U.S.A. and N. Africa from Italy 6,187,000
Christiania
Göteborg
Copenhagen
Malmö
Glasgow
Edinburgh
Belfast
Newcastle
Sunderland
Dublin
Manchester
Bolton
Liverpool
Salford
Bradford
Leeds
Hull
Sheffield
Stoke
Walsall
Derby
Birmingham
Cardiff
Bristol
London
Portsmouth
Kiel
Lübeck
Hamburg
Bremen
Stettin
Amsterdam
The Hague
Rotterdam
Utrecht
Hanover
Bielefeld
Brunswick
Berlin
Münster
Magdeburg
Antwerp
Ghent
Tourcoing
Roubaix
Lille
Brussels
Liège
Charleroi
Namur
Aachen
Verviers
Krefeld
Duisburg
Essen
Bochum
Dortmund
Wuppertal
Dusseldorf
Cologne
Kassel
Leipzig
Dresden
Erfurt
Chemnitz
Cherbourg
Le Havre
Rouen
Amiens
Brest
Paris
Reims
Wiesbaden
Frankfurt
Prague
Longwy
Hayange
Metz
Nancy
Strasbourg
Mannheim
Stuttgart
Nuremberg
Rennes
Nantes
Loire
Tours
Seine
Meuse
Rhine
Augsburg
Munich
Linz
Mulhouse
Montbéliard
Basle
Zurich
Fourchambault
Le Creusot
Commentery
Limoges
Geneva
Clermont Ferrand
Lyon
St. Etienne
Firminy
Grenoble
Decazeville
Bordeaux
Garonne
Toulouse
Rhône
Marseilles
Toulon
Nice
Varese
Milan
Bergamo
Brescia
Turin
Venice
Trieste
Graz
Po
Genoa
Savona
Bologna
Livorno
Florence
Piombino
Terni
Rome
Naples
Sassari
Cagliari
Palermo
Catania
Oviedo
Gijon
Santander
Bilbao
San Sebastian
Oporto
Duero
Valladolid
Saragossa
Ebro
Madrid
Tagus
Toledo
Barcelona
Lisbon
Valencia
Seville
Cordoba
Alicante
Murcia
Cartagena
Jerez
Cadiz
Malaga
Marbella
Almeria
Algiers
Oran
Tunis

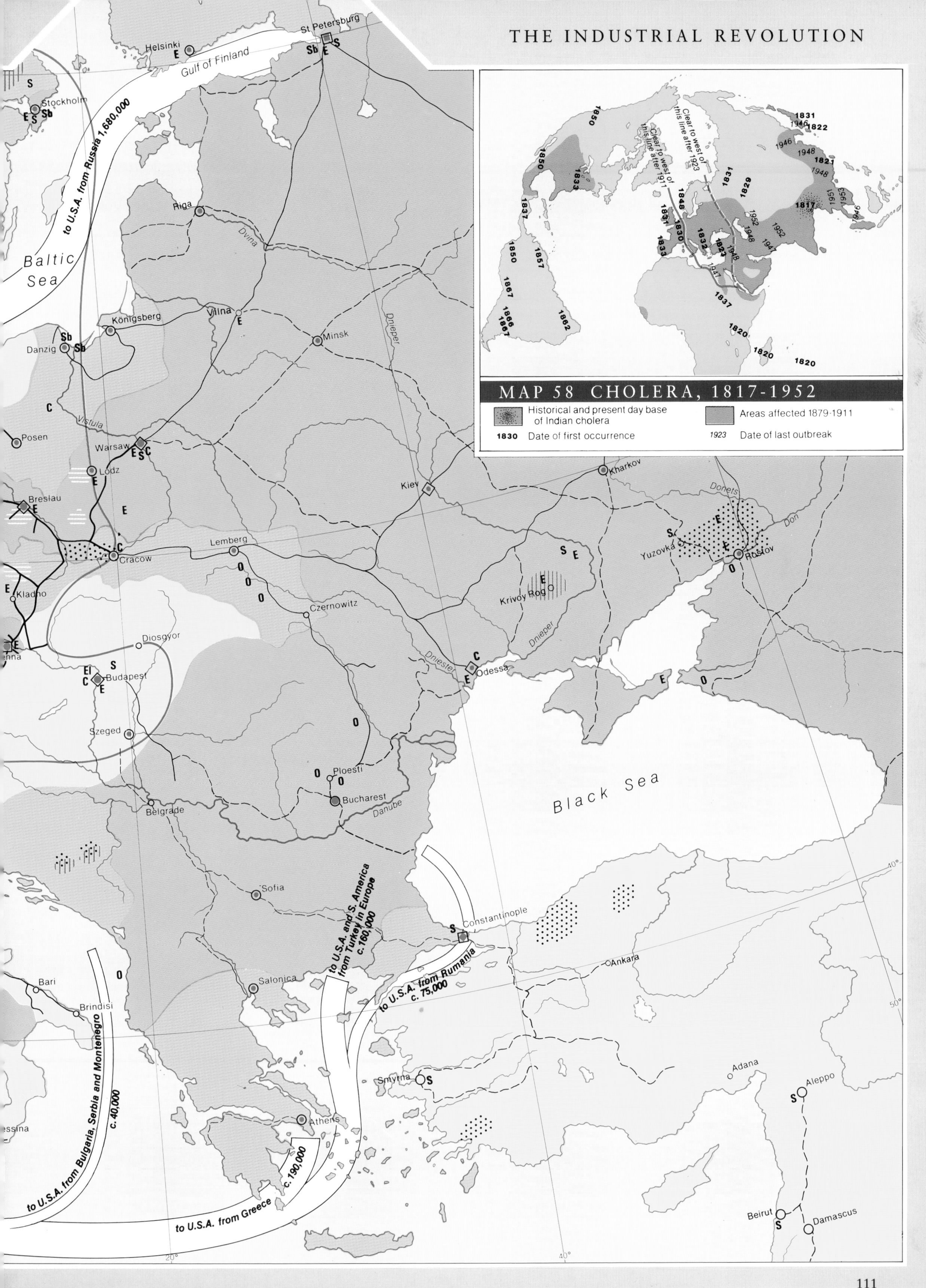
MAP 58 CHOLERA, 1817-1952
Historical and present day base of Indian cholera
Areas affected 1879-1911
1830 Date of first occurrence
1923 Date of last outbreak
Clear to west of this line after 1911
Clear to west of this line after 1923
Baltic Sea
Gulf of Finland
Black Sea
to U.S.A. from Russia 1,680,000
to U.S.A. and S. America from Turkey in Europe c.160,000
to U.S.A. from Rumania c. 75,000
to U.S.A. from Greece c. 190,000
to U.S.A. from Bulgaria, Serbia and Montenegro c. 40,000
St Petersburg
Helsinki
Stockholm
Riga
Königsberg
Vilna
Minsk
Danzig
Posen
Warsaw
Lodz
Breslau
Cracow
Lemberg
Kiev
Kharkov
Czernowitz
Krivoy Rog
Yuzovka
Rostov
Odessa
Diosgyor
Budapest
Szeged
Ploesti
Bucharest
Belgrade
Sofia
Constantinople
Ankara
Salonica
Bari
Brindisi
Athens
Smyrna
Adana
Aleppo
Beirut
Damascus
Dvina
Dnieper
Vistula
Dniester
Donets
Don
Danube

The age of European supremacy 8

LIBERALISM AND NATIONALISM

Although reaction appeared triumphant in the aftermath of 1815, as conservative rule was restored to most of Europe (Map 60), the twin forces of liberalism and nationalism which had been unleashed by the French revolution continued their volcanic rumblings beneath the surface of international politics.

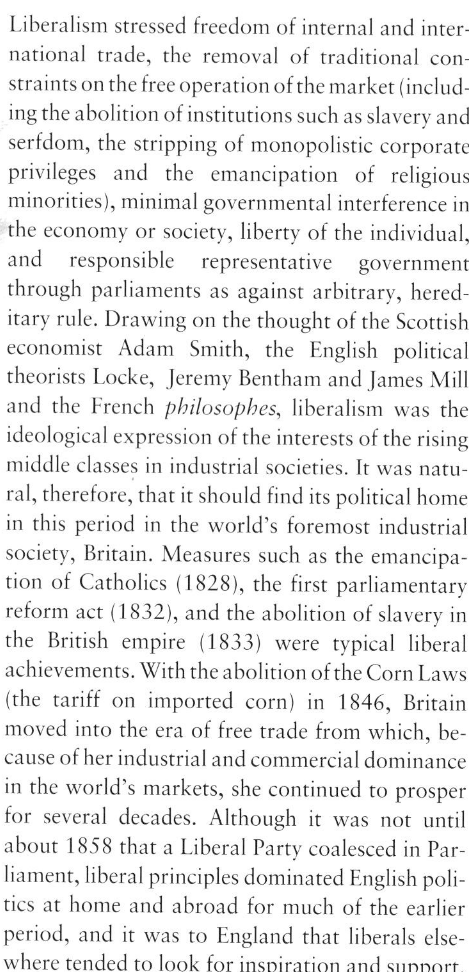

Liberalism stressed freedom of internal and international trade, the removal of traditional constraints on the free operation of the market (including the abolition of institutions such as slavery and serfdom, the stripping of monopolistic corporate privileges and the emancipation of religious minorities), minimal governmental interference in the economy or society, liberty of the individual, and responsible representative government through parliaments as against arbitrary, hereditary rule. Drawing on the thought of the Scottish economist Adam Smith, the English political theorists Locke, Jeremy Bentham and James Mill and the French *philosophes*, liberalism was the ideological expression of the interests of the rising middle classes in industrial societies. It was natural, therefore, that it should find its political home in this period in the world's foremost industrial society, Britain. Measures such as the emancipation of Catholics (1828), the first parliamentary reform act (1832), and the abolition of slavery in the British empire (1833) were typical liberal achievements. With the abolition of the Corn Laws (the tariff on imported corn) in 1846, Britain moved into the era of free trade from which, because of her industrial and commercial dominance in the world's markets, she continued to prosper for several decades. Although it was not until about 1858 that a Liberal Party coalesced in Parliament, liberal principles dominated English politics at home and abroad for much of the earlier period, and it was to England that liberals elsewhere tended to look for inspiration and support.

A striking example was the liberation of Latin America from Spanish and Portuguese colonial rule (*Map 59*). The leaders of the liberation movement, Francisco de Miranda, Simón Bolívar, and José de San Martín, were much influenced by the ideas of English liberalism, and by the American and French revolutions. After the collapse of the short-lived first Venezuelan republic, proclaimed in 1811, Miranda was imprisoned in Spain (dying in gaol in 1816), while Bolívar fled to neighbouring New Granada, and thence after 1814 to Jamaica and Haiti. During the next three years he organized his army anew, and in 1817 he returned to Venezuela, landing at Angostura. From there he led his troops (among whom were several thousand European, particularly British, volunteers) in a series of epic campaigns through difficult country, capturing Bogotá in 1819, and Quito in 1822. Meanwhile in the south of the continent San Martín had formed his 'Army of the Andes' in Argentina. In one of the most remarkable campaigns in military history, San Martín led his forces across the Andes and into Chile, fewer than half surviving the journey. After inflicting defeat on the Spaniards at the battle of Chacabuco, he was able to proclaim the independence of Chile in 1818. By 1821 he had made a triumphal entry into Lima after a thousand-mile sea voyage with his men in a fleet commanded by the British admiral, Lord Cochrane. The two liberators met at Guayaquil in 1822, but they fell out, and Bolívar wrested leadership of the movement from his rival. After 1825, with the liberation of the sub-continent virtually complete, Bolívar devoted his energies to preserving the unity of 'Gran Colombia' – but in vain. By the time of his death in 1830 the former Spanish empire had fragmented into small units. By contrast the former Portuguese territory of Brazil remained united after its bloodless separation from Portugal in 1822 under the Emperor Pedro I. The liberation process had received strong support from the USA, whose President, James Monroe, in 1823 enunciated his celebrated 'doctrine' prohibiting European intervention against the nascent republics, and from Britain, whose Foreign Secretary, Canning, in 1826 declared that he had 'called the New World into being to redress the balance of the Old'.

In the Old World, however, liberals faced more formidable opposition as conservative governments concerted their defensive measures in the 'congress system'. This was the term applied to the four-power alliance of Britain, Russia, Prussia, and Austria, in November 1815, whereby the signatories agreed to meet periodically in congress to discuss common measures to preserve the *status quo* as enshrined in the Treaty of Vienna (*Map 60*). However, as the system, masterminded by the Austrian statesman Metternich, was rapidly revealed to be a 'Holy Alliance' of conservative forces determined to crush liberal tendencies throughout Europe, Britain gradually dissociated herself from the arrangement. Britain objected to the French military intervention in Spain in 1822, conducted with the blessing of the Holy Alliance, which repressed a liberal revolt there. Austrian intervention in Italy to crush liberal rebellions, particularly those of the secret nationalist society, the *Carbonari*, further aroused British indignation. The marriage of liberalism and nationalism found its ultimate consummation in the Greek War of Liberation between 1821 and 1829 (*Map 63*). Romantic revolutionaries from all over Europe, among them Lord Byron, flocked to the Greek cause and sang its praises. Russia, stealing a further march on the Turks, supported the Greeks. In the naval battle of Navarino (1827) British, French, and Russian forces defeated the Turks. With conservatism now in some disarray, the liberals took an important stride forward in 1830, when the last

Above: Simon Bolívar (1783-1830).

59 Independent Latin America
Protected from hostile European intervention by Britain and America (the Monroe doctrine was proclaimed in 1823), the liberation movements ended the Spanish American empire, but failed to create a united republic – Bolívar's Gran Colombia – in its place. Disputes over land, minerals and access to the coast continued to weaken and divide the new states.

60 Reaction and revolution in Europe
The revolutions of 1848, though directly responsible for a change of regime only in France, marked a decisive stage in the progress of liberal ideas and the aspirations of national minorities. These had presented a growing and increasingly successful challenge to the *status quo* imposed by the Congress of Vienna of 1815.

Atlantic Ocean
Pacific Ocean
To Brazil: 3m. 1835-1913 from Portugal, Spain, Italy
To Uruguay from Italy, Spain
To Argentine: 4.5m. 1857-1913 from Italy, Spain
Canal Zone (U.S. occ. 1903)
PANAMA 1903
COLOMBIA 1819
VENEZUELA 1830
ECUADOR 1830
PERU 1821
BOLIVIA 1825
CHILE 1818
ARGENTINA 1810
PARAGUAY 1811
URUGUAY 1828
BRAZIL 1822
GREATER COLOMBIA 1819-30
FEDERATION OF PERU AND BOLIVIA 1836-39
BRITISH GUIANA
DUTCH GUIANA
FRENCH GUIANA
Curaçao
Margarita
Trinidad
Maracaibo
Cartagena
Panama
Mompós
Caracas
Carabobo 1821
San Carlos
Angostura
Boyacá 1819
Bogotá
Bombona 1822
Pichincha 1822
Quito
Guayaquil
Georgetown
Paramaribo
Cayenne
Gurupá
Belém
Manaus
Maranhão
Ceará
Pernambuco
Bahia
Minas Novas
Diamantina
Sao Paulo
Santos
Rio de Janeiro
Porto Alegre
Montevideo
Buenos Aires
Rosario
Santa Fé
Córdoba
San Luis
Mendoza
Chacabuco 1817
Maipú 1818
Valparaiso
Santiago
Concepción
Valdivia
La Serena
Copiapó
Antofagasta
Jujuy
Salta
Tucumán
Asunción
Corumbá
Iquique
Arica
Tacna
La Paz
Chuquisaca
Potosí
Cuzco
Ayacucho 1824
Junín 1824
Lima
Callao
Pisco
Trujillo
Patagonia
Tierra del Fuego
Falkland Islands (Br. 1833)
River Plate
Orinoco
Negro
Amazon
Xingu
Tocantins
S. Francisco
PARÁ
MARANHÃO
CEARÁ
RIO GRANDE DO NORTE
PARAIBA
PERNAMBUCO
ALAGÔAS
BAHIA
GOIÁS
MATO GROSSO
MINAS GERAIS
ESPIRITO SANTO
SÃO PAULO
SANTA CATARINA
RIO GRANDE DO SUL
RIO NEGRO
ACRE
CHACO
Coffee
Cattle
Sugar
Sheep
Bananas
TIMBER
RUBBER
Cotton
Cocoa
Tobacco
COPPER
SILVER
NITRATES
GUANO
TIN
MANGANESE
Cereals
1 to Brazil 1905
2 to Brazil 1904
3 to Ecuador 1880-1922
4, 5 to Ecuador 1880-1942
6 to Peru 1942
7 to Brazil 1904-5
8 to Brit. Guiana 1899
9 to Brazil 1900
10, 11 to Bolivia 1867-1903
12 to Bolivia 1867
13 to Bolivia 1867-1909
14 to Bolivia 1867-1902
15 to Brazil 1927
16 to Paraguay 1935
17 to Bolivia 1880-1935
18 to Chile 1883
19, 20 to Brazil 1870
21 to Argentina 1874
22 to Brazil 1895
23 to Chile 1884
24 to Argentina 1874
25 to Argentina 1881
26 to Chile 1902
27 to Argentina 1881
Mountain
Desert and semi-desert
Temperate forest and scrub
Tropical forest and scrub
Grasslands
Population:
c.1880 c.1910
100,000 and over
200,000 and over
1,000,000 and over
Other towns under 100,000
Main railways c.1910
Bolivar's route 1817-24
San Martin's route 1817-22
Borders c.1830
Subsequent border changes
Border of Greater Colombia, 1819-30 and border of Federation of Bolivia and Peru, 1835-39
European immigration (showing country of origin)
0 1000 km
0 600 miles

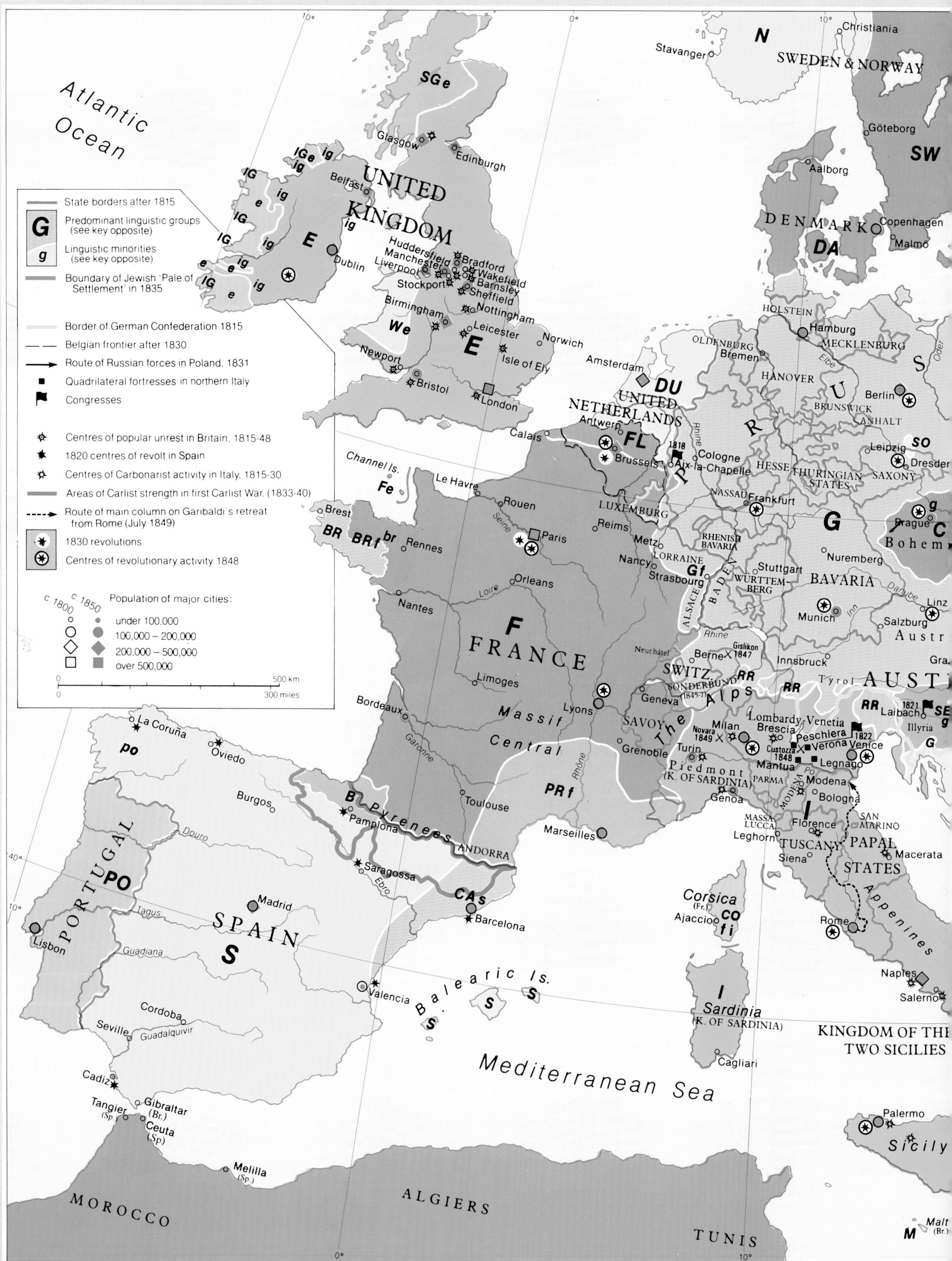
State borders after 1815
Predominant linguistic groups (see key opposite)
Linguistic minorities (see key opposite)
Boundary of Jewish 'Pale of Settlement' in 1835
Border of German Confederation 1815
Belgian frontier after 1830
Route of Russian forces in Poland, 1831
Quadrilateral fortresses in northern Italy
Congresses
Centres of popular unrest in Britain, 1815-48
1820 centres of revolt in Spain
Centres of Carbonarist activity in Italy, 1815-30
Areas of Carlist strength in first Carlist War, (1833-40)
Route of main column on Garibaldi's retreat from Rome (July 1849)
1830 revolutions
Centres of revolutionary activity 1848
Population of major cities:
c. 1800
c. 1850
under 100,000
100,000 – 200,000
200,000 – 500,000
over 500,000
500 km
300 miles
Atlantic Ocean
UNITED KINGDOM
FRANCE
SPAIN
PORTUGAL
SWEDEN & NORWAY
DENMARK
UNITED NETHERLANDS
BAVARIA
SWITZ.
Mediterranean Sea
MOROCCO
ALGIERS
TUNIS
KINGDOM OF THE TWO SICILIES
PAPAL STATES
TUSCANY
Piedmont (K. OF SARDINIA)
Lombardy-Venetia
Corsica (Fr.)
Sardinia (K. OF SARDINIA)
Balearic Is.
Pyrenees
Massif Central
The Alps
Appenines

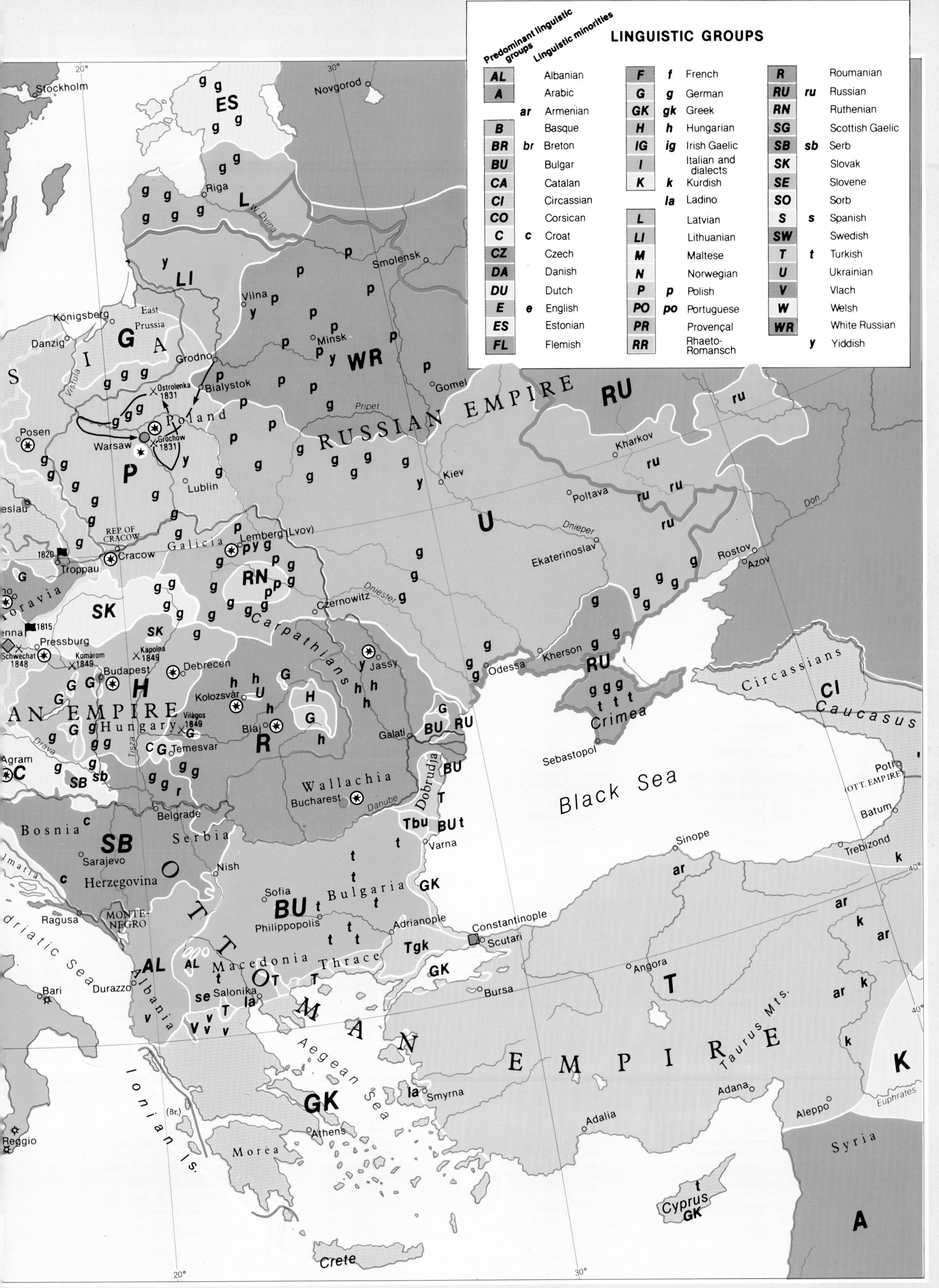
LINGUISTIC GROUPS
Predominant linguistic groups
Linguistic minorities
AL Albanian
A Arabic
ar Armenian
B Basque
BR br Breton
BU Bulgar
CA Catalan
CI Circassian
CO Corsican
C c Croat
CZ Czech
DA Danish
DU Dutch
E e English
ES Estonian
FL Flemish
F f French
G g German
GK gk Greek
H h Hungarian
IG ig Irish Gaelic
I Italian and dialects
K k Kurdish
la Ladino
L Latvian
LI Lithuanian
M Maltese
N Norwegian
P p Polish
PO po Portuguese
PR Provençal
RR Rhaeto-Romansch
R Roumanian
RU ru Russian
RN Ruthenian
SG Scottish Gaelic
SB sb Serb
SK Slovak
SE Slovene
SO Sorb
S s Spanish
SW Swedish
T t Turkish
U Ukrainian
V Vlach
W Welsh
WR White Russian
y Yiddish
Stockholm
Novgorod
Riga
W. Dvina
Smolensk
Vilna
Königsberg
East Prussia
Danzig
Minsk
Grodno
Vistula
Bialystok
Ostrolenka 1831
Gomel
Poland
Posen
Warsaw
Grochow 1831
Pripet
RUSSIAN EMPIRE
Kharkov
Kiev
Lublin
Poltava
Don
eslau
REP. OF CRACOW
Galicia
Lemberg (Lvov)
Dnieper
Ekaterinoslav
1820
Cracow
Troppau
Rostov
Azov
Moravia
Dniester
Czernowitz
Carpathians
1815
Pressburg
Schwechat 1848
Komárom 1849
Kápolna 1849
Budapest
Debrecen
Jassy
Odessa
Kherson
Crimea
Circassians
Caucasus
Kolozsvár
Hungary
Világos 1849
Blaj
Tisza
Temesvar
Drava
Agram
Galati
Sebastopol
Black Sea
Wallachia
Bucharest
Danube
Dobrudja
Poti (OTT. EMPIRE)
Batum
Belgrade
Bosnia
Serbia
Varna
Sinope
Trebizond
Sarajevo
Herzegovina
Nish
Sofia
Bulgaria
Ragusa
MONTENEGRO
Philippopolis
Adrianople
Constantinople
Scutari
Adriatic Sea
Macedonia
Thrace
Angora
Bari
Durazzo
Salonika
Bursa
Albania
OTTOMAN EMPIRE
Taurus Mts.
Aegean Sea
Ionian Is.
(Br.)
Smyrna
Adana
Aleppo
Euphrates
Reggio
Athens
Adalia
Syria
Morea
Cyprus
Crete
20°
30°
40°

of the French Bourbons, the archreactionary Charles X, was overthrown in the 'July Revolution' and replaced by the Orleanist dynasty of Louis Philippe. Shortly afterwards a liberal revolution in Belgium dissolved the union with Holland, and the new state received guarantees of its independence and neutrality by the Treaty of London (1839). The success of the July Revolution gave rise to further revolts, but these were crushed by conservative governments. A Polish attempt to regain independence was extinguished by the Russians. Under the July Monarchy, France pursued a guardedly liberal course in home politics, a *rapprochement* with Britain abroad, a policy of imperial expansion in Algeria (where a vicious colonial war was waged to subdue local resistance which endured until 1847), and an economic policy which, while it enriched sections of the bourgeoisie, left France lagging further behind Britain in industrial development (*compare Maps 56 and 57*). The Orleanist regime was increasingly criticized for its corruption, and a severe economic crisis in 1846-7 sounded its death-knell.

The year 1848, the year of revolutions throughout Europe, was the supreme crisis of conservatism (*Map 60*). Beginning in Sicily in January, a wave of revolutions swept through the continent, throwing nearly all conservative governments off balance, and giving a fresh impetus to democratic and nationalist ideals. In France the July Monarchy was replaced by the short-lived Second Republic, which, after the suppression of radical left-wing elements in June 1848, elected Louis Napoleon (nephew of the first Emperor) as President. By 1852 he had transformed the regime into the Second Empire, styling himself Napoleon III, and maintaining a firm grip on power, by a mixture of populism, authoritarianism, and opportunism, until 1870. In Prussia popular disturbances led King Frederick William IV to agree to 'merge Prussia into Germany' and to reign as a constitutional monarch. Similar movements were sparked off in the smaller German states, and a Constituent National Assembly met at Frankfurt from May 1848 to April 1849. Meanwhile the revolutionary surge had reached the Austrian empire where an uprising in Vienna in March 1848 led to the fall of Metternich. A Constituent Assembly in Vienna emancipated the peasantry from surviving feudal burdens. In June 1848 a Slav Congress in Prague demanded national rights for the subject peoples of the empire. However, resolute military action by the Austrian general Windischgraetz crushed the revolution in Prague and later in Vienna. Under the leadership of Schwarzenberg, Hapsburg power was restored. In Hungary a nationalist revolution led by Kossuth was repressed by 1849 after the Hungarians had been defeated by Austrian, Croat, and Russian forces. Revolution against Austrian rule in Italy, supported by King Charles Albert of Piedmont, was defeated, though the Venetian republic held out until August 1849. By then the revolutionary surge had subsided, and conservative governments nearly everywhere had reasserted control. But 1848 had demonstrated the vulnerability of reactionary regimes, and the year of revolutions marked a decisive stage on the road to nationhood of several peoples, most notably those of Italy and Germany.

The *Risorgimento*, the movement for Italian unification, was a diversified and at times incoherent movement, whose supporters often differed over both means and ends, even over the practicability and desirability of the complete unification of the peninsula. The liberal constitutionalists, among whom the Piedmontese statesman Cavour was outstanding, proved to be the dominant group, but they were challenged by the republicans, whose leaders Mazzini and Garibaldi inspired revolutionaries everywhere, the former by his speeches and writings, the latter by his romantic heroism. A third group, the 'neo-Guelphs', believed that the Papacy was the natural head of a united Italy, and this notion was given some stimulus by the early actions of Pope Pius IX, elected in 1846. However, in the revolution of 1848 Pius fled from Rome, and returned only after Garibaldi's Roman Republic had been destroyed by French troops. The political unification of Italy took place in several stages (*Map 62*). The first, and most important, took place in 1859-60 when France, in alliance with Piedmont, defeated Austria in war, and secured the liberation of Lombardy and its union with Piedmont. In return Napoleon exacted his *'pourboire'* ('tip') in the form of the cession of Savoy and Nice to France by Piedmont. The independent northern duchies decided to join the union. Cavour was inclined to call a halt at this stage, but his hand was forced by Garibaldi who sailed for Sicily with his 'thousand', and, in a brilliant campaign, conquered Sicily and moved up through Naples towards Rome. In order to forestall an attack by Garibaldi on Rome (which, it was feared, would bring about outside intervention), the Piedmontese king Victor Emmanuel II moved south to block the way against Garibaldi. Rome and Venetia remained outside the kingdom of Italy proclaimed in 1861. Further attempts by Garibaldi in 1862 and 1867 to seize Rome were thwarted. In 1866 Venetia fell into Italian hands as a result of the defeat of Austria by Prussia, but it was not until 1870, after the French defeat by Prussia, that Rome was at last captured and the *Risorgimento* appeared complete.

The *Risorgimento* was the foremost example of the union of liberalism and nationalism. By contrast the process of German unification (*Map 61*) was marked by the gradual divorce of the two movements, particularly after 1848, as nationalism came to be increasingly aligned with conservative elements. Italian unification, it was sometimes said, was merely a mask for Piedmontese expansion. There was some truth in this (as was shown by the failure of the new Italy to prevent the ever-widening divergence between the developed north and the primitive south); but in the case of Germany there could be no doubt that the country was united primarily in the form of conquest by Prussia. The dominant genius of German unification was Bismarck (Prussian minister-president 1862-7 and federal chancellor 1867-90) who towered over international politics in the later part of the century even more effectively than had Metternich earlier. Bismarck proceeded, like Cavour, by a deft mixture of diplomacy and war. Unlike Cavour he had, in the Prussian army, a military machine which could win decisive victories without heavy reliance on allies. Prussian victories in three wars within seven years secured German unification. The war with Denmark in 1864 secured Austro-Prussian occupation of the duchies of Schleswig and Holstein. The war with Austria in 1866 saw the decisive defeat of Austria at Sadowa-Königgrätz, the formation of the North German Confederation of German states under Prussian leadership, and the eclipse of Hapsburg aspirations to German leadership. Henceforth it was certain that Prussia would dominate Germany and that Austria would be excluded from the new national state. The final stage came in 1870-1 with the victory over France at Sedan which brought the collapse of the Second French Empire, and the birth of the new German Empire which incorporated not only the south German states but also the annexed French provinces of Alsace and Lorraine, with their substantial German-speaking populations. In January 1871 the Prussian king William I was proclaimed German Emperor in a ceremony held at Versailles. The dream of the romantic German nationalists of the early part of the century seemed fulfilled. But the methods by which German unification had been brought about, and the type of state which was now established, socially conservative and politically authoritarian, hardly fulfilled the hopes of the German liberals. Henceforth nationalism was increasingly to be the handmaiden not of liberalism but of reactionary forces, notably imperialism.

Above left: The 1848 revolution in Italy.

61 The unification of Germany
Under the leadership and, after the defeat of Austria in 1866, the domination of Prussia, Germany was unified to form a highly centralized and authoritarian state, and the leading military and industrial power of continental Europe.

62 The unification of Italy
Despite the brilliance and international fame of the republican heroes Mazzini and Garibaldi, the traditional leadership of Piedmont retained effective control of the Italian *Risorgimento.* After 1870 the benefits of political unity were limited by deep and persistent economic and social divisions.

63 The Balkans in the nineteenth century
As the Ottoman empire retreated, the rise of nationality in the Balkans led through provincial autonomy and war to independence. The political and strategic interests of the great powers ensured their constant, often dangerous, and eventually fatal intervention.

Further reading: Owen Chadwick, *The Secularization of the European Mind in the Nineteenth Century* (Cambridge U.P. 1975); J.H. Lynch, *The Spanish American Revolutions* (Weidenfeld & Nicolson 1973; Norton); P.N. Stearns, *The Revolutions of 1848* (Weidenfeld & Nicolson 1974; Norton); James J. Sheehan, *German History, 1770-1866* (Oxford U.P. 1990); D. Mack Smith, *The Making of Italy, 1796-1870* (Michigan U.P. 1959); Ernest Gellner, *Nations and Nationalism* (Basil Blackwell 1983).

Border of German Confederation 1815
Border of North German Confederation 1867
Border of German Empire 1871
Prussia 1815
Prussian gains by 1867
German States still independent 1867-71
Battle
150 km
100 miles
A Anhalt
B Brunswick
Ha Hamburg
H Hanover
MS Mecklenburg-Strelitz
O Oldenburg
P Prussia
TS Thuringian States
SWEDEN
Baltic Sea
North Sea
DENMARK
Copenhagen
SCHLESWIG
Flensburg
Schleswig
Kiel
Heligoland (Br. to 1890)
HOLSTEIN
Lübeck
LÜBECK
MECKLENBURG-SCHWERIN
Rostock
Cuxhaven
Hamburg
HAMBURG
Wilhelmshaven
Frisian Is.
Oldenburg
OLDENBURG
BREMEN
Bremen
Stettin
MECKLENBURG-STRELITZ
Pomerania
Danzig
Memel
Tilsit
Königsberg
East Prussia
West Prussia
Vistula
Warsaw
Posen
RUSSIAN EMPIRE
Poland
Wittenberg
Brandenburg
Berlin
HANOVER
Hanover
Brunswick
BRUNSWICK
SCHAUMBURG-LIPPE
LIPPE-DETMOLD
Detmold
Osnabrück
Amsterdam
NETHERLANDS
The Hague
Münster
Westphalia
Magdeburg
Dessau
ANHALT
Halle
Saxony
Leipzig
Göttingen
Dortmund
Essen
WALDECK
Kassel
Düsseldorf
Dresden
SAXONY
Breslau
Silesia
REP. OF CRACOW (to Austria 1846)
Cracow
Galicia
Antwerp
Brussels
BELGIUM
Cologne
ELte. OF HESSE
Erfurt
THURINGIAN STATES
Marburg
GR. D. OF HESSE
Fulda
Karlsbad
Prague
Sadowa Königgratz 1866
Olmütz
Bohemia
Moravia
RHENISH PRUSSIA
Coblenz
NASSAU
FRANKFURT-AM-MAIN
Frankfurt
Mainz
GR. D. OF HESSE
Würzburg
Pilsen
Brünn
LUXEMBURG
(to Belgium 1839)
Sedan 1870
Luxemburg
Trier
LICHTENBERG
Mannheim
Ludwigshafen
Heidelberg
Fürth
Nuremberg
RHENISH BAVARIA
Saarbrücken
Metz
Lorraine
(From Fr. 1871)
Regensburg
Danube
AUSTRIAN EMPIRE
Lower Austria
Karlsruhe
Stuttgart
WÜRTTEMBERG
BAVARIA
Linz
Vienna
Pressburg
Nancy
Strasbourg
BADEN
Ulm
Augsburg
Munich
HOHENZOLLERN
FRANCE
Alsace
Upper Austria
Salzburg
Budapest
Hungary
Freiburg
Mulhouse
Belfort
Lake of Constance
Constance
Basel
Zurich
Innsbruck
Graz
Styria
Tyrol
LIECHTENSTEIN
Neuchâtel (Pr. 1815-57)
Bern
SWITZERLAND
The Alps
Carinthia
Drava
Lausanne
L. Geneva
Laibach
Carniola
Trieste
Fiume
Venice
Milan
Lyon
Croatia
Adriatic Sea
Grenoble
Turin
Rhône
Rhine
Elbe
Oder
Weser
Main
Mosel
Meuse
Inn
Po

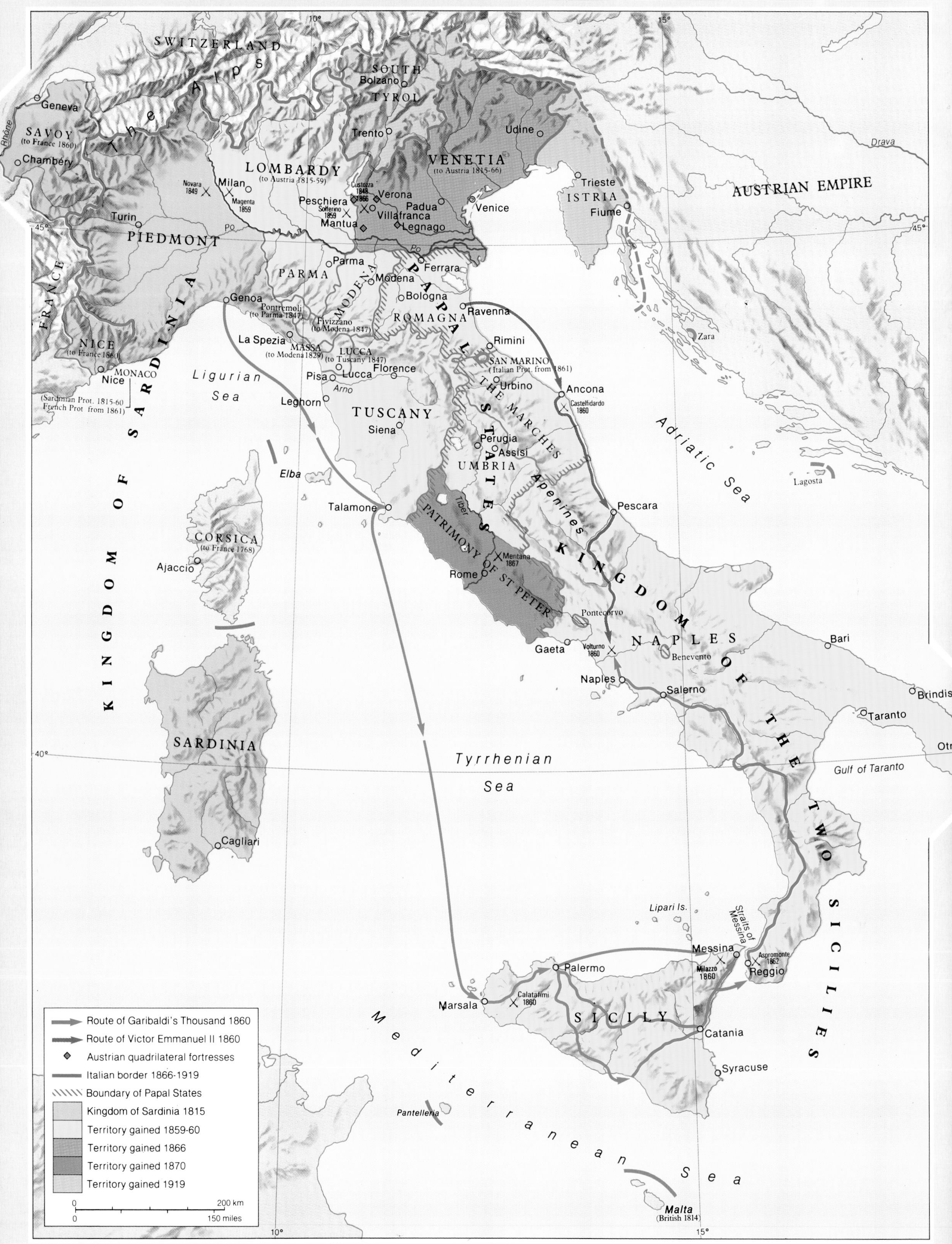
SWITZERLAND
The Alps
SOUTH TYROL
Bolzano
Trento
Udine
Geneva
SAVOY (to France 1860)
Chambéry
LOMBARDY (to Austria 1815-59)
VENETIA (to Austria 1815-66)
Novara 1849
Milan
Magenta 1859
Custozza 1848 1866
Peschiera
Verona
Padua
Solferino 1859
Villafranca
Mantua
Legnago
Venice
Trieste
ISTRIA
Fiume
AUSTRIAN EMPIRE
Drava
Turin
PIEDMONT
Po
FRANCE
Parma
PARMA
MODENA
Modena
Ferrara
Bologna
Genoa
Pontremoli (to Parma 1847)
Fivizzano (to Modena 1847)
ROMAGNA
Ravenna
PAPAL STATES
NICE (to France 1860)
MONACO
Nice
(Sardinian Prot. 1815-60 French Prot. from 1861)
La Spezia
MASSA (to Modena 1829)
LUCCA (to Tuscany 1847)
Lucca
Pisa
Florence
Arno
Rimini
SAN MARINO (Italian Prot. from 1861)
Urbino
Ancona
Castelfidardo 1860
Zara
Ligurian Sea
Leghorn
TUSCANY
Siena
THE MARCHES
Perugia
Assisi
UMBRIA
Adriatic Sea
Lagosta
KINGDOM OF SARDINIA
Elba
Talamone
Tiber
PATRIMONY OF ST PETER
Apennines
Pescara
CORSICA (to France 1768)
Ajaccio
Mentana 1867
Rome
KINGDOM OF THE TWO SICILIES
Pontecorvo
NAPLES
Gaeta
Volturno 1860
Benevento
Bari
Naples
Salerno
Brindisi
Taranto
SARDINIA
Tyrrhenian Sea
Gulf of Taranto
Cagliari
Lipari Is.
Straits of Messina
Messina
Milazzo 1860
Aspromonte 1862
Reggio
Palermo
Calatafimi 1860
Marsala
SICILY
Catania
Syracuse
Mediterranean Sea
Pantelleria
Malta (British 1814)
10°
15°
45°
40°
Route of Garibaldi's Thousand 1860
Route of Victor Emmanuel II 1860
Austrian quadrilateral fortresses
Italian border 1866-1919
Boundary of Papal States
Kingdom of Sardinia 1815
Territory gained 1859-60
Territory gained 1866
Territory gained 1870
Territory gained 1919
0 200 km
0 150 miles

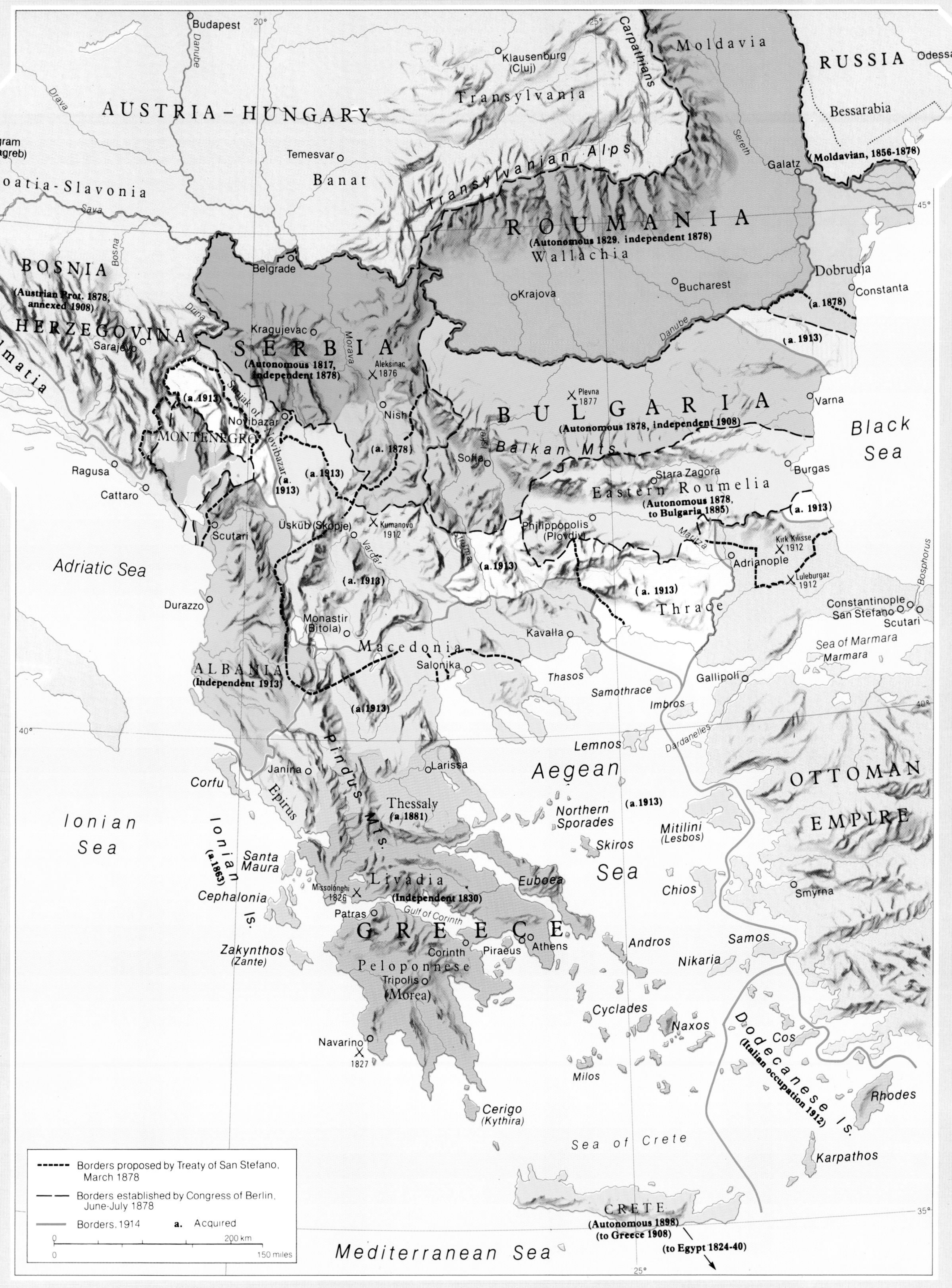
AUSTRIA-HUNGARY
RUSSIA
ROUMANIA
(Autonomous 1829, independent 1878)
SERBIA
(Autonomous 1817, independent 1878)
BULGARIA
(Autonomous 1878, independent 1908)
BOSNIA
(Austrian Prot. 1878, annexed 1908)
HERZEGOVINA
MONTENEGRO
ALBANIA
(Independent 1913)
GREECE
OTTOMAN EMPIRE
Eastern Roumelia
(Autonomous 1878, to Bulgaria 1885)
Livadia
(Independent 1830)
Thessaly
(a. 1881)
CRETE
(Autonomous 1898)
(to Greece 1908)
(to Egypt 1824-40)
Dodecanese Is.
(Italian occupation 1912)
Ionian Is.
(a. 1863)
Moldavia
Bessarabia
(Moldavian, 1856-1878)
Transylvania
Wallachia
Banat
Croatia-Slavonia
Dobrudja
Macedonia
Thrace
Epirus
Peloponnese
(Morea)
Black Sea
Adriatic Sea
Ionian Sea
Aegean Sea
Sea of Marmara
Sea of Crete
Mediterranean Sea
Budapest
Klausenburg (Cluj)
Odessa
Temesvar
Galatz
Belgrade
Bucharest
Krajova
Constanta
Kragujevac
Sarajevo
Aleksinac 1876
Plevna 1877
Nish
Novibazar
Varna
Sofia
Burgas
Stara Zagora
Ragusa
Cattaro
Scutari
Üsküb (Skopje)
Kumanovo 1912
Philippopolis (Plovdiv)
Kirk Kilisse 1912
Adrianople
Luleburgaz 1912
Constantinople
San Stefano
Durazzo
Monastir (Bitola)
Kavalla
Salonika
Gallipoli
Janina
Larissa
Corfu
Missolonghi 1826
Patras
Corinth
Piraeus
Athens
Tripolis
Navarino 1827
Smyrna
Agram (Zagreb)
Carpathians
Transylvanian Alps
Balkan Mts
Pindus Mts.
Danube
Drava
Sava
Bosna
Drina
Morava
Vardar
Struma
Maritza
Sereth
Sanjak of Novibazar
Dalmatia
Dardanelles
Bosphorus
Gulf of Corinth
Thasos
Samothrace
Imbros
Lemnos
Northern Sporades
Skiros
Mitilini (Lesbos)
Chios
Euboea
Andros
Samos
Nikaria
Cyclades
Naxos
Milos
Cos
Rhodes
Karpathos
Cerigo (Kythira)
Santa Maura
Cephalonia
Zakynthos (Zante)
(a. 1878)
(a. 1913)
Borders proposed by Treaty of San Stefano, March 1878
Borders established by Congress of Berlin, June-July 1878
Borders, 1914
a. Acquired
200 km
150 miles

The age of European supremacy 9

THE AGE OF IMPERIALISM

The late nineteenth and early twentieth centuries witnessed an unprecedented extension of European power over non-Europeans. Hence the frequent characterization of the period as an 'age of imperialism'. This was, however, as much a time of imperial decline as of imperial expansion. Indeed, the debilitation of the older imperial systems – most notably those of Austria, Ottoman Turkey, and China – and the ensuing diplomatic rivalries, were two of the primary causes of the imperial expansion of countries such as Britain and France.

Above: Pu Yi (on the right), the last emperor of China, ascended to the throne at the age of two.

64 European penetration of the Far East
The 'Opium War' of 1839-42 demonstrated the inability of the Manchu (Ch'ing) empire to withstand the expansion of the European powers. Their domination of the Far East was established as much by exacting commercial privileges as by territorial occupation.

The vulnerability of the old empires became steadily more apparent in the course of the nineteenth century. Austria, bludgeoned into submission by Prussia, not only lost most of its lands in Italy and its position as the leading German power (*Maps 61 and 62*) but was compelled by resurgent Hungarian nationalism to acquiesce in 1867 to the *Ausgleich* ('compromise') whereby the empire was transformed into a 'Dual Monarchy' based on the joint domination of Germans and Hungarians over Slavs. Although unity under Austro-Hungarian rule made considerable economic sense (as was proved when the area broke up into several states after 1918 – *Map 77*) Austro-Hungarian output and industrialization lagged far behind that of Germany. While the Hapsburg regime continued to command impressive reserves of institutional and ideological strength, the nationalist Revolutions of 1848-9 and 1866-7 had demonstrated its essential frailty. The spread of the ideas of romantic nationalism and the rise of Pan-Slav feeling championed by Russia rendered the Austro-Hungarian system increasingly unstable.

Slav opposition to the Hapsburgs was heightened by the success of Slav and other subject nationalities in south-east Europe in gaining independence from the Turks (*see Map 63*). The long territorial retreat of the Ottoman Empire, which had begun in 1699, greatly accelerated in the nineteenth century. The Empire made repeated attempts to recover its strength by internal reforms and modernization, and it enjoyed strong support from other powers (especially Britain, which sought to maintain Ottoman integrity for fear of Russian encroachment on Constantinople and the Dardenelles). Nevertheless one after another of the European subject nationalities wrested autonomy and eventually independence from the Turks. In 1830, after a bitter struggle, Greece won its independence, and by 1878 Serbia and Romania were independent and Bulgaria virtually so.

Meanwhile Ottoman power on the southern shore of the Mediterranean was also disappearing. France conquered Algeria between 1830 and 1848, annexed Tunis in 1881, and harboured ambitions in Morocco (which, however, preserved a precarious independence until 1912) – *see Maps 66 and 74*. Egypt had asserted its autonomy under Muhammad Ali in the early nineteenth century, but his successors drove the country into bankruptcy and financial submission to Britain and France. With the construction of the Suez Canal (opened in 1869) the British began to fear that control of the area by a hostile power might endanger the security of their communications with India. The outbreak of an Egyptian nationalist revolution in 1881 was the occasion for the occupation of the country by British forces the following year. Although successive British governments affirmed their intention to withdraw, a 'veiled protectorate', in which Egypt became in all but name a British possession, endured for nearly three-quarters of a century.

It was, as Gallagher and Robinson point out, 'more than any other cause, the danger of a general Ottoman collapse [which] set off the partition of Africa and brought on the rise of new European empires in north and tropical Africa'. The 'scramble for Africa' (*see Map 74*) in the 1880s and 1890s saw nearly the whole continent subjected to European rule. Britain secured the lion's share of the territorial spoils as she expanded up the Nile valley into east Africa and inland from the west African coast. In southern Africa the discovery of gold and diamonds led to a vast influx of European capital and labour and laid the foundations of the greatest economic power on the continent. An elaborate railway system was constructed, and British rule was extended northward beyond the Zambeze to the shores of Lakes Nyasa and Tanganyika. The French too moved into the hinterland from their north and west African coastal footholds and established their suzerainty over most of the Sahara and as far south as the Congo basin. Other European powers nibbled at more modest morsels. Bismarck, although sceptical of the value of imperial possessions, gained the German annexation of Tanganyika, Togoland, Kamerun and South-West Africa. Portugal, deprived of her former vast dominion in Brazil (*Map 59*), consoled her national pride by consolidating her position in Portuguese West Africa (Angola) and Mozambique, rebuffing the rapacious advances of acquisitive European rivals. Italy too, disillusioned with the failure of the post-*Risorgimento* regime to recreate Italian greatness, tried her hand at empire-building, only to encounter humiliating disaster when her army was defeated at Adowa by the army of Abyssinia, the one indigenous imperial system in Africa to survive into the twentieth century.

In East Asia (*see Map 64*) the decline of the Ch'ing (Manchu) empire in China afforded the opportunity for rapid European expansion into the area as the decline of the Mughal empire had already done in India (*see Map 65*). In 1839 an attempt by the Chinese Government to enforce a prohibition on the importation of opium led to war with Britain. By the Treaty of Nanking in 1842 China was obliged to cede Hong Kong to Britain and to make a series of commercial concessions, including the opening of several ports to British traders. The T'ai P'ing Rebellion (1850-64), a popular upheaval which convulsed sixteen of China's eighteen provinces, provided the pretext for further European intervention. Anglo-French victories between 1856 and 1860 led to further 'unequal treaties' which extended European commercial and cultural penetration of China. The decrepitude of the Ch'ing Empire made possible the expansion of French sovereignty from its base at Saigon to the whole of Indo-China. Defeated by

MAP 64 EUROPEAN PENETRATION OF THE FAR EAST

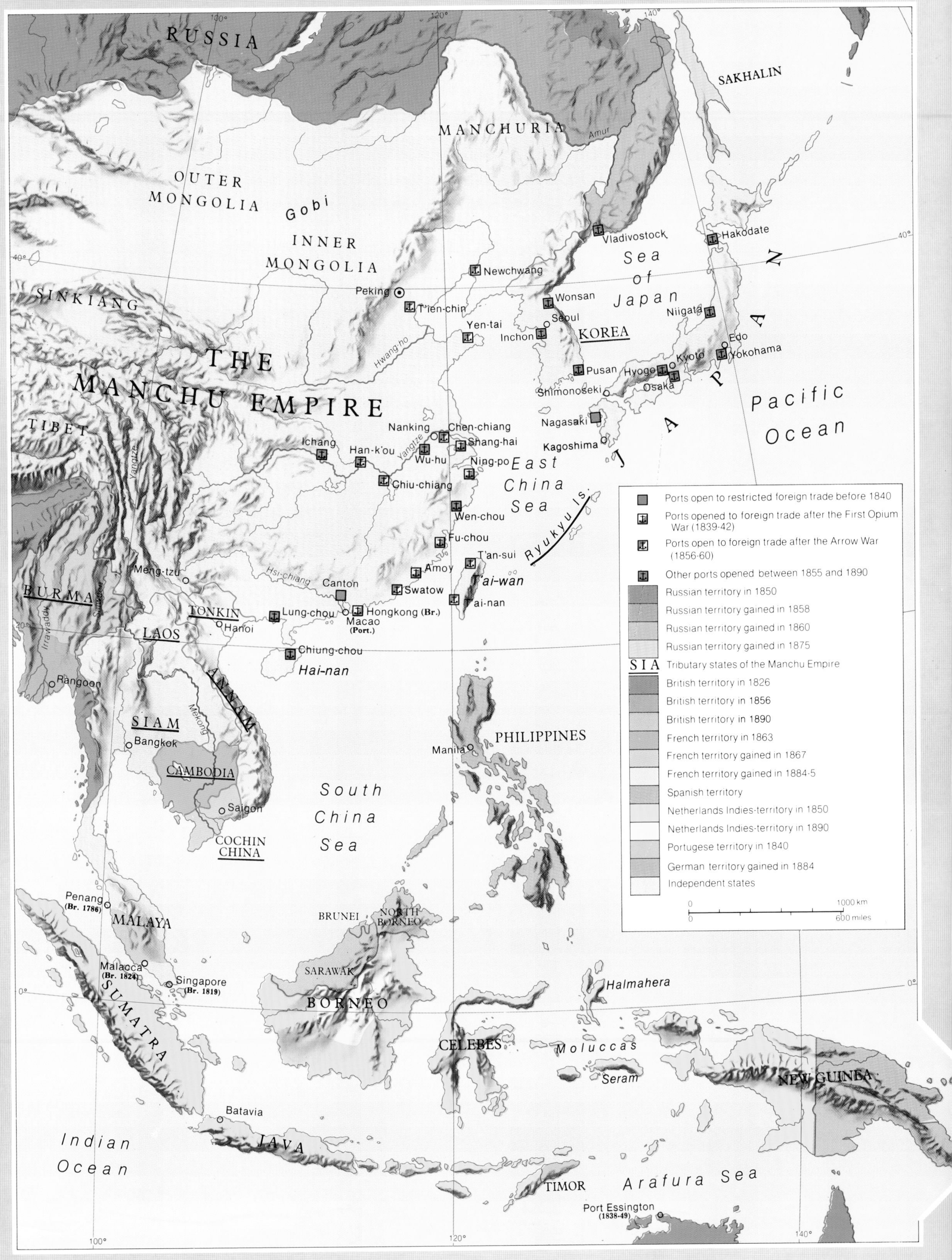
RUSSIA
SAKHALIN
MANCHURIA
Amur
OUTER MONGOLIA
Gobi
INNER MONGOLIA
SINKIANG
THE MANCHU EMPIRE
TIBET
Vladivostock
Hakodate
Sea of Japan
JAPAN
Newchwang
Peking
T'ien-chin
Wonsan
Seoul
Yen-tai
Inchon
KOREA
Niigata
Edo
Yokohama
Kyoto
Hwang-ho
Pusan
Hyogo
Osaka
Shimonoseki
Pacific Ocean
Nagasaki
Nanking
Chen-chiang
Shang-hai
Kagoshima
Ichang
Han-k'ou
Yangtze
Wu-hu
Ning-po
East China Sea
Chiu-chiang
Wen-chou
Ryukyu Is.
Fu-chou
T'an-sui
Amoy
T'ai-wan
Meng-tzu
Hsi-chiang
Canton
Swatow
T'ai-nan
BURMA
TONKIN
Lung-chou
Hongkong (Br.)
Macao (Port.)
Hanoi
LAOS
Irrawaddy
Chiung-chou
Hai-nan
Rangoon
ANNAM
Mekong
SIAM
Bangkok
PHILIPPINES
Manila
CAMBODIA
South China Sea
Saigon
COCHIN CHINA
Penang (Br. 1786)
MALAYA
BRUNEI
NORTH BORNEO
Malacca (Br. 1824)
Singapore (Br. 1819)
SARAWAK
Halmahera
SUMATRA
BORNEO
CELEBES
Moluccas
Seram
NEW GUINEA
Batavia
Indian Ocean
JAVA
TIMOR
Arafura Sea
Port Essington (1838-49)
Ports open to restricted foreign trade before 1840
Ports opened to foreign trade after the First Opium War (1839-42)
Ports open to foreign trade after the Arrow War (1856-60)
Other ports opened between 1855 and 1890
Russian territory in 1850
Russian territory gained in 1858
Russian territory gained in 1860
Russian territory gained in 1875
SIA Tributary states of the Manchu Empire
British territory in 1826
British territory in 1856
British territory in 1890
French territory in 1863
French territory gained in 1867
French territory gained in 1884-5
Spanish territory
Netherlands Indies-territory in 1850
Netherlands Indies-territory in 1890
Portugese territory in 1840
German territory gained in 1884
Independent states
0 1000 km
0 600 miles

Japan in 1894-5, China was compelled to yield up her suzerainty over the tributary state of Korea. The Sino-Japanese war was the signal for a 'scramble for China' in the late 1890s, in which the imperial powers vied for railway and other concessions and occupied Chinese ports (*see Map 73*). Chinese resentment of European encroachments found expression in the so-called 'Boxer Rebellion'. This eruption of anti-foreign feeling, spearheaded by a secret society of 'Righteous and Harmonious Fists', enjoyed the support of a faction of the imperial government. In 1900 a multinational military expedition relieved a siege of the foreign legations in Peking. The vindictive terms subsequently imposed by the imperial powers appeared to spell the doom of the Ch'ing dynasty.

Although formal European rule had not been extended to the greater part of the country, and in spite of American attempts to preserve Chinese integrity by the enunciation of the 'open door' principle in 1899, the Chinese government had by the end of the century effectively been deprived of mastery in its own house. China was thus an outstanding example of 'informal imperialism', the process whereby imperial powers secured commercial, legal, or diplomatic privileges which gave them influence, in some cases a predominant voice, in the internal affairs of nominally independent states. Another such case was Persia where Britain and Russia carved out spheres of influence in the declining Qajar empire.

The weakening of the old empires, and the consequent power vacuums in much of Asia and

MAP 65 SOUTH ASIA AROUND 1900

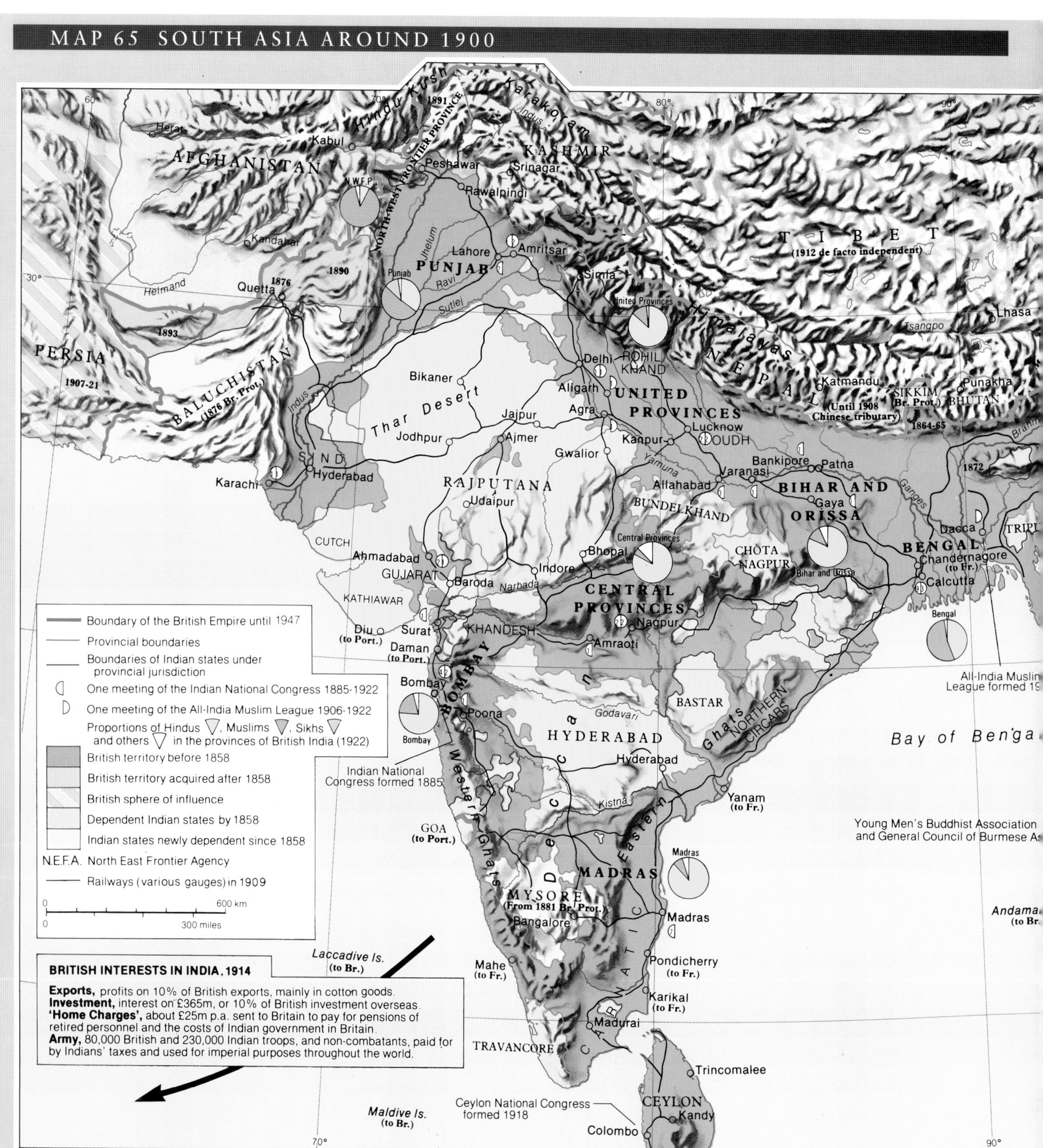

Africa, cannot alone explain the phenomenal growth of European imperialism in the late nineteenth century. A number of further explanations have been advanced. Imperialism, it is suggested, was the result of a search for outlets for 'surplus capital'. Was it rather a necessary consequence of heightened trade rivalries and moves towards protectionism in Europe? Or did it derive from the need of manufacturing economies for assured sources of supply of cheap raw materials? Or from the need of rapidly expanding populations to find outlets for emigration and settlement? Some historians tend to discount economic motives and stress rather the more purely political origins of the imperial urge. It is thus portrayed as a stepchild of frustrated nationalisms, as a plaything of diplomatic rivalries, or as an attempt by ruling élites to siphon off internal social unrest by the stimulation of 'jingoist' imperial enthusiasms. Although there are grains of truth in several of these suggested causes the search for a 'general theory' of imperialism has been unsuccessful – perhaps not surprisingly in the case of such a far-flung and variegated phenomenon.

Just as there is no historical consensus as to the causes of imperialism, so views diverge as to its nature and effects. Some emphasize its negative aspects: the use of force and repression to establish and maintain imperial rule; the barbarities perpetrated in some colonies by imperialist agents and officials (as in the Congo, governed for a time as the private estate of the King of the Belgians); the distortion of colonial economies to meet the needs of metropolitan countries; the subordination of the interests of indigenous peoples to those of European settlers; the racialism of most imperial powers; the extinction of some non-European cultures; the alienation and psychological dislocation arising from the sudden imposition of westernization. Against all this it is argued that imperialism did not rely only on brute force but in many cases constructed sophisticated governmental systems incorporating indigenous institutions and co-opting local élites. Moreover, it was the imperial powers, led by Britain, that sought (with considerable success) to eliminate the African slave trade in the course of the nineteenth century (*compare Map 51*). Also on the positive side are often added the development of modern economic infrastructures, the spread of education and literacy, the application of modern medical techniques to the battle against disease (*compare Map 66*), the unification of large areas containing diverse religions, tribes, and ethnic groups into single units, and the establishment of the rule of law.

Resistance to imperialism reflected its ambivalent impact, for opposition to colonial incursions tended to be more effective the more it borrowed from the ideas and techniques of imperial societies themselves. The British victories over the Indian mutiny (1857-9), the Ashanti of the Gold Coast (1874), the Zulus of South Africa (1879), and the Mahdist forces in the Sudan (1885) showed that technologically inferior anti-imperialist forces might win occasional battles but could not expect enduring success against imperial armies in straightforward military confrontations. By contrast, the Indian National Congress (founded in 1885), based on a marriage of western with Indian techniques of political mobilization, and profoundly influenced by British liberalism, succeeded in compelling the Government of India (which had replaced the East India Company after the mutiny as the agency of British rule) to concede a growing share of political power to Indians (*Map 65*). In this respect the Indian experience served as a model for some other anti-imperial movements and some other (particularly British) colonial administrations. A similarly ambiguous response to European penetration may be detected in the declining old empires: the constitutional revolution in Persia in 1905, the Young Turk revolution in the Ottoman Empire in 1908, and the republican revolution in China led by Sun Yat-Sen in 1911, were at once against western imperial domination and in themselves evidence of the impact of western political and social ideas.

Among all the imperial powers, one held for a while almost undisputed predominance. Britain indeed attained in the third quarter of the nineteenth century a position more nearly approaching world mastery than perhaps has ever been achieved by any other power in history. It was not merely that Britain had amassed what was territorially the largest empire ever known (*see Map 67*). Britain maintained its long lead over competitors in industrial innovation and production almost until the end of the century. Until the 1870s she produced more coal than all other countries put together. She was similarly dominant in the production of iron. Britain produced one-third of the world's industrial output in 1870. Britain's foreign trade (in which Lancashire cotton was the largest single element) was greater than that of any two other countries until the 1890s. The pound sterling remained the basis of the international payments system until well into the twentieth century. Britain was the world's largest foreign investor until the First World War (most of the exported capital flowing to the Americas, India, and South Africa, rather than to the new empire). Britain dominated the world's system of transport and communications: herself possessed of the world's best network of roads and railways, she supplied the capital and the technology for the construction of railways in five continents; she owned the majority of the world's submarine cables. Above all, she dominated world shipping: until almost the eve of the First World War the British merchant fleet comprised a larger tonnage than that of all other countries put together. Shielding this massive aggregation of economic might was the Royal Navy, the world's most powerful seaborne force. The age of imperialism was, truly, the British era.

Nevertheless, by the turn of the century Britain's overwhelming predominance was beginning to be eroded. By 1890 the USA had overtaken Britain in the production of iron, and by 1900 in the production of coal and steel (*Map 69*). Germany too had outstripped Britain in industrial production by the turn of the century (*Map 57*). By 1913 the USA was producing more than one-third of the world's manufactured goods, whereas Britain's share of world output had slipped below one-tenth. By 1900 Britain was the only major nation which still adhered to free trade, and although Britain still dominated world trade some voices began to be raised in favour of protectionism. Nor was it only economically that Britain now began to appear vulnerable. Britain, alone among the European

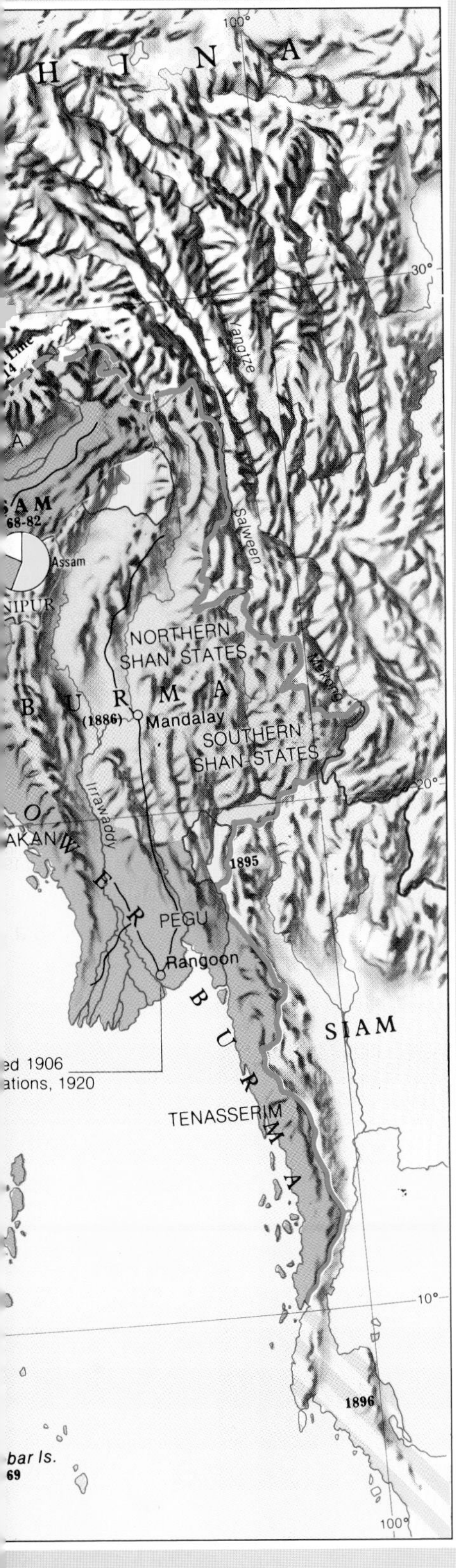

65 South Asia around 1900
India became a British Crown Colony after the suppression of the mutiny of 1857-59. Territorial consolidation, the importation of British administrative and educational institutions and economic development (which, however, destroyed the self-sufficiency of the village economies and opened the way to chronic rural over-population) had created by 1900 Britain's greatest imperial possession and a growing independence movement.

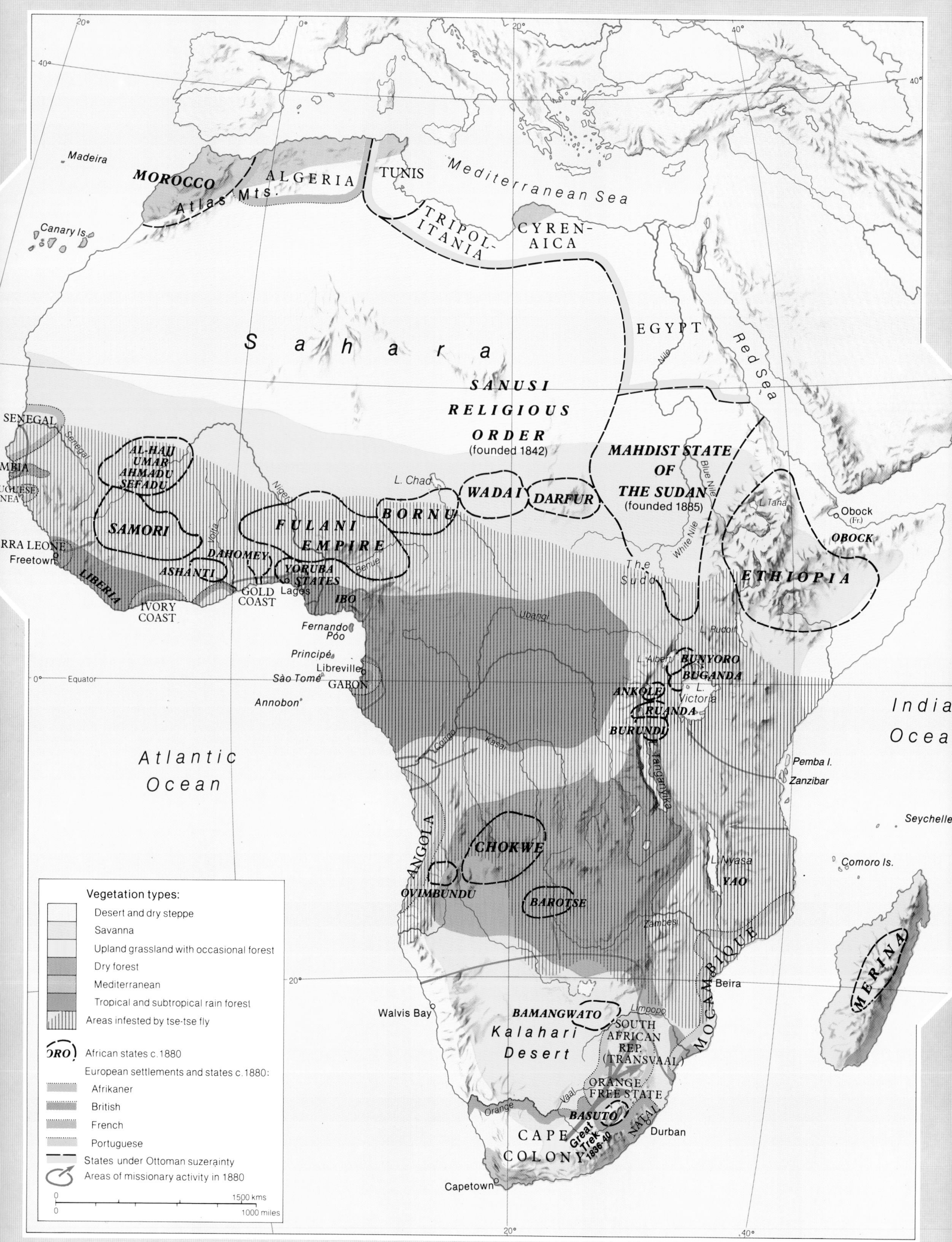
Madeira
MOROCCO
Atlas Mts.
ALGERIA
TUNIS
Mediterranean Sea
TRIPOLITANIA
CYRENAICA
Canary Is.
Sahara
EGYPT
Nile
Red Sea
SANUSI RELIGIOUS ORDER
(founded 1842)
SENEGAL
Senegal
AL-HAJJ UMAR AHMADU SEFADU
Niger
L. Chad
WADAI
DARFUR
MAHDIST STATE OF THE SUDAN
(founded 1885)
Blue Nile
White Nile
L. Tana
Obock
(Fr.)
OBOCK
ETHIOPIA
SAMORI
FULANI EMPIRE
BORNU
Volta
DAHOMEY
ASHANTI
YORUBA STATES
Benue
LIBERIA
Freetown
GOLD COAST
Lagos
IBO
IVORY COAST
The Sudd
Fernando Póo
Príncipe
Libreville
Sào Tomé
GABON
Annobon
Ubangi
L. Rudolf
L. Albert
BUNYORO
BUGANDA
ANKOLE
L. Victoria
RUANDA
BURUNDI
Equator
India Ocea
Atlantic Ocean
Congo
Kasai
Tanganyika
Pemba I.
Zanzibar
Seychelle
ANGOLA
CHOKWE
OVIMBUNDU
L. Nyasa
YAO
Comoro Is.
BAROTSE
Zambesi
MOÇAMBIQUE
MERINA
Beira
Walvis Bay
BAMANGWATO
Limpopo
Kalahari Desert
SOUTH AFRICAN REP. (TRANSVAAL)
ORANGE FREE STATE
Vaal
Orange
BASUTO
Great Trek 1836-40
NATAL
Durban
CAPE COLONY
Capetown
Vegetation types:
Desert and dry steppe
Savanna
Upland grassland with occasional forest
Dry forest
Mediterranean
Tropical and subtropical rain forest
Areas infested by tse-tse fly
African states c.1880
European settlements and states c.1880:
Afrikaner
British
French
Portuguese
States under Ottoman suzerainty
Areas of missionary activity in 1880
0
1500 kms
0
1000 miles

Right: For many Cecil Rhodes, a key British player in the scramble for Africa embodied the spirit of imperialism.

66 Africa on the eve of the scramble
Before 1880 most of the African continent was unknown to Europeans, and very little of it ruled by them. They were confined to the coast by disease (also the greatest obstacle to African development), the hostility generated by the slave trade and the fact that comparable profits from other sources seemed unlikely.

powers, had no system of conscription and no large standing army. Between 1899 and 1902 she suffered a shattering blow to her prestige in the Boer War: although she was ultimately victorious her difficulties in crushing the Dutch colonists in South Africa cruelly exposed her military weakness and her diplomatic isolation. British policy-makers now began to wonder whether the vast territorial acquisitions of the late nineteenth century had not extended the empire beyond Britain's capacity to sustain or defend it. In 1905 the head of the British Foreign Office suggested that the British Empire might give the appearance 'of some huge giant sprawling over the globe, with gouty fingers and toes stretched in every direction, which cannot be approached without eliciting a scream'.

British paramountcy was further challenged by the development of European alliance systems. In 1879 Bismarck had formed a 'Dual Alliance' between Germany and Austria-Hungary. In 1882 this was expanded to a 'Triple Alliance' by the addition of Italy. Meanwhile Bismarck sought to contain Russia by drawing her into a *Dreikaiserbund* (League of Three Emperors) in company with Austria-Hungary. The heightening of Balkan rivalries between Russia and Austria-Hungary made this impossible to preserve intact, and in 1887 Bismarck replaced it with the so-called 'Re-insurance Treaty', a bipartite arrangement between Germany and Russia. However, in 1890 Bismarck was dismissed by the new German Emperor, William II. The delicate balance of Bismarck's alliance system collapsed with him: Germany now jettisoned Russia and threw in her lot wholeheartedly with Austria-Hungary. This led between 1891 and 1894 to what Bismarck had always feared most and what his entire diplomacy had been concerned to prevent – the crystallization of a Russo-French alliance which presented Germany with the danger of a war on two fronts.

Although the phrase 'splendid isolation', as sometimes applied to British foreign policy in the late nineteenth century, is misleading if taken literally, it is true that Britain in the 1890s held aloof from either camp. The traditions of her foreign policy earlier in the century had been anti-Russian rather than anti-German. It was against Russia that Britain had combined with France, Turkey, and Sardinia to fight in the Crimean War (1854-6). At the Congress of Berlin in 1878 the British prime minister, Disraeli, had helped to deprive Russia of the fruits of her victory in the Russo-Turkish war, and had secured a reversal of the Treaty of San Stefano which Russia had sought to impose on Turkey (*see Map 63*). Throughout the period Britain had been concerned by the apparent threat to her Indian empire posed by Russian advances in central Asia (*Map 70*) – which stimulated Britain too to advance her frontiers in northern India (*see Map 65*). Britain was further inhibited from identifying herself with the Russo-French alliance by colonial disputes with France, particularly over North Africa. In 1898 a minor Anglo-French confrontation at Fashoda (*see Map 74*) blew up into a serious crisis which seemed to bring Britain and France to the brink of war.

Nevertheless, by the end of the century it was the German empire, with its dynamic economy, its thrusting foreign policy, its assertive demand for a 'place in the sun', and its expanding naval programme which seemed to represent the chief threat to Britain's international hegemony. Although Anglo-German discussions about a possible alliance continued until 1901, it became apparent that the fundamental interests and sympathies of the two powers were diverging. It is the Anglo-Japanese alliance, concluded in 1902, which is traditionally held to mark the end of Britain's 'isolation', but this did not commit Britain to either of the main European power blocs. Even the '*ententes*' signed with France in 1904 and with Russia in 1907 were ostensibly concerned merely with the settlement of outstanding colonial disputes. But they were followed by naval and military conversations which, although short of an alliance, insensibly drew Britain closer to France and Russia. In the diplomatic crises of 1905 and 1911 over Morocco and of 1908 and 1912-13 over the Balkans the lines hardened between the 'Triple Entente' and the 'central powers'. In the years before 1914 all the European powers greatly increased their expenditure on armaments. Meanwhile, as the struggle for mastery in Europe intensified, the rise of new powers on the periphery of the international system foreshadowed the sudden collapse, at the moment of its greatest imperial extension, of Europe's mastery of the world.

67 Foundations of a world economy
European colonial expansion created a world economy united not only by the establishment of regular communications (telegraph cables joined most parts of the civilized world by 1900) and the exchange of goods and people, but by financial ties through capital investment even more widespread than territorial dominion.

Further reading A. J. P. Taylor, *The Struggle for Mastery in Europe* (Oxford University Press, 1954); John Gallagher and Ronald Robinson, *Africa and the Victorians,* (Macmillan, 1961); J. Berque, *Egypt Imperialism and Revolution* (Faber 1972);John K. Fairbank, *The Great Chinese Revolution, 1800-1985* (Harper & Row 1986, Picador); C. A. Bayly, *Indian Society and the Making of the British Empire* (Cambridge U. P. 1988); Eric Hobsbawm, *The Age of Empire* (Weidenfeld & Nicolson 1987; Random House); D. K. Fieldhouse *Economics and Empire* (2nd ed Macmillan1984). *China and the West* (Hutchinson, 1979).

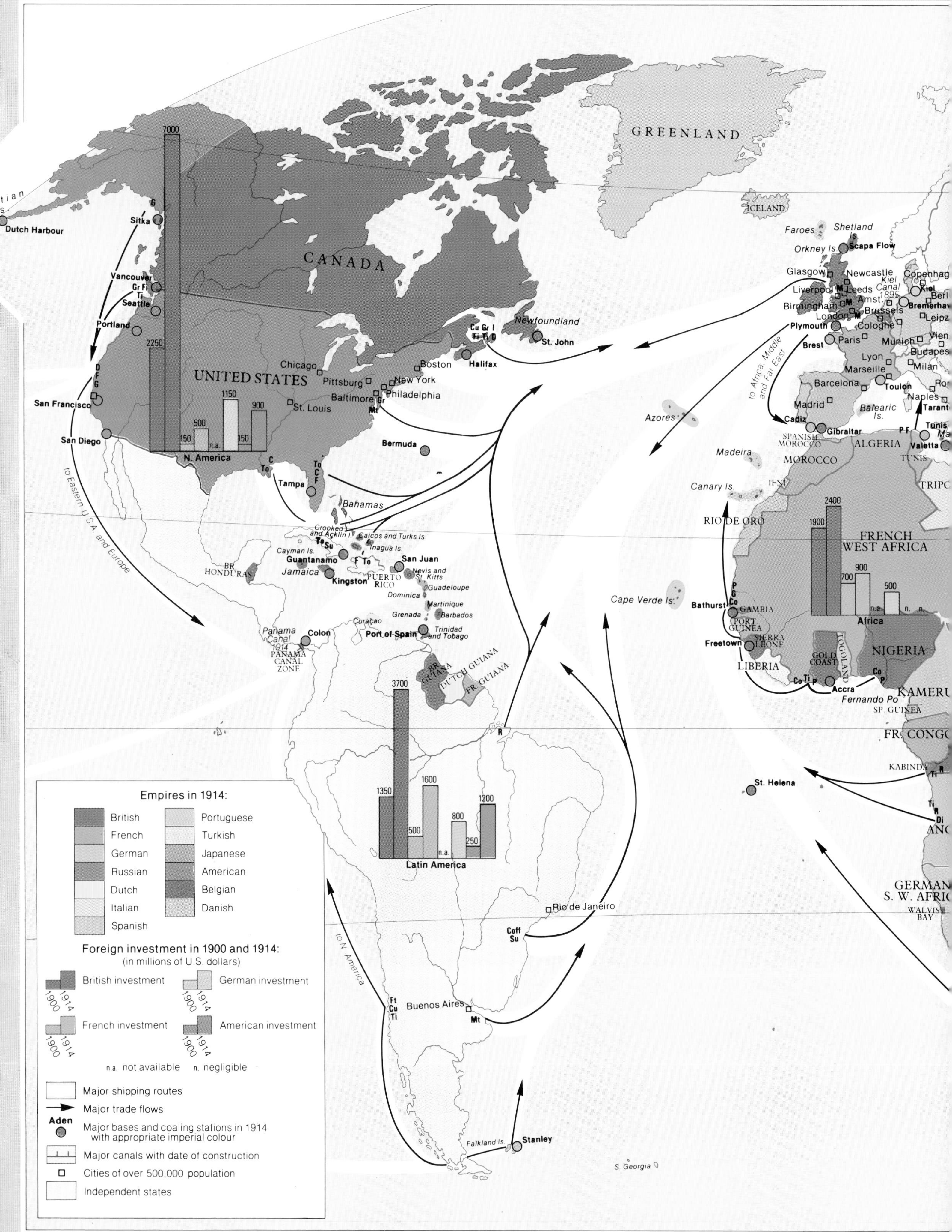
GREENLAND
CANADA
UNITED STATES
ICELAND
Dutch Harbour
Sitka
Vancouver
Seattle
Portland
San Francisco
San Diego
Chicago
Pittsburg
Boston
New York
Philadelphia
Baltimore
St. Louis
Halifax
Newfoundland
St. John
Bermuda
Tampa
Bahamas
Cayman Is.
Guantanamo
Jamaica
Kingston
San Juan
PUERTO RICO
BR. HONDURAS
Panama Canal 1914
PANAMA CANAL ZONE
Colon
Port of Spain
Trinidad and Tobago
BR. GUIANA
DUTCH GUIANA
FR. GUIANA
Rio de Janeiro
Buenos Aires
Falkland Is.
Stanley
S. Georgia
St. Helena
Cape Verde Is.
Azores
Madeira
Canary Is.
Faroes
Shetland
Orkney Is.
Scapa Flow
Glasgow
Newcastle
Liverpool
Leeds
Birmingham
London
Plymouth
Brest
Paris
Kiel Canal 1895
Amst.
Brussels
Cologne
Lyon
Marseille
Toulon
Barcelona
Madrid
Cadiz
Gibraltar
Balearic Is.
Naples
Valetta
Tunis
SPANISH MOROCCO
MOROCCO
ALGERIA
IFNI
RIO DE ORO
FRENCH WEST AFRICA
Bathurst
GAMBIA
PORT. GUINEA
SIERRA LEONE
Freetown
LIBERIA
GOLD COAST
TOGOLAND
NIGERIA
Accra
Fernando Po
KAMERUN
SP. GUINEA
FR. CONGO
KABINDA
GERMAN S. W. AFRICA
WALVIS BAY
to Eastern U.S.A. and Europe
to N. America
to Africa, Middle and Far East
N. America
7000
2250
150
500
n.a.
1150
150
900
Latin America
1350
3700
500
1600
n.a.
800
250
1200
Africa
1900
2400
700
900
n.a.
500
n.
Empires in 1914:
British
French
German
Russian
Dutch
Italian
Spanish
Portuguese
Turkish
Japanese
American
Belgian
Danish
Foreign investment in 1900 and 1914:
(in millions of U.S. dollars)
British investment
German investment
French investment
American investment
1900 1914
n.a. not available
n. negligible
Major shipping routes
Major trade flows
Aden
Major bases and coaling stations in 1914 with appropriate imperial colour
Major canals with date of construction
Cities of over 500,000 population
Independent states

Commodities:
C Cotton
Co Cocoa
Coff Coffee
Cu Copper ore
D Dairy produce
Di Diamonds
F Fruit
Fi Fish
Ft Fertiliser
G Gold
Gr Grain
I Iron ore
J Jute
M Manufactured goods
Mt Meat
O Oil
P Palm products (palm oil, etc.)
R Rubber
Ri Rice
S Silk
Sp Spices
Su Sugar
T Tea
Ti Timber
To Tobacco
W Wool
4700
4100
2500
1000
700
50
n.a.
Europe
Archangel
Moscow
RUSSIA
Odessa
Istanbul
TURKISH EMPIRE
Dodecanese Is.
Limasol
Cyprus
Port Said
Alexandria
Suez Canal 1869
Cairo
EGYPT
Bahrain
ANGLO-EGYPTIAN SUDAN
ERITREA
Massawa
Aden
Obok
FRENCH SOMALILAND
BR. SOMALILAND
Socotra
ABYSSINIA
IT. SOMALILAND
UGANDA
BRITISH EAST AFRICA
Mombasa
Zanzibar
BELGIAN CONGO
GERMAN EAST AFRICA
NYASALAND
RHODESIA
MOZAMBIQUE
Beira
Comoro Is.
MADAGASCAR
Réunion
Mauritius
Seychelles
UNION OF SOUTH AFRICA
Durban
Cape Town
Karachi
INDIAN EMPIRE
Calcutta
BURMA
Bombay
GOA
Hyderabad
Madras
Andaman Is.
CEYLON
Colombo
Maldive Is.
Rangoon
3500
1700
1200
500
700
100
n.a.
Asia
Peking
Tientsin
Port Arthur
Wei Hai Wei
Tsingtao
KOREA
Vladivostok
KARAFUTO
Tokyo
Osaka
Yokohama
Shanghai
Hangchow
MANCHU EMPIRE
Foochow
FORMOSA
Ryukyu Is.
Canton
Hong Kong
Macao
Kwangchow
FRENCH INDO-CHINA
Hué
Bangkok
Manila
PHILIPPINE IS.
Guam
Palau Is.
Caroline Is.
MALAYA
Singapore
BRUNEI
N. BORNEO
SARAWAK
NETHERLANDS INDIES
Batavia
TIMOR
Bismark Arch.
KAISER WILHELMSLAND
PAPUA
Darwin
2200
1600
100
n.
AUSTRALIA
Oceania and Australasia
Fremantle
Sydney
Melbourne
Noumea
Auckland
NEW ZEALAND
Wellington

The emergence of the modern world 1

RIVALS TO EUROPEAN SUPREMACY

The sudden eclipse of European world power in the mid-twentieth century was foreshadowed by the emergence as potential 'super-powers' of the USA, Russia, and Japan. Although each of them followed a very different path of development, they shared certain general characteristics. All three underwent vast expansion in population, territory and production.

They industrialized on a massive scale, transforming themselves in the process from overwhelmingly rural to predominantly urban societies. In each the rapid pace of economic and social change led to acute strains between traditional and modernizing institutions and ideologies. And all three alternated between periods of expansionist involvement in international politics and periods of self-absorption and isolationism.

No nation in modern history can match the phenomenal growth of the USA within a few generations from the small agrarian community of the thirteen colonies (*Map 53*) to a continental civilization commanding the world's greatest concentration of economic and military power. The territorial expansion of the USA westwards to the Pacific (*see Map 68*) proceeded in three broad stages. By 1819 all of the region between the old seaboard states and the Mississippi had been admitted to the Union except Michigan (admitted in 1837) and Wisconsin (admitted in 1848). By 1858 five states had been carved out of the vast hinterland of the Louisiana Purchase obtained by Jefferson from France in 1803 for approximately $15,000,000 and admitted to the Union. In addition, Florida, purchased from Spain in 1819, attained statehood in 1845. The third stage was the settlement of the south-western lands detached from Mexico. Texas revolted against Mexico in 1836 and constituted an independent state until it was admitted to the Union in 1845; American

Opposite page top: Immigrants on the move in Nebraska, 1886.

Opposite page below: A native American Indian photographed on a reservation in Idaho.

68 The westward growth of the USA. Systematic extension of its territory by diplomacy, purchase and conquest both within and beyond its frontiers transformed the United States from a small agrarian community into a major continental civilization. The arid high plains beyond the Mississippi constituted the principal barrier to the settlement of the newly acquired lands.

MAP 68 THE WESTWARD GROWTH OF THE USA

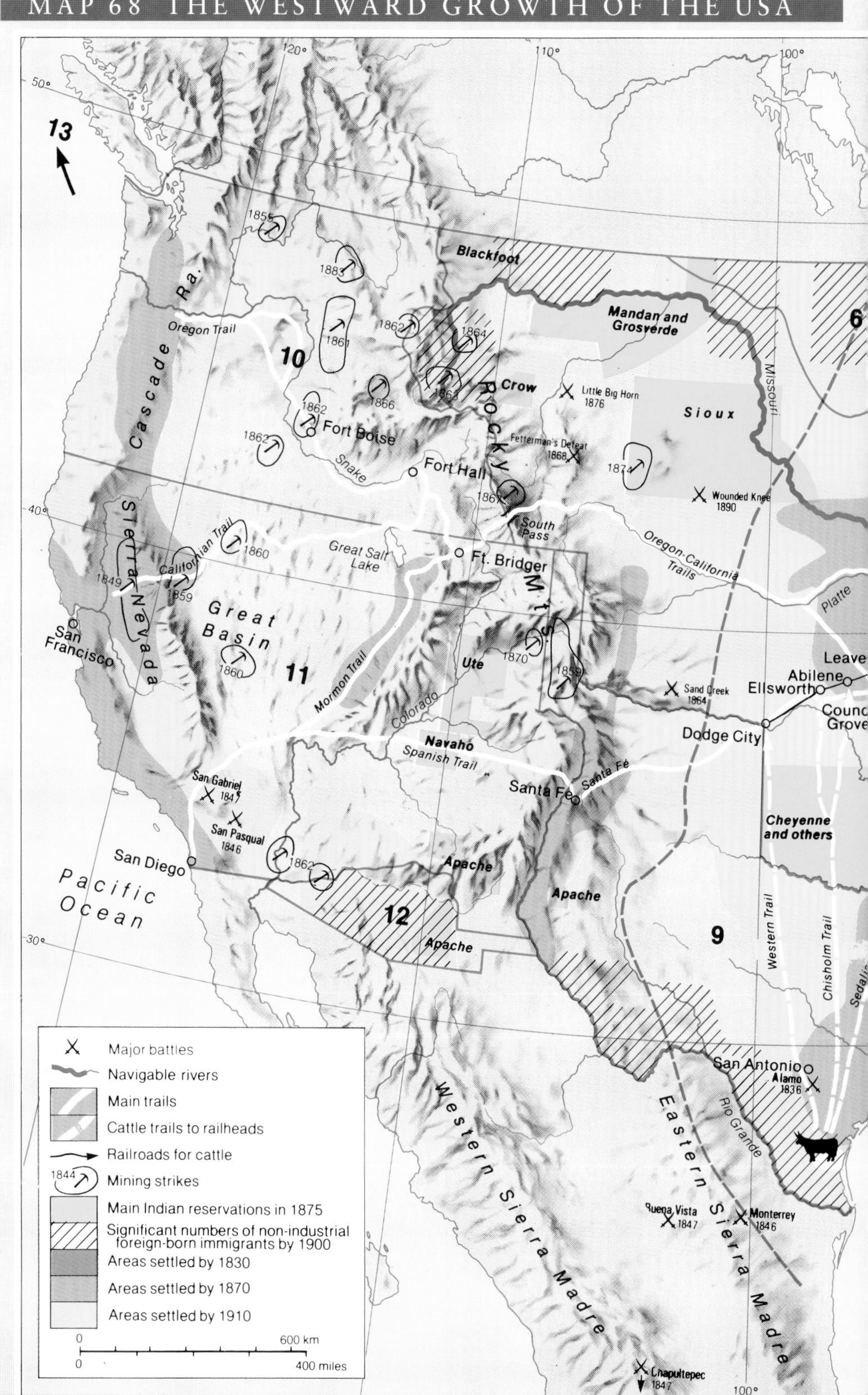

victory in war against Mexico (1846-8) added the present states of Arizona, Nevada, California, and Utah, plus other areas; and the Gadsden Purchase of 1853 acquired a further small strip (now the southern parts of Arizona and New Mexico). Meanwhile a dispute with Britain over the Oregon Territory was settled in 1846 by the concession to the USA of the mainland as far north as the 49th Parallel. Finally, in 1867 Alaska was purchased from Russia for $7,200,000.

Territorial expansion depended on settlement, which proceeded against formidable physical and

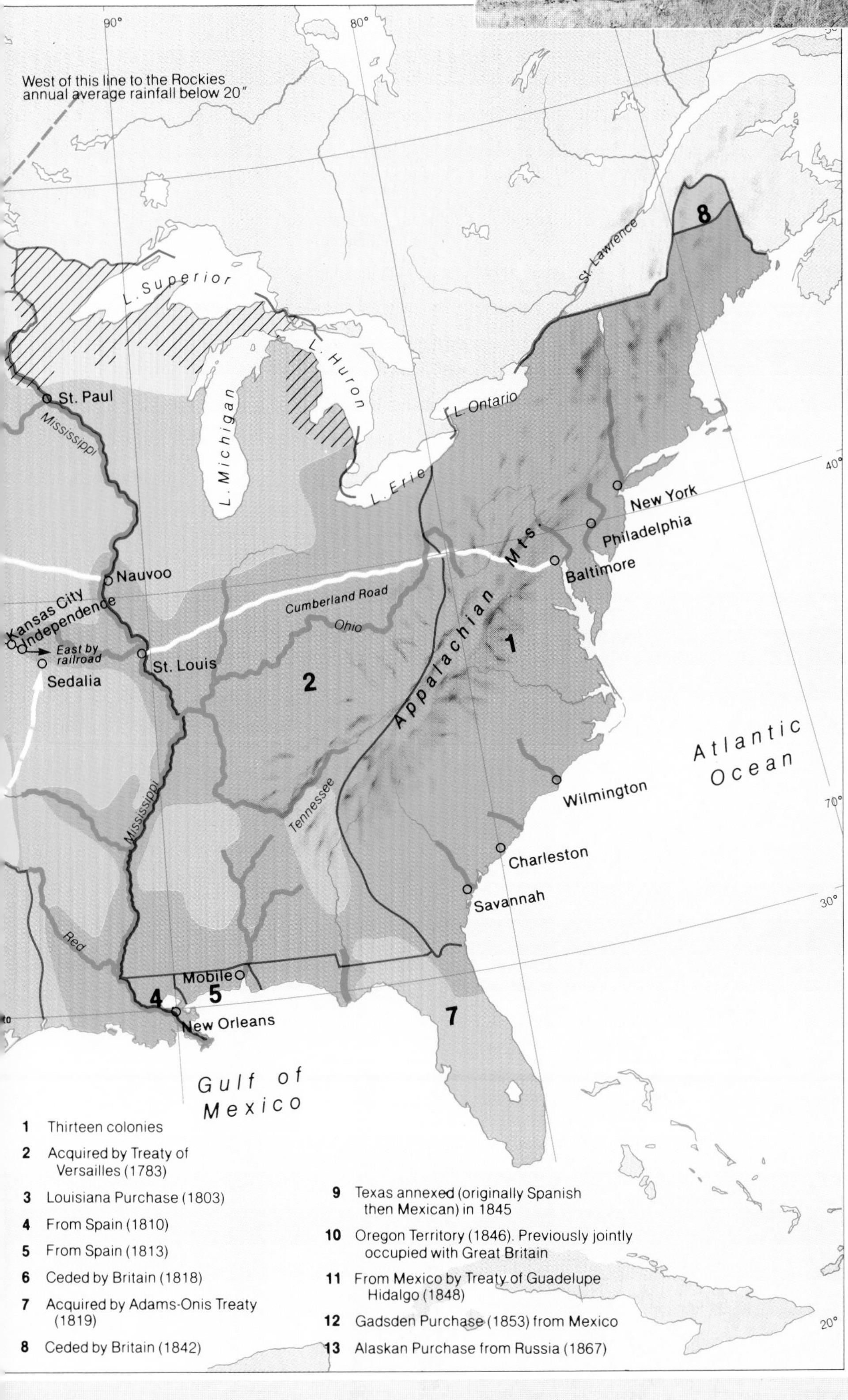

West of this line to the Rockies annual average rainfall below 20″

1 Thirteen colonies
2 Acquired by Treaty of Versailles (1783)
3 Louisiana Purchase (1803)
4 From Spain (1810)
5 From Spain (1813)
6 Ceded by Britain (1818)
7 Acquired by Adams-Onis Treaty (1819)
8 Ceded by Britain (1842)
9 Texas annexed (originally Spanish then Mexican) in 1845
10 Oregon Territory (1846). Previously jointly occupied with Great Britain
11 From Mexico by Treaty of Guadelupe Hidalgo (1848)
12 Gadsden Purchase (1853) from Mexico
13 Alaskan Purchase from Russia (1867)

human obstacles. The fast-flowing, navigable rivers eastwards from the Mississippi Valley were vital in locating ports and creating subject economic hinterlands. In the more arid and gently sloping high plains of the trans-Mississippi west, trails rather than rivers marked the lines of movement and settlement. *Map 68* shows how aridity delayed agricultural settlement on the high plains; the wave of migrants leapt across to the west (often encouraged by gold and silver strikes), leaving the interstices to be filled in from the 1870s onwards. Settlement was encouraged by the sale of federal land for as little as $1.25 an acre. After the Homestead Act of 1862 lots of up to 160 acres could be acquired for nothing after 5 years of continuous residence. The human obstacle of the indigenous Amerindian population was overcome by ruthless expropriation and mass murder. By 1838 most of the remaining Indians from the east had been moved to the Indian territory of Oklahoma. In a series of wars (1861-68 and 1875-90) the

Left: Immigrants waiting for the ferry from Ellis Island to New York.

Below left: An Italian family arriving at Ellis Island, New York.

69 The industrial growth of the USA
Abundant mineral resources, a limitless supply of labour from the surplus populations of the Old World and great agricultural wealth, brought together by a transcontinental railway system completed in its essentials in the 1890s, made the United States the greatest industrial power in the world by the early twentieth century .

western tribes were subjugated and confined to reservations.

The growth of the USA's population was no less spectacular. The population was 3,929,000 in 1790; by 1830 it was 12,866,000; by 1880 it was 50,155,000; and 105,710,000 by 1920. Immigration rose to an annual average of over a million by the peak decade before 1914 (*see Map 57*). After 1881 the massive flow of 'new immigration' came from southern and eastern Europe. Within the country there was huge internal migration from east to west and from south to north. The overwhelming majority of the migrants settled in towns, so that the urban population of the USA, which was only 3.3% of the total in 1790, increased to 16% by 1860 and to 33% by 1900. By 1920 the majority of Americans lived in towns .

The transition from an agrarian to an urban vision of society was perhaps the most revolutionary change in the American consciousness. The

Civil War of 1861-65, in which eleven southern states attempted to secede from the Union and form a separate 'Confederacy', was in essence a conflict between a traditional agrarian society and a dynamic industrial community. Slavery was not really the issue: emancipation was more a consequence than a cause of the war. At first President Abraham Lincoln, the leader of the northern states, stressed that he did not seek to abolish slavery in the south. But he insisted that he was under solemn oath to 'preserve, protect, and defend' the Union. Only in January 1863 did he issue the Proclamation of Emancipation. The defeat of the Confederacy in April 1865 came five days before the assassination of Lincoln. The Civil War was the costliest in American history, leaving over 600,000 dead, but it welded the nation together indissolubly and helped to determine the direction of American social and economic development. The abolition of slavery, confirmed by the northern victory, brought new forms of economic exploitation and misery to the freed slaves from which their descendants began to escape only after the 1930s when large-scale negro migration to the north began. But the war destroyed the power of 'King Cotton'. As Arthur M. Schlesinger Sr. wrote: 'The collapse of plantation capitalism signalized the rise of industrial capitalism.'

The industrialization of the USA (*see Map 69*) was based on a perpetually replenished pool of immigrant labour, on the discovery and exploitation of the continent's tremendous concentration of natural resources, on the development of a sophisticated system of communications, and on the rapid application to industry of technological innovations by dynamic and ruthless entrepre-

MAP 69 THE INDUSTRIAL GROWTH OF THE USA

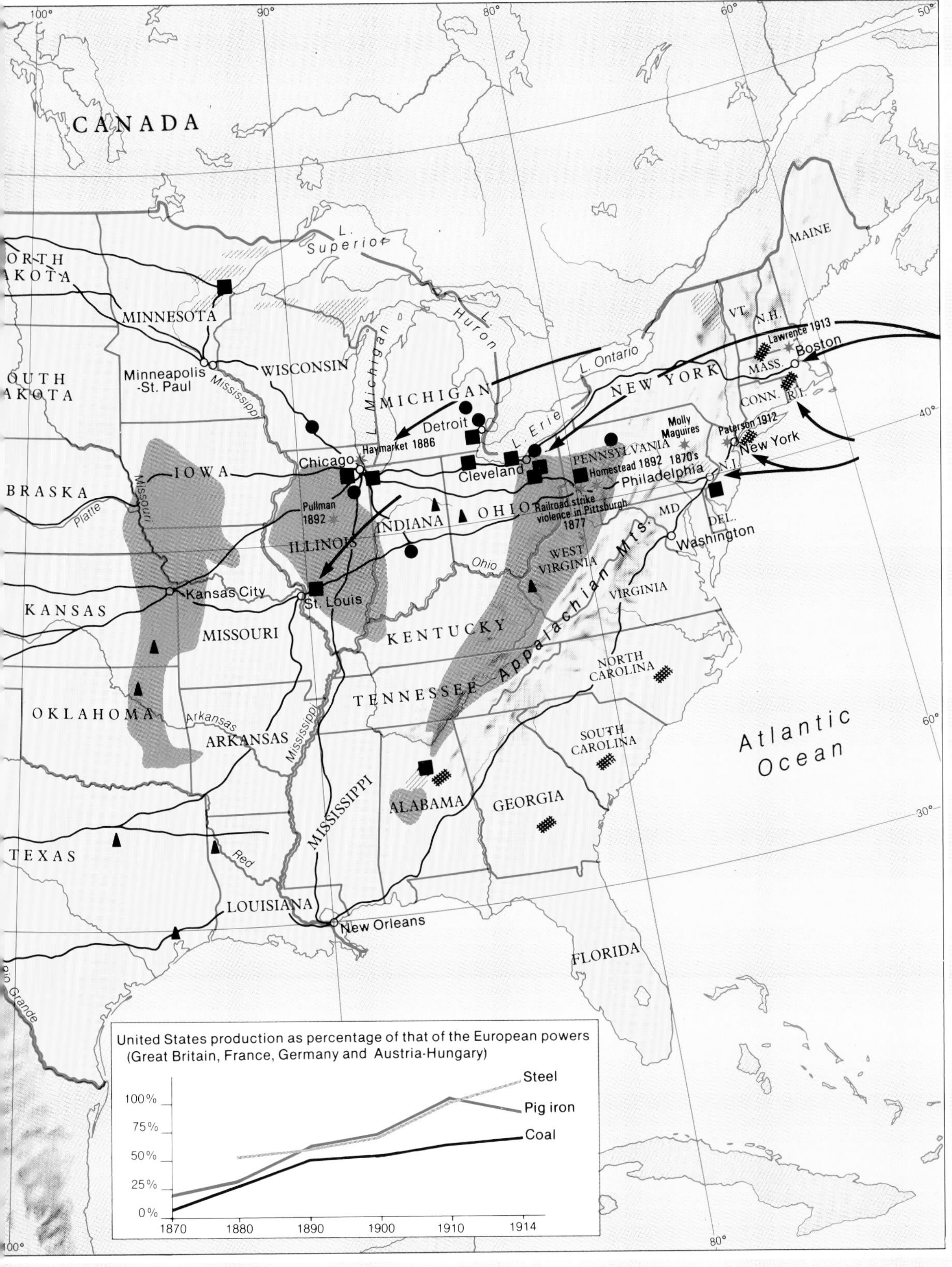

neurs. Between 1860 and 1890 coal production increased more than tenfold and iron production nearly elevenfold. By 1910 US production of iron and steel exceeded that of Britain, France, Germany, and Austria-Hungary put together and by the 1920s the USA produced (and consumed) about three-quarters of the world's oil. New industries rose in the early twentieth century, most notably automobile manufacture. The mass production of motor cars, pioneered by Henry Ford, transformed American (and eventually world) society as well as the economy: the 'assembly line' became the characteristic form of factory organization. The stream of immigrant labour for long hampered the growth of effective labour unions in the USA. Resentment of the activities of the 'robber barons' (magnates of railroads, oil, steel, meatpacking and high finance) and fear of the trend towards economic concentration in 'trusts' and combines led to sporadic industrial unrest, sometimes violent. But labour union membership and power remained much weaker than in many other industrial countries. Nevertheless, an inchoate but widespread desire to tame 'big business' and to humanize untrammelled capitalism helped give rise to the Progressive movement which dominated American politics in the early twentieth century. As the USA emerged as the world's greatest economic power she took a more outward-looking and expansive role in world affairs. As a result of victory in the Spanish-American War (1898), she acquired Cuba, Hawaii, and the Philippines (*see Map 85*). Having thus joined the ranks of imperial powers the USA became, particularly under Presidents Theodore Roosevelt (1901-9) and Woodrow Wilson (1913-21), a major actor in international diplomacy.

Although Russia, unlike the USA, was already a major power in the early nineteenth century, her development lagged far behind that of America. Indeed, a sense of 'backwardness' and of social and cultural inferiority haunted many Russian thinkers and politicians in the nineteenth century, and contrasted markedly with the thrusting self-confidence of maturing American capitalism. From the 1840s onwards Russian social thought was dominated by the debate between the 'Slavophiles', who believed that Russia's salvation lay in a return to her Orthodox religious traditions, and 'Westernizers', such as Belinsky and Herzen, who attacked religion and adopted many of the liberal and radical ideas of western Europe. The absence in Russia of a substantial mercantile and industrial bourgeoisie, however, prevented liberalism from becoming a major force in Russian politics. The autocracy, until its demise in 1917, consequently played a much more central and directing role in social and economic development than did governments in most other major countries (*see Map 71*).

More than anything else it was the overwhelming agrarian problem which dominated economic and political discussion in Russia. In 1861 the 'Tsar-Liberator', Alexander II, promulgated the emancipation of the serfs. But Alexander's emancipation decree, as much a symbolic watershed as Lincoln's, proved as much a disappointment. The peasants remained burdened by the large redemption payments which they were compelled to make for their lands. The communal system of tenure tied the peasant to the land and perpetuated primitive techniques of cultivation. By the end of the century the rapid rise in the rural population of European Russia from fifty million in the early 1860s to eighty-two million by 1897 had produced a crisis of rural over-population (*see Map 57*). The establishment of a Peasant Land Bank in 1882 and the encouragement of emigration to the virgin lands of Siberia (to which some three million peasants had moved by 1914) hardly touched the surface of the problem (*Map 70*). The legislation inspired by P. A. Stolypin between 1906 and 1911 represented the most serious effort by the tsarist regime to come to grips with the agrarian problem. Stolypin announced that he proposed to back 'the sound and the strong'. His legislation was designed to encourage a shift from communal to private tenure, the consolidation of land into compact units, the movement of surplus population from the country to the towns, the promotion of more advanced techniques of cultivation, and the creation of a surplus of agrarian income, beyond bare subsistence, to create a market in the country for the manufactured products of the towns. Significant progress had been achieved by 1914 but war, revolution, and civil war led to a collapse of the rural economy (*see Map 76*). The Bolshevik Revolution of 1917 made the peasants proprietors of the land, but only in the late 1920s did agricultural

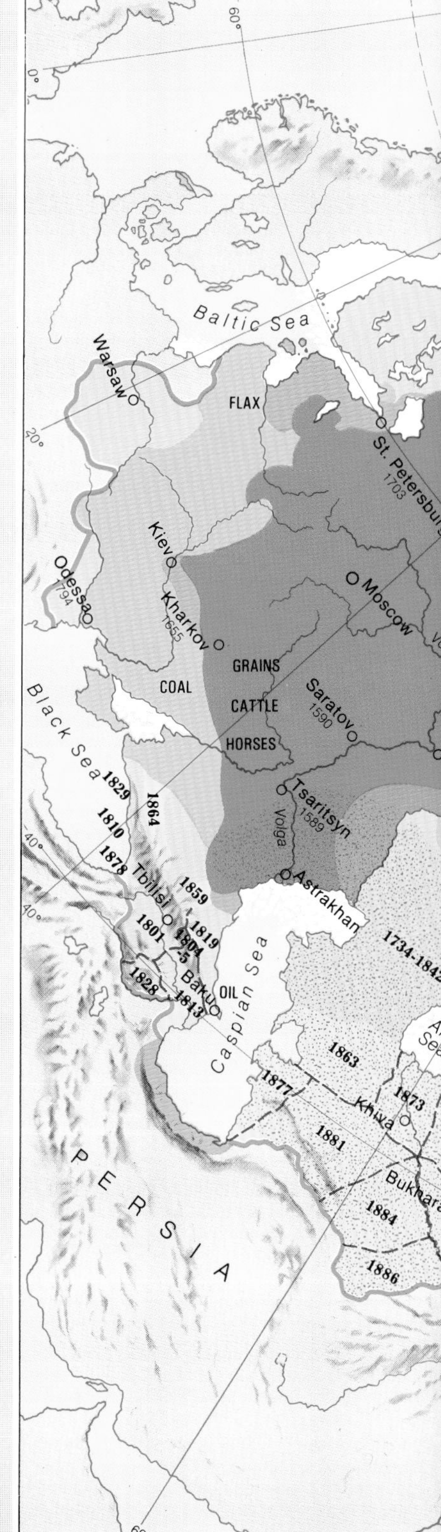

Above: Prisoners building a railway near Nertschinsk in Siberia, 1898.

70 Russian expansion into Asia
In the nineteenth century the long expansion of Russia into Asia, in quickening pursuit of land, minerals and icefree ports, brought her into conflict with the Middle Eastern and Asian interests of the European powers, and eventually with Japan. Behind the moving frontier colonization by migrants from European Russia steadily encroached upon the nomadic peoples.

production again reach pre-war levels. Stalin's programme forced collectivization after 1929, accompanied by mass murder of recalcitrants, plunged Russian agriculture once again into chaos. Russian agricultural productivity remained far behind that of western Europe and North America, and Russia, an exporter of grain before the revolution, was compelled in the 1970s to import large quantities of grain from her capitalist rivals, the USA and Canada.

Russian industrial development was far more impressive and was indeed the foundation of her emergence as a 'super-power'. Throughout the nineteenth century, Russian industry remained primitive and expansion slow. Only towards the end of the century was there really significant development and growth. Russian industrialization was characterized by a very high reliance on foreign (particularly French) capital, by a stress on mining and metallurgy, by concentration in large units of production, and by heavy state involvement in industrial development. All of these characteristics except the first endured into the post-revolutionary period (*Map 71*). The foremost exponent of industrialization under the old regime was S. Y. Witte who presided over economic policy for most of the period between 1892 and 1906. These were years of very swift economic expansion, with an average annual growth rate in the 1890s of 8%. A renewed surge of growth took place between 1906 and 1913. The dislocations of war between 1914 and 1921 were catastrophic for Russian industry. 'War communism' between 1918 and 1921 brought overnight nationalization, attempts to introduce workers' control, and near-total economic collapse. The 'New Economic

MAP 70 RUSSIAN EXPANSION INTO ASIA

Policy' (NEP) after 1921 permitted a limited return to capitalism, and by 1929 industrial production had surpassed the pre-war level. The 'five-year plan' instituted by Stalin in 1929 marked the beginning of the most intensive period of industrial expansion – particularly striking because it took place against a background of economic depression in the capitalist world (*Map 78*). Although official Soviet figures are dubious there is no question that during this period Russia was ruthlessly propelled into the front ranks of industrial producers. The progress continued after the Second World War, and between 1950 and 1980 the Soviet economy grew from about one-third to more than two-thirds the size of that of the USA. However, much of Soviet industry remained relatively primitive, and it was notable that in the 1960s Russia once again began to rely on large-scale imports of foreign capital and advanced western technology.

The eastward territorial expansion of Russia in the nineteenth century (*see Map 70*) was no less impressive than that of the USA to the west. But Russian imperialism encountered serious internal and external difficulties. The empire contained vast numbers of non-Russian subject nationalities, many (in the east) educationally and socially backward, others (in the west) relatively advanced, most resentful of Russification and highly nationalistic. The Jews, confined to the so-called 'Pale of Settlement' (*see Map 60*), were particularly prominent in the revolutionary socialist movement which grew rapidly after the 1890s. Defeat by Japan in 1904-5 (*Map 73*) was the catalyst for revolution in 1905, which came close to toppling the regime. The concession of a Duma (Parliament) in 1905 was soon whittled away by the autocracy which retreated into hidebound conservatism. The liberal-democratic interlude of the February Revolution in 1917 gave way by October to a 'proletarian dictatorship' which by the late 1920s had degenerated into an autocracy far more brutal than that of the tsars.

Top: Forced labour in Siberia.

Above: Widows and orphans at a mass grave following the goldminers' rebellion and ensuing Lena Goldfields Massacres in Siberia (1912).

71 The emergence of modern Russia
After the checks imposed by war and revolution the industrialization of Russia, which had progressed very rapidly from the 1890s to 1914, was resumed with the first five-year plan in 1929. At the same time the beginning of forced collectivization – reversing the movement towards individual peasant proprietorship in the decades immediately before and after the revolution – further depressed the low levels of agricultural productivity which dogged both the old and the new regime.

The modernization of Japan, like that of Russia, was closely bound up with her relationship with the rest of the world. Until the mid-nineteenth century Japan had kept herself largely insulated from contact with other powers. But in 1853 an American naval squadron under Commodore Perry visited Japan. This marked the start of the opening of Japan to foreign trade and foreign influences (*see Map 64*). In 1858 Russia, Britain, the USA and France imposed 'unequal treaties' on Japan which, although much resented by the Japanese, confirmed foreign influence in the country.

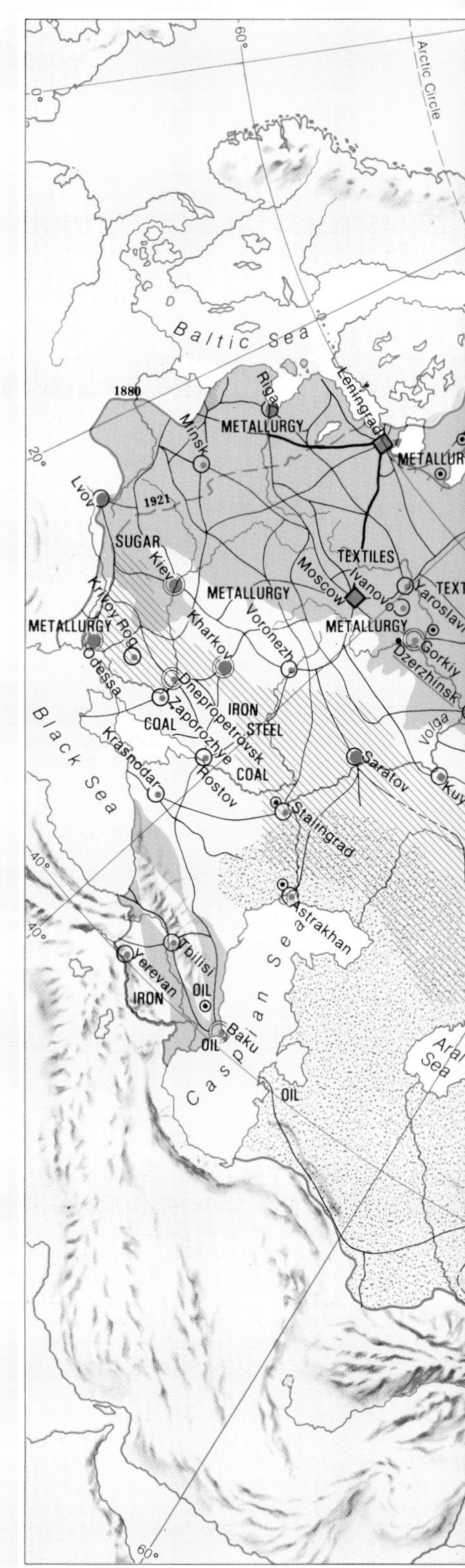

Isolation from the outside world had not preserved Japan from change. The Tokugawa peace tightly controlled the *daimyo* and their families, and drew the samurai to the courts of their lords. The unintended consequence was the creation of a class of idle and status-conscious consumers which stimulated dramatic urban expansion and a rapid growth of population. By the eighteenth century Edo had more than a million inhabitants, Osaka and Kyoto four hundred thousand each, and four million Japanese, perhaps 15% of the population, lived in cities. Their needs were supplied by a panoply of trades and crafts, among which textiles, notably silk, and mining and metal work of every kind were particularly thriving. The buying and selling, investing, transporting and brokering which all this demanded nourished effective communications, widespread literacy and numeracy, and a vigorous and sophisticated merchant class. The intensification of agriculture necessary to feed such a rapidly-growing, non-productive population led to substantial gains in efficiency, including the training of much of the work force in disciplines not (it has been argued)

72 The modernization of Japan
The Meiji restoration of 1868 ended the traditional seclusion of Japan and returned power to the imperial government. A deliberate programme of westernization in government and society was accompanied by a state-directed transformation of the economy to make Japan a modern industrial power.

73 The Far East around 1900
After defeating China in the war of 1894-5 Japan competed with the western powers and Russia in a 'scramble for China' which the imperial government, paralysed by corruption and internal dissension, was powerless to resist. Japan confirmed its new status as a world power by overwhelming Russia in the war of 1904-5.

MAP 71 THE EMERGENCE OF MODERN RUSSIA

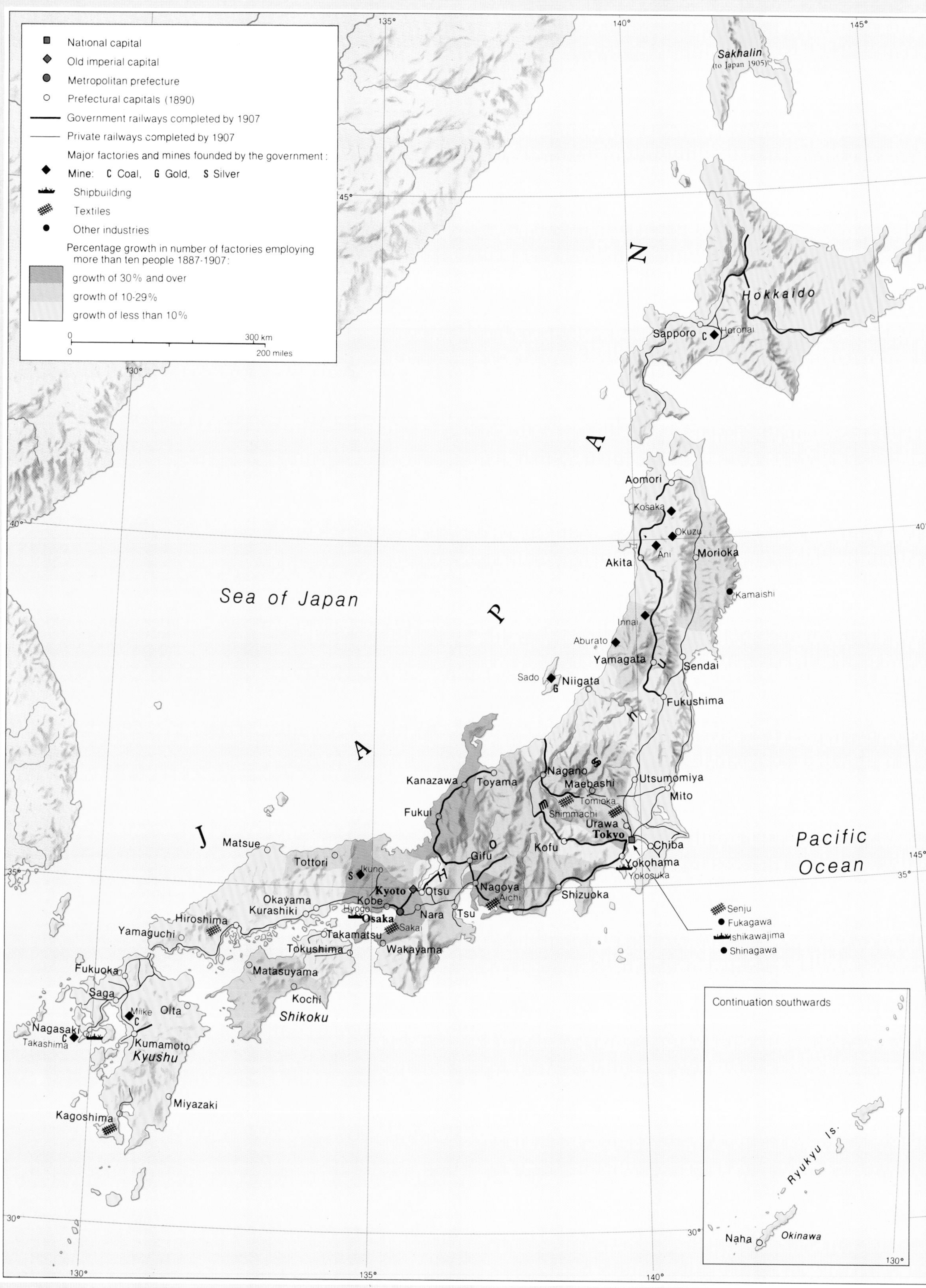

National capital
Old imperial capital
Metropolitan prefecture
Prefectural capitals (1890)
Government railways completed by 1907
Private railways completed by 1907
Major factories and mines founded by the government:
Mine: C Coal, G Gold, S Silver
Shipbuilding
Textiles
Other industries
Percentage growth in number of factories employing more than ten people 1887-1907:
growth of 30% and over
growth of 10-29%
growth of less than 10%
300 km
200 miles
Sakhalin (to Japan 1905)
Hokkaido
Sapporo
Horonai
JAPAN
Aomori
Kosaka
Okuzu
Ani
Morioka
Akita
Kamaishi
Sea of Japan
Innai
Aburato
Yamagata
Sendai
Sado
Niigata
Fukushima
HONSHU
Kanazawa
Toyama
Nagano
Maebashi
Utsunomiya
Mito
Tomioka
Shimmachi
Urawa
Tokyo
Chiba
Fukui
Kofu
Yokohama
Yokosuka
Pacific Ocean
Matsue
Tottori
Ikuno
Gifu
Kyoto
Otsu
Nagoya
Aichi
Shizuoka
Okayama
Kurashiki
Kobe
Hyogo
Osaka
Sakai
Nara
Tsu
Hiroshima
Yamaguchi
Takamatsu
Tokushima
Wakayama
Senju
Fukagawa
Ishikawajima
Shinagawa
Matasuyama
Kochi
Shikoku
Fukuoka
Saga
Miike
Oita
Nagasaki
Takashima
Kumamoto
Kyushu
Miyazaki
Kagoshima
Continuation southwards
Ryukyu Is.
Naha
Okinawa

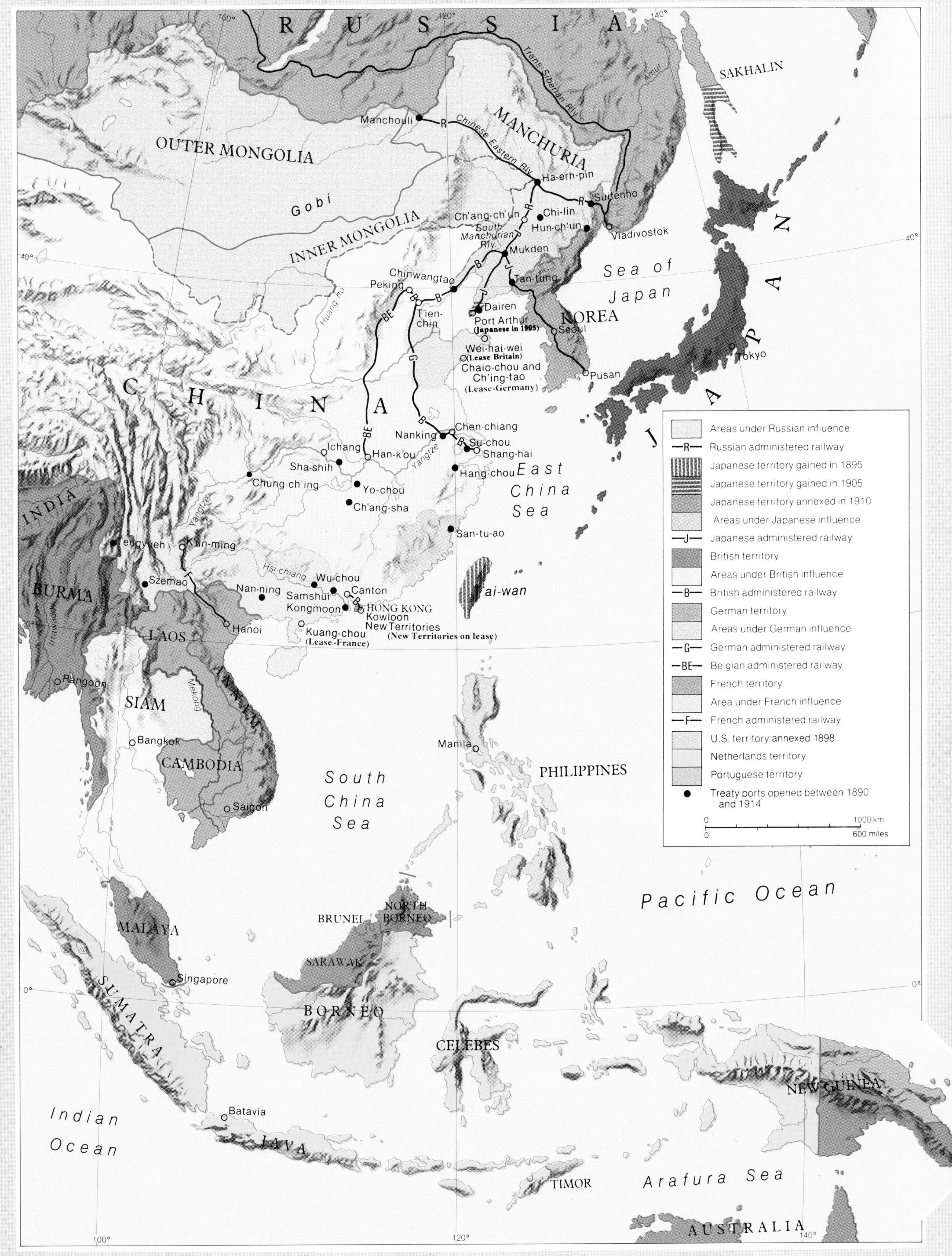

RUSSIA
SAKHALIN
Trans-Siberian Rly.
Amur
Manchouli
Chinese Eastern Rly.
MANCHURIA
OUTER MONGOLIA
Ha-erh-pin
Suifenho
Gobi
Ch'ang-ch'un
Chi-lin
Hun-ch'un
Vladivostok
South Manchurian Rly.
INNER MONGOLIA
Mukden
Sea of Japan
Chinwangtao
Peking
Tan-tung
T'ien-chin
Dairen
Port Arthur (Japanese in 1905)
KOREA
Seoul
Wei-hai-wei (Lease Britain)
Chaio-chou and Ch'ing-tao (Lease-Germany)
Pusan
Tokyo
JAPAN
CHINA
Huang ho
Chen-chiang
Nanking
Su-chou
Shang-hai
Ichang
Han-k'ou
Sha-shih
Yangtze
Hang-chou
East China Sea
Chung-ch'ing
Yo-chou
Ch'ang-sha
INDIA
San-tu-ao
Tengyueh
Kun-ming
Hsi-chiang
Wu-chou
Szemao
Nan-ning
Canton
Samshui
T'ai-wan
BURMA
Kongmoon
HONG KONG
Kowloon
New Territories (New Territories on lease)
Irrawaddy
Hanoi
LAOS
Kuang-chou (Lease-France)
Rangoon
SIAM
Mekong
ANNAM
Bangkok
Manila
CAMBODIA
PHILIPPINES
South China Sea
Saigon
Pacific Ocean
NORTH BORNEO
BRUNEI
MALAYA
SARAWAK
Singapore
SUMATRA
BORNEO
CELEBES
NEW GUINEA
Indian Ocean
Batavia
JAVA
TIMOR
Arafura Sea
AUSTRALIA
100°
120°
140°
40°
20°
0°
Areas under Russian influence
—R— Russian administered railway
Japanese territory gained in 1895
Japanese territory gained in 1905
Japanese territory annexed in 1910
Areas under Japanese influence
—J— Japanese administered railway
British territory
Areas under British influence
—B— British administered railway
German territory
Areas under German influence
—G— German administered railway
—BE— Belgian administered railway
French territory
Area under French influence
—F— French administered railway
U.S. territory annexed 1898
Netherlands territory
Portuguese territory
Treaty ports opened between 1890 and 1914
0 1000 km
0 600 miles

unlike those which would be required by an industrializing economy.

Although the boom in population seems to have levelled off after about 1700 it left a society which was, by current world standards, not only prosperous and firmly governed but highly urbanized and commercialized, with a capable and self-confident managerial élite and a skilled, diverse and well educated work force. On the other hand, since the social values and pretensions of the redundant warrior aristocracy remained intact while their real importance declined along with the value of their incomes, which were fixed in rice, the widening discrepancy between the real and theoretical power and status of different groups in society engendered growing tension and impatience with the political stalemate which the regime so determinedly maintained. Perry's brusque demonstration of modern military power and the diplomatic reverses of the following years pointed irresistably to the conclusion that for Japan the alternative to change was the fate of China.

The modern history of Japan is generally seen as dating from 1868 when the Tokugawa shogunate ended and authority reverted to the young Meiji emperor. The 'Meiji Restoration' began with an explicit statement of receptiveness to foreign ideas pronounced in the emperor's 'Charter Oath': 'Knowledge', he declared, 'shall be sought from all over the world and thus shall be strengthened the foundations of the imperial polity.' There followed soon afterwards the abolition of feudalism, the surrender of fiefs into the hands of the Emperor clearing the way for the establishment of bureaucratic government in the western manner. A centralized system of coinage and taxation was set up. After a short interval local government was placed in the hands of prefects appointed in Tokyo (as Edo had been renamed). Banks and railways, postal and telegraph services, newspapers and printing presses, were rapidly introduced. The early years of modernization bore heavily on the peasantry as rents remained high and the cost of living rose, and on the many thousands of samurai who could not find a place for themselves in the new world. Widespread revolts, culminating in the savage Satsuma rebellion of 1877, were suppressed, and the government continued a wide-ranging programme of modernizing reforms. In 1885 a cabinet system of government was established, and in 1889 a westward-looking constitution was adopted; this led to thc convening of a legislative assembly in 1890. The legal codes were revised, occidental fashions in ideas, clothes, and food spread, and the foundations of a mass education system were laid. By 1905 over 90% of children attended primary schools. Secondary and higher education (particularly technical colleges) developed rapidly after the turn of the century. A modern army and navy were established.

The basis for these reforms was the transformation of the economy of Japan. Industrialization, in which the government played a major role, was concentrated particularly in strategic industries such as munitions and ship-building and in textiles (*see Map 72*). There was a twentyfold expansion in the export of finished goods between 1868 and 1897. The late 1890s and the years after 1895 were boom periods; the outbreak of the First World War led to greatly increased demand for Japanese goods, and the period 1915-20 saw a huge spurt forward. Between 1900 and the late 1930s output of manufactured goods increased more than twelvefold. By 1936 Japan had overtaken Britain as the world's leading exporter of cotton piece goods. By the late 1930s Japan had developed what was in many ways a mature and diversified industrial economy. Industrialization naturally led to rapid urbanization: whereas in 1895 only 12% of the population lived in towns, by the mid-1930s the urban population had increased to 45% of the total. But the Japanese economy had certain weaknesses. On the one hand there were large numbers of small, relatively primitive units of production; on the other, there developed the *zaibatsu*, massive industrial conglomerates, of which the most important in the 1920s and 1930s were Mitsui and Mitsubishi, which were probably the two largest private economic empires in the world. The zaibatsu, by means of corruption and other forms of covert control, exercised a generally baneful influence over Japanese politics and society. But the most serious weakness of the Japanese economy was her increasing dependence on imported raw materials: by 1930 she was a net importer of coal, and depended on imports for 85% of her iron and steel, 79% of her oil, and a large part of her food. The desire to break out of this apparent stranglehold helped to strengthen imperialist elements in Japan.

Japanese imperialism was in large measure a response to the imperialism of western powers. It began in the 1870s with the incorporation of the Ryuku Islands into Japan and the imposition of an 'unequal treaty' on Korea (*see Map 73*). Rivalry with China in Korea was largely responsible for the outbreak of the Sino-Japanese War in 1895 in which Japan won a stunnng victory. But pressure from Russia, France, and Germany compelled Japan to yield up her claim to have won Port Arthur and the Liaotung Peninsula. The seizure of the peninsula by Russia only three years later aroused strong Japanese animosity, and the conclusion of the alliance with Britain in 1902 placed Japan in a position to confront Russia without fear of intervention. In 1904 she attacked Russia, won another startling victory, and regained the leasehold of the Liaotung Peninsula, and control of south Sakhalin and the Russian-built railways in southern Manchuria. Russia further recognized Japanese paramountcy in Korea, and by 1910 Japan felt strong enough to annex Korea outright.

The emergence of the USA, Russia, and Japan as powers of the first rank was, therefore, already far advanced by 1914 when there began the series of cataclysmic shocks which, within little more than a generation, was to shatter the old European-dominated world order.

Above: The first Japanese diplomatic delegation in Paris, 1862.

74 European imperialism in Africa
The partition of Africa in the 'scramble' ot 1880-1914 was less a development of earlier activity there than an extension of the rivalries of the Great Powers in Europe. The new political geography had little correspondence with African reality; nevertheless it largely survived the decolonization of the 1950s, 60s and 70s.

Further reading: Hugh Brogan, *History of the United States of America* (Longman 1985; Viking Penguin); Richard Hofstader, *The Age of Reform* (Random House 1955; Cape); Hugh Seton-Watson, *The Russian Empire 1801-1917* (Oxford U P); L. Kochan and R. Abraham, *The Making of Modern Russia* (second ed. Penguin 1983); Jack Gray, *Rebellions and Revolutions: China from the 1800s to the 1980s* (Oxford U.P. 1990); Richard Storry, *A History of Modern Japan* (Penguin 1982 edn.).

Borders in 1914
Battle
Siege
Railways c. 1914
1884 Date of imperial acquisition
Belgian territory in 1914
British territory " "
French territory " "
German territory " "
Italian territory " "
Portuguese territory " "
Spanish territory " "
Independent states in 1914
Europeans under 1% of population 1939
Europeans 1%-5% of population 1939
Europeans 5%-10% of population 1939
Europeans over 10% of population 1939
Borders in 1987
1958 Date of independence in colour of last ruling colonial power
0 1500 kms
0 1000 miles
Mediterranean Sea
Atlantic Ocean
Indian Ocean
Red Sea
Libyan Desert
Sahara
Kalahari Desert
Madeira 1418
Canary Is. 1496
Tangier
Casablanca
Marrakesh 1912
Agadir
IFNI 1860
SPANISH MOROCCO 1912
Fez
Oran
Algiers
MOROCCO 1956
Atlas Mts.
SPANISH SAHARA 1912
RIO DE ORO 1884
ALGERIA 1830 1962
Tunis 1881 1956
TUNISIA
Malta 1815 1964
Tripoli
Benghazi
LIBYA 1911
Marzuk 1951
(Br. and Fr. administration, 1941-51)
Alexandria
Port Said
Suez Canal (opened 1869)
Suez
Cairo
EGYPT (Br. occ. 1882) 1922
1893 1960
MAURETANIA
FRENCH SUDAN 1960
Timbuktu
FRENCH WEST AFRICA 1893/1904
1899/1912 1960
NIGER
Senegal
SENEGAL 1960 1637/1889
UPPER VOLTA 1896 1960
FRENCH GUINEA 1843 1958
SIERRA LEONE 1787 1961
Freetown
LIBERIA
Monrovia 1847
IVORY COAST 1842/82
Bingerville 1960
GOLD COAST 1820/74 1957
TOGOLAND 1894 1960
DAHOMEY 1851/93 1960
Accra
Lomé
Porto Novo
Lagos
NIGERIA 1861/1900 1960
Benue
L. Chad
CHAD 1884 1960
Fort Lamy
KAMERUN 1884 1960
Douala
Fernando Póo
1483 1975 Principé
São Tomé
RIO MUNI 1843 1968
Annobon 1778
GABON 1884 1960
MIDDLE CONGO
Brazzaville
FR. EQUATORIAL AFRICA
UBANGI SHARI 1884 1960
Ubangi
Equator
Congo
Cabinda
Leopoldville
Kasai
BELGIAN CONGO 1885/1908 1960
Stanleyville
L. Albert
SUDAN (Anglo-Egyptian Condominium 1899) 1956
Khartoum
Omdurman 1898
Blue Nile
White Nile
Nile
Fashoda
The Sudd
(Br. administration, 1941-52)
Asmara
ERITREA 1889
Adowa 1896
L. Tana
Gondar
Djibouti 1977
Berbera
Harar
BR. SOMALILAND 1884 1960
Addis Ababa
ABYSSINIA (It. occ. 1935-41)
ITALIAN SOMALILAND 1889 1960
Mogadishu
L. Rudolf
UGANDA 1890/94 1962
1888 1963
EAST AFRICA
L. Victoria
Nairobi
RUANDA URUNDI 1962 1962
Mwanza
Mombasa
Pemba I.
Tanga
Ujiji
Tabora
L. Tanganyika
GERMAN EAST AFRICA 1890 1961
ZANZIBAR 1890 1963
Dar es Salaam
Aldabra Is.
Luanda
ANGOLA 1885/1905 1975
Benguela
Moçâmedes
Elisabethville
NORTHERN RHODESIA 1891 1964
Lusaka
Zambezi
NYASALAND 1891 1964
Nyasa
Blantyre
MOZAMBIQUE 1891 1975
Moçambique
Beira
Comoro Is. 1841/86 1975
Diégo Suarez
MADAGASCAR 1885/1896 1960
Tananarive
Fort Dauphin
Caprivi Strip
SOUTHERN RHODESIA 1888 (Auton. 1923) 1980
Salisbury
SOUTH-WEST AFRICA 1884
Windhoek
Walvis Bay (S.A. 1910 - 1910)
BECHUANALAND 1885 1966
Limpopo
Mafeking 1899-1900
Pretoria
Johannesburg
Vereeniging
Majuba Hill 1881
Lourenço Marques
SWAZILAND 1903 1968
Blood River 1839
Isandhlwana 1879
Ulundi 1879
Rorke's Drift 1879
Bloemfontein
Vaal
Orange
Kimberley 1899-1900
Ladysmith 1899-1900
BASUTOLAND 1868 1966
Pietermaritzburg
Durban
UNION OF SOUTH AFRICA 1814/1902 1910
East London
Port Elizabeth
Cape Town
20° 0° 20° 40°
40°

The emergence of the modern world 2

THE FIRST WORLD WAR AND ITS AFTERMATH

The outbreak of the First World War in August 1914 may be explained as first and foremost the product of a German bid for world power.

The immense growth of German industrial and military might since 1871 (*see Map 57*) had nourished the development of dynamic political ambitions for a German-dominated 'Mitteleuropa', a colonial empire including a German 'Mittelafrika' (*see Map 74*), and the permanent subjugation of all Germany's potential European rivals. Underlying all this was hatred of the Slavs, fear of 'encirclement' by the Triple Entente, and resentment of Britain's empire, of her navy, and of her dominance of world trade and of the international capital market (*Map 67*). The German government intended, by means of a war, to establish the Reich as a superpower on a par with Britain. By 1914 the Germans, conscious that they would have to fight in both the east and west, and aware of Russia's programme of military modernization, felt it was 'now or never'. The opportunity came in June with the assassination by Serbs of the Austrian Archduke Franz Ferdinand in Sarajevo. Austria, encouraged by Germany, sent Serbia an ultimatum designed to be so harsh as to ensure rejection. The Serbs, although they were fired by a burning Slav nationalism, and were confident of Russian support, accepted nearly all Austria's demands. But the Austrians, under German influence, nevertheless declared war on Serbia. Russia's immediate decision to mobilize dispelled any prospect of localization of the conflict, and Germany quickly declared war on Russia and France. German violation of Belgian neutrality led Britain to join Russia and France. The Ottoman Empire, fearing partition by the Entente powers, allied itself with Germany. The Entente powers were joined by Japan in August 1914, and by Italy in May 1915, and, after German U-boat (submarine) attacks on merchant shipping, by the USA in April 1917.

The First World War was more catastrophic in its impact on nearly every sphere of human activity than any previous war. Although some fighting occurred in Asia and Africa and at sea, the conflict was at its most intense in Europe (*Map 75*). Relying on the pre-war Schlieffen plan, the Germans launched a sweeping thrust through Belgium into France, hoping to knock her out in six weeks, thus enabling Germany to turn her full strength against Russia. However the German army was halted at the River Marne, and the war in the west settled down to static trench warfare for four years, leaving millions of German, French and British dead. In the east the conflict was more mobile but no less bloody. With the issue unresolved on the two central fronts both sides sought alternative strategies. But neither the British landing at Gallipoli in 1915-16 nor the German attempt to starve Britain into surrender by blockade was successful in breaking the impasse.

In its military character (although not its scale) the war was in general fought by traditional means, the key elements being infantry, cavalry, and artillery. But the war boosted technological innovation, and the appearance of tanks and warplanes, although in limited numbers, was a portent of the revolution in warfare of the mid-twentieth century. In most belligerent countries, particularly in Europe, the war had a shattering impact on society, economy, and government. Conscription, food shortages, attacks on civilian populations, war propaganda and hysteria were nothing new in human warfare. But what rendered this perhaps the first 'total war' in history was the vast expansion in the role of government in directing social and economic organization: *laissez-faire* was dead.

By late 1917 Germany had won the war in the east and in March 1918 imposed the draconian Treaty of Brest-Litovsk on Russia (*Map 76*). But although Germany was now free to concentrate on the western front, the entry of the USA to the war, with its huge reservoir of manpower and resources, ensured an eventual Allied victory. By late 1918 a final German push in the west had failed, her allies Austria-Hungary and Turkey had collapsed, and revolution had broken out in Germany. Although no enemy armies were yet on German soil, an armistice took effect on November 11 1918.

The war had convulsive effects on the old empires. In Russia the Tsar abdicated after a liberal revolution in March 1917 (the February Revolution after the Old Style calendar then still used in Russia). The new Provisional Government determined to keep Russia in the war, but it was discredited and demoralized by continuing defeat, desertion, and dislocation, and by a rising demand for peace. The ascent to power of Lenin's Bolsheviks (the extreme left wing of the Russian Social Democratic Party) in November 1917 (the 'October Revolution') was founded on his promise of 'peace, bread, and land.' Although defeated in elections in December 1917, and forced to surrender large areas in the west to the Germans at Brest-Litovsk, the Bolsheviks clung to power and by 1921 had defeated both their internal enemies and interventionist armies of capitalist powers. In the last days of the war the German and Austrian emperors were swept off their thrones by revolution. Short-lived socialist republics in eastern and central Europe soon collapsed, however, leaving Russia for the next quarter-century as the sole exemplar of a communist state. Perhaps the most momentous of the anti-imperial revolutions was that of Mustafa Kemal (later known as Ataturk). From 1919 onwards he drove Greek forces out of Asia Minor, to be followed by the enforced exodus of the ancient Greek communities of the Black Sea and Aegean littorals (*Map 5*). He expelled all occupying forces, reversed the imposed peace treaty, deposed the Sultan, and pronounced the end of the Islamic Caliphate (symbol of Islamic political unity since the death of the Prophet). Ataturk

MAP 75 THE FIRST WORLD WAR

Opposite page above: The landscapes of Europe, as well as human beings, were devastated by heavy shelling shown in this picture of a woodland battleground in France.

75 The First World War
The supremacy of defensive over offensive techniques made the Great War one of relatively little movement, especially on the Western Front, and enormous casualties, engaging armies many times larger than ever before. The resources of the belligerent powers were deployed and their civilian populations involved to a quite unprecedented degree, making this the first 'total' war.

consolidated Turkey as a national state, and propelled her on a path of modernization which was to inspire a later generation of post-colonial politicians in Asia and Africa.

Allied war aims, as enunciated in the American President Wilson's 'Fourteen Points', had presaged a relatively generous peace. In the event the treaties imposed on the defeated powers after a peace conference at Paris in 1919 humiliated the vanquished without in the long run benefiting the victors. Germany, convicted in the Treaty of Versailles of 'war guilt', was forced to cede territory in the east and the west, to pay massive reparations, and to constrict her armed strength within narrowly defined limits (*Map 77*). East Prussia was divided from the rest of Germany by a narrow strip of land gained by the new Polish state – the 'Polish corridor'. Austria, reduced to a German-speaking rump around Vienna, was barred from uniting with Germany. Hungary too was diminished to a small national state, losing two-thirds of her pre-war territory and population. The old empires were replaced by a patchwork of small 'successor states', formed in ostensible accordance with the principle of 'national self-determination'. But far from resolving national problems the new political structure in Europe aggravated them. All the new states contained substantial national minorities; the defeated powers resented the 'dictated peace' and itched to regain lost territories; the successor states lived in terror of the 'revisionist' ambitions of their former masters. Outside Europe too the peace treaties helped to stimulate local nationalisms. The Anglo French carve-up of the ex-Ottoman Fertile Crescent provoked Arab unrest. The Chinese, who had hoped that the 'Fourteen Points' would lead

MAP 76 REVOLUTION IN EUROPE

German occupation line. Treaty of Brest-Litovsk. March 1918
Curzon line 1919
Furthest advance of white and interventionist forces
Seized by Poland 1920
Polish advance to Russia, May 1920
Bolshevik advance into Poland, Aug. 1920
Russo-Polish frontier, Treaty of Riga, Oct. 1920
Roumanian occupation line in Hungary 1919
Interventionist naval forces
Railways in Russia
European frontiers 1923
Centres of revolutionary activity outside Russia
0 600 km
0 400 miles

the western powers to treat them on a basis of equality, resented the transfer to Japan of former German territories in China. Wilson, disillusioned by the selfish aggrandizement of his allies, acceded to their demands in order to gain their acquiescence to the Covenant of the League of Nations, the world organization which he hoped would guarantee peace. However the League's prospects were gravely damaged by the US Senate's repudiation of the Charter. The USA remained outside the League and embarked on an 'isolationist' course for the next two decades.

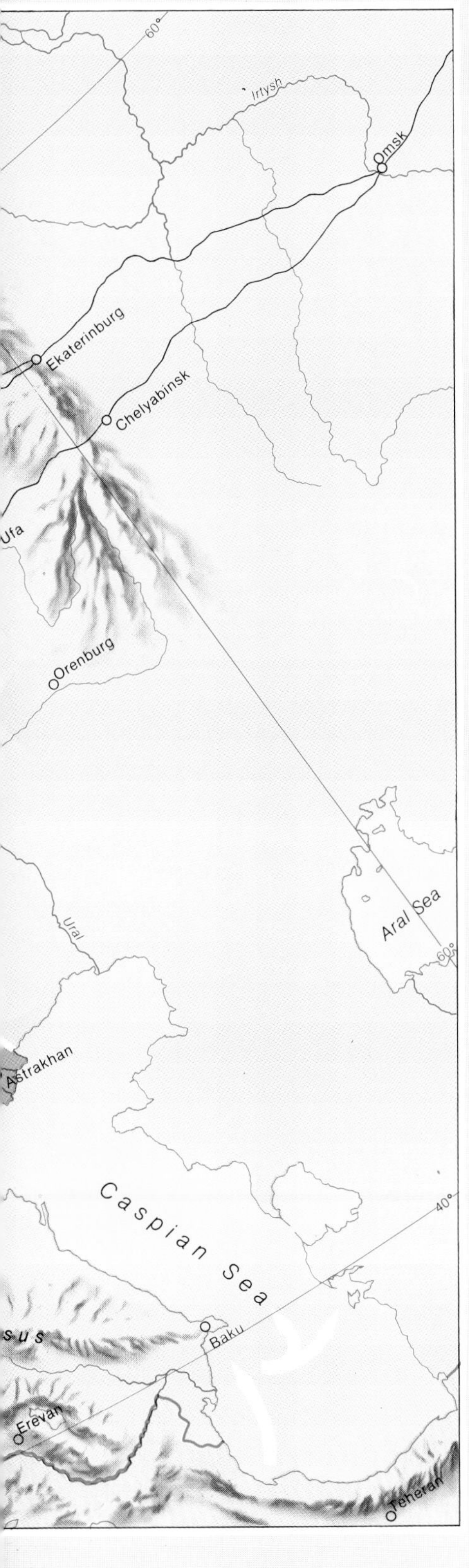

The international economic order, shattered by the war, never fully recovered. Britain's former pre-eminence as a producing, trading, and investing centre was in tatters. In company with others Britain was humiliatingly obliged to 'renegotiate' her war debts to the USA. The victorious powers had hoped to finance their debt payments out of German reparations, but these were not forthcoming, and even the French occupation of the Ruhr in 1923 failed to secure payment on the desired massive scale. Germany, together with most of central and eastern Europe after the war, was gripped by hyperinflation which had profoundly unsettling social effects. During the middle and late 1920s a partial recovery of the international economy occurred. But the crash on the New York Stock Exchange in 1929 was the signal for descent into the most severe economic crisis of the century, by which only Soviet Russia and some undeveloped countries remained unafflicted (*Map 78*). Banks failed, stock markets collapsed, businesses were bankrupted, international trade slumped, demand for all types of goods plummeted, and further millions were thrown out of work. Everywhere confidence in liberal capitalism was shaken, and the general reaction was to resort to protectionist, beggar-my-neighbour policies with competitive devaluations and high tariff walls. The British, American, and French currencies were forced off the gold standard. Even Britain abandoned free trade in 1932. Some measure of recovery was achieved in the later 1930s, but a functioning international economic system was not resurrected. Meanwhile the insecurities induced by the Great Depression had helped to engender political deformations which wrecked the flimsy constructions of the peace treaties.

Economic recession and aggressive nationalism, heightened by frustration with the consequences of the peace treaties, led to the rise of violent authoritarian movements and their seizure of the reins of government. Demagogic militarist dictatorships became the order of the day. Mussolini's fascist movement in Italy, which took power in 1922, formed the prototype for such regimes, with its accent on brute force, national prestige, and imperial expansion, and its contempt for intellectuals and for parliamentary democracy. The insecure Weimar constitution in Germany was by 1933 reeling under the impact of economic collapse (with six million unemployed) and fierce rivalry between communists and socialists. In 1933, after emerging in free elections as the largest party in Germany, Hitler's National Socialists (Nazis) took power with the support of conservatives. A ruthless totalitarian state apparatus replaced the rickety Weimar structure: Jews, socialists, trade unionists and liberal intellectuals were attacked and placed in concentration camps, the *Reichstag* (Parliament) was burned down, books were thrown on bonfires, and a pagan, racialist, anti-democractic ideology was inculcated by state propaganda. The economy was regenerated by massive expansion of the armaments industries. The bourgeois decencies of imperial and Weimar Germany gave way to the cult of 'blood and soil' and to hysterical mob adulation of the leader. Authoritarian regimes, often with a similar tinge, sprang up in much of Europe, notably in Spain after the bloody civil war of 1936-9 (*see Map 80*). In Soviet Russia too a savage despotism developed, with the usual apparatus of secret police, censorship, torture, prison camps, repression of all opposition, rule through a single party, and stress on economic self-sufficiency (*Map 71*). Stalin, who by the late 1920s had eliminated all potential rivals for power in the USSR, launched the country on a hectic course of heavy industrialization, collectivization of agriculture, and military reinforcement, accompanied by mass murder of kulaks (peasant proprietors), 'purges' of dissidents, and show trials. Japan, severely affected by the Depression, descended into the 'dark valley' of militarism. The efforts of thc *Kuomintang* government of China to counter fragmentation into regional warlordism by unifying the country economically and politically evoked fears of a threat to Japanese economic interests and helped to stimulate Japanese expansionism into Manchuria and China (*Map 79*). On the other side of the Pacific also, democracy failed to withstand the impact of economic crisis, with dictators assuming power in Brazil and Argentina after military coups in 1930. Only in the states around the North Atlantic seaboard did liberal democracy survive in the late 1930s as the characteristic form of government, and even here economic enfeeblement, social malaise, and fear of war seemed to portend collapse in the face of totalitarian attack.

76 Revolution in Europe
In the civil war which followed the Russian revolution of October 1917 the 'White' (anti-Bolshevik) forces were supported by the western powers, and especially by Poland which, its independence confirmed by the Congress of Versailles, sought territorial expansion. Elsewhere in Europe revolutionary outbreaks were widespread from the last months of the Great War, but were ultimately abortive.

77 Central Europe between the wars
The peace treaties divided the old dynastic empires into what purported to be nation-states but in fact contained large national minorities. In consequence they engaged in continuous border disputes while living in perpetual dread that the defeated powers, Germany, Hungary and Bulgaria, would seek to overturn what they regarded as a dictated peace.

78 The Depression
The crash of the New York Stock Exchange in October 1929 was followed by the collapse of businesses and of financial confidence all over the developed world. While new industries developed in many regions the high unemployment and acute depression which followed, especially in areas dependent on traditional industries, imposed additional strains on democratic regimes, many of which failed to survive.

Further reading: B. H. Liddell Hart, *The First World War* (second ed. Cassell 1970); E. H. Carr, *The Russian Revolution from Lenin to Stalin* (Macmillan, 1979); J. K. Galbraith, *The Great Crash* (third edn. Houghton Mifflin 1972; Hamish Hamilton); A.J. Nicholls, *Weimar and the Rise of Hitler* (second edn. Macmillan 1979); A. Polonsky, *The Little Dictators* (Routledge 1975); Anthony Copley, *Ghandhi: Against the Tide* (Basil Blackwell 1987); Edgar Snow, *Red Star over China* (second edn. Gollancz 1968; Grove Weidenfeld).

Major alliance systems
French alliances
German alliances
Polish alliances
Balkan Pact (1934)
Italian alliances
Little Entente (1922)
Baltic Entente (1934)
National divisions c. 1930
POLAND
POLES 69%
UKRAINIANS 10%
WHITE RUSSIANS 4%
JEWS 9%
OTHERS 8%
HUNGARY
MAGYARS 85%
JEWS 6%
OTHERS 9%
RUMANIA
RUMANIANS 71%
MAGYARS 9%
GERMANS 4%
JEWS 5%
OTHERS 11%
CZECHOSLOVAKIA
CZECHS 46%
SLOVAKS 20%
GERMANS 22%
OTHERS 12%
YUGOSLAVIA
SERBS 45%
CROATS 24%
SLOVENES 8%
BOSNIAN MOSLEMS 6%
OTHERS 17%
BULGARIA
BULGARIANS 88%
TURKS AND TARTARS 10%
OTHERS 2%
Other countries over 90% nationally homogeneous
Borders in 1924
Border changes by 1939 (with arrows showing destination and date)
Demilitarised zones to 1936
Nazi-Soviet demarcation line in Poland 1939
Percentage of population employed in agriculture c. 1930:
70% and over
50% – 70%
30% – 50%
less than 30%
Cities with Jewish population of more than 100,000 c. 1935
Other major Jewish communities
Internationalised waterways
500 km
300 miles
North Sea
Baltic Sea
Black Sea
Adriatic Sea
Tyrrhenian Sea
Gulf of
NETHERLANDS
BELGIUM
LUX.
SAAR
GERMANY
DENMARK
SWEDEN
ESTONIA
LATVIA
LITHUANIA
East Prussia
POLAND
U.S.S.R.
CZECHOSLOVAKIA
SUDETENLAND
Protectorate of Bohemia and Moravia 1939
Slovakia (Independent 1939)
Ruthenia
AUSTRIA
SWITZERLAND
HUNGARY
RUMANIA
YUGOSLAVIA
BULGARIA
ALBANIA
GREECE
TURKEY
ITALY
FRANCE
Danzig (Free city)
Istanbul (Constantinople)
Edirne (Adrianople)

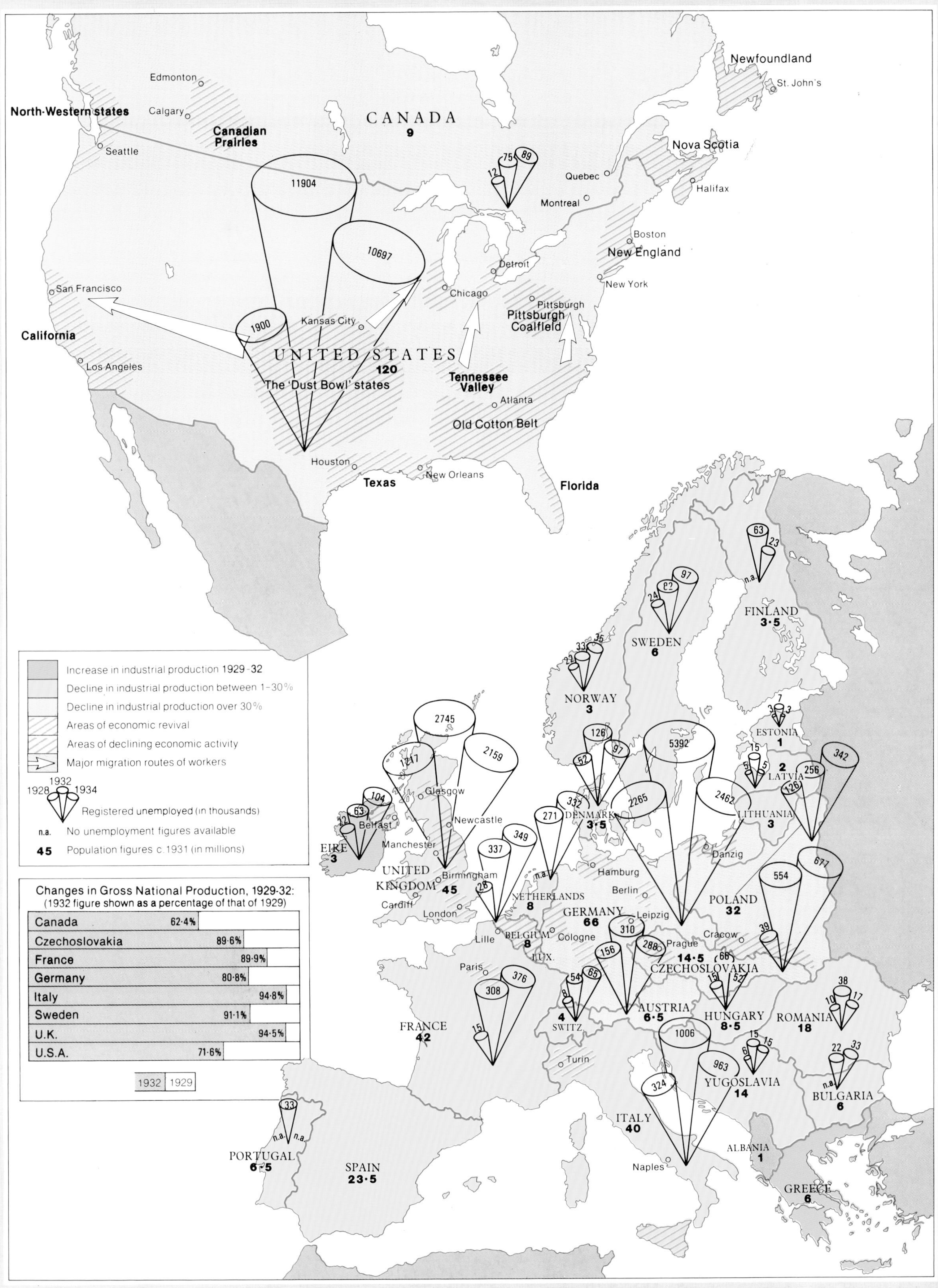

Newfoundland
St. John's
Edmonton
Calgary
North-Western states
Canadian Prairies
CANADA
9
Seattle
Nova Scotia
Quebec
Halifax
Montreal
11904
12
75
89
Boston
New England
10697
Detroit
San Francisco
Chicago
New York
Pittsburgh
Pittsburgh Coalfield
1900
Kansas City
California
UNITED STATES
120
The 'Dust Bowl' states
Los Angeles
Tennessee Valley
Atlanta
Old Cotton Belt
Houston
New Orleans
Texas
Florida
Increase in industrial production 1929-32
Decline in industrial production between 1-30%
Decline in industrial production over 30%
Areas of economic revival
Areas of declining economic activity
Major migration routes of workers
1928 1932 1934
Registered unemployed (in thousands)
n.a. No unemployment figures available
45 Population figures c.1931 (in millions)
Changes in Gross National Production, 1929-32:
(1932 figure shown as a percentage of that of 1929)
Canada 62·4%
Czechoslovakia 89·6%
France 89·9%
Germany 80·8%
Italy 94·8%
Sweden 91·1%
U.K. 94·5%
U.S.A. 71·6%
1932 1929
FINLAND
3·5
63
23
n.a.
SWEDEN
6
24
82
97
NORWAY
3
22
33
35
ESTONIA
1
LATVIA
2
LITHUANIA
3
342
256
126
5392
2265
2462
2745
1217
2159
Glasgow
Newcastle
Belfast
104
63
32
EIRE
3
Manchester
UNITED KINGDOM
45
Birmingham
Cardiff
London
126
52
97
332
DENMARK
3·5
271
n.a.
337
349
28
NETHERLANDS
8
BELGIUM
8
LUX.
Lille
Hamburg
Berlin
Danzig
GERMANY
66
Leipzig
Cologne
554
677
39
POLAND
32
310
288
156
Prague
14·5
66
CZECHOSLOVAKIA
Cracow
Paris
308
376
15
FRANCE
42
54
65
8
4
SWITZ.
AUSTRIA
6·5
15
52
HUNGARY
8·5
38
10
17
ROMANIA
18
1006
963
324
15
6
15
YUGOSLAVIA
14
22
33
n.a.
BULGARIA
6
Turin
ITALY
40
Naples
ALBANIA
1
GREECE
6
33
n.a.
n.a.
PORTUGAL
6·5
SPAIN
23·5

The emergence of the modern world 3

THE SECOND WORLD WAR

79 The Far East 1931-45
With the invasion of Manchuria in 1931 Japan, increasingly under the domination of its military leaders, and badly affected by the Depression, embarked upon a programme of military expansion designed to secure its domination of Asia and especially to eliminate western economic influence. The Far East consequently became a major theatre of the Second World War.

The Second World War was more truly a global conflict than the first. In a sense it consisted of three wars, intertwined but distinct.

These centred around: the Japanese attempt to build an East Asian empire which brought her into conflict with China and the western powers which had interests in the area; the German ambition to dominate continental Europe (coupled with the Italian desire to render the Mediterranean an Italian lake) which led to war with Britain and France; and the German attack on the Soviet Union which made Russia the ally of Britain and the USA.The roots of the Far Eastern war lay in the aim of the Japanese militarists to establish a 'New Order in East Asia' – a sphere of Japanese paramountcy in which western interests would be eliminated, and economic resources exploited to Japan's exclusive benefit. The invasion of Manchuria in 1931 marked the beginning of the descent to war (*Map 79*). The League of Nations was a broken reed, unable to compel Japan to withdraw from Manchuria – although Japan withdrew from the League. A puppet state, Manchukuo, was erected under the nominal suzerainty of the last Chinese emperor, in reality under the supervision of Tokyo. Japan's twenty-year alliance with Britain had been permitted to lapse in 1922, and in 1936 Japan's new diplomatic alignment was sealed by the Anti-Comintern Pact with Nazi Germany.

The Japanese invasion of China in 1937 is sometimes held to mark the real beginning of the Second World War. However, the British Empire and the USA were not at this stage engaged, and Japan did not declare war on Britain upon the outbreak of the European war in September 1939, nor on the USSR after Hitler's attack in mid-1941. Nevertheless further Japanese incursions in China and French Indo-China provoked an American, British, and Dutch economic embargo which led to the fatal decision in December 1941 to attack the US naval base at Pearl Harbor (in Hawaii), thus drawing the USA into both the Pacific and the European wars.

The war in Europe also arose out of the bid for imperial aggrandizement of an authoritarian regime. Hitler's Nazi movement had cultivated the myth of the 'stab in the back' (the notion that Germany had not been militarily defeated by the Allies in 1918 but had been the victim of internal conspiracy by socialists and Jews). The Nazis had played on the widespread resentment in Germany of the punitive impositions of the Versailles Treaty. Massive rearmament in breach of the treaty was accompanied by the demand for *lebensraum* ('living-space'), revision of borders, and the inclusion within the fatherland of the substantial German minorities outside the Third Reich (*Map 77*). The remilitarization of the Rhineland (in further breach of the treaty) in March 1936 failed to evoke an effective response from Britain and France. In late 1936 Hitler and Mussolini allied in the so-called 'Rome-Berlin Axis'. Meanwhile Italian forces attacked the ancient and backward empire of Abyssinia (Ethiopia), providing a further demonstration of the ineffectualness of the League. Both Italy and Germany sent forces to aid the fascists in the Spanish Civil War, which was seen as an ideological and military testing-ground between 1936 and 1939. Russia sent some aid to the Spanish Republican government, but France (although ruled by a left-wing 'Popular Front' government) and Britain enunciated the doctrine of 'non-intervention', which effectively ensured a fascist victory.

The 'appeasement' policy of the democracies was the product of a profound horror of war on the part of a generation traumatized by the nightmare of 1914-18, compounded by the isolationism of the USA, the slowness to rearm of Britain, and the deep internal divisions in France. Moreover, the suggestion of an alliance with Bolshevik Russia was anathema to many conservatives. Hitler's annexation of Austria in 1938 (the *Anschluss*), and his demand for territorial concessions from Czechoslovakia brought matters to a head. At the Munich conference in September 1938, Britain and France avoided war by conceding Hitler's demands and permitting the emasculation of Czechoslovakia. Six months later the rump of Czechoslovakia was occupied by Germany, and Hitler turned his attention east towards Poland. Undeterred by a British guarantee to Poland, Hitler demanded the redress of various grievances concerning Danzig and the Polish corridor (Poland's link with the Baltic coast). In August 1939 he scored a diplomatic coup with the surprise conclusion of the Nazi-Soviet pact, under which Germany and Russia secretly agreed to a renewed partition of Poland. This was a *carte blanche* for the German attack on Poland on September 1 1939, which induced the British empire and France to declare war on Germany.

Germany conquered western Poland in a fortnight, and the USSR then occupied the eastern portion and later took the opportunity to attack Finland and swallow the Baltic republics of Latvia, Lithuania, and Estonia (*Map 81*). After September 1939 a period known as the 'phoney war' ensued, in which little fighting occurred and there was even the whisper of a negotiated peace. But in May 1940 Germany attacked the Low Countries and France, and in a spectacular seven-week '*Blitzkrieg*' won a smashing victory which made her the dominant power in Europe, and attracted Italy into the war as a junior ally eager to share the spoils.

Britain now stood alone under the inspiring leadership of Churchill, Prime Minister from May 1940. In the aerial 'Battle of Britain' the Royal Air Force prevented the Luftwaffe from gaining mastery of the skies, and thereby thwarted Hitler's cross-Channel invasion plans. Meanwhile the American President Roosevelt, although conscious of what was still a strongly isolationist mood in Congress and among public opinion, nudged the USA closer to war with the 'Lend-Lease' agreement, by which the USA agreed to 'lend' Britain fifty surplus destroyers in return for long-term 'leases' on bases in the Caribbean and western Atlantic (*Map 85*).

In April 1941 Germany moved into Yugoslavia and Greece in a campaign which, although it inflicted further painful humiliations on Hitler's enemies, delayed (and thereby gravely imperilled) his most ambitious, and ultimately fatal, gamble – the attack on the Soviet Union on June 22 1941. This turned Stalin into the involuntary ally of Churchill and Roosevelt and inaugurated the critical phase of the war.

Even more than the First World War this was 'total war' – more extensive in its scope, more intensive in its impact, producing breathtakingly rapid innovations in military technique, scientific invention, and economic and social organization. Unlike its predecessor the Second World War was

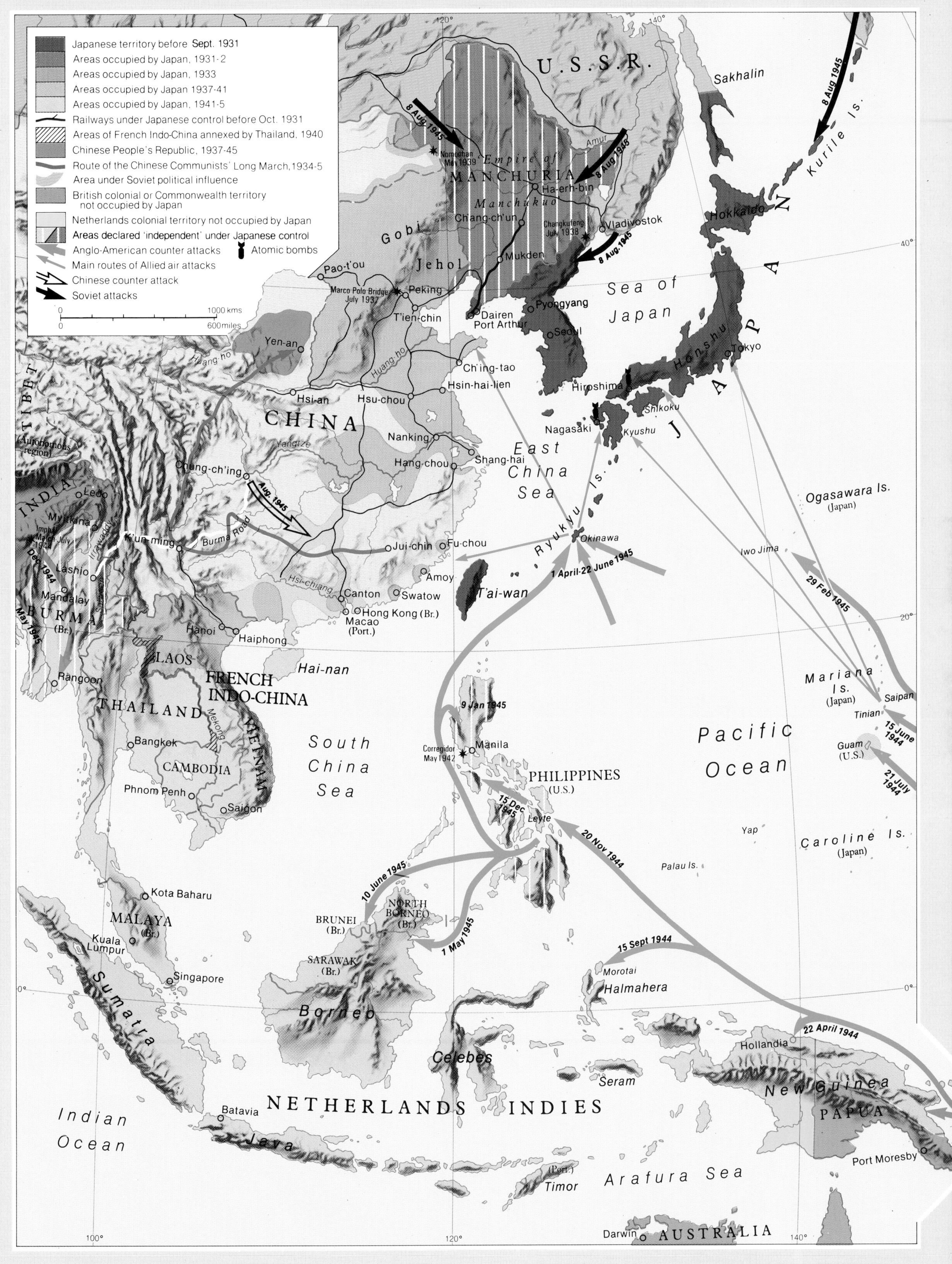

Japanese territory before Sept. 1931
Areas occupied by Japan, 1931-2
Areas occupied by Japan, 1933
Areas occupied by Japan 1937-41
Areas occupied by Japan, 1941-5
Railways under Japanese control before Oct. 1931
Areas of French Indo-China annexed by Thailand, 1940
Chinese People's Republic, 1937-45
Route of the Chinese Communists' Long March, 1934-5
Area under Soviet political influence
British colonial or Commonwealth territory not occupied by Japan
Netherlands colonial territory not occupied by Japan
Areas declared 'independent' under Japanese control
Anglo-American counter attacks
Atomic bombs
Main routes of Allied air attacks
Chinese counter attack
Soviet attacks
1000 kms
600 miles
U.S.S.R.
Sakhalin
Kurile Is.
8 Aug 1945
Empire of Manchuria
Manchukuo
Nomonhan May 1939
Amur
Ha-erh-bin
Ch'ang-ch'un
Changkufeng July 1938
Vladivostok
Mukden
Gobi
Jehol
Pao-t'ou
Marco Polo Bridge July 1937
Peking
T'ien-chin
Dairen
Port Arthur
Pyongyang
Seoul
Sea of Japan
Hokkaido
Honshu
Tokyo
JAPAN
Hiroshima
Shikoku
Kyushu
Nagasaki
Yen-an
Huang ho
Ch'ing-tao
Hsin-hai-lien
Hsi-an
Hsu-chou
CHINA
TIBET (Autonomous region)
Yangtze
Nanking
Shang-hai
Hang-chou
East China Sea
Ch'ung-ch'ing
Aug. 1945
INDIA
Ledo
Myitkyina
Imphal March-July 1944
Dec 1944
Irrawaddy
K'un-ming
Burma Road
Jui-chin
Fu-chou
Ryukyu Is.
Okinawa
1 April-22 June 1945
Lashio
Mandalay
Salween
BURMA (Br.)
May 1945
Hsi-chiang
Canton
Amoy
Swatow
T'ai-wan
Hong Kong (Br.)
Macao (Port.)
Hanoi
Haiphong
LAOS
Rangoon
Hai-nan
FRENCH INDO-CHINA
THAILAND
Mekong
VIETNAM
Bangkok
CAMBODIA
Phnom Penh
Saigon
South China Sea
9 Jan 1945
Corregidor May 1942
Manila
PHILIPPINES (U.S.)
15 Dec 1945
Leyte
20 Nov 1944
Ogasawara Is. (Japan)
Iwo Jima
29 Feb 1945
Mariana Is. (Japan)
Saipan
Tinian
15 June 1944
Guam (U.S.)
21 July 1944
Pacific Ocean
Yap
Caroline Is. (Japan)
Palau Is.
Kota Baharu
MALAYA (Br.)
Kuala Lumpur
Singapore
10 June 1945
NORTH BORNEO (Br.)
BRUNEI (Br.)
1 May 1945
SARAWAK (Br.)
15 Sept 1944
Morotai
Halmahera
Sumatra
Borneo
Celebes
22 April 1944
Hollandia
Seram
New Guinea
PAPUA
Port Moresby
Indian Ocean
Batavia
NETHERLANDS INDIES
Java
(Port.) Timor
Arafura Sea
Darwin
AUSTRALIA
100°
120°
140°
40°
20°
0°

pre-eminently a war of movement in which the characteristic forms of locomotion were not infantry or cavalry but motorized armour and warplanes. Warfare in East Asia and Africa still provided some scope for human ingenuity in 'guerrilla' campaigns with only limited mechanization, but in general the capability to invent, construct, deploy and operate machines and sophisticated instruments became the determining element in the war. Britain and the USA in particular gained the edge in scientific warfare, most notably with their 'Manhattan Project' for the manufacture of the atomic bomb (in which they were greatly aided by intellectual emigrants from Nazi Europe).

Remarkably, in spite of their authoritarian regimes, the Axis powers were less successful in gearing their economies to the requirements of total war. Germany sought to exploit the resources of occupied Europe to the full, but her ruthless 'New Order' in Europe did not succeed in creating a coherently integrated continental war economy. Even Germany attained her full productive capacity only in 1944. The Japanese 'Co-Prosperity Sphere' in East Asia (*Map 79*) embittered occupied populations and failed to produce vitally needed goods: by early 1943 Japan was losing ten times as much shipping sunk as was being replaced by new building. In contrast the Allies not only succeeded in concentrating their productive efforts more intensively and rationally, but also pooled their (potentially far greater) resources in what was, particularly in the case of Britain and the USA, very intimate co-ordination. Indeed, although the Russians stood somewhat apart, the co-operation of the Allies in every sphere – economic, military, and diplomatic – contrasted tellingly with the wary suspiciousness of one another with which the Axis powers fought their separate wars. Beyond the battlefield, the factory, and the laboratory, the

MAP 80 FASCIST EUROPE

arena of conflict extended into men's minds. This was an ideological struggle in which the wireless, the printed word, and the cinema were potent weapons.

If the war stimulated sophisticated technological and scientific advances, it also discredited the outlook, hitherto widespread, which equated the material civilization of the white races with moral superiority. For the war was conducted with a ruthless ferocity and disregard of humane values which dwarfed the horrors of all previous conflicts. Civilian populations were drawn into the struggle as never before. German, Japanese, and Russian treatment of prisoners-of-war was often brutal. Terror bombing of cities, a tactic initiated by Germany but adopted also by the Allies, left hundreds of thousands of dead. The age-old distinction between combatants and civilians was blurred, especially in those areas of occupied Europe where anti-Nazi resistance movements sought to conduct guerrilla warfare, which in some areas developed into internecine conflict between resistance forces and 'collaborators' or between communists and anti-communists.

Inspired by Hitler's obsessive anti-semitism, the Nazis (often, particularly in eastern Europe, with the active support of local populations) gathered together the Jews of Europe in 'ghettos' or forced-labour concentration camps (*see Map 80*). Hundreds of thousands of Jews were murdered during the early years of the war by special killing squads ('*Einsatzgruppen*') or by other military and paramilitary units. Later special mass murder centres were established in eastern Europe, such as the Auschwitz camp, to which millions of Jews and others were deported, killed in gas chambers, and cremated. Resistance, such as the revolt of the Jews in the Warsaw Ghetto in 1943, was hopeless. Nor did the Allies take effective action to admit significant numbers of refugees from the holocaust or seek to blunt its impact.

In spite of initial German and Japanese successes, the tide of the war had begun to turn by early 1943. In June 1942 American air and naval forces in the central Pacific won an important victory over the Japanese in the Battle of Midway Island, which for the first time threw the Japanese on to the defensive (*Map 79*). In November 1942 British forces defeated a German army at el Alamein in Egypt, thereby preventing German capture of the Suez Canal, vital to British imperial communications (*Map 81*). Still more significant was the dramatic Russian stand in defence of Stalingrad, where in February 1943 large German armies capitulated, decisively halting the German advance into the USSR.

Thenceforth the stubborn resistance of the Axis powers was slowly ground down. The first to collapse was Italy where in mid-1943 Mussolini was overthrown and replaced by a government which surrendered to the Allies. However, before the Allied forces in southern Italy could capitalize fully on this success, the Germans had occupied the northern half of the peninsula whence they were dislodged only after long and gruelling battles in 1944 and 1945. The crucial battles were fought elsewhere. During 1944 the Red Army steadily pressed the Germans back on the eastern front while demanding that the western allies open a 'second front' in north-west Europe. After some delays this was at last secured on 6 June 1944 ('D-Day'), when American and British troops landed in Normandy. By late 1944 nearly the whole of France had been liberated, although even now German resistance was such that in December 1944 a surprise German offensive in the Ardennes achieved temporary success. But this was soon reversed, and by early 1945 the Allies in the west were advancing into Germany on a broad front. In late April they met the Russians at the Elbe, and by May 8 were able to celebrate V-E (Victory in Europe) Day.

Japan now faced certain defeat, but continued to defy her enemies even after Germany's collapse. Japanese surrender on August 14 1945 came only after the USA had dropped atomic bombs on Hiroshima and Nagasaki causing huge, hideous casualties. The world war thus terminated, but the mushroom cloud of Hiroshima cast a shadow over the moral quality of the victory, and darkened the prospects of post-war international harmony, perhaps even of long-term human survival.

Above: The sinking of the *USS California* at Pearl Harbor, December 7 1942. The USS California settling into mud

80 Fascist Europe
The violent authoritarian movements which, assisted by economic recession and resentment of the Versailles settlement, seized power in much of inter-war Europe, shared an aggressive nationalism and brutal hostility to minorities. These reached a peak in Nazi Germany.

81 The Second World War in Europe
The second great war of the century was shaped this time by the rapid movement of both land and air forces, with correspondingly widespread devastation. The European powers exhausted one another and domination passed to the USA and Russia, whose intervention had decided the outcome of the war.

Further reading: Akira Iriye, *The Origins of the Second World War in Asia and the Pacific* (Longman 1987); A. Bullock, *Hitler and Stalin* (Collins 1991); Ian Kershaw, *The Hitler Myth* (Oxford U. P. 1987); G. Wright, *The Ordeal of Total War* (Harper & Row, 1968); W.L.S. Churchill, *The Second World War* (Cassell, 1945-54); Martin Gilbert, *The Holocaust* (Collins 1986).

To North America
To Murmansk and Archangel
British landings in Norway April 1940
NORWAY
SWEDEN
Stockholm
Skagerrak
Kattegat
Göteborg
Copenhagen
DENMARK
9·4·40
UNITED KINGDOM
Aberdeen
Glasgow
Edinburgh
Belfast
Newcastle
Dublin
EIRE
Manchester
Liverpool
Leeds
Hull
Sheffield
Birmingham
Norwich
Coventry
Swansea
Cardiff
London
Southampton
Plymouth
Exeter
Dover
North Sea
Atlantic Ocean
NETHERLANDS
Amsterdam
Rotterdam
Arnhem
Bremerhaven
Kiel
Lübeck
Peenemünde
Hamburg
Bremen
Hanover
Berlin
Potsdam
Posen
GERMANY
Elbe
Rhine
Oder
Essen
Düsseldorf
Cologne
Antwerp
Brussels
BELGIUM
Dunkirk
Calais
Lille
Boulogne
Amiens
English Channel
6·6·44
Cherbourg
Dieppe
Le Havre
Brest
Late June 1944
Caen
Rouen
Seine
Paris
Reims
Ardennes
11·6·40
Metz
10·5·40
Leipzig
Dresden
1·9·39
Breslau
Frankfurt
Schweinfurt
Karlsruhe
Mannheim
Nuremberg
Stuttgart
Strasbourg
Munich
May 1945
Pilsen
Prague
Lidice
CZECHOS
Brno
Bratislava
Vienna
Sopron
Danube
Le Mans
Alençon
Angers
Troyes
Nancy
Dec. 1944
Loire
Orléans
Nantes
FRANCE
Poitiers
Dijon
Mulhouse
Bay of Biscay
22·6·40
Vichy
Berne
SWITZ.
Innsbruck
Bordeaux
Lyon
The Alps
Bolzano
Graz
6·4·41
Drava
Ljubljana
Zagreb
Trieste
Milan
Turin
Grenoble
Garonne
Rhône
Po
Venice
Genoa
21·6·40
Bologna
Bilbao
Oporto
Pyrenees
Toulouse
Douro
La Spezia
December 1944
Marseille
Nice
Toulon
Ancona
YUGO
Sarajevo
PORTUGAL
Lisbon
Madrid
Tagus
SPAIN
Guadiana
Barcelona
Corsica
Ajaccio
late June 1944
ITALY
Apennines
Adriatic Sea
Vis
Dubrovnik
15·8·44
Rome
Monte Cassino
Anzio
Dec. 1943
Foggia
Bari
Balearic Is (Sp.)
Seville
Guadalquivir
Sardinia
Caserta
Naples
Salerno
Brindisi
Taranto
Tyrrhenian Sea
22·1·44
Cagliari
9·9·43
Mediterranean Sea
Gibraltar (Br.)
Malaga
8·11·42
Tangier
Rabat
Casablanca
SP. MOROCCO
Fez
Oran
Algiers
Messina
Reggio
Palermo
3·9·43
Sicily
Catania
Syracuse
Ionian
Bizerta
Constantine
Tunis
MOROCCO (France)
Atlas Mts.
ALGERIA (France)
TUNISIA
Pantelleria
10·7·43
Malta (Br.)
Sahara
November 1942
Tripoli
LIBYA
March 1941

German invasions with dates
Axis advance by date shown
Allied invasions with dates
Allied advance by date shown
Allied convoy routes
Major German air raids
Major Allied air raids
Oil wells
Oil pipelines
Neutral states
300 kms
200 miles
U. S. S. R.
Black Sea
Caspian Sea
Mediterranean Sea
Aegean Sea
TURKEY
ROUMANIA
BULGARIA
GREECE
SYRIA (France)
IRAQ
IRAN
PALESTINE (Br. mandate)
TRANS-JORDAN
EGYPT
Cyrenaica
Crimea
Caucasus
Ukraine
White Russia
Estonia
Latvia
Lithuania
Pripet Marshes
Carpathians
Taurus Mts.
Quttara Depression
December 1941
November 1942
December 1943
late June 1944
December 1944
22-6-41
6-4-41
17-4-41
20-5-41
25.8.41
10.5.41
8-6-41
April 1941
Nov. 1942
Moscow
Leningrad
Stalingrad
Kiev
Kharkov
Smolensk
Minsk
Rostov
Odessa
Sebastopol
Yalta
Ploiesti
Bucharest
Istanbul
Ankara
Athens
Crete
Cyprus
Beirut
Damascus
Haifa
Jerusalem
Baghdad
Mosul
Kirkuk
Tobruk
El Alamein
Alexandria
Cairo
Port Said
Suez

The emergence of the modern world 4

82 Post-war Europe, 1945-1991
After 1945 the areas of Europe which had been controlled by the armed forces of the USSR and by those of the western democracies confronted one another in parallel political, economic and military blocs. By 1990 the nations of the west had secured prosperity and considerable political and economic integration, while the Communist regimes of the east collapsed in poverty and chaos.

THE POST-WAR WORLD

Even before the end of the Second World War the new pattern of international relations was beginning to emerge. Of the five 'great powers' in the victorious wartime coalition, three had been disastrously weakened and two immeasurably strengthened by the years of struggle.

Britain was economically exhausted by the war, and its post-war Labour government, preoccupied with social reform at home, was compelled to cut a much-reduced figure on the diplomatic stage. The claim of France to 'great power' status was barely conceded by her allies, and accorded ill with France's impoverished condition after the trauma of Nazi occupation. China's 'great power' status was thrown into question as the *Kuomintang* government's grip on power became ever more tenuous (*see Map 85*). By contrast the USA and the USSR had emerged by 1945 as the unquestioned 'super-powers' of the post-war era. Of the two the USA was by far the more powerful. Her prodigious wartime economic growth rendered her by 1945 the producer of over half the world's manufactured goods. Moreover she possessed nuclear weapons, whereas the USSR detonated its first atomic bomb only in 1949.

Mutual suspicions as to post-war ambitions had been evident at the 'big three' wartime conferences at Tehran in 1943, Yalta in February 1945, and Potsdam in July 1945. The severe strains between the USSR and the western allies had surfaced in mid-1944, particularly over the Russian refusal to allow adequate aid to be given to the anti-Nazi rising of the (anti-communist) Polish underground movement in Warsaw. At the end of the war communist and western forces confronted one another in a great arc stretching from central Europe through the middle east to east Asia (*Map 84*). The United Nations, successor to the now-defunct League of Nations, was established at the San Francisco Conference in mid-1945, with the primary aim of preserving world peace. Although the UN succeeded, unlike the League, in securing the

MAP 82 POST-WAR EUROPE, 1945-1991

adhesion of nearly all independent states, it soon became apparent that world politics would henceforth be dominated by the east-west rivalry for power, influence, and prestige, a contest dubbed after 1947 the 'cold war'.

The 'iron curtain' which descended across Europe generally followed the lines secured by Russian and western forces at the end of the war (*Map 81*). Determined to establish firm buffers against any possible threat to the USSR, Stalin annexed large territories from Finland, East Prussia, Poland, Czechoslovakia, and Romania. In Poland, Romania, Bulgaria, and Hungary non-communist elements were squeezed out and communist-dominated 'puppet' regimes took office under Russian supervision. In Czechoslovakia in February 1948 democratic politicians were eliminated and a communist-directed 'coalition' government installed. Only in Yugoslavia, where the resistance forces headed by Josip Broz (Tito) assumed power, was a communist government successful in maintaining independence from Moscow. In Greece a bitter civil war broke out late in 1944. British troops supported the anti-communists, while Stalin, as he had promised in October 1944, refrained from intervention. After renewed fighting in 1947-9 the pro-western groups achieved victory.

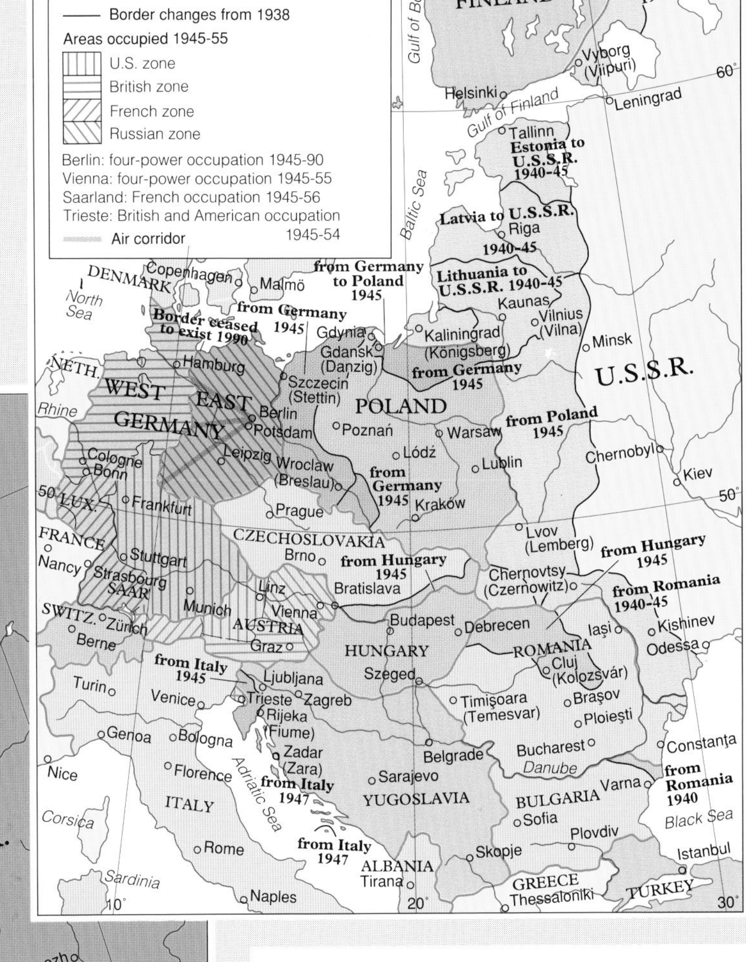

In the immediate aftermath of the war the democratic governments of western Europe were heavily dependent on American military protection and

83 Population and movements of people after 1945
Economic opportunity, poverty, war and persecution have made the second half of the twentieth century an age of mass migration on a scale quite unknown in any previous epoch, both reflecting and reinforcing the national and international tensions from which it has arisen.

84 Great power conflicts since 1945
The mutual distrust of the USA and USSR divided much of the post-war world into opposing camps in a series of occupations and military alliances, and produced a succession of confrontations when war seemed imminent. A period of relaxation after the Cuba crisis of 1962 was followed in the early 1980s by a massive arms race, before political and economic crisis in the USSR effectively brought the cold war to an end.

Indonesia 0·5
Netherlands
Poland
U.S.S.R.
Romania
Czech.
Hungary
Yugoslavia
(total 14·0)
Italy
Yugoslavia
Turkey
(total 3·0)
E. Germany 3·0
W. Germany
Bangladesh
E. Africa
Ireland
W. Indies
Pakistan
India
(total 2·0)
U.K.
Portugal
Spain
Italy
Morocco
Tunisia
Algeria
(total 2·0)
France
Greece
Germany
France
U.S.A.
Italy
Britain
(total 2·0)
Canada
Germany 0·75
Italy 0·5
Poland 0·3
U.K. 0·5
Mexico 1·1
Canada 0·5
W. Indies 1·1
Puerto Rico
Cuba 0·4
illegal immigrants 5·0
U.S.A.
Yugoslavia 0·4
Italy
Chad 0·1
Cameroon
Angola
Uganda
Rwanda
Burundi
(total 0·3)
Zaire
Zaire
Namibia
(total 0·6)
Angola
Vancouver
Edmonton
Seattle
Portland
Winnipeg
San Francisco
Los Angeles
Denver
Phoenix
Kansas City
St Louis
Memphis
Dallas
Houston
New Orleans
Atlanta
Miami
Minneapolis-Saint Paul
Milwaukee
Chicago
Indianapolis
Cincinnati
Detroit
Cle.
Pitt.
Toronto
Buffalo
Montreal
Ottowa
Boston
New York
Philadelphia
Baltimore
Washington D.C.
Monterrey
Guadalajara
Mexico City
Havana
Santo Domingo
Maracaibo
Caracas
Medellin
Bogotá
Cali
Quito
Lima
La Paz
Belém
Fortaleza
Recife
Salvador
Brasilia
Belo Horizonte
Rio de Janeiro
São Paulo
Porto Alegre
Cordoba
Valparaiso
Santiago
Montevideo
Buenos Aires
Glasgow
Belfast
Dublin
Leeds
Man.
Liverpool
Birmingham
London
Paris
Lyon
Bordeaux
Madrid
Lisbon
Barcelona
Marseille
Copenhagen
Oslo
Stockholm
Amst.
Brussels
Prague
Munich
Vienna
Milan
Turin
Naples
Algiers
Tunis
Casablanca
Ibadan
Accra
Lagos
Kinshasa
Cape Town
0.1
0.2
22.8
213.6
60.1
0.2
9.1
4.6
4.7
3.1
2.0
0.1
5.3
3.0
4.0
2.2
2.0
11.7
12.0
29.7
0.8
0.4
0.1
6.7
15.8
107.1
5.6
2.6
10.3
3.1
25·4
56.0
5.1
13.7
16.9
61.8
52.9
6.4
7.5
55.8
35.5
8.8
4.0
8.2
16.8
5.8
17.3
1.3
5.7
4.6
4.1
0.5
0.5
6.0
4.4
3.1
69.2
2.8
6.7
9.9
2.2
1.7
6.4
0.3
0.5
Percentage population growth, 1945-75
under 25%
25-50%
50-100%
over 100%
Density of population, 1975: (persons per sq. km.)
0-10
10-50
50-100
over 100
1945
1975
Population of selected cities
under ½ million
½-1 million
over 1 million
15.9 Population 1975 (millions)
Volume of Migration: (showing origin and destination of migrants)
17 million
17·1
Estimated numbers (in millions) from selected sources
1 million

N. Korea 3·0
China 2·9
S.E. Asia 0·7
Korea 0·9
Philippines
U.S.S.R. 0·5
Australia
Afghanistan 1·0
Middle East
Israel 1·0
Asia and Africa
C. and E. Europe
(total 1·4)
W. Pakistan
India 7·2
E. Pakistan
India 1·3
India
E. Pakistan 12
W. Pakistan 5·1
China 2·0
Vietnam 0·26
Cambodia
Vietnam
Laos
(total 0·3)
Vietnam
Cambodia
Philippines
(total 0·1)
Yemen 1
Egypt 0·5
Ethiopia 1·5
Ethiopia 0·4
Uganda
Chad
Zaire
Rwanda
Zaire
(total 0·1)
Rwanda
Burundi
(total 0·15)
G.B.
Italy
Yugoslavia
Greece
(total 2·0)
Arctic Circle
Tropic of Cancer
Equator
Tropic of Capricorn

Soviet-American Nuclear Balance

	USA	U.S.S.R.
1986 Nuclear warheads deployed	12,846	10,716
1991 START treaty ceilings	10,360	8,040

U.S.S.R.
(5,130)
Moscow 1972, 1988, 1991
INLAND
(35)
Porkkala (to 1955)
MONGOLIA
(25)
CHINA
(2,950)
1945-9
TIBET
1950
JAPAN
(243)
NORTH KOREA
[1,340]
SOUTH KOREA
(601)
Vladivostok 1974
Port Arthur (to 1955)
Yokosuka
Okinawa
Midway Is.
Pearl Harbor
1969
1950
TURKEY
(654) 1960, 1980
GREECE
CYPRUS
Akrotiri
LEB
SYRIA
(392)
1961
1975-91
ISRAEL
[704]
IRAQ
(800)
1958
JORDAN
(70)
KUWEIT
1961
1991
Suez (to 1956)
EGYPT
(445)
1952
SAUDI ARABIA
(67)
Daharan (to 1962)
Bahrain (to 1971)
Sharjah (to 1971)
UN. ARAB EMIRATES
OMAN
SOUTH YEMEN
1965-75
Aden (to 1967)
1962
Socotra
DJIBOUTI
Dahlak Is.
ETHIOPIA
(227)
1974,1991
SOMALIA
(43)
SUDAN
(57)
1985
IRAN
(705)
1945-6
1979
1978
AFGHANISTAN
(50)
Kabul
PAKISTAN
(481)
1977
NEPAL
INDIA
(1,260)
BANGLADESH
1971
SRI LANKA
(38)
1983-
Diego Garcia
BURMA
(MYANMAR)
(186)
1962
1988
THAILAND
(256)
(to 1976)
1991
LAOS
VIETNAM
(1,155)
1945-75
1953-75
CAMBODIA
1970-
1970
1964
Da Nang (to 1972)
Cam Ranh Bay
Hong Kong
TAIWAN
(424)
1979
PHILIPPINES
(113)
1986
Clark (to 1991)
Subic Bay
Guam
MALAYSIA
(110)
1948-60
Singapore (to 1976)
INDONESIA
(281)
1965
PAPUA NEW GUINEA
AUSTRALIA
(70)
North West Cape
New Caledonia
NEW ZEALAND
(13)
KENYA
(14)
UGANDA
(6)
1971
RWANDA
BURUNDI
1966
TANZANIA
(40)
AIRE (CONGO)
(50)
1960-3
ZAMBIA
(16)
1964-
1976-9
ZIMBABWE
(RHODESIA)
(42)
MOZAMBIQUE
(28)
MADAGASCAR
(21)
1973
BOTSWANA
OUTH AFRICA
(106)
monstown (to 1957)
AFRICAN REP
1965,
1979
LAND
1968
1956
1956
1989
ROMANIA
BULGARIA
1964
1958
Bases/Military Action
U.S.S.R.
US
UK
France
USSR/US/UK/Fr
UN
Other communist countries
Borders in 1987
Major powers' summit conferences
Revolutions and civil wars
'Iron Curtain'
US blockade
USSR blockade
Declared nuclear powers by 1987
(67) [1100] x 10³
Total armed forces
Rapidly mobilised reserves
Power Blocs in 1987
Warsaw Pact 1955-1991
Other Communist States
N. Atlantic Treaty Organisation
U.S. Allies
Organisation of American States
Organisation of African Unity
Arab League
Other States

THE DISINTEGRATION OF THE SOVIET UNION

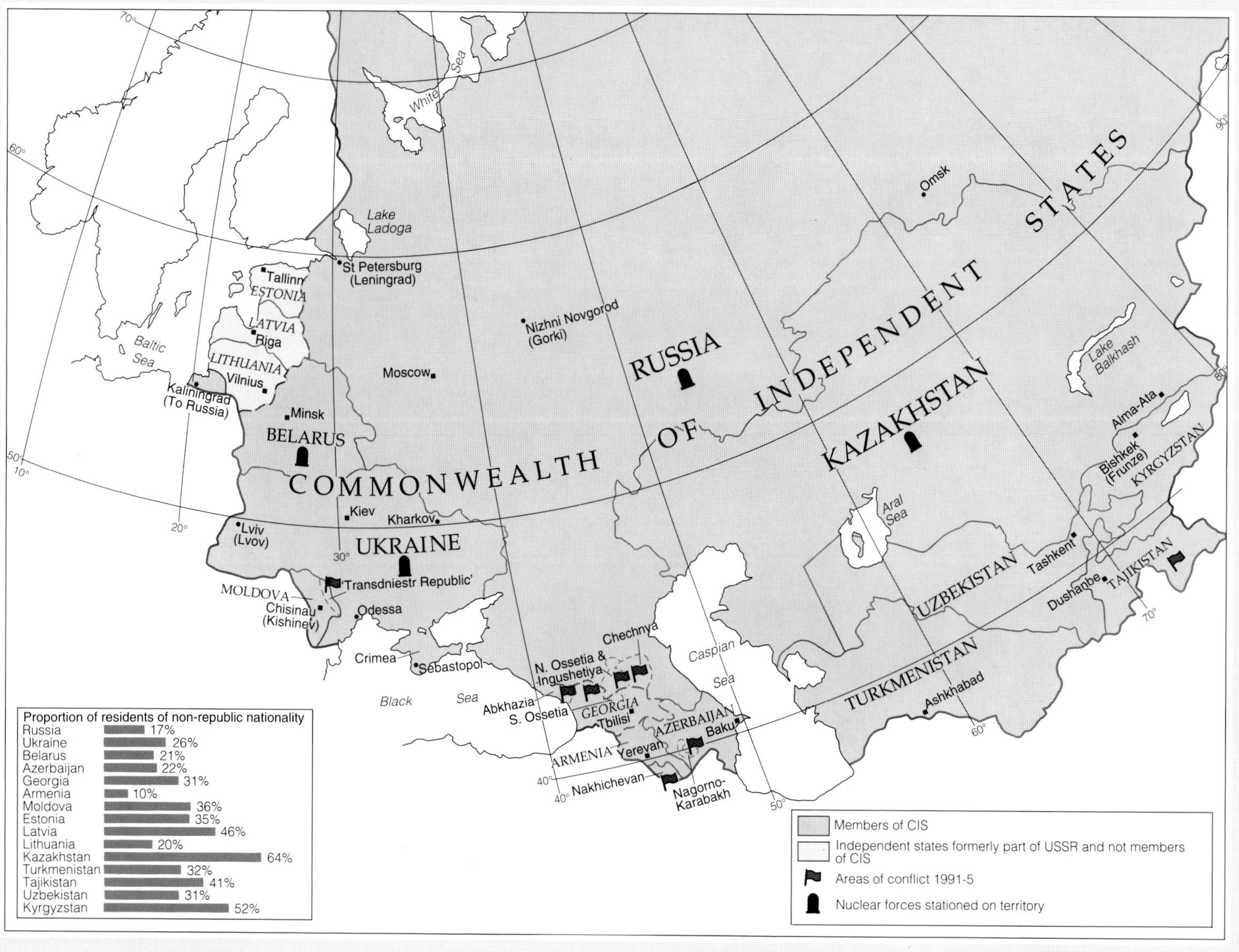

economic aid. The Marshall Plan, inaugurated by the US Secretary of State George Marshall in June 1947, provided their war-ravaged economies with assistance worth $17,000 million, stimulating their rapid recovery. Under Russian influence, however, the east European states rejected American aid. In 1949 most west European states joined the USA in the North Atlantic Treaty Organization (NATO) with the aim of 'containing' the Soviet Union. The Warsaw Pact of 1955 formalized the military alliance of the USSR with its east European satellites, whose economies were subordinated to Russian interests.

The focus of the cold war in Europe was on Berlin and the fate of Germany. In its old form the German problem was solved after the war. Over thirteen million Germans were expelled from eastern Europe (*see Map 83*), the majority moving to western Germany in the greatest European population movement of the century. Poland shifted west, being compensated for her eastern losses to the USSR by western gains at the expense of Germany (*see Map 82*). Germany, shorn of these lands and of East Prussia, was divided into four occupation zones. In 1949 the American, British, and French zones united to form the Federal Republic of Germany which was granted full independence in 1955. The communist German Democratic Republic (GDR) was established in the Russian-occupied zone. The position of West Berlin, as an enclave within East Germany, gave rise to three major international crises. In 1948-9 a western airlift defeated a Russian land blockade of West Berlin. Ten years later a Russian ultimatum (rejected by the western powers) demanded that western forces leave West Berlin. In August 1961 the East German government, alarmed at the huge exodus of its citizens to the west, erected a wall separating East from West Berlin. After severe economic tribulations in the late 1940s both German states made dramatic recoveries from the 1950s onwards to emerge among the industrial leaders of their respective blocks, the GDR being absorbed into the Soviet orbit while the Federal Republic, led by Chancellor Konrad Adenauer, pursued a pro-western course.

Although the Russo-American rivalry in East Asia never produced direct fighting between the superpowers, the cold war in this area was punctuated by a series of bitter localized wars. The Chinese civil war ended in 1949 in total victory for the communist forces headed by Mao Tse-tung (*Map 85*). The rump of the anti-communist armies withdrew to the island of Formosa (Taiwan) where they remained under American protection. In 1950 North American forces, joined by small contingents from their allies, intervened to resist the invasion of South Korea by communist North Korea, itself aided by Chinese troops. The war ground to a halt along the original partition line of the 38th parallel in 1953. The 'loss of China', as it was seen in the USA, helped to engender a profound anti-communist reaction among Americans, culminating in the hysteria of 'McCarthyism' (after the anti-communist demagogue, Senator Joseph McCarthy) in the early 1950s. However, the USA remained determined to maintain its influence in East Asia, and in 1954 formed the South-East Asia Treaty Organization (SEATO) with Britain, France, and several Asian states.

The cold war reached its climax in the late 1950s and early 1960s as both super-powers developed hydrogen bombs and inter-continental missile delivery systems. The poisoning of the atmosphere by above-ground nuclear tests, the building-up of vast arsenals of hydrogen bombs capable of destroying nearly all human beings, and the danger of nuclear 'proliferation' to smaller powers cast over the world a shadow of prospective self-immolation. For one week in late October 1962 it seemed to shudder on the brink of catastrophe as a result of a

Right: August 1961: East German troops close the Berlin border. A trench is dug straight through tram lines on the Friedrich-Ebert Straße.

Opposite page above: In December 1991 the USSR split into fifteen independent republics, of which eleven agreed to form the Commonwealth of Independent States (Georgia joined later). Ethnic conflicts, particularly in the Caucasus, threatened the stability of the new states.

Russo-American conflict over Cuba. The USSR had sought to install offensive missiles armed with nuclear warheads on Cuba, where a revolutionary movement headed by Fidel Castro had in 1959 ousted a pro-American dictatorship. The American President, John F. Kennedy, blockaded the island and demanded the removal of the missiles. The crisis ended when the Russian leader, Nikita Khrushchev, yielded to the American demands.

With the resolution of the Cuban crisis the cold war gradually eased, giving way to a period of 'détente', while new powers challenged and steadily eroded the predominance of the super-powers, heralding the end of the 'bi-polar' era.

In western Europe renewed economic strength and moves towards economic integration provided a basis for foreign policies more independent of the USA. In 1951 France, Germany, Italy and the Benelux countries formed the European Coal and Steel Community, and by the Treaty of Rome in 1957 created a European Economic Community (EEC) involving an unprecedented measure of economic integration between major sovereign states (*Map 82*). The EEC enjoyed spectacular growth in production and trade in the 1960s. Britain joined, after two unsuccessful attempts, in 1972, at the same time as Ireland and Denmark, and by 1986 Greece, Portugal and Spain, having rid themselves of dictatorships, had become members. Agreement to abolish internal tariffs by 1992 heralded a further large step towards European economic and political integration.

In the communist world too the overwhelming dominance of the super-power diminished. From 1960 onwards China engaged in a virulent ideological conflict with the USSR, whose leaders were denounced by Mao Tse-tung as 'revisionists'. Ideological warfare intensified between 1966 and 1969 during the internal upheaval in China known as the 'cultural revolution'. That the conflict was a serious threat to world peace became clear with the development of armed skirmishes along the disputed Russo-Chinese border and with the emergence of China as a nuclear power in the late 1960s.

As the Sino-Soviet conflict deepened the USSR and later China moved into a period of cautious 'détente' with the western powers. In 1963 the USA, USSR, and UK (but not France or China) signed a partial nuclear test ban treaty. The persistent irritant of the German question was eased after 1969 by the conciliatory '*Ostpolitik*' of the socialist West German Chancellor, Willy Brandt. In 1972 and 1979 the two super-powers signed agreements on the limitation of strategic weapons. From the early 1970s China too moderated her hostility to the western powers, re-opening relations with the USA and seeking closer links with western Europe. The Soviet invasion of Afghanistan in 1979 and the installation of a new 'hard-line' American administration in 1981 was reflected in a massive super-power arms race in the 1980s which threatened to upset the delicate equilibrium of the 'balance of terror' that had kept a tenuous peace for more than three decades.

The death of Stalin in 1953 had excited hopes of democratization in eastern Europe, but his successors sought to maintain a firm grip on power over other communist states. In November 1956 Russian troops crushed a brief attempt by Hungary to withdraw from the Warsaw Pact. In August 1968 the USSR again used armed strength to destroy the democratic reforms which had been introduced by the Czechoslovak communists headed by Alexander Dubcek. Nevertheless there was an easing of the atmosphere in eastern Europe as the grim Stalin years gave way to a period of relative economic prosperity. Yugoslavia maintained its independence of Moscow, and Soviet power was further challenged in the ideological domain by the increased tendency of west European communist parties (most notably the Italian) to defy directives from Moscow.

In March 1985 Mikhail Gorbachev took over as leader of a Soviet Union whose economy and political institutions betrayed signs of serious weakness. Gorbachev instituted a far-reaching programme of internal political and economic reforms, under the slogan of *perestroika* (reconstruction). He withdrew Soviet troops from Afghanistan by 1989. He opened the door to the collapse of the Soviet-imposed communist regimes in eastern Europe before the new 'springtime of the peoples' in 1989. The decisive moment came with the peaceful breach of the Berlin Wall in November 1989. This was followed in rapid succession by the collapse of communist regimes throughout eastern Europe and the reunification of Germany in October 1990.

Across most of eastern Europe democratic elections produced anti-communist governments that proceeded to dismantle the centralized command economy. Ethnic tensions, long suppressed under Communism, bubbled once again to the surface. In Czechoslovakia these were resolved peacefully but at the price of the separation of Slovakia from the Czech lands in 1993. In Yugoslavia a bitter civil war broke out in 1991, first between Serbs and Croats, then pitting both against Bosnian Muslims. The war produced tens of thousands of dead and millions of refugees.

In the Soviet Union too bureaucratic sclerosis, economic strains, and nationalistic assertiveness, particularly in the Baltic states, combined to bring about a new political order. Central power proved increasingly unable to assert control over outlying provinces. A botched coup attempt by a Communist rearguard in August 1991 heralded the imminent collapse of the system. In December Gorbachev resigned and the USSR dissolved into fifteen independent republics, ten of which joined Russia to form a loosely defined Commonwealth of Independent States (Georgia joined later). In Russia reformist elements headed by Boris Yeltsin took power and achieved unsteady progress towards market-style reforms. But severe internal conflicts continued, leading to the forcible suppression of the Russian parliament by presidential forces in October 1993, and an armed invasion of the secessionist Chechen republic in January 1995. Heightened ethnic antagonisms, growing social inequalities, spiralling inflation, a precipitous decline in production, and a startling increase in crime in the CIS states in the early 1990s darkened their prospects for peaceful transition to a dimly perceived liberal order.

Further reading: Daniel Yergin, *Shattered Peace* (Houghton Mifflin 1977; Penguin); Derek W. Urwin *Western Europe since 1945* (4th ed. Longman 1989); Geoffrey Hosking, *The First Socialist Society* (2nd ed., Harvard U.P. 1990); William Shawcross, *Alexander Dubcek* (2nd edn. Hogarth 1990; Simon & Schuster); Misha Glenny, *The Fall of Yugoslavia* (Penguin, 1992)

The emergence of the modern world 5

THE FAR EAST SINCE 1945

At the close of the Second World War China was a victorious ally of the United States, and Japan a defeated enemy.

Opposite page above: Car factory in Pusan, South Korea, 1987.

Opposite page below: Tokyo Stock Exchange, where more than one million shares – five times the volume of the New York Stock Exchange – are traded daily.

Below: Vietnamese government troops on an anti-Communist mission in August 1962.

But within four years China had fallen to a Communist revolution (*Map 85*) and Japan had become essential to America's anti-Communist strategy. Japan's former colony, Korea, had been divided into American and Soviet zones, while Formosa and Okinawa became bases for United States forces.

Initially America's occupation of Japan sought to weaken and pacify a potential enemy. However, her desire for trade and fear of Communism soon produced policies to stimulate Japan's economic recovery. In contrast, the founding of the People's Republic of China in October 1949 created a government which criticized American 'imperialism', occupied Tibet, and looked to the Soviet Union for political and military support. In June 1950 pro-Soviet North Korean forces invaded the pro-American South, and United States and Chinese forces soon intervened. Tension between Washington and Peking was heightened and their embittered relations further increased Japan's military importance. America encouraged the beginnings of Japanese re-armament and in September 1951 forty-eight non-Communist powers signed a peace treaty with Japan. In April 1952 Japan's political independence was formally restored.

Japan's economic recovery continued throughout the 1950s and by 1956 her standard of living surpassed that of the pre-war years. Some Japanese resented their country's dependence on the United States and others feared that their country might be drawn into a war between the super-powers, but government and industry believed that only the United States could provide the markets and protection necessary for continued prosperity.

For China problems of reconstruction, modernization and agricultural improvement were

85 The retreat of imperialism in Asia
The Japanese victories of the Second World War destroyed the prestige of the European powers in Asia and opened the way to rapid decolonization in the post-war years, but continuing Great-Power intervention prolonged the bitter struggles between the successor states and exacerbated political and social instability, most tragically in South-East Asia.

Further reading: Jonathan D. Spence, *The Search for Modern China* (Norton 1990; Century Hutchinson); John Gittings, *China Changes Face: the Road from Revolution, 1949-1989* (Oxford U.P. 1990); Anthony Short, *The Origins of the Vietnam War* (Longman 1989); Roger Buckley, *Japan Today* (Cambridge U. P. 1990); R. Drifte, *Japan's Foreign Policy* (Routledge/RIIA 1989).

immense but the Communist government secured a greater degree of order and unity than had existed for more than a century. The Soviet Union assisted the new regime in many industrial and agricultural projects, but by 1960 China's more revolutionary ideology and her militant foreign policy led to worsening relations with the Soviet Union.

In China domestic policies often underwent drastic changes of style and direction as leaders sought to combine economic progress with revolutionary enthusiasm. These dramatic fluctuations reached their peak in the 'Cultural Revolution', which began in 1966. This nationwide movement combined social turmoil and revolutionary ardour. In these same years America's involvement in the Vietnam War stimulated Russian and Chinese help for Hanoi and temporarily concealed the depth of hostility between Moscow and Peking.

By 1972 the Cultural Revolution and the Vietnam War had diminished in intensity, while China's fear of Moscow led to policies based on anti-Soviet strategy rather than Communist ideology. China now formally forgave Japan for her aggression in the 1930s (*Map 79*), and mutual trade increased rapidly. This improvement in Sino-Japanese relations soon received further stimulus from decisions in America and the Middle East. America's failure in Vietnam led her to reduce her military presence in East Asia, and in 1971 the success of Japanese goods in the American market led to President Nixon's measures to restrict the entry of Japanese products. The return of Okinawa to Japanese administration in 1972 was less important than Japan's doubts regarding the future openness of the American market and the dependability of American military protection. In 1973 the high price and restricted supply of oil which followed the Arab-Israeli war further threatened Japan's economy, and led her to seek alternative oil supplies and markets in China and South-East Asia.

In these years China felt increasingly insecure in her relations with the Soviet Union, while the death of Mao Tse-tung, in 1976, and the removal of the radical 'gang of four', in 1977, made it easier for China's leaders to replace policies based upon ideology by the 'Four Modernizations'. These new policies aimed to increase China's economic well-being and her ability to defend herself against the Soviet Union. By 1978 Japan's need for markets and China's need for modern technology had produced a mutual agreement which provided for large increases in trade and Japanese help in the development of China's industry and natural resources. Perhaps surprisingly, Soviet policy in East Asia showed little sign of major changes. The USSR, like China, attempted to secure Japanese help in the exploitation of her underdeveloped territories (*see Map 71*), but Japanese officials and businessmen doubted the reliability of Soviet undertakings and feared that Moscow might draw them into its dispute with Peking. Indeed, while Japan's relations with China underwent rapid improvement, those with the Soviet Union appeared frozen in the patterns of the cold war. Not only did the Soviet Union take a particularly severe attitude in fishery negotiations, but she still refused to return four small islands – Habomai, Shikotan, Kunashiri and Etorufu – which Japan claimed were part of her national territory.

During the 1980s the shared interests of China and Japan produced a cordiality in their relations that was almost without precedent in the twentieth century. Japan feared the growing power of the Soviet navy and China resented the growth of Russian influence in Vietnam; as a result, both criticized Russia's intervention in Afghanistan and her support for Hanoi's occupation of Kampuchea. In 1989 Sino-Japanese relations deteriorated somewhat temporarily following the massacre of students in Tienanmen Square but economic imperatives soon dictated the restoration of good relations between Peking and Tokyo.

By 1990 the effective ending of the cold war between the United States and the USSR finally removed the perceived Soviet threat to northern Japan, although Gorbachev's visit to Tokyo in 1991 failed to resolve the long-standing territorial dispute which continued to plague Soviet-Japanese relations. In the Korean peninsula friction between North and South continued, but South Korea's prestige rose rapidly. Seoul's remarkable economic growth led Moscow to seek closer ties with the South, leaving North Korea increasingly isolated from her previous ally and patron.

U.S.S.R.
Caspian Sea
Aral Sea
Tashkent
Ulan Bator
MONGOLIA
1949
IRAN
AFGHANISTAN
Herat
Hindu Kush
Kabul
Kandahar
Quetta
Peshawar
Islamabad
KASHMIR
Lahore
Amritsar
PAKISTAN
1947
Indus
TIBET
1951
Himalaya
NEPAL
Kathmandu
Lhasa
Thimbu
BHUTAN
Delhi
Lucknow
Ganges
Brahmaputra
Karachi
Rann of Kutch
Allahabad
Patna
Dacca
INDIA
1947
Chandernagore
(1950)
Calcutta
BANGLADESH
(E. PAKISTAN
until 1971)
BURMA
Mandalay
Irrawaddy
1948
Salween
Dien Bi
1954
LAOS
Vientiane
Diu
(1961)
Daman
(1961)
Nagpur
Bombay
Arabian Sea
Hyderabad
Bay of Bengal
Yanam
(1954)
Rangoon
THAILAND
Goa
(1961)
Bangkok
Laccadive Is.
(India)
Madras
Andaman Is.
(India)
Pondicherry
(1954)
Mahé
(1954)
Karikal
(1954)
SRI LANKA
(Ceylon)
Colombo
1948
Nicobar Is.
(India)
Maldive Is.
Malé
1965
MALAYA
Kuala Lumpur
1957
Singapore
1963
Sumatra
Indian Ocean

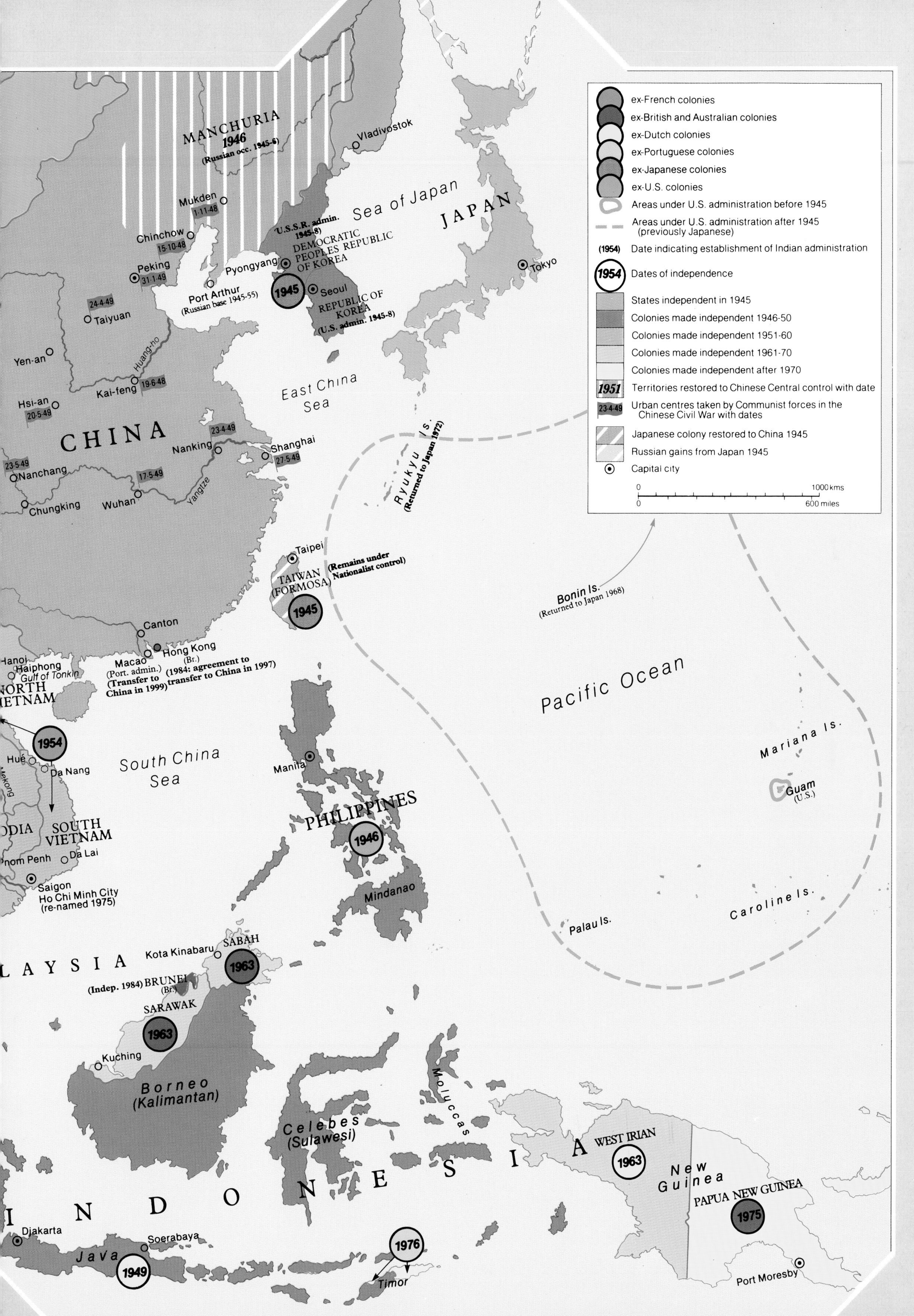

ex-French colonies
ex-British and Australian colonies
ex-Dutch colonies
ex-Portuguese colonies
ex-Japanese colonies
ex-U.S. colonies
Areas under U.S. administration before 1945
Areas under U.S. administration after 1945 (previously Japanese)
(1954) Date indicating establishment of Indian administration
1954 Dates of independence
States independent in 1945
Colonies made independent 1946-50
Colonies made independent 1951-60
Colonies made independent 1961-70
Colonies made independent after 1970
1951 Territories restored to Chinese Central control with date
23-4-49 Urban centres taken by Communist forces in the Chinese Civil War with dates
Japanese colony restored to China 1945
Russian gains from Japan 1945
Capital city
0 1000 kms
0 600 miles
MANCHURIA
1946
(Russian occ. 1945-6)
Vladivostok
Mukden
1-11-48
Chinchow
15-10-48
Sea of Japan
JAPAN
U.S.S.R. admin. 1945-8)
DEMOCRATIC PEOPLES REPUBLIC OF KOREA
Pyongyang
Peking
31-1-49
Port Arthur
(Russian base 1945-55)
1945
Seoul
REPUBLIC OF KOREA
(U.S. admin. 1945-8)
Tokyo
24-4-49
Taiyuan
Yen-an
Huang-ho
Kai-feng
19-6-48
Hsi-an
20-5-49
East China Sea
CHINA
23-4-49
Nanking
Shanghai
27-5-49
23-5-49
Nanchang
17-5-49
Chungking
Wuhan
Yangtze
Ryukyu Is.
(Returned to Japan 1972)
Taipei
TAIWAN (FORMOSA)
(Remains under Nationalist control)
1945
Bonin Is.
(Returned to Japan 1968)
Canton
Hong Kong
(Br.)
Macao
(Port. admin.)
(Transfer to China in 1999)
(1984: agreement to transfer to China in 1997)
Hanoi
Haiphong
Gulf of Tonkin
NORTH
ETNAM
1954
Pacific Ocean
Hue
Da Nang
South China Sea
Manila
Mariana Is.
Guam
(U.S.)
DIA
SOUTH VIETNAM
PHILIPPINES
1946
nom Penh
Da Lai
Saigon
Ho Chi Minh City
(re-named 1975)
Mindanao
Caroline Is.
Palau Is.
Kota Kinabaru
SABAH
LAYSIA
1963
(Indep. 1984) BRUNEI
(Br.)
SARAWAK
1963
Kuching
Borneo
(Kalimantan)
Moluccas
Celebes
(Sulawesi)
WEST IRIAN
INDONESIA
1963
New Guinea
PAPUA NEW GUINEA
1975
Djakarta
Soerabaya
Java
1949
1976
Timor
Port Moresby

The emergence of the modern world 6

CONTEMPORARY SOCIETY

Contemporary history is dominated by the heightened competition of a rapidly growing population for control of the Earth's territory and resources.

A series of local and regional power struggles erupted in the aftermath of the collapse of European imperialism. The inability of many post-colonial societies to conquer endemic poverty, famine and over-population exacerbated ethnic, religious and economic divisions within and between new states. In decolonized Asia and Africa (as in interwar Europe) independence seemed to increase rather than diminish human aggression, giving rise to vast refugee movements (*see Map 83*), mass murder of civilians, and relapse to authoritarian forms of government. The obstinately persistent gap between wealthy societies (mainly in the northern hemisphere) and the 'Third World' was visible not only in figures for per capita national income but also by such measures as life expectancy at birth (*see Map 87*).

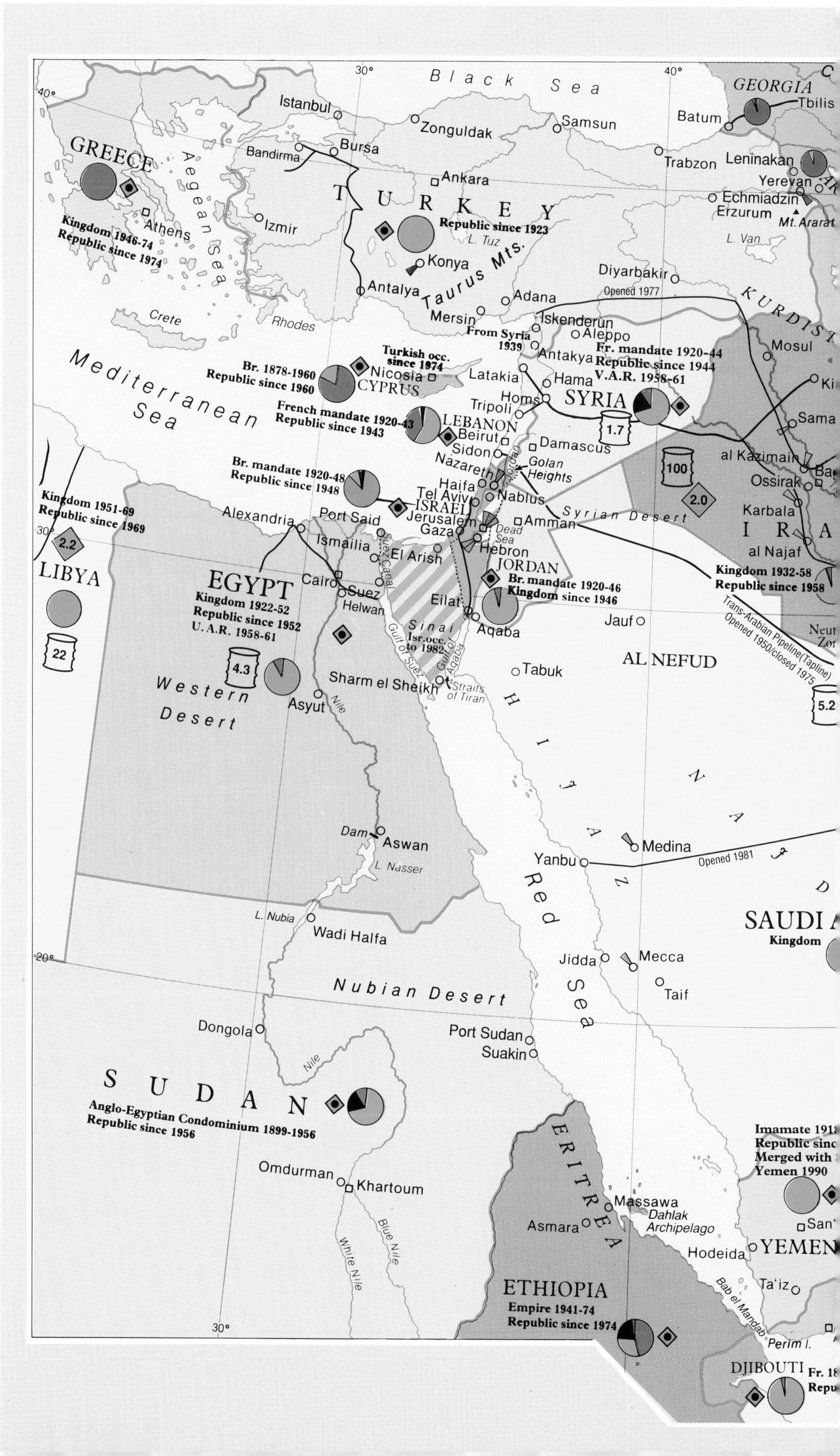

The Second World War shattered the prestige of many of the imperial powers, helping to stimulate anti-colonial nationalisms and force the pace of European withdrawal from Asia and Africa. In 1947 Britain accorded independence to India. The sub-continent split into two sovereign states. The smaller, Muslim state of Pakistan was formed out of north-western India and east Bengal, the two portions of the new country being separated by a thousand miles of territory belonging to the larger, secular state of India (*Map 85*). Partition was accompanied by massive bloodshed and huge movements in population. Pakistan initially pursued a pro-American foreign policy, while India, under the leadership of Gandhi's disciple, Jawaharlal Nehru, followed a 'neutralist' course. A military government took power in Pakistan by 1958, whereas India was one of the few post-colonial states to preserve parliamentary democracy. Relations between India and Pakistan remained sour, embittered in particular by a dispute over Kashmir. In 1965 they fought an inconclusive war. A fierce civil war in Pakistan in 1971 broadened into another Indo-Pakistani conflict in which India won a decisive victory. East Pakistan, under Indian protection, became the new, independent state of Bangladesh.

The British withdrawal from India marked the start of a general European evacuation of South Asia (*see Map 83*). The most humiliating colonial ejection from the region was that of France from Indo-China after defeat at Dien Bien Phu in 1954. Independent states were formed in Laos, Cambodia, and Vietnam, which was partitioned at the 17th Parallel between a communist north and a non-communist south. American efforts in the 1960s to shore up the South Vietnamese regime against communist revolution aided by attack from the north gave rise to a murderous war involving, at its peak in 1968, more than half a million American troops. Strong opposition to the war in the USA helped bring about a gradual American military withdrawal, completed by 1973. By 1975 communist forces had ousted the South Vietnamese regime and had taken power in Laos and Cambodia as well. In Cambodia the victorious revolutionaries perpetrated a ruthless 'pastoralization' of the cities, resulting in millions of deaths and the destruction of the country's economy and social organization. In 1977 Vietnam invaded Cambodia, eventually occupying most of the country and installing a government of its own choosing. But guerrilla warfare between rival factions, often backed by outside powers, continued in the 1980s.

During the decade after 1957 most of the British and French colonies in Africa achieved independence. France had already recognized the independence of Morocco and Tunisia in 1956, but she clung doggedly to Algeria in the face of an increasingly bloody nationalist revolution there. The Algerian war culminated in 1958 in the collapse of the Fourth French Republic and the return to power of General De Gaulle as President. He consolidated the institutions of the Fifth Republic in a presidential regime, and in 1962 granted independence to Algeria. In west and east Africa colonial rule was shaken off with little or no bloodshed (*Map 74*). In the Belgian Congo, however, chaos followed the sudden Belgian withdrawal in 1960. Powerful western economic interests sponsored the formation of an independent state in the mineral-rich southern province of Katanga. Order was eventually restored by an international force dispatched by the United Nations. A civil war broke out also in Nigeria in 1966, ending in 1970 with victory for the central government over the army of the secessionist eastern region, 'Biafra'.

White rule in southern Africa held out a little longer. Portugal, which had held coastal areas of Angola and Mozambique for more than three centuries (compare Map 36), engaged in an increasingly costly struggle during the 1960s and early 1970s to repress nationalist guerrillas. As in France in 1958, colonial warfare led to political upheaval at home: in 1974 a military junta carried out a peaceful 'revolution of flowers'. The new democratic government speedily conceded independence to nearly all Portugal's colonies. But the anti-colonial struggle in Angola was transformed into a fierce civil war between rival factions, drawing the intervention on opposing sides of Cuban and South African forces. Meanwhile Rhodesia (formerly Southern Rhodesia), ruled by a small white minority, had issued a 'unilateral declaration of independence' in November 1965. With South African support the Rhodesian whites succeeded for a time in defying United Nations economic sanctions and maintained their oligarchic society intact. But by 1980 they too were compelled to accept black majority rule.

MAP 86 THE MIDDLE EAST, 1945-1994

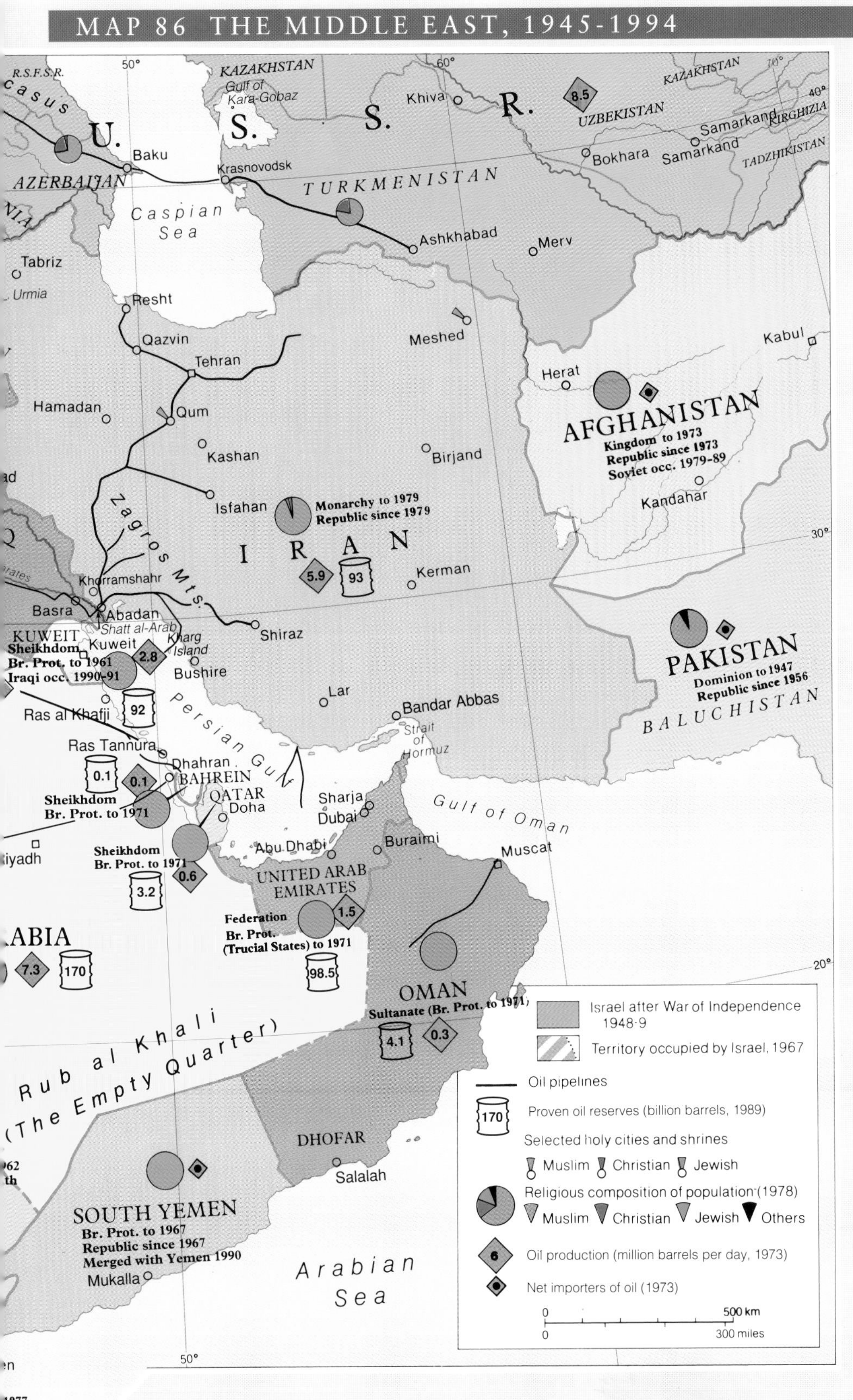

Opposite page: Celebrating independence, Algiers July 6 1962.

86 The Middle East, 1945-1994
With the decline of British power, especially after the abortive Anglo-French invasion of Egypt in 1956 and the growing dependence of the developed world on imported oil, the USA and USSR became the main external forces in the Middle East, where the creation of Israel in 1948 had led to four Arab-Israeli wars by 1973.

87 Foundations of a post-imperial world
By the later twentieth century the growth of population, especially in the poorest regions, presented the world with acute difficulties. They were heightened by the decline of the traditional industrial powers and the high political and economic costs of energy, control of which seemed certain to be a decisive factor in any new international order.

GREENLAND
ICELAND
5
CANADA
438
UNITED STATES
4,864
MEXICO
152
BERMUDA
1.4
CUBA
27
0.3
BELIZE
HONDURAS
4.1
JAMAICA
2.6
HAITI
2.2
DOMINICAN REP.
4.7
PUERTO RICO
GUATAMALA
7.6
EL SALVADOR
4.8
NICARAGUA
2.9
COSTA RICA
4.7
PANAMA
5.1
TRINIDAD
4.2
VENEZUELA
59
GUYANA
0.3
SURINAM
1.1
FR. GUIANA
COLOMBIA
37
ECUADOR
11
BRAZIL
329
PERU
29
BOLIVIA
3.9
PARAGUAY
4.8
CHILE
19
ARGENTINA
83
URUGUAY
7.4
NORWAY
84
SWEDEN
DENMARK
95
U.K.
730
EIRE
27
NETH
215
BELG
144
GERMANY
1,290
LUX
FRANCE
899
SWIT
178
AUST
765
117
ITALY
PORTUGAL
37
SPAIN
302
MOROCCO
18
TUNISIA
69
ALGERIA
58
WESTERN SAHARA
MAURITANIA
MALI
1.8
NIGER
2.2
SENEGAL
4.5
GAMBIA
0.2
GUINEA-BISSAU
BURKINA FASO
2
GUINEA
2.3
SIERRA LEONE
8.6
5.6
1.5
NIGERIA
32
LIBERIA
IVORY COAST
GHANA
TOGO
BENIN
CAMEROON
11
EQUATORIAL GUINEA
0.1
GABON
3.2
CONGO
ANGOLA
6.9
NAMIBIA
1.5
Life expectancy at birth, c.1983
(by country)
45 years or less
46-64 years
65 years or more
Not available
Gross National Product per capita, c.1984
(dollars)
Less than 400
401 - 1000
1001 - 5000
Over 5000
Gross National Product c.1988
(billions of dollars)
328
BRAZIL

U.S.S.R.
2,500
FINLAND
92
HUNGARY
65
ROMANIA
79
BULGARIA
51
TURKEY
52
GREECE
48
CYPRUS
38
LEB.
SYRIA
20
ISRAEL
4.4
JORDAN
IRAQ
41
IRAN
94
KUWEIT
26
UN. ARAB EMIRATES
24
EGYPT
33
SAUDI ARABIA
87
OMAN
7.1
YEMEN
5.7
SOUTH YEMEN
1
SUDAN
8.1
ETHIOPIA
5.8
SOMALIA
1
KENYA
8.3
UGANDA
4.5
RWANDA
BURUNDI
ZAIRE
5.7
TANZANIA
3.8
ZAMBIA
2.2
MALAWI
ZIMBABWE
6.1
MOZAMBIQUE
1.6
BOTSWANA
1.2
SWAZILAND
SOUTH AFRICA
78
LESOTHO
MADAGASCAR
2.1
MONGOLIA
3.6
AFGHANISTAN
3.1
PAKISTAN
37
NEPAL
BHUTAN
CHINA
357
INDIA
271
BANGLADESH
18
SRI LANKA
7
BURMA (MYANMAR)
7.4
LAOS
THAILAND
55
VIETNAM
13
CAMBODIA
0.6
MALAYSIA
32
SINGAPORE
24
BRUNEI
3.1
NORTH KOREA
20
SOUTH KOREA
150
JAPAN
2,757
TAIWAN
125
HONG KONG
55
PHILIPPINES
38
INDONESIA
76
PAPUA NEW GUINEA
2.9
AUSTRALIA
204
NEW ZEALAND
32

After 1980 only South Africa (and its appendage of South-West Africa or Namibia) remained under white domination. By far the richest country on the continent, South Africa was ruled after 1948 by the Nationalist Party which pursued the policy of *apartheid* or 'separate development'. This sought to maintain white supremacy by the enforcement of discriminatory laws directed against the black majority and by racial segregation. Scattered undeveloped tracts of land were set aside as 'Bantustans' and granted nominal independence. Bloodshed in 1960 and again in 1976 heightened international criticism. From 1984 onwards severe internal violence convulsed the country and evoked fierce government counter-measures. The white minority regime, bolstered by powerful armed forces and by the country's rich mineral resources and highly developed economy, remained entrenched in power. International isolation and domestic unrest finally drove the regime, under President F. W. de Klerk, to seek an accommodation with the African National Congress whose leader, Nelson Mandela, was released from prison in February 1990 and, after the first free all-race elections in 1994, assumed office as the country's first black President.

Latin America in the post-war period remained closely tied, politically and economically, to the United States. In this region in particular, the refusal of the Roman Catholic church to sanction artificial methods of birth control contributed to the rapid population growth rate which overwhelmed the social and economic resources of many countries. Nearly all countries on the South American mainland succumbed to military rule at some stage in the post-war period. In 1973 the left-wing government of Salvador Allende in Chile was deposed by an American-inspired coup and replaced by a brutal military dictatorship. Argentina returned to democratic rule when a similar regime collapsed after its attempt to buttress its position by occupying the Falkland Islands (Malvinas) in 1982 ended in defeat by British expeditionary forces. By the mid-1980s military regimes in Latin America and the Caribbean had, with few exceptions, given way to elected civilian governments. But these confronted almost insuperable problems of massive inflation, towering foreign debt, and deep cleavages between wealthy elites and poverty-stricken masses. The exploitation of natural resources such as oil brought a modicum of prosperity to some countries like Venezuela, but even oil failed to lift Mexico (or little Trinidad) out of the mire of economic backwardness and social misery. American interventions in Guatemala in 1954, the Dominican Republic in 1965, Grenada in 1983 and Panama in 1989 ensured that those countries remained in the pro-American camp. For long Cuba was the only state in the region openly to defy the United States. But in 1979 the pro-American Somoza dictatorship in Nicaragua was overthrown by leftist revolutionaries who succeeded in maintaining power in spite of raids by American surrogates operating from Honduras, until they surrendered it voluntarily, following electoral defeat, in February 1990.

In the Middle East, as elsewhere after the Second World War, British and French imperialism collapsed, although not without severe withdrawal pains. France withdrew from Syria and Lebanon at the end of the war. Upon Britain's withdrawal from Palestine in 1948 a bitter Arab-Jewish war resulted in the establishment of the State of Israel. In 1956 Israel joined Britain and France in invading Egypt. Israel scored a swift victory, but Britain and France suffered a humiliating political defeat. The Suez affair was held to be definite proof that the age of European imperialism was past. Further Arab-Israeli wars in 1967 and 1973 led to renewed Israeli victories. For three decades the Arab states refused to accept the existence of Israel, but in 1977, in a startling *volte-face*, President Sadat of Egypt visited Israel and started a process which led to the signature of an Egyptian-Israeli peace treaty in 1979. Other Arab states, however, denounced the treaty as a betrayal. In 1982 Israel intervened in Lebanon, where a bloody civil war had raged since 1975. Israel withdrew most of her forces by 1985, but the Lebanese civil war continued until 1991, horrifying the world with the spectacle of a society in a Hobbesian state of disintegration. From 1987 onwards serious civil unrest, known as the *intifada*, disrupted the Israeli-occupied territories on the West Bank of the Jordan and the Gaza strip. Secret talks in Oslo between Israel and the Palestine Liberation Organization led to an agreement, signed in Washington in September 1993. Although progress towards implementation proved disappointingly slow, an end to the long Arab-Israeli conflict at last seemed in sight.

International attention was focused on the Middle East in the 1970s and 1980s above all because of the heightened importance of the region's oil reserves, by far the largest in the world. In 1960 the major oil-producing states had formed a cartel known as the Organization of Petroleum Exporting Countries (OPEC). The economic boom of the late 1960s and early 1970s, and the loss of self-sufficiency in oil by the world's largest consumer, the USA, created a great increase in demand which enabled OPEC to demand vast price increases, particularly after 1973. Another steep increase took place in 1979 following the revolution in Iran, in which the pro-American Shah was ousted by Islamic nationalists.

Greed for the oilfields at the head of the Persian Gulf twice tempted the Iraqi dictator Saddam Hussein, to invade his neighbours. In 1980 he precipitated eight years of desperately bloody but ultimately profitless war with Iran. Six weeks were sufficient for a United Nations force under American leadership to dislodge him from Kuwait, which he had occupied in August 1990. Iraq suffered total and devastating military defeat, but Saddam survived to wreak savage vengeance against his Kurdish and Shi'ite subjects.

The dramatic oil price rises of the 1970s were one of the major causes of the world-wide recession after 1974. This, the worst 'slump' since the 1930s, produced widespread unemployment, high levels of inflation, rocketing interest rates, wildly fluctuating currency values, and a halt to the rapid economic growth of the post-war period. The poorest countries were often the hardest hit. Although some economies (notably the United States) had recovered by the mid-1980s, and in spite of the dramatic collapse of the oil cartel after 1985, there was no return to the more settled economic conditions of the pre-1973 era. The recession of the early 1990s even affected the hitherto impregnable German and Japanese economies. Among the ex-Communist states only Poland, Hungary and the Czech Republic showed signs of making an effective transition to a market economy. In much of Africa millions hovered on the verge of starvation. Pressures everywhere towards economic nationalism represented perhaps the gravest threat to international order. In what was now a global market, if not yet in any real sense an international community, man faced anew, though with no great certainty of solution, the fundamental questions of survival and social organization with which he had grappled since the dawn of civilized life on earth.

Above: Burning oil wells in Kuwait two months after the end of the Gulf War, as trouble continued.

Further reading: Geoffrey Barraclough, *An Introduction to Contemporary History* (second edn. Viking Penguin 1968); M.E. Yapp, *The Near East since the First World War* (Longman 1990); Judith M. Brown, *Modern India: Origins of an Asian Democracy* (Oxford U. P. 1985); Alistair Horne, *A Savage War of Peace: Algeria, 1954-62* (Macmillan 1977; Viking Penguin); R.B. Smith, *An International History of the Vietnam War: 1, Revolution versus Containment, 1955-61; 2, The Struggle for Southeast Asia, 1961-65* (Macmillan, 1983, 1985; St Martin's Press); Shaul Bakhash, *The Reign of the Ayatollahs* (second edn. Basic Books 1986; Unwin).

United States historical maps

INTRODUCTION

The search for adventure, wealth, and freedom has inspired those coming to America since the discovery of the New World.

The Spaniard Cortez, confessing to a "sickness of the soul only gold could cure," exemplified the early explorer who set out to claim land and gold for his king and riches for himself. But Great Britain soon discovered that true wealth lay in the land itself, and in North America chose colonization as the road to political and economic power. The maps that follow chronicle the remarkable development of Britain's one-time colony – the United States. Covering eight historical periods, the maps illustrate the country's foundation and expansion westward, its richly varied population, and three major conflicts – the Revolutionary and Civil wars and World War II. The maps portray these developments in a vivid, colorful style, depicting often overlapping events, such as the construction of transcontinental railways and the rise and fall of the great cattle empires. Short summaries accompanying each map provide more detailed information of each historical period. A series of tables at the end of this section list the entry of the states into the union, the flow of immigrants by nationality, and recent shifts in regional population.

From the beginning, the vastness of the continent challenged the imaginations of early settlers. The new land offered not only abundant natural resources but the opportunity to experiment with various social, religious, and political ideals. Freed from traditional European constraints, Americans rapidly created an economy and industry that outstripped the combined production of Europe. These successes built into the national character expectations for a continually rising standard of living and unlimited opportunity.

But the nation's growth was not always a steady progress forward. Native Americans and other racial minorities have long struggled for an equal place in American society. And as far back as the early 1800s, some people felt the nation's emphasis on commercial development meant neglecting the long-term consequences of uncontrolled growth. Finally, the legacy of World War II – that America would enjoy continued political and economic expansion – left the country somewhat unprepared for the problems that emerged only decades later. Conflicts abroad, increasing international economic competition, as well as domestic concerns affecting the well-being of all its citizens are major issues that challenge the United States.

Yet the maps show the development of a confident and energetic people. Perhaps the national experience of taming a continent, creating a vast industry, and absorbing millions of newcomers into the culture may prove to be adequate preparation for meeting the problems of today. It has seemed, in the past, that the nation is never more resourceful than when facing a difficult challenge.

THE AMERICAN COLONIES, 1700

The fabulous wealth discovered by Spain in Central and South America touched off a race among other nations – chiefly France and England – to share in the riches of the New World.

By the early 1600s, French holdings in North America reached from the Appalachian Mountains to the western plains and north beyond the Great Lakes; while Spain claimed the south and southwest regions. As the map on the following page shows, Great Britain possessed only a narrow strip along the Atlantic seaboard and a small area in the northwest.

Dreams of finding easy treasure faded; England and France began to realize the commercial and military value of colonizing these lands. Except for the settlements at Québec, Trois-Rivières, and Montréal, however, few people immigrated to the French regions. In contrast, America fired the imaginations of the English people. Even so, the early settlers of Jamestown and similar camps barely survived the "starving times," when disease and lack of food decimated the small population. The settlements slowly began to prosper as more immigrants arrived, bringing with them a complex array of religious, social, and political beliefs.

Most of the settlements were clustered near waterways and along the sea coast, leaving large inland areas virtually uninhabited. Provincetown, Plymouth, Philadelphia, and the Chesapeake settlements – founded as religious communities – became thriving commercial centers by the late 1600s. Boston and New York prospered as port cities, and towns scattered along the coast benefited from a growing fishing industry. The rich farmlands of Maryland, Virginia, and the Carolinas proved ideal for valuable cash crops such as cotton and tobacco. As the transplanted European population grew, native Indian tribes were forced out of coastal areas and pushed further west. By 1700, the colonies were loosely organized into eleven provinces. The population, with its unusual social, political, and religious makeup, was already markedly different from any society in Europe.

England was clearly winning the race to settle and develop its colonies. With the eventual defeat of France in the French and Indian War (1754-63), Great Britain became the dominant power in North America.

INDEPENDENCE, 1775-1783

To many historians, the Revolutionary War remains the single most important event in American history, instilling in the people a sense of their nation's special destiny. The war arose from conflicts between a diverse, fiercely independent colonial population and a British government determined to tighten its control over King George's colonies. Americans viewed the revenue acts passed to subsidize Britain's colonial army as a threat to their political and economic freedoms. Mounting hostility finally erupted in the Boston Massacre of 1770. By 1775, colonial resistance had become armed rebellion. The map on page 169 depicts the major battles and strategies of the war.

Expecting easy victories at Lexington, Concord and Bunker Hill, the British, instead, suffered heavy losses defeating the Yankee militia. Action in the western regions remained indecisive for both sides. By July, 1776, Britain was mounting a full-scale military effort to end the rebellion. Though well equipped and trained, the British army often had to deal with a largely hostile population and fight in wilderness terrain. In contrast, the Americans, outnumbered and poorly equipped, were fighting for their own land.The British sought to divide the colonies by isolating New England. They defeated George Washington's Continental Army at Long Island and New York; but at the end of 1776, Continental troops had captured Princeton and Trenton. The American victory at Saratoga in October, 1777, dealt a final blow to Britain's northern strategy. And by the following year, France had allied itself with the American cause.

From 1778 onward, Britain concentrated on the South and the sea coast. British Commander Cornwallis captured Savannah, Charleston, and Camden, but could not secure the countryside. American irregular forces continually harassed the British army until it withdrew to the coast. Finally, in October, 1781, Cornwallis surrendered his entire command to Washington and Rochambeau, Commander of the French forces dispatched to aid Americans, at Yorktown.

The peace treaty of 1783 recognized American independence and more than doubled the size of the former territory. The victorious Americans believed that their emerging nation was destined to lead the world toward liberty.

MAP LEGEND

- Settled area: each dot represents 500 rural population.
- ● More than 5,000 people
- ○ Less than 5,000 people
- *Huron* Indian Tribe
- (1634) Founding Date

SCALE

miles 0 50 100 150

kilometers 0 50 100 150 200

Québec
Dec. 1775
Montgomery Aug.-Dec. 1775
Montréal
Nov. 1775
Arnold Sept.-Dec. 1775
MASS.
(District of Maine)
St. Leger July 1777
Lake Champlain
Fort Ticonderoga
May 1775
Burgoyne June 1777
Falmouth
NEW HAMPSHIRE
Fort Stanwix
Aug. 1777
Fort Oswego
July 1777
Fort Niagara
Saratoga
Oct. 1777
Manchester
Stark
Bennington
Aug. 1777
Oriskany
Aug. 1777
Fort Herkimer
Loyalists & Brant
Herkimer & Arnold
Gates
Albany
Howe to Halifax Mar. 1776
Fort Pontchartrain
Geneseo
Cherry Valley
Nov. 1778
Loyalists & Brant
Lexington & Concord
April 1775
Bunker Hill
June 1775
Johnson & Indians
Newtown
Aug. 1779
NEW YORK
MASS.
Boston
Mar. 1776
Providence
CONN.
R.I.
Loyalist & Indian raid
Fort Sandusky
Wyoming Valley
July 1778
Sullivan
New Haven
Washington
White Plains
Oct. 1776
Fort Lee
Nov. 1776
Easton
New York
Sept. 1776
PENNSYLVANIA
Fort Pitt
Princeton
Jan. 1777
Long Island Aug. 1776
Cornwallis
Howe from Halifax July 1776
Germantown
Oct. 1777
Monmouth June 1778
Trenton Dec. 1776
Clark to Fort Vincennes Feb. 1778
Valley Forge
Brandywine
Sept. 1777
Washington
Philadelphia Nov. 1777
Wilmington
Forts Mercer & Mifflin
Nov. 1777
MD.
Baltimore
NEW JERSEY
Proclamation Line 1763
VIRGINIA
DEL.
Washington & Rochambeau (Fr.) Aug.-Sept. 1781
APPALACHIAN MOUNTAINS
Boonesborough
Howe from New York July-Aug. 1777
Graves from New York
Charlottesville
Tarleton June 1781
Lafayette June-Sept. 1781
Richmond
Petersburg
Cornwallis May 1781
Yorktown
Aug.-Oct. 1781
Norfolk
Off the Chesapeake Capes
Sept. 1781
De Grasse (Fr.) from West Indies Sept. 1779
Guilford Courthouse
Mar. 1781
Salem
Cornwallis April 1781
N.C.
Frontier Settlers
Cornwallis Jan. 1781
Ferguson
King's Mountain
Oct. 1780
Charlotte
Cowpens
Jan. 1781
Morgan Dec. 1780
S.C.
Cornwallis Aug. 1780
Moore's Creek Bridge
Feb. 1776
Tarleton Jan. 1781
Winnsboro
Gates
Fort Ninety Six
June 1781
Greene Mar. 1781
Camden
Aug. 1780
Wilmington
Ft. Augusta
Feb. 1779
Rawdon
Eutaw Springs
Sept. 1781
Georgetown
Asche Feb. 1779
Briar Creek
Feb. 1779
Campbell Feb. 1779
Charles Town
May 1780
Clinton & Cornwallis from New York Jan. 1780
Campbell from New York Dec. 1778
GEORGIA
Prevost May 1779
Lincoln Oct. 1779
Savannah
Dec. 1778
Oct. 1779
D'Estaing (Fr.) from West Indies Sept. 1779
Prevost Jan. 1779
42°
40°
38°
36°
34°
32°
70°
80°
78°
76°
74°
72°
Copyright © by Rand McNally & Co.
Made in U.S.A. All rights reserved.
MAP LEGEND
American Colonies
Indian Reserve
British Occupied City
American Occupied City
British Held Fort
American Held Fort
British Victory
American Victory
British Forces
American Forces
SCALE
miles 0 50 100 150
kilometers 0 50 100 150 200

The rallying cry of "Manifest destiny!" reflected the American belief that providence itself had granted the United States exclusive right to settle North America.

The country's rapidly expanding population and commercial development, the flood of European immigrants, and a growing transportation system all played a part in the first great western migration.

In 1803, Thomas Jefferson, deeply concerned about European influence on the continent, made the bold step of purchasing the Louisiana Territory from France – in one stroke doubling the nation's size. Early explorers such as Zebulon Pike and Meriwether Lewis and William Clark brought back glowing reports of the territory's rich land and abundant fur trade. In 1819, Spain ceded the remainder of Florida to the Republic. For many people in the crowded eastern states, including hundreds of Irish and German immigrants, the new lands represented opportunities for a better life. Soon a complex network of turnpikes, canal and river systems, and railroads carried settlers into the Mississippi Valley and parts of Texas, and opened the lands to eastern markets.

As the Louisiana Territory became more densely settled, pioneers began to push beyond the formal borders of the country. By the early 1840s, the St. Joseph, Missouri rail line served as a starting point for wagon trains heading west over the Oregon, Santa Fe, Fremont, and California trails. Mexico, attempting to stop the flow of settlers into its lands, soon found itself at war with the Americans, losing Texas in 1836 and its vast southwestern territories in 1848. The Gadsden Purchase of 1853 completed America's southernmost border. In the Pacific Northwest, early explorers and settlers had strengthened American claims to the Oregon Territory, held jointly with Great Britain. The two countries agreed in 1848 to divide the land at the 49th Parallel. As more settlers poured into these territories, native Indian tribes were forced off their lands and eventually moved to reservations.

In little over half a century, America had fulfilled its manifest destiny on the continent. Seventeen new states had joined the Republic, eight of them west of the Mississippi. Only the deepening conflict over slavery seemed to dim the nation's brilliant future.

MAP LEGEND

- ▲ Port Cities
- ● Other Cities
- States as of 1803
- Roads
- Canals
- Railroads
- Width of flow lines are proportional to actual numbers of immigrants entering the United States through the ports indicated during the period 1840-1855.

SCALE

miles 0 100 200 300 400

kilometers 0 200 400 600

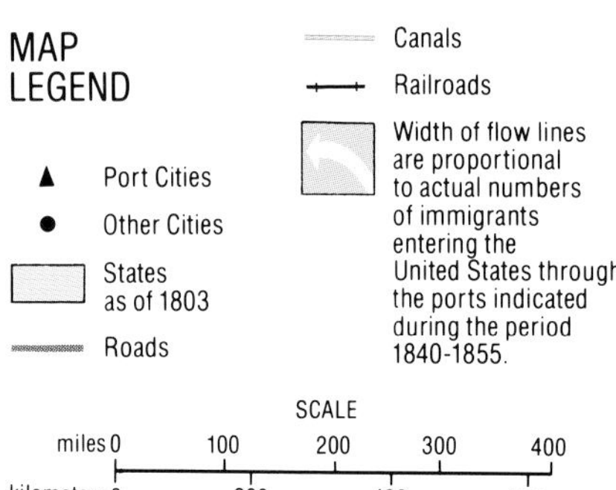

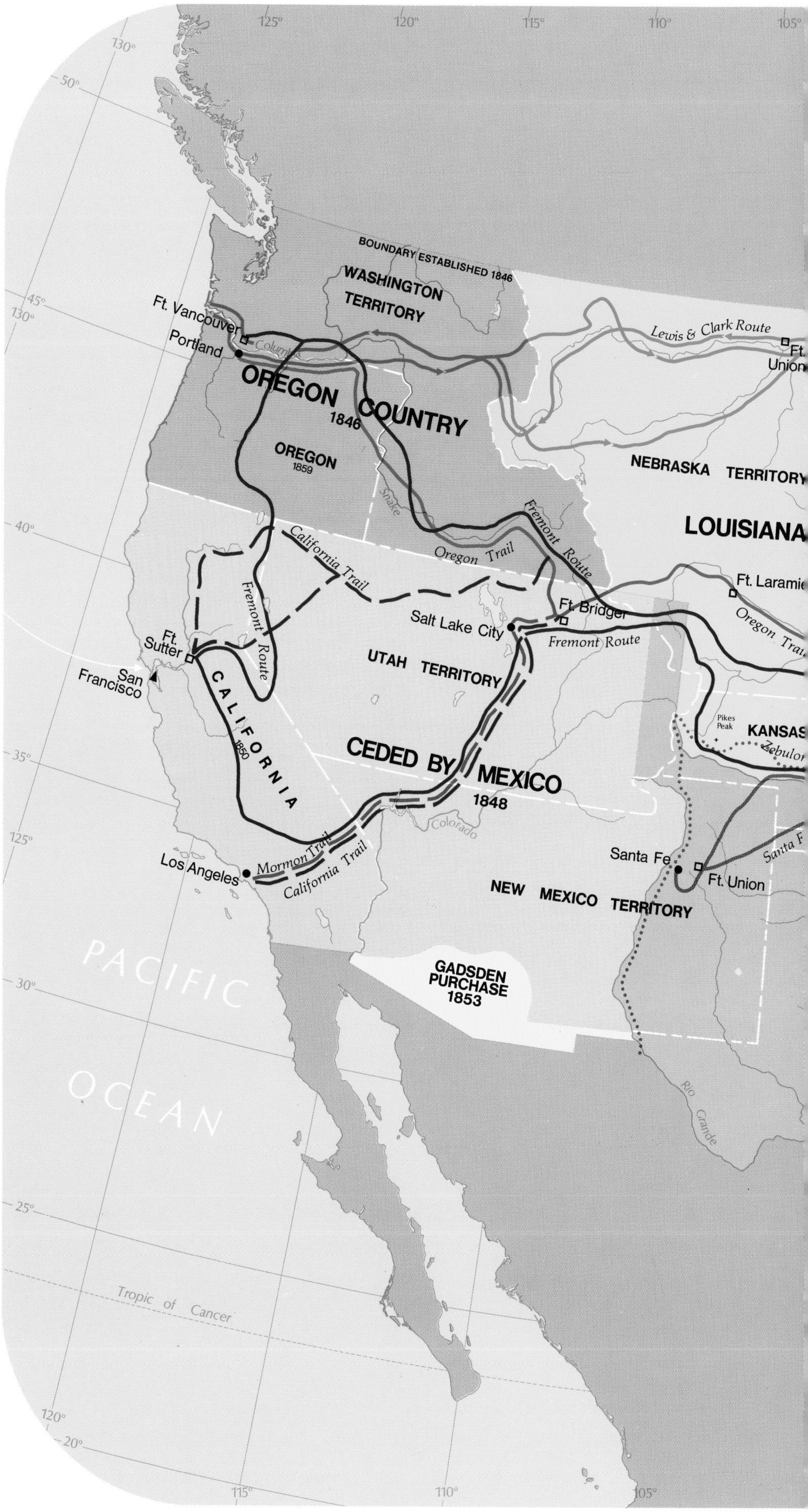

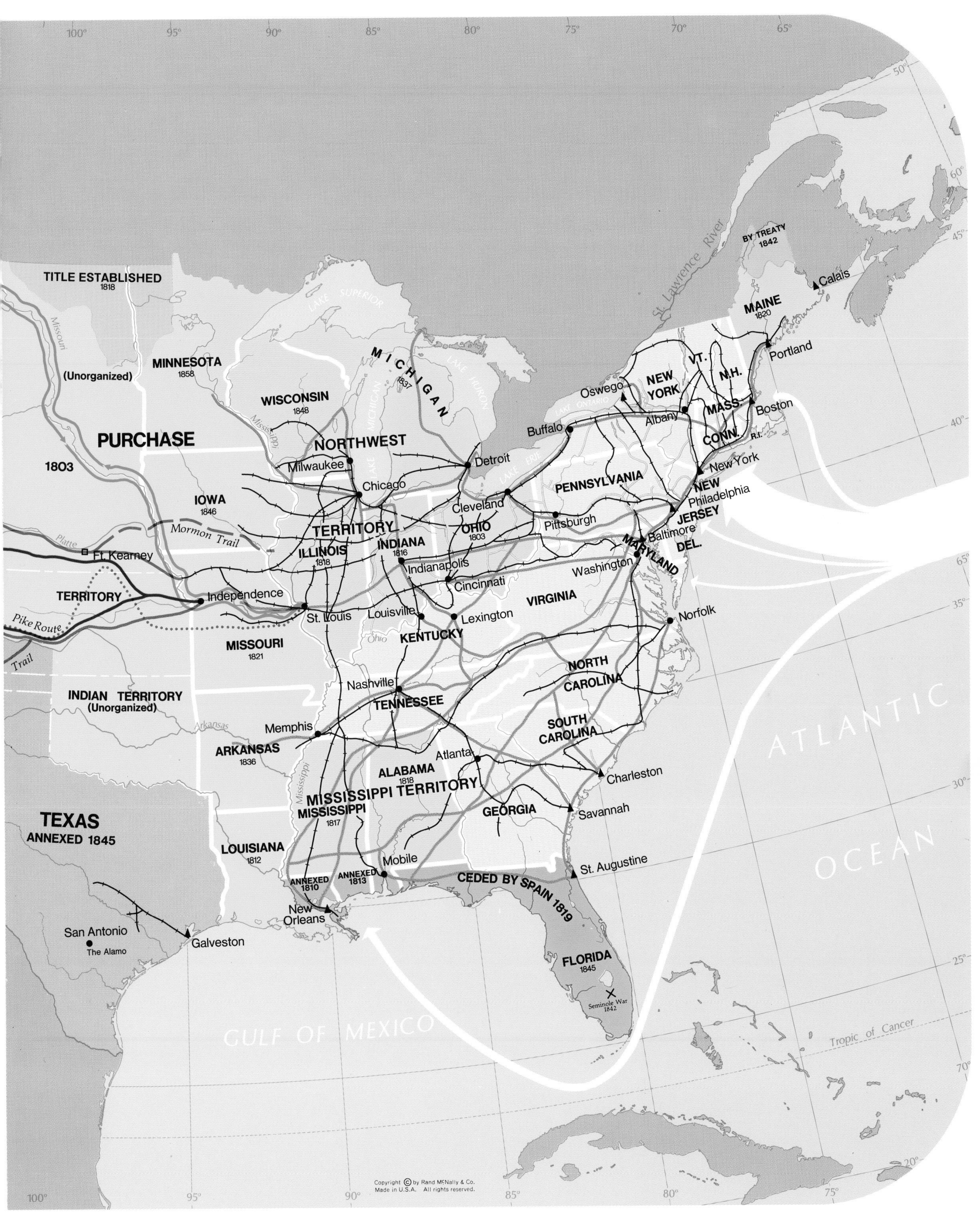
TITLE ESTABLISHED 1818
(Unorganized)
MINNESOTA 1858
PURCHASE
1803
WISCONSIN 1848
MICHIGAN 1837
NORTHWEST
TERRITORY
IOWA 1846
Mormon Trail
Platte
Ft. Kearney
TERRITORY
Independence
Pike Route
Trail
Missouri
ILLINOIS 1818
INDIANA 1816
OHIO 1803
Milwaukee
Chicago
Detroit
Cleveland
Indianapolis
Cincinnati
St. Louis
Louisville
Lexington
KENTUCKY
Ohio
MISSOURI 1821
INDIAN TERRITORY (Unorganized)
Arkansas
Memphis
Nashville
TENNESSEE
ARKANSAS 1836
Atlanta
ALABAMA 1818
MISSISSIPPI TERRITORY
MISSISSIPPI 1817
Mississippi
GEORGIA
TEXAS
ANNEXED 1845
LOUISIANA 1812
ANNEXED 1810
ANNEXED 1813
Mobile
New Orleans
San Antonio
The Alamo
Galveston
CEDED BY SPAIN 1819
FLORIDA 1845
Seminole War 1842
St. Augustine
Savannah
Charleston
SOUTH CAROLINA
NORTH CAROLINA
VIRGINIA
Norfolk
Washington
MARYLAND
Baltimore
DEL.
NEW JERSEY
Philadelphia
PENNSYLVANIA
Pittsburgh
Buffalo
Oswego
NEW YORK
Albany
New York
VT.
N.H.
MASS.
CONN.
R.I.
Boston
MAINE 1820
Portland
Calais
BY TREATY 1842
St. Lawrence River
LAKE SUPERIOR
LAKE MICHIGAN
LAKE HURON
LAKE ERIE
LAKE ONTARIO
ATLANTIC OCEAN
GULF OF MEXICO
Tropic of Cancer
100°
95°
90°
85°
80°
75°
70°
65°
60°
50°
45°
40°
35°
30°
25°
20°

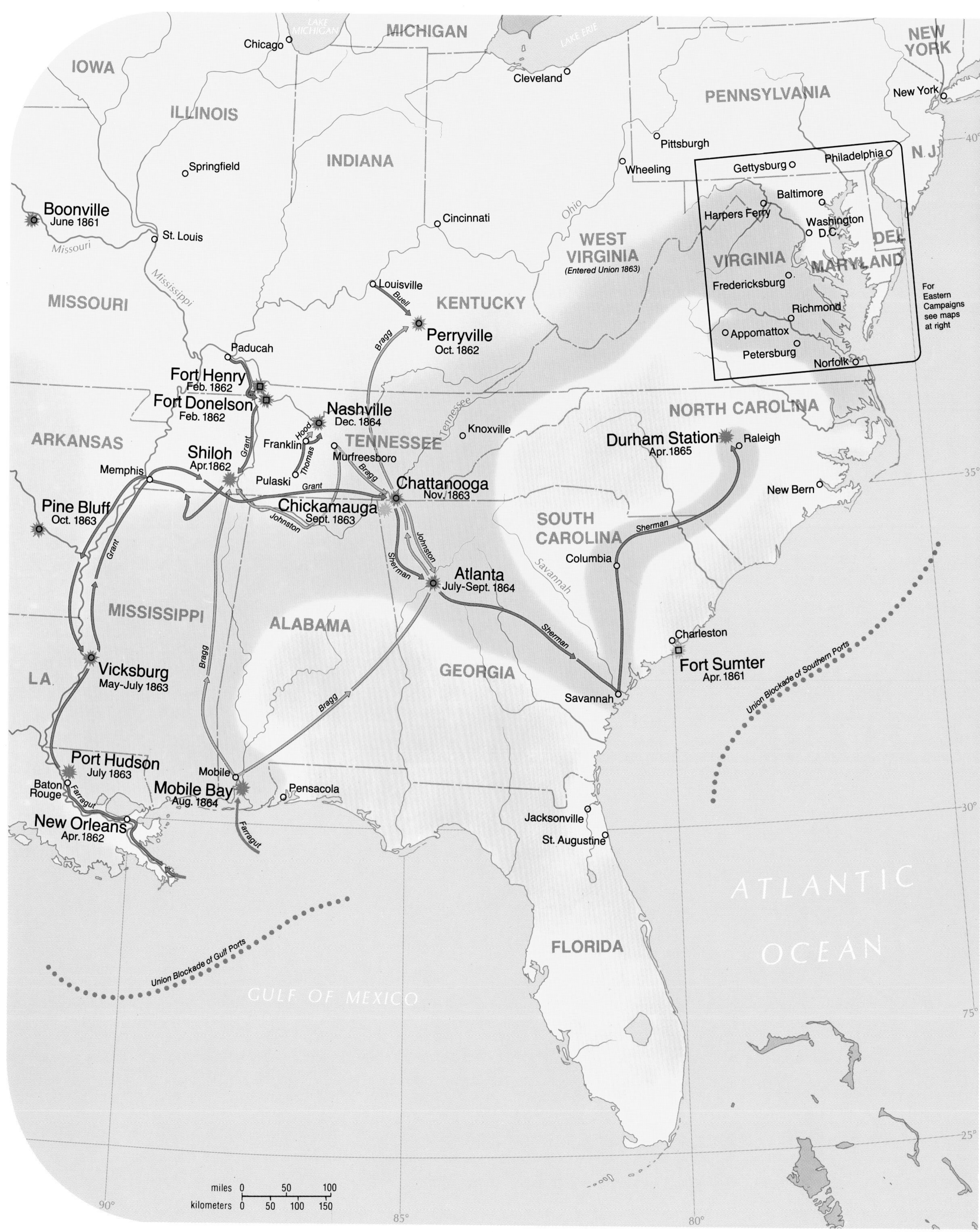
IOWA
ILLINOIS
INDIANA
MICHIGAN
Chicago
Cleveland
PENNSYLVANIA
NEW YORK
New York
N.J.
Pittsburgh
Wheeling
Philadelphia
Gettysburg
Baltimore
Harpers Ferry
Washington D.C.
DEL
VIRGINIA
MARYLAND
Fredericksburg
Richmond
Appomattox
Petersburg
Norfolk
For Eastern Campaigns see maps at right
Springfield
Boonville
June 1861
St. Louis
Missouri
Mississippi
Cincinnati
Ohio
WEST VIRGINIA
(Entered Union 1863)
MISSOURI
Louisville
Buell
KENTUCKY
Perryville
Oct. 1862
Bragg
Paducah
Fort Henry
Feb. 1862
Fort Donelson
Feb. 1862
Nashville
Dec. 1864
Hood
Franklin
Thomas
ARKANSAS
Shiloh
Apr. 1862
Grant
Memphis
Pulaski
Murfreesboro
TENNESSEE
Tennessee
Knoxville
NORTH CAROLINA
Durham Station
Apr. 1865
Raleigh
Chattanooga
Nov. 1863
Chickamauga
Sept. 1863
Johnston
Pine Bluff
Oct. 1863
New Bern
SOUTH CAROLINA
Sherman
Columbia
Savannah
Atlanta
July-Sept. 1864
MISSISSIPPI
ALABAMA
GEORGIA
Charleston
Fort Sumter
Apr. 1861
Union Blockade of Southern Ports
LA.
Vicksburg
May-July 1863
Savannah
Port Hudson
July 1863
Baton Rouge
Farragut
Mobile
Mobile Bay
Aug. 1864
Pensacola
New Orleans
Apr. 1862
Jacksonville
St. Augustine
ATLANTIC OCEAN
FLORIDA
Union Blockade of Gulf Ports
GULF OF MEXICO
miles 0 50 100
kilometers 0 50 100 150
90°
85°
80°
75°
40°
35°
30°
25°

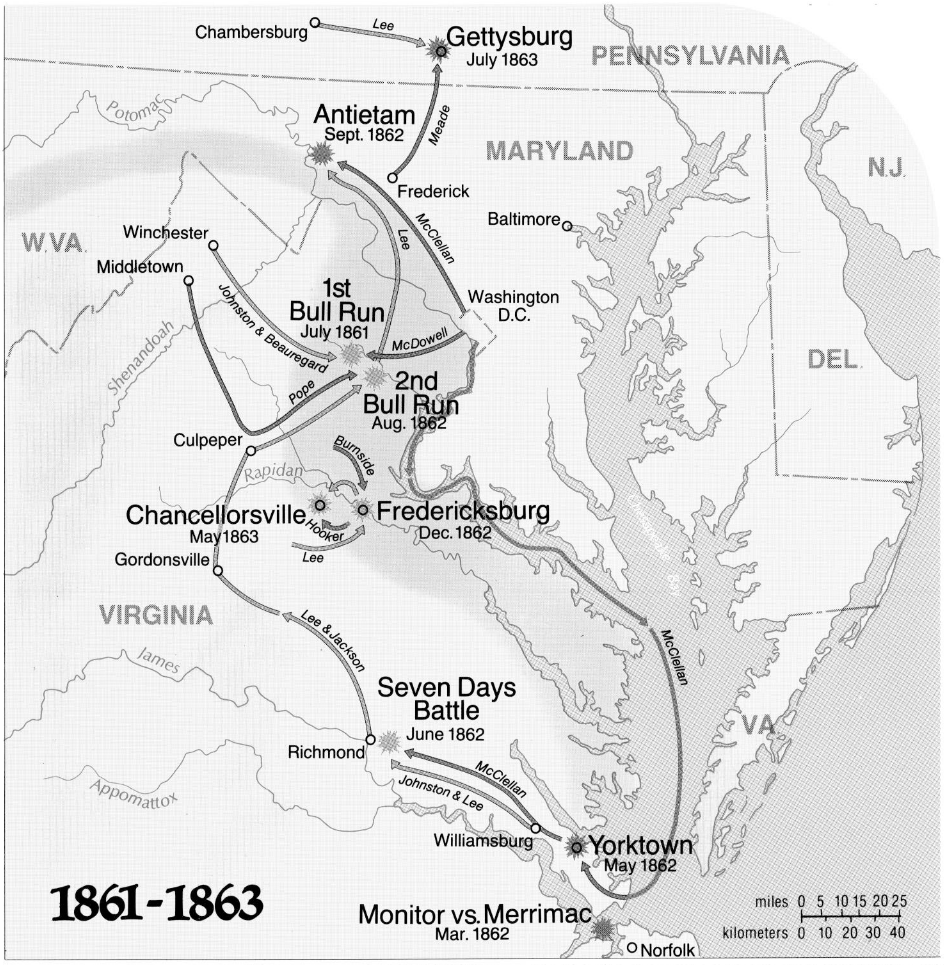

1861-1863

1864-1865

By the 1860 presidential election, it was clear that compromise on the issue of slavery could no longer hold the nation together.

While the North vehemently denounced slave holding, the South as passionately defended its way of life against a "despotic" federal authority. Soon after Abraham Lincoln was elected president, the South seceded from the union and chose Jefferson Davis to head a new government in Richmond, Virginia. By May, 1861, the United States and the Confederacy were at war.

Both sides expected a quick end to the conflict. But after the decisive Confederate victory at Bull Run in July, the war bogged down. Not until early 1862 did the Union army, under George Brinton McClellen and Ulysses S. Grant, take the offensive, winning in the west at Fort Henry, Fort Donelson, and Shiloh. McClellen's subsequent move against Richmond, though supported by the Navy, was stopped by Confederate forces under the command of Robert E. Lee in the Seven Days battle. With the Union offensive stalled, Lee and Pope launched a Confederate invasion of the North, reaching Antietam before being pushed back into Virginia. But the Union losses at Fredericksburg and Chancellorsville encouraged Lee to attempt a second invasion. In July, 1863, he was defeated at Gettysburg in the most decisive battle of the war. That same month, Grant captured Vicksburg, and joining William Tecumseh Sherman, Commander of the Tennessee troops, went on to win at Chattanooga, driving the Confederate troops back into Georgia.

By 1864, the North's economic superiority and the Union naval blockade had become critical factors in the war. In May of that year, Grant and George Meade, Commander of the Army of the Potomac, made the final march on Richmond. Although defeated by Lee in the battle of the Wilderness, and again at Spotsylvania and Cold Harbor, Grant's well-supplied troops continued to press toward Richmond and Petersburg. In a coordinated effort, Sherman began his march to the sea, capturing Atlanta, Savannah, and Columbia before turning north to Raleigh. On April 9, 1865, Lee finally surrendered to Grant at Appomattox Court House: The Union had been preserved.

When the war ended, the nation had undergone profound changes. The Emancipation Proclamation had abolished slavery; the South's agricultural economy lay in ruins. But the conflict had awakened the industrial might of the North. If one way of life had been lost, another was already rising to take its place.

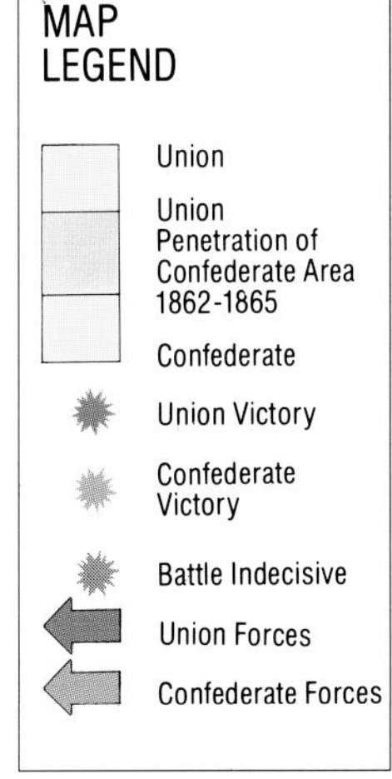

The final settlement of the West involved the greatest movement of people in the nation's history. In only thirty years – one generation after the Civil War – the "Great American Desert" had been transformed into the mineral and agricultural empire of the Republic.

The railroad boom of this era soon opened the plains and mountain-desert regions to settlement. Between 1869 and 1884, four transcontinental railways were built; along with the overland stage, they linked the industrial East to the West. In a few years, the railroads were shipping cattle and grain east, carrying mail and payrolls, helping to supply the frontier army, and bringing settlers, many of them immigrants, into western territories.

The first wave of settlers were miners. In the 1860s and '70s, gold and silver strikes in the Black Hills, Nevada, Colorado, Arizona, and Montana brought thousands of prospectors swarming into Indian lands. Inevitably, war broke out with tribes in the north and southwest. Although the Indians won isolated battles – the most famous at Little Big Horn – they could not prevail against the army's superior weapons. By 1887, the Indians and buffalo were gone from the open range.

Ranchers and farmers soon followed in the miners' wake. From the mid-1860s to the late 1880s, a vast cattle empire dominated Texas, Wyoming, and Montana. Cattle drives up the Chisholm and Sedalia trails helped inspire the romance of the cowboy, a figure that, like the notorious western outlaw, quickly passed into American legend. But the open range was short-lived. Sheepherders soon challenged the ranchers, and farmers began fencing off grazing land and planting crops in the semi-arid soil. In the end, windmills and barbed wire tamed the West as effectively as the railroads and Colt repeating revolver.

By 1890, an almost continuous line of settlement stretched from the Midwest to the Pacific, and population in the territories had soared. The "frontier" had all but disappeared. Ten new states joined the Union, bringing with them the regional flavor of the West. Only the great waves of immigration in the early 1900s would compare with the extensive migration of this era.

MAP LEGEND

- Settled by 1890
- Indian Reservations 1880
- Railroads
- Trails West
- Buffalo Herds 1870
- Cattle Trails
- Mining
- Indian Battle
- Incident of Violence
- 1867 Dates of Admission

SCALE

miles 0 50 100 150 200 250

kilometers 0 100 200 300 400

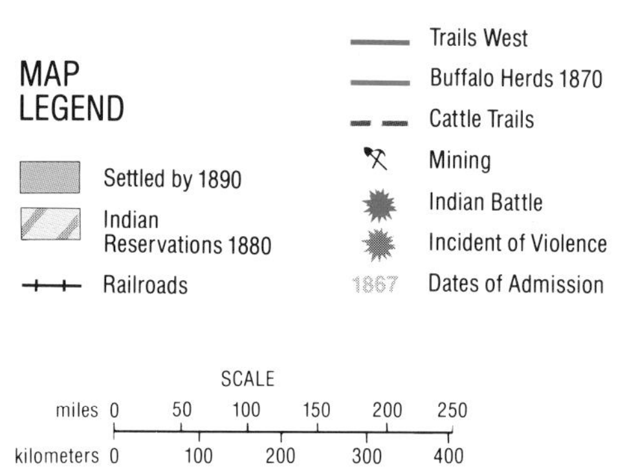

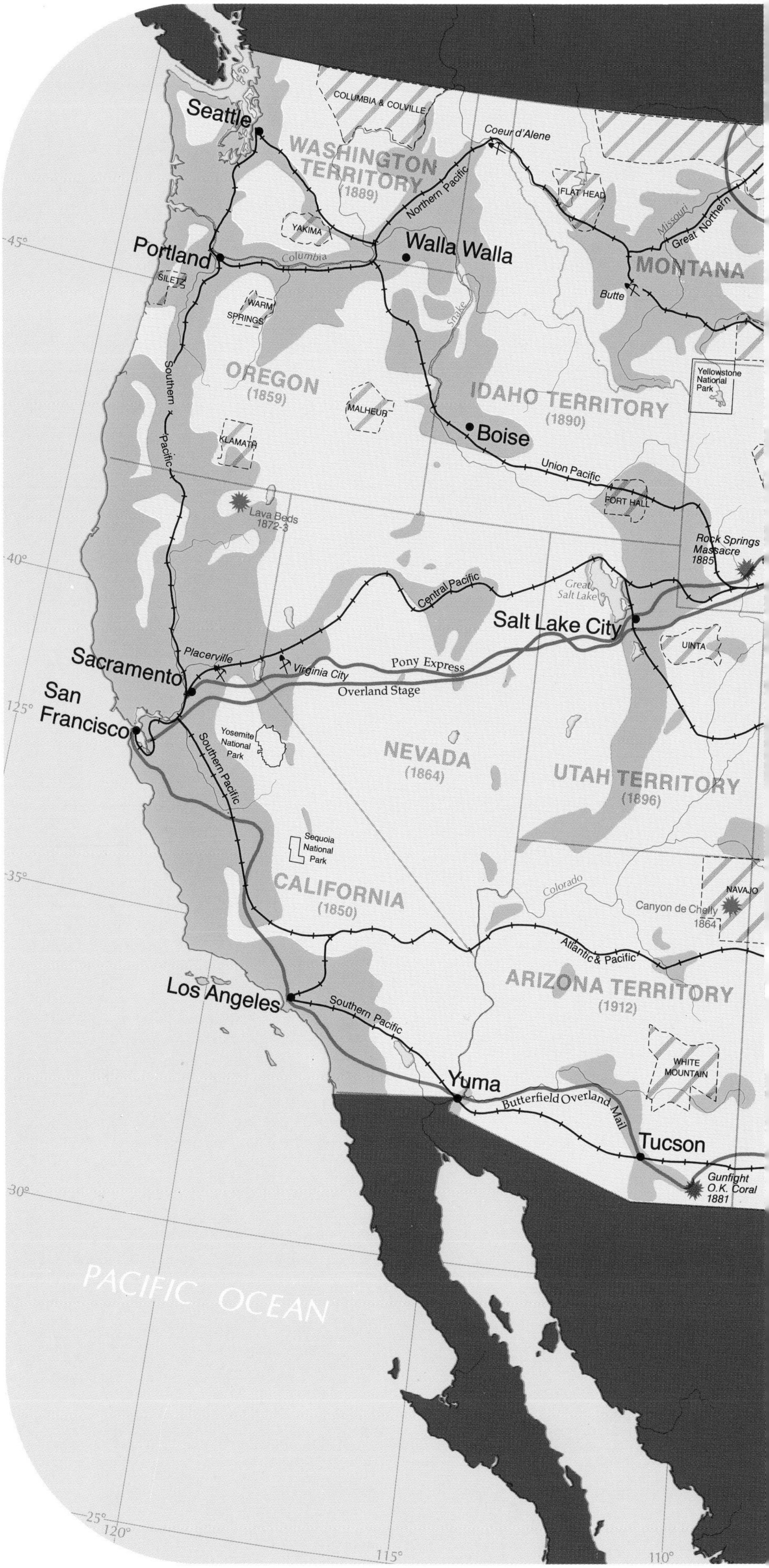

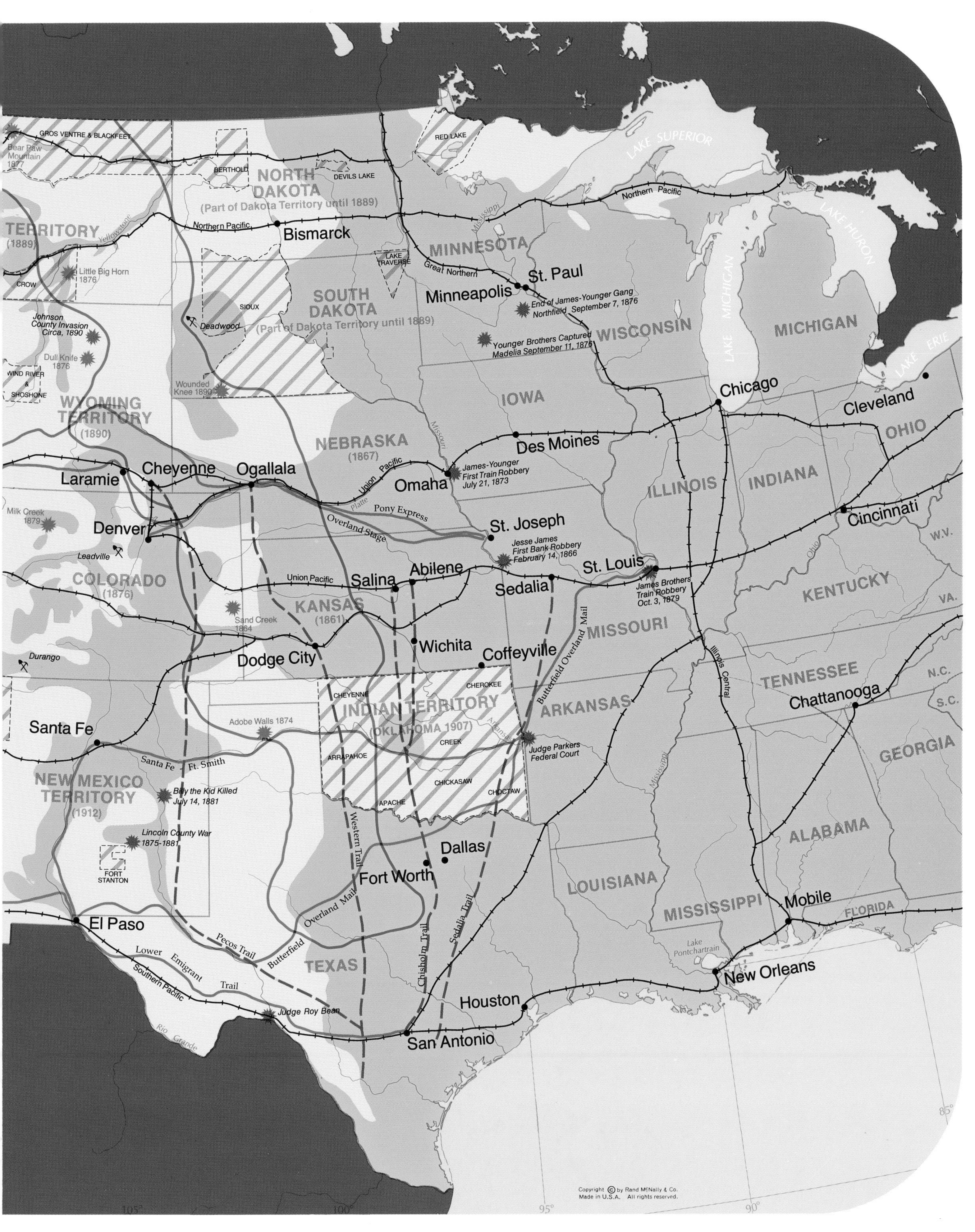
GROS VENTRE & BLACKFEET
Bear Paw Mountain 1877
TERRITORY (1889)
Yellowstone
Little Big Horn 1876
CROW
Johnson County Invasion Circa, 1890
Dull Knife 1876
WIND RIVER & SHOSHONE
WYOMING TERRITORY (1890)
BERTHOLD
NORTH DAKOTA
(Part of Dakota Territory until 1889)
DEVILS LAKE
RED LAKE
Northern Pacific
Bismarck
LAKE TRAVERSE
SOUTH DAKOTA
(Part of Dakota Territory until 1889)
SIOUX
Deadwood
Wounded Knee 1890
MINNESOTA
Great Northern
Mississippi
St. Paul
Minneapolis
End of James-Younger Gang Northfield September 7, 1876
Younger Brothers Captured Madelia September 11, 1876
WISCONSIN
LAKE SUPERIOR
LAKE HURON
LAKE MICHIGAN
MICHIGAN
LAKE ERIE
Chicago
Cleveland
OHIO
IOWA
Des Moines
NEBRASKA (1867)
Missouri
Union Pacific
Omaha
James-Younger First Train Robbery July 21, 1873
Platte
Pony Express
Overland Stage
Laramie
Cheyenne
Ogallala
Denver
Milk Creek 1879
Leadville
COLORADO (1876)
Union Pacific
Salina
Abilene
KANSAS (1861)
Sand Creek 1864
St. Joseph
Jesse James First Bank Robbery February 14, 1866
Sedalia
St. Louis
James Brothers Train Robbery Oct. 3, 1879
ILLINOIS
INDIANA
Cincinnati
Ohio
W.V.
KENTUCKY
VA.
MISSOURI
Butterfield Overland Mail
Illinois Central
Wichita
Coffeyville
Dodge City
Durango
CHEYENNE
CHEROKEE
INDIAN TERRITORY (OKLAHOMA 1907)
CREEK
ARRAPAHOE
CHICKASAW
APACHE
CHOCTAW
Arkansas
Judge Parkers Federal Court
ARKANSAS
TENNESSEE
Chattanooga
N.C.
S.C.
GEORGIA
ALABAMA
Santa Fe
Adobe Walls 1874
Santa Fe
Ft. Smith
NEW MEXICO TERRITORY (1912)
Billy the Kid Killed July 14, 1881
Lincoln County War 1875-1881
FORT STANTON
Western Trail
Dallas
Fort Worth
Overland Mail
Butterfield
Chisholm Trail
Sedalia Trail
LOUISIANA
MISSISSIPPI
Mississippi
Mobile
FLORIDA
Lake Pontchartrain
New Orleans
El Paso
Pecos Trail
Lower Emigrant Trail
Southern Pacific
TEXAS
Houston
Judge Roy Bean
San Antonio
Rio Grande
105°
100°
95°
90°
85°
Copyright © by Rand McNally & Co. Made in U.S.A. All rights reserved.

For the first one hundred years of its history, the United States opened its doors to all nationalities. Often war, famine, or oppression drove millions of people from their homelands to American shores.

The accompanying map depicts where these immigrants and the children of mixed or foreign parentage had settled by 1910.

European immigrants who arrived before, and two decades after, the Civil War, came primarily from England and Ireland, Scandinavia, and Germany. While the Irish tended to remain in the eastern cities, other immigrants seized the chance to journey westward to Oregon, then later to the northern plains states and parts of Texas and California. Many were skilled farmers and artisans, and blended quickly into the mainstream of American life. By the early 1900s, however, the character of immigration had changed considerably. Conditions in eastern and southern Europe led over eight million people to make the arduous journey across the Atlantic. Most of these immigrants, illiterate and unskilled, crowded into the poorer sections of industrial cities such as New York, Boston, and Chicago, creating ethnic communities that insulated them from the language and customs of their new country. Yet they answered industry's insatiable demand for labor, and filled the factories, mines, textile and steel mills, stockyards and railroads, helping to build the industrial might of the nation.

On the West Coast, the Chinese and Japanese did not fare as well. Their numbers alarmed American workers, and in 1882, the first in a series of immigration laws was passed, restricting the entry of Asians into the United States. Mexicans and Latin Americans entering California and the southwestern states often encountered the same resistance and hostility.

In contrast, since the South lacked both heavy industry and available land, immigrants tended to bypass this region in favor of the North and West. Also, restrictive state immigration laws made it difficult for the foreign-born to settle in the South.

The constant stream of newcomers helped create a rich and varied culture in America, making it truly a "nation of nations." Immigrants, and the children of immigrants, contributed immeasurably to the country's industry, science, and arts, and in two world wars, served their new country with distinction.

MAP LEGEND

Immigrants

Foreign born whites and children of foreign or mixed parentage; by counties.

Source: U.S. Decennial Census, 1910

- Less Than 10%
- 10% To 25%
- 25% To 50%
- 50% To 75%
- 75% & Over

MONTANA 94,713 Total Foreign born population in 1910

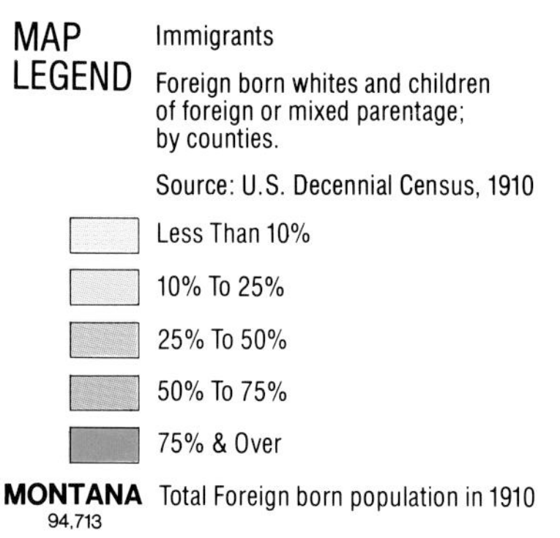

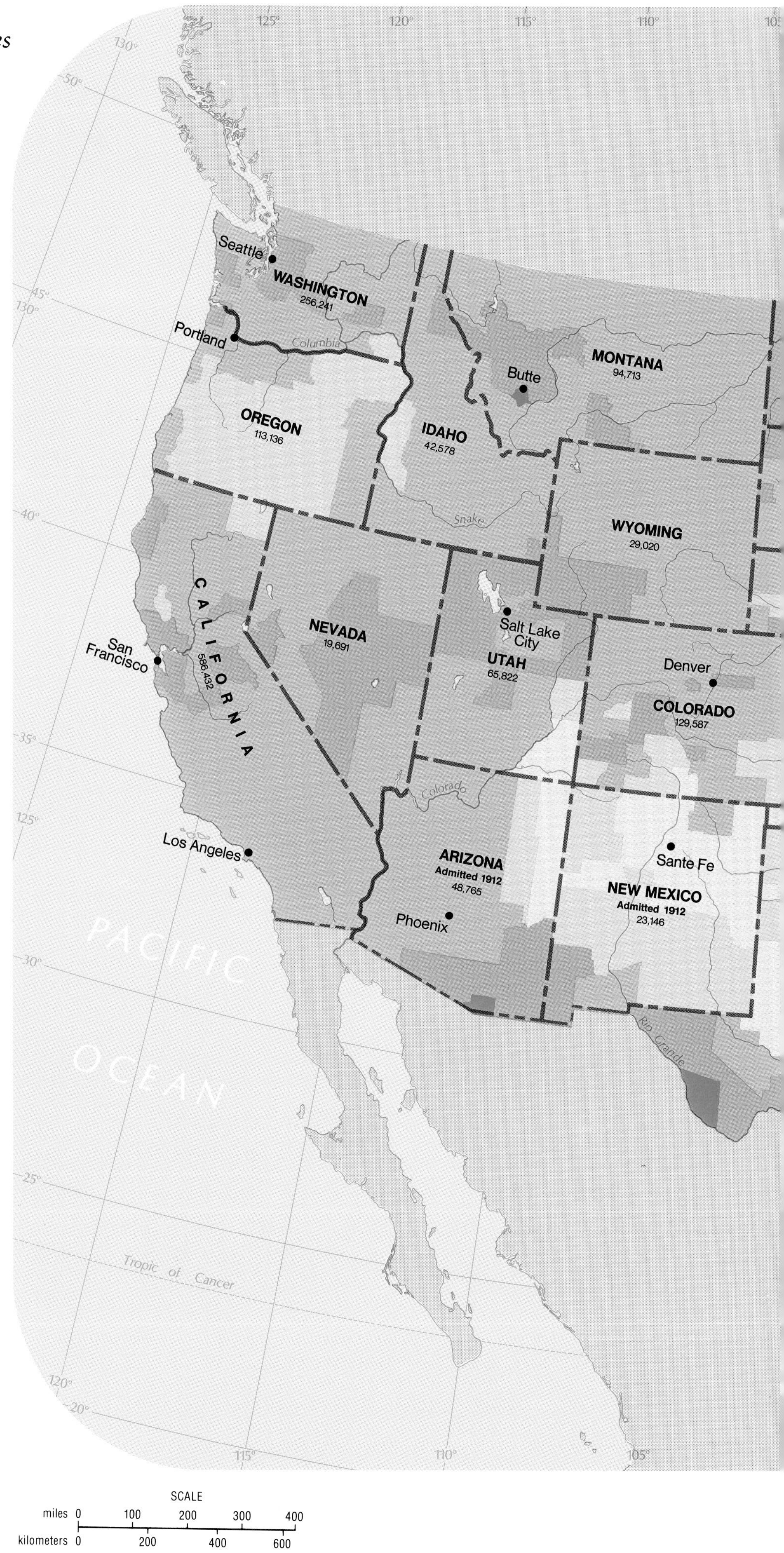

NORTH DAKOTA
156,654
MINNESOTA
543,595
Minneapolis
SOUTH DAKOTA
100,790
WISCONSIN
512,865
Milwaukee
MICHIGAN
597,550
Detroit
IOWA
273,765
NEBRASKA
176,662
Chicago
ILLINOIS
1,205,314
INDIANA
159,663
OHIO
598,374
Cleveland
Cincinnati
Kansas City
KANSAS
135,450
MISSOURI
229,779
St. Louis
KENTUCKY
40,162
WEST VIRGINIA
57,218
VIRGINIA
27,057
Washington D. C.
24,902
MARYLAND
104,944
Baltimore
DEL.
17,492
Philadelphia
N.J.
560,788
Newark
New York
PENNSYLVANIA
1,442,374
Pittsburgh
NEW YORK
2,748,011
Buffalo
CONN.
329,574
R.I.
179,141
MASS.
1,059,245
Boston
VT.
49,921
N.H.
96,667
MAINE
110,562
LAKE SUPERIOR
LAKE MICHIGAN
LAKE HURON
LAKE ONTARIO
LAKE ERIE
Missouri
Ohio
Mississippi
Nashville
TENNESSEE
18,607
NORTH CAROLINA
6,092
SOUTH CAROLINA
6,179
OKLAHOMA
40,442
ARKANSAS
17,046
Atlanta
MISSISSIPPI
9,770
ALABAMA
19,286
GEORGIA
15,477
TEXAS
241,938
LOUISIANA
52,766
Jacksonville
FLORIDA
40,633
New Orleans
San Antonio
GULF OF MEXICO
ATLANTIC
OCEAN
Tropic of Cancer
100°
95°
90°
85°
80°
75°
70°
65°
60°
50°
45°
40°
35°
30°
25°
20°

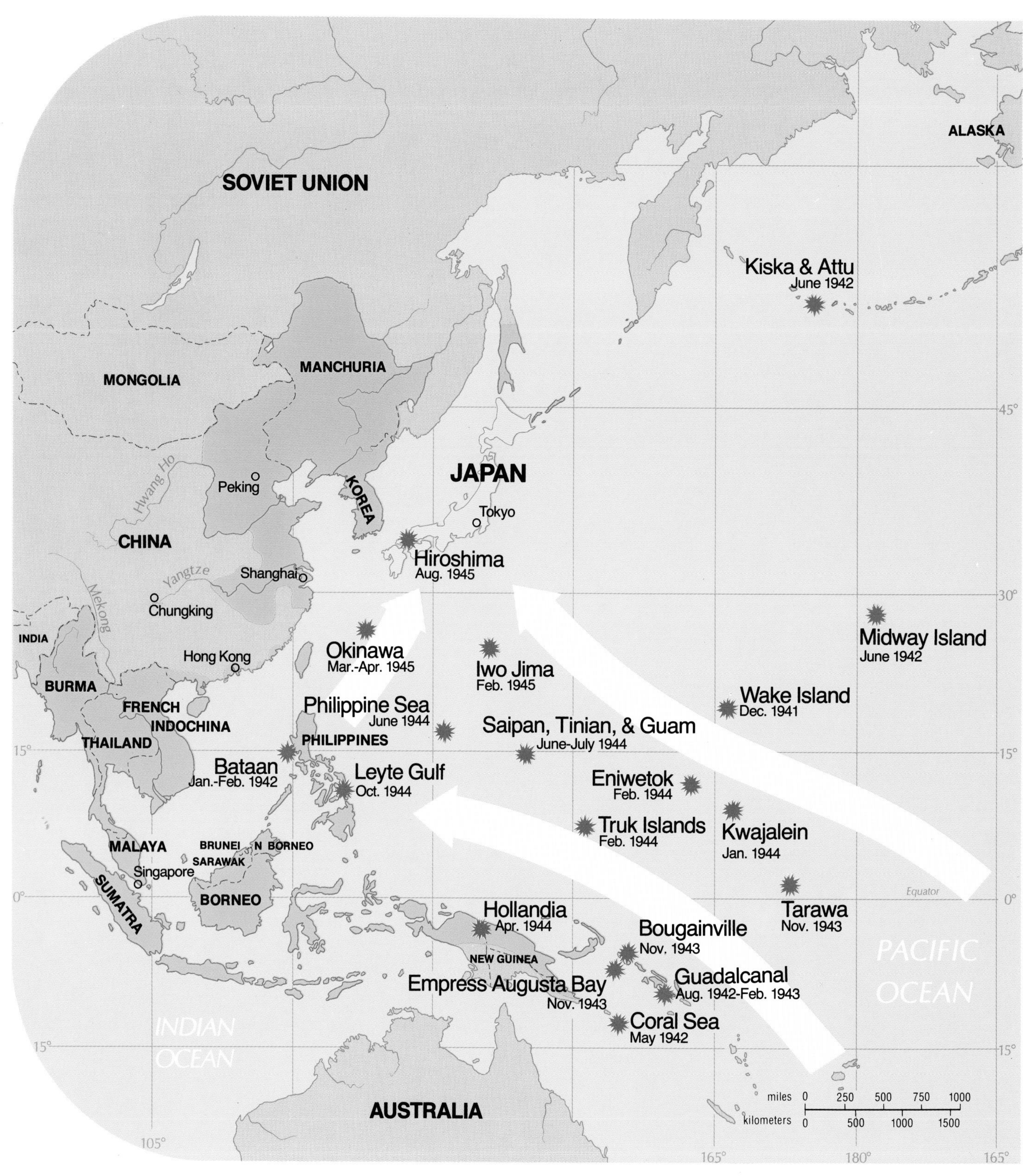

The United States entered World War II almost totally unprepared to fight on the two fronts of Europe and the Pacific. Yet its vast industrial capacity proved to be a decisive factor in the Allied victory, and eventually thrust America into a position of world leadership.

Early in the war, however, the Axis alliance seemed invincible. By 1942, Germany had swept through most of Europe, isolated Great Britain, and launched an invasion of Russia. In North Africa, Rommel, Commander of German forces, threatened the vital Suez Canal. Russian leader, Joseph Stalin desparately called for a "second front" in Europe to relieve his hard-pressed troops, but the Allies were unprepared to invade the continent. Instead, in November, 1942, Dwight D. Eisenhower, U.S. General and Allied Supreme commander in North Africa, led a coordinated attack on Morocco and Algeria, and by May of the next year had driven the Axis powers out of North Africa. Bolstered by American material, Soviet troops regained the offensive in the 1942-43 winter war and began forcing the Germans back toward Berlin. Finally, after

an ill-advised invasion of Sicily, the Allies landed on the beaches of Normandy and southern France in June, 1944. Caught between advancing Russian and Allied troops, Germany surrendered on May 7, 1945.

In the early months of the Pacific war, Japan had quickly overrun Manchuria, Southeast Asia, Singapore, and Indonesia and gained control of the seas. But by 1942, Allied forces had defeated the Japanese navy at Coral Sea, Midway, and Solomon Islands, and in 1944, destroyed the remaining fleet at Leyte Gulf. Douglas MacArthur, Commander of the U.S. Forces in the Far East, liberated the Philippines in October of that year and, with Chester Nimitz, Commander of the U.S. Pacific Fleet, launched a two-pronged attack toward Japan. Capturing one island after another, American forces were soon poised to invade the Japanese mainland. Instead, in early August, 1945, the first atomic bombs were exploded over Hiroshima and Nagasaki. Japan surrendered on August 14.

The war had profoundly changed the world. The United States and Russia now faced one another as rival superpowers over a divided Europe, and the spectre of the atom bomb haunted the world. As people returned to peacetime, it was hoped that the newly chartered United Nations would provide a forum for all nations to seek peaceful solutions to world problems and to begin to build a more lasting peace throughout the world.

Over 250 million people lived in the United States in 1990. Metropolitan areas were home to 77 % of those Americans.

Through most of the twentieth century, metropolitan areas have been centers of population growth. Though rates of growth have slowed, these areas continue to attract people in search of greater economic opportunities. The accompanying map shows the distribution of population and the dense concentration of Americans in major urbanized areas.

Until the late 1950s, the Industrial belt – stretching from the Northeast to St. Louis – continued to attract businesses and labor. Thousands of blacks from the South and whites from Appalachia migrated North to the great cities, while inner-city whites moved to the rapidly growing suburbs. By the late 1950s and early 1960s, many light industries were also leaving the inner city not only for the suburbs but for the Sunbelt of the West and South where labor and energy costs were lower and tax incentives more attractive. In addition, a growing aerospace and electronics industry drew a large, highly skilled work force to Florida, Texas, and California.

Changing American lifestyles also contributed to the exodus to warmer climates. The ecology movement of the 1960s that carried into the 1990s encouraged people to escape from crowded industrial areas to less developed sections in the Southwest and Pacific states. In contrast, rural areas – particularly the drier western states – were losing population as people sought employment in cities and the new industrial regions. More retired people looked to the Sunbelt as a place to enjoy their later years. The retirement and leisure communities that grew up in Florida, Arizona, and California continue to attract people at a greater rate than cities in the North.

The latter decades of the century have witnessed a wave of immigrants from Asia and Latin America that has contributed to the ethnic variety as well as to the growth of the nation.

This growing nation, aided by a well-developed communication and transportation system and a substantial resource base, continued to move, settle, and redefine the American society of the 1990s.

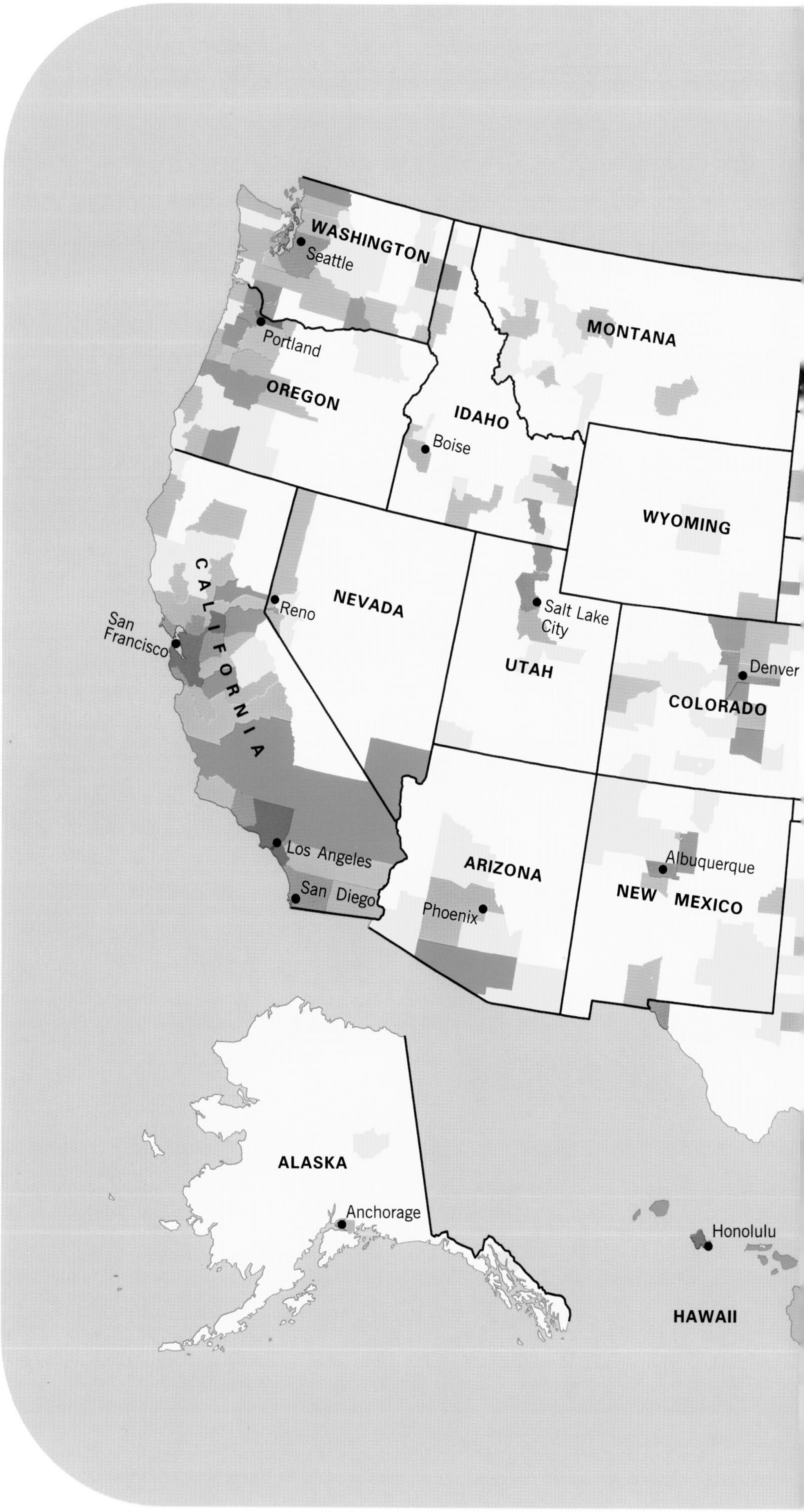

MAP LEGEND

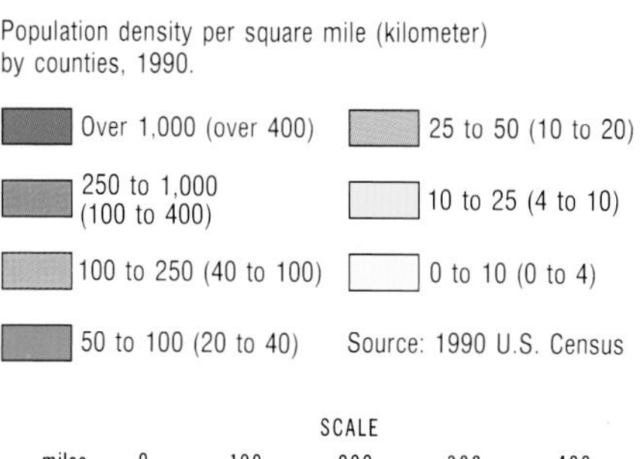

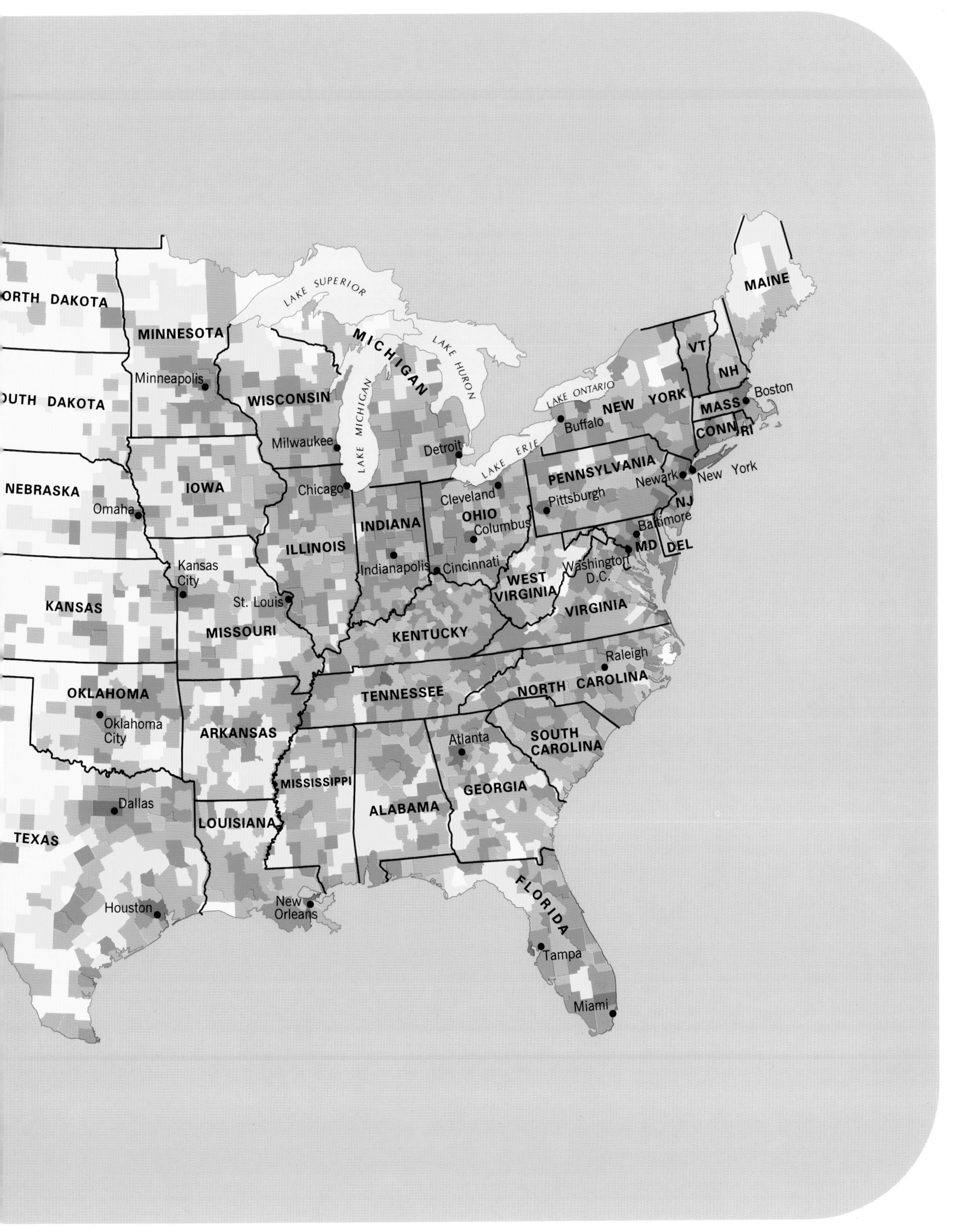
ORTH DAKOTA
MINNESOTA
Minneapolis
OUTH DAKOTA
WISCONSIN
LAKE SUPERIOR
MICHIGAN
LAKE HURON
LAKE MICHIGAN
Milwaukee
Detroit
LAKE ONTARIO
LAKE ERIE
MAINE
VT
NH
MASS
Boston
NEW YORK
Buffalo
CONN
RI
NEBRASKA
IOWA
Chicago
Omaha
PENNSYLVANIA
Newark
New York
Pittsburgh
Cleveland
OHIO
Columbus
INDIANA
ILLINOIS
NJ
Baltimore
MD
DEL
Indianapolis
Cincinnati
Washington D.C.
Kansas City
WEST VIRGINIA
KANSAS
St. Louis
VIRGINIA
MISSOURI
KENTUCKY
Raleigh
OKLAHOMA
TENNESSEE
NORTH CAROLINA
Oklahoma City
ARKANSAS
SOUTH CAROLINA
Atlanta
MISSISSIPPI
GEORGIA
Dallas
ALABAMA
LOUISIANA
TEXAS
FLORIDA
Houston
New Orleans
Tampa
Miami

The tables below reflect three major movements im American History – the filling out of the nation's boundaries, the flow of immigrants entering the United States, and the latest trends in population shifts. These figures depict a nation in a state of constant change and development.

THE EXPANDING NATION

State	Date Admitted	No.	State	Date Admitted	No.	State	Date Admitted	No.
Alabama	Dec. 14, 1819	22	Louisiana	April 30, 1812	18	Ohio	March 1, 1803	17
Alaska	Jan 3, 1959	49	Maine	March 15, 1820	23	Oklahoma	Nov. 16, 1907	46
Arizona	Feb. 24, 1912	48	Maryland	April 28, 1788	7	Oregon	Feb. 14, 1859	33
Arkansas	June 15, 1836	25	Massachusetts	Feb. 6, 1788	6	Pennsylvania	Dec. 12, 1787	2
California	Sept. 9, 1850	31	Michigan	Jan. 26, 1837	26	Rhode Island	May 29, 1790	13
Colorado	Aug. 1, 1876	38	Minnesota	May 11, 1858	32	South Carolina	May 23, 1788	8
Connecticut	Jan. 9, 1788	5	Mississippi	Dec. 10, 1817	20	South Dakota	Nov. 2, 1889	40
Delaware	Dec. 7, 1787	1	Missouri	Aug. 10, 1821	24	Tennessee	June 1, 1796	16
Florida	March 3, 1845	27	Montana	Nov. 8, 1889	41	Texas	Dec. 29, 1845	28
Georgia	Jan. 2, 1788	4	Nebraska	March 1, 1867	37	Utah	Jan. 4, 1896	45
Hawaii	Aug. 21, 1959	50	Nevada	Oct. 31, 1864	36	Vermont	March 4, 1791	14
Idaho	July 3, 1890	43	New Hampshire	June 21, 1788	9	Virginia	June 25, 1788	10
Illinois	Dec. 3, 1818	21	New Jersey	Dec. 18, 1787	3	Washington	Nov. 11, 1889	42
Indiana	Dec. 11, 1816	19	New Mexico	Jan. 6, 1912	47	West Virginia	June 20, 1863	35
Iowa	Dec. 28, 1846	29	New York	July 26, 1788	11	Wisconsin	May 29, 1848	30
Kansas	Jan. 29, 1861	34	North Carolina	Nov. 21, 1789	12	Wyoming	July 10, 1890	44
Kentucky	June 1, 1792	15	North Dakota	Nov. 2, 1889	39			

A NATION OF IMMIGRANTS: 1851-1988

Region	1851-70	1871-90	1891-1910	1911-30	1931-50	1951-70	1971-88
Europe—Northern and Western Belgium, England, Denmark, Finland, France, Germany, Ireland, Netherlands, Norway, Scotland, Sweden, Switzerland	4,463,000	5,849,000	3,553,500	2,298,200	693,900	1,498,800	469,100
Europe—Southern and Eastern Austria, Bulgaria, Czechoslovakia, Greece, Hungary, Italy, Poland, Portugal , Romania, Spain, Turkey, U.S.S.R., Yugoslavia	54,900	1,158,600	8,140,700	4,525,100	261,100	983,300	790,200
Asia China, India, Iran, Japan, Korea, Laos, Philippines, Vietnam	106,000	187,800	195,900	172,500	32,700	398,300	3,029,200
America Canada, Latin America, Mexico, West Indies	241,300	831,000	400,900	2,660,400	514,800	2,576,300	3,800,600
Other Countries African countries, Australia, New Zealand, Pacific Islands	47,700	26,300	72,300	38,300	31,500	121,900	291,300

REGIONAL TRENDS IN POPULATION: 1970-2000

Region	1970	1980	1990	2000	Per Cent Change 1970-1980	Per Cent Change 1980-1990	Per Cent Change (Projected) 1990-2000
Northeast Connecticut, Maine, Massachusetts, New Hampshire, New Jersey, New York, Pennsylvania, Rhode Island, Vermont	49,061,000	49,137,000	50,809,000	51,810,000	0.2%	3.4%	2.0%
North Central Illinois, Indiana, Iowa, Kansas, Michigan, Minnesota, Missouri, Nebraska, North Dakota, Ohio, South Dakota, Wisconsin	56,590,000	58,854,000	59,669,000	59,596,000	4.0	1.4	-0.1
South Alabama, Arkansas, Delaware, District of Columbia, Florida, Georgia, Kentucky, Louisiana, Maryland, Mississippi, North Carolina, Oklahoma, South Carolina, Tennessee, Texas, Virginia, West Virginia	62,813,000	75,349,000	85,446,000	96,919,000	20.0	13.4	13.4
West Alaska, Arizona, California, Colorado, Hawaii, Idaho, Montana, Nevada, New Mexico, Oregon, Utah, Washington, Wyoming	34,838,000	43,165,000	52,786,000	59,422,000	23.9	22.3	12.6

This index includes the major places, events, peoples and activities to be covered by the text and maps. For the most part individual towns have not been included. References to the map numbers are listed in **bold** type; references to the text are in roman type, and indicate the relevant page numbers.

A

B

C

D

E

F

G

H

INDEX OF ALTERNATIVE PLACE NAMES

There has been no attempt to standardize the spelling of place names in this Atlas. Many places have changed their names in the course of history; many different forms of transcription or romanization have been used for oriental names; and many places, especially the best-known ones, are more familiar to English-speaking readers in their modern, Anglicized form than in the vernacular which may be more common for their less-well-known neighbours. The maps in this Atlas reflect this diversity. Rather than attempt to impose any rule of thumb such as modern internationally-accepted spellings the editor has asked the contributors to use the spellings and forms which students in their particular fields are most likely to encounter in their reading on the subject. Thus two maps of the same area, separated in date by two or three hundred years, may show minor differences. Sometimes, also, local forms are shown, sometimes Anglicized ones. It is hoped that these differences will be aids to general clarity rather than confusion.

The list that follows is intended to be a guide to the major places that have changed their names significantly over the centuries. Minor variations, modernizations or Anglicizations have been ignored; but where cultural, political or linguistic developments have given rise to entirely new names, these are listed below. The modern forms, given in bold type, are those usually to be found in The Times Atlas of The World (6th ed., 1980);the variants are mostly to be found on the maps in the present volume. The main entry for each place is listed under its modern spelling with its variants in roughly chronological order; a major (though not necessarily the only) map reference has also been given.

Only town names, sites of battles, archaeological sites and some rivers have been included in this list. The names of regions and countries, which have changed in both name and area too much to be included in a list of this kind, are to be found in the main index.

A

Aachen (Germany) – Aquigranum, Aix-la-Chapelle 22
Abarshahr *see* Neyshabur
Abila Syria – Seleuceia 9
Aboba *see* Pliska
Abrotonum *see* Sabratah
Abydus *see* Çanakkale
Acre *see* 'Akko
Adalia *see* Antalya
Adana (Turkey) – Antiocheia 9
Adrianople *see* Edirne
Aela *see* Aqaba
Aelia Capitolina *see* Jerusalem
Afamiyah (Syria) – Apamea 26
Agedincum *see* Sens
Agram *see* Zagreb
Agrigento (Sicily) – Agrigentum, Acragas 8
Ahvāz (Iran) – Ahwāz 27
Aix-en-Provence – Aquae, Aquae, Sextiae 25
Aix-la-Chapelle *see* Aachen
Ajodhan *see* Pakpattan
Akhtiar *see* Sebastopol
'Akko (Israel) – Acre, Ptolemais, St Jean d'Acre 26
Akşehir (Turkey) – Philomelium 19, 26
Alaşehir (Turkey) – Philadelphia 26
Alba Iulia (Romania) – Apulum, Gyulaféhrvár, Karlsburg 12
Albany (New York, USA) – Fort Orange 44
Aleppo (Syria) – Beroea, Ḥalab 86
Alexandretta *see* Iskenderun
Alexandria *see* Arbil, Ghazni, Herat
Alexandria (Egypt) – El Iskandariya 19
Alexandria in Arachosia *see* Kandahar
Alexandria Troas *see* Eski Stambul
Alexandrov (USSR) – Alexandrovskaya Sloboda 41
Al-Faramah *see* Pelusium
Algiers (Algeria) – Icosium, Alger 74
Aligarh (Rajasthan, India) – Koil 29
Al Khal *see* Hebron
Allahabad (Uttar Pradesh, India) – Prayaga 65
Alma-Ata (Kazakhstan, USSR) – Vernyy 71
Al Quds *see* Jerusalem
Amasra (Turkey) – Amastris 19
Ambiani *see* Amiens
Ambon (Moluccas) – Amboina 37
Amfissa (Greece) – Salona 26
Amga (USSR) – Amginsk 70
Amid, Amida *see* Diyarbakir
Amiens (France) – Samarobriva, Ambian 25
Amisea *see* Amasya
Amisus *see* Samsun
'Ammān (Jordan) – Philadelphia 86
Ammochostos *see* Famagusta
Amphipolis *see* Thapsacus
Anazarbus *see* Dijhan
Anas, R *see* Guadiana, R
Ancyra *see* Ankara
An-i *see* Ho-tung
Ankara (Turkey) – Ancyra 86
'Annaba (Algeria) – Hippo Regius, Bône 17
An-ping (Taiwan) – Anpeijo 37
Antakya (Turkey) – Antiochia, Antioch 26
Antalya (Turkey) – Attalia, Adalia 26
Antietam *see* Sharpsburg
Antiocheia *see* Adana, Antakya, Gerasa, Mallus, Mary, Nusaybin, Tarsus Cayi
Antiocheia-Edessa *see* Urfa
Antiochia in Pisidia *see* Yalvac
Apamea *see* Afamiyah, Celaenae, Kala'at el Medik, Mudanya
Aparri (Philippines) – Kagayan 37
Apulum *see* Alba Iulia
'Aqaba (Jordan) – Aela 86
Aquae, Aquae Sextiae *see* Aix-en-Provence
Aquileia *see* Cividale del Friuli
Aquincum *see* Budapest
Aquisgranum *see* Aachen
Arausio *see* Orange
Arbil (Iraq) – Arbela, Alexandria 6
Archangel *see* Arkhangelsk
Arelate *see* Arles
Argentoratum *see* Strasbourg
Ariha *see* Jericho
Ariminum *see* Rimini
Arkhangelsk (USSR) – Archangel 70
Arles (France) – Arelate 25
Arsinoe *see* Patara
Artashat (Armenia, USSR) – Artazata 12
Arvad *see* Arwad
Arwad (Syria) – Arvad, Ruad, Rowad 26
Ashdod (Israel) – Azotus 9
Ash Sham *see* Damascus
Ashur *see* Sharqat
Ashqelon (Israel) – Ascalon, Ashkelon, Tel Ashqelon 26
Asido *see* Medina Sidonia
Atri (Italy) – Hadria 8
Attalia *see* Antalya
Augsburg (Germany) – Augusta Vindelicorum 28
Augst (Switzerland) – Augusta Rauricorrum 8
Augusta Taurinorum *see* Turin
Augusta Treverorum *see* Trier
Augusta Vindelicorum *see* Augsburg
Auschwitz *see* Oswiecim
Auximium *see* Osimo
Avaricum *see* Bourges
Avignon (France) – Avenio 54
Avlona *see* Vlorë
Aylah *see* Elat
Azotus *see* Ashdod

B

Baalbek (Lebanon) – Heliopolis 8
Bactria *see* Balkh
Baeterrae *see* Béziers
Baile Átha Cliath *see* Dublin
Balchik (Bulgaria) – Dionysiopolis 18
Balkh (Afghanistan) – Bactria 27
Bambyce *see* Membij
Bangkok (Thailand) – Krung Thep 85
Banjul (The Gambia) – Bathurst 74
Banten (Java, Indonesia) – Bantam 37
Bardaa *see* Dashkesan
Barygaza *see* Bharuch
Batavia *see* Djakarta
Bathurst *see* Banjul
Bayonne (France) – Lapurdum 54
Beç *see* Vienna
Beijing (China) – Khanbalik, Peking 38
Beja (Portugal) – Pax Iulia 8
Bejaïa (Algeria) – Bougie 28
Belgrade *see* Beograd
Belkis (Turkey) – Cyzicus 14
Belostok *see* Bialystok
Belvoir (Israel) – Kaukab 26
Benares *see* Varanasi
Beograd (Yugoslavia) – Singidunum, Belgrade 63
Berenice (Egypt) – Berghazi
Bergama (Turkey) – Pergamum 8
Bergen *see* Mons
Berghāzi *see* Berenice
Beyrouth (Lebanon) – Berytus, Laodiceia 86
Berroea *see* Aleppo, Stara Zagora
Berytus *see* Beyrouth
Beseire (Iraq) – Circesium 14
Béziers (France) – Baeterrae 14
Bharuch (Gujarat, India) – Barygaza, Broach 65
Bialystok (Poland) – Belostok 77
Bioko (Equatorial Guinea) – Fernando Poo, Macias Nguema 46
Bishapur *see* Shapur
Bitola (Yugoslavia) – Monastir 63
Bituriges *see* Bourges
Bizerte (Tunisia) – Hippo Zarytus, Bizerta 81
Black Sea – Pontus Euxinus 39
Boğazkale (Turkey) – Hattusha, Hattushash, Pteria 4
Bologna (Italy) – Bononia, Felsina 33
Bône *see* Annaba
Bononia *see* Bologna, Boulogne, Vidin
Bor (Turkey) – Tyana 19, 26
Bordeaux (France) – Burdigala 12, 14
Borysthenes, R *see* Dnepr/Dnieper, R
Bosporus *see* Kerch
Bougie *see* Bejaïa 28
Boulogne (France) – Bononia, Gesoriacum 14
Bourges (France) – Avaricum, Bituriges 14
Braga (Portugal) – Bracara 14
Braşov (Romania) – Kronstadt 52
Bratislava (Czechoslovakia) – Pressburg 77
Braunschweig (Germany) – Brunswick 52
Brecia *see* Wroclaw
Breslau *see* Wroclaw
Bressanone (Italy) – Brixen 33
Brindisi (Italy) – Brundisium 62
Brixen *see* Bressanone
Brno (Czechoslovakia) – Brünn 77
Broach *see* Baruch
Brundisium *see* Brindisi
Brünn *see* Brno
Brunswick *see* Braunschweig
Budapest (Hungary) – Aquincum 77
Buffavento (Cyprus) – Koützivendi 21
Bulandshahr (Uttar Pradesh, India) – Baran 29
Burdigala *see* Bordeaux
Byblos *see* Jubail
Byzantium *see* Istanbul

C

Cádiz (Spain) – Gades 32
Caerleon (Wales) – Isca 12, 14
Caernarvon (Wales) – Segontia 25
Caesaraugusta *see* Zaragoza
Caesarea *see* Cherchell, Viayspri
Caesarodunum *see* Tours
Cairo (Egypt) – Fustat 19
Calah *see* Nimrud
Calicut (Kerala, India) – Kozhikode 29
Callinicium *see* Raqqa
Camulodunum *see* Colchester
Çanakkale (Turkey) – Abydus 26
Çanakkale Boğazi *see* Dardanelles
Candia *see* Iraklion
Canterbury (England) – Cantuaria 25
Canton *see* Guangzhou
Cantuaria *see* Canterbury
Carrhae (Turkey) – Haran, Altinbasak 8
Cartagena (Spain) – Carthago Nova 32
Carthago Nova *see* Cartagena
Castabala (Turkey) – Hierapolis 9
Castra Regina *see* Regensburg
Cawnpore *see* Kanpur
Celaenae (Iran) – Apamea 9
Cenabum *see* Orléans
Cenevo *see* Cherven
Cerigo *see* Kíthira
Cernauti *see* Chernovtsy
Ceuta (North Africa) – Sebta, Septem 27
Chalcedon *see* Kadiköy, Usküdar
Chalcis (Greece) – Negroponte 26
Ch'ang-an *see* Xian
Chemnitz *see* Karl-Marx-Stadt
Cherchell (Algeria) – Caesarea 17
Chernovtsy (Ukraine, USSR) – Cernauti, Czernowitz 76
Cherven (USSR) – Cenevo 19
Chester (England) – Deva 25
Chittaurgarh (Rajasthan, India) – Chitor 29
Chiu-yuan (North China) – Wu-yuan 13
Christiania *see* Oslo
Chu (North China) – Tzu-ch'uan 13
Chü-yen *see* Hsi-hai
Circesium *see* Beseire
Cirta *see* Constantine
Citium *see* Larnaka
Cividale del Friuli (Italy) – Aquileia 33
Claudiopolis *see* Bolu, Mut
Cluj (Romania) – Klausenburg, Kolozsvár 81
Colchester (England) – Camulodunum 8
Cologne *see* Köln
Colonia Agrippina *see* Köln
Constanţa (Romania) – Tomi 77
Constantia *see* Famagusta
Constantine (Algeria) – Cirta 8
Constantinople, Constantinopolis *see* Istanbul
Corcyra *see* Corfu
Córdoba (Spain) – Córdova, Karmona 32
Corfu (Greece) – Corcyra, Kerkira 63
Cracow *see* Kraków
Crocodilopolis *see* Patara
Ctesiphon *see* Madain
Cuddalore *see* Fort St David
Cursat *see* Quseir, El
Cyrene *see* Shahhat
Czernowitz *see* Chernovtsy

D

Dabiq *see* Kilis
Dagon *see* Rangoon
Dakar (Senegal) – Goree 46
Damascus (Syria) – Ash Sham, Dimashq 87
Damietta *see* Dumyât
Da Nang (Vietnam) – Suran, Tourane 37
Danube, R – Danuvius, Ister, R 76
Danzig *see* Gdansk
Dara *see* Mardin
Dardanelles (Turkey) – Hellespont, Çanakkale Boğazi 63
Dasapura *see* Mandasore
Dashkesan (Azerbaijan, USSR) – Bardaa 27
Denizli (Turkey) – Laodicea 18
Detroit (Michigan, USA) – Fort Pontchartrain 69
Deva *see* Chester
Dibse (Syria) – Thapsacus, Amphipolis 9
Dijhan (Turkey) – Anazarbus 14
Dimashq 86
Dionysiopolis *see* Balchik
Diyarbakir (Turkey) – Amida, Amid 14, 17, 19
Djakarta (Java, Indonesia) – Batavia, Sunda Kalapa, Jakarta 37, 46, 73
Dnepr/Dnieper, R (USSR) – Borysthenes, R
Dnepropetrovsk (Ukraine, USSR) – Yekaterinoslav, Ekaterinoslav 81
Dnestr, R (USSR) – Tgras, R
Donetsk (Ukraine, USSR) – Stalino, Yuzovka 83
Dorylaeum *see* Eskisehir
Dorystolum *see* Silistra
Dover (England) – Dubris 25
Dovin (Armenia, USSR) – Dvin 18
Dublin (Irish Republic) – Baile Atha Cliath 25
Dubrovnik (Yugoslavia) – Ragusa 28
Dumyât (Egypt) – Damietta 28
Dura-Europos *see* Qal'at as-Sālihīyah
Durius, R *see* Douro, R
Durocortorum *see* Reims
Durrës (Albania) – Epidamnus, Dyrrachium, Durazzo 77
Dvin *see* Dovin
Dyrrachium *see* Durrës

E

Eboracum *see* York
Ebro, R (Spain) – Iberus, R 60
Eburacum *see* York
Ebusos *see* Ibiza

INDEX OF ALTERNATIVE PLACE NAMES

ACKNOWLEDGEMENTS

It would be quite impossible to list all the sources which have been consulted in the preparation of these maps. Among general works of reference, those much used include:

Atlas zur Geschichte (2 vols., Leipzig 1976).

C.M Cipolla, ed., *The Fontana Economic History of Europe* (6 vols., London 1972-)

H.C Darby and H Fullard, eds., *The New Cambridge Modern History Vol. XIV, Atlas* (Cambridge, 1970).

M.Gilbert, *Atlas of American History* (London, Weidenfeld and Nicolson, 1968).

Grosser Historischer Weltatlas, ed. J.Engel (3 vols., Munich 1953-70).

A.Herrmann, *An Historical Atlas of China* (Edinburgh, 1966). *The International Atlas* (New York, Rand MacNally, 1974).

H.Jedin, K.S Latourette and J. Martin, *Atlas zur Kirchengeschihte* (Freiburg, 1970).

H.Kinder and W.Hilgemann, *The Penguin Atlas of World History* (2 vols., London, 1974, 1978)

C.McEvedy and R.Jones, *Atlas of World Population History* (London, Penguin Books 1978).

W.H McNeill, *The Rise of the West* (Chicago, Chicago U.P., 1968)

B.R Mitchell, *European Historical Statistics*, 1750-1970 (London, 1975).

W.G Moore, *The Penguin Encyclopedia of Places* (London, 1971).

Ramsey Muir, *Historical Atlas*, ed. R.F Treharne and H Fullard (London, Philip, 1966).

D.E Pitcher, *An Historical Geography of the Ottoman Empire* (Leiden, 1973).

The New Oxford Atlas (Oxford, 1975).

J.M Roberts, *The Hutchinson History of the World* (London, 1976).

The Statesman's Yearbook.

The Times Atlas of the World, comprehensive edition (London, 1976).

The United Nations Yearbook.

G Westermann, *Grosser Atlas zur Weltgeschichte* (Brunswick, 1976).

The Editor and contributors are also grateful to acknowledge specific obligations in respect of the following:

Map 17: 'Frontier of literacy' – P Riché, *Education and Culture in the Barbarian West* (Engl. trans., Columbia, South Carolina U.P., 1976), pp 177-183.

Map 21: states of Kievan Russsia – G Vernadsky, *A History of Russia* 2 (New Haven, Yale U.P., 1948), endpaper; use of Glagolitic rite – A.P Vlasto, *The Entry of the Slavs into Christendom* (Cambridge, Cambridge U.P., 1970), p 204.

Map 22, 24: itineraries – Carlrichard Bruhl, *Fodfum, Gistum, Servitium Regis* (Köhn, Böhlau, 1968), vol. II.

Map 23: Viking graves – D.M Wilson, 'Scandinavian Settlement in the North and West of the British Isles', *Transactions of the Royal Historical Society* 5th series 26 (1976), pp 108-9.

Map 26: Latin sees in Frankish Greece – P Fedelto, *La chiesa Latina in Oriente* (Verona, 1973-76), II: *Hierarchia Latina Orientis, Studi Religiosi*, 3.

Map 28: Pegolotti – J.K Hyde, *Society and Politics in Medieval Italy* (London, Macmillan, 1973), Map 6.

Map 31: Mongol strategy – O Lattimore, *'The Geography of Chingis Khan'*, Geographical Journal CXXIX, 1963, 1-7.

Map 36: distribution of peoples – G.W Hewes, *A Conspectus of the World's Cultures in 1500 A.D.*

Map 38: economic regions – G William Skinner, ed., *The City in Late Imperial China*, (Stanford, Stanford U.P., 1977), pp 214-15; couriers – Y.W Cheng, *Postal Communication in China and its modernisation*, 1860-96 (Cambridge, Mass., Harvard U.P. for East Asian Research Center, 1970), pp 11,22.

Map 40: Mughal service élite – M Athar Ali, *'Towards an interpretation of the Mughal Empire'*, Journal of the Royal Asiatic Society, 1976, No.1, p45.

Map 42: Origins of Hapsburg infantry – G Parker, *The Army of Flanders and the Spanish Road*, (Cambridge, Cambridge U.P., 1972), p28 Fig. iv.

Map 43: population figures – P Channu, *Amérique et les Amériques* (Paris, 1964), p22. Other estimates differ widely.

Map 45: imports of slaves – P Curtin, *The Atlantique Slave Trade* (Madison, Milwaukee and London, 1969), p268.

Map 47: currency – F Braudel and L Spooner, 'Movements of Prices, 1450-1650' in *Cambridge Economic History of Europe*IV, ed.E.E Rich and C.H Wilson (Cambridge, Cambridge U.P., 1967), p463; Dutch engineers – J van Deem, *Dredge, Drain, Reclaim* (The Hague, Nijhoff, 1962).

Map 48: iconoclastic riots in Netherlands – G Parker, *The Dutch Revolt* (London, Allen Lane, 1977), p77; dissemination of printing – L Febvre and H.J Martin, *L'apparition du livre* (Paris, Albin Michel,1958), map opposite p272.

Map 52: T Bestermann, ed. *The complete Works of Voltaire* (Geneva, 57 vols., 1968-); P.M Scholes, ed., *Dr. Charles Burney's Musical Tours in Europe* (London, Oxford U.P., 1969); C.B Oldham ed., *The Letters of Mozart and his Family (London, 1938).*

Map 54: Great Fear – G.Lefebvre, *The Great Fear of 1789 – Rural Panic in Revolutionary France* (Engl. trans. London, New Left Books, 1970), p4; town councils – L.A Hunt, *Revolution and Urban Politics in Provincial France, Troyes and Reims 1786-1790* (Stanford, Stanford U.P., 1978), p136; federalist revolts – original material supplied by Paul Hansen (University of California at Berkeley) from his thesis in progress, *The Federalist Revolt of 1793: a Comparative Study of Caen and Limoges.*

Map 55: departmental government – J Godechot, *Les institutions de la France sous la révolution et l'empire* (Paris, 1968), p112.

Map 57: railways in 1848 – J Jouffroy, *'Aperçu du développement du réseau ferré en Europe'*, *Annales de Géographie xl* (1931), pp 504-18.

Picture Acknowledgments

The publishers wish to thank the following organisations and individuals for their kind permission to reproduce the photographs in this book: • ET Archive: 25, 48, 101, 149 / British Museum: 58, / Museum of Fine Art, Boston: 34 • Mary Evans Picture Library: 93, 116 • French Picture Library / Barrie Smith: 32 • Hirmer Fotoarchiv: 15 • Michael Holford: 16 • Hulton Picture Library: 2, 12, 14, 120, 129 top, 130 bottom, 138, 163 / Bettman: 130 top • Imperial War Museum: 140 • David King Collection: 134 top, 134 bottom • Magnum Photos Ltd / René Burri: 161 top, 161 bottom / Salgado: 166 • Mansell Collection: 102, 108, 112 • National Maritime Museum: 71 • Oxford Picture Library / Chris Andrews: 60 • Peter Newark's Pictures: 132 • Christine Osborne Pictures: 44 top • Paul Popper: 84 • Tony Stone Associates: 44 bottom • Topham Picture Library: 79, 159, 160 • Werner Forman Archive: 74 • Zefa Picture Library: 129 bottom.

Editors: Frances Adlington, Jackie Hoy, Caz Philcox, Carolyn Pyrah   Art editor: James Hughes   Picture researchers: Jenny Faithfull, Christine Rista